Justice In-Between

OXFORD MONOGRAPHS ON CRIMINAL LAW AND JUSTICE

Series Editor:
Jeremy Horder LLD, FBA, Professor of Criminal Law, London School of Economics

This series aims to cover all aspects of criminal law and procedure including criminal evidence. The scope of this series is wide, encompassing both practical and theoretical works.

OTHER TITLES IN THIS SERIES

Criminal Fraud and Election Disinformation
Law and Politics
Jeremy Horder

Policing the Borders Within
Ana Aliverti

Criminalizing Sex
A Unified Liberal Theory
Stuart P. Green

Reasons to Doubt
Wrongful Convictions and the Criminal Cases Review Commission
Carolyn Hoyle and Mai Sato

Fitness to Plead
International and Comparative Perspectives
Ronnie Mackay and Warren Brookbanks

Criminal Misconducts in Office
Law and Politics
Jeremy Horder

The Preventive Turn in Criminal Law
Henrique Carvalho

Criminal Justice and Taxation
Peter Alldridge

In Search of Criminal Responsibility
Ideas, Interests, and Institutions
Nicola Lacey

Preventive Justice
Andrew Ashworth and Lucia Zedner

Character in the Criminal Trial
Mike Redmayne

Homicide and the Politics of Law Reform
Jeremy Horder

The Insecurity State
Vulnerable Autonomy and the Right to Security in the Criminal Law
Peter Ramsay

Manifest Madness
Mental Incapacity in the Criminal Law
Arlie Loughnan

The Ethics of Plea Bargaining
Richard L. Lippke

Prosecuting Domestic Violence
A Philosophical Analysis
Michelle Madden Dempsey

Abuse of Process and Judicial Stays of Criminal Proceedings
Second Edition
Andrew L.-T. Choo

A Philosophy of Evidence Law
Justice in the Search of Truth
H. L. Ho

The Criminal Justice System and Health Care
Charles A. Erin and Suzanne Ost

Excusing Crime
Jeremy Horder

Justice In-Between

A Study of Intermediate Criminal Verdicts

FEDERICO PICINALI

OXFORD
UNIVERSITY PRESS

OXFORD
UNIVERSITY PRESS

Great Clarendon Street, Oxford, OX2 6DP,
United Kingdom

Oxford University Press is a department of the University of Oxford.
It furthers the University's objective of excellence in research, scholarship,
and education by publishing worldwide. Oxford is a registered trade mark of
Oxford University Press in the UK and in certain other countries

First Edition published in 2022

Impression: 1

Published in the United States of America by Oxford University Press
198 Madison Avenue, New York, NY 10016, United States of America

British Library Cataloguing in Publication Data

Data available

Library of Congress Control Number: 2022932463

ISBN 978–0–19–886459–2

DOI: 10.1093/oso/9780198864592.001.0001

Printed and bound by
CPI Group (UK) Ltd, Croydon, CR0 4YY

A mia mamma,
che da sempre mi racconta il diritto.

A mio papà,
che mi ha mostrato come si studia con dedizione.

A Dora e a Leila,
perchè scelgano liberamente,
ma facciano con impegno ciò che han scelto.

Acknowledgements

I first entertained the idea of researching intermediate criminal verdicts in 2014, during a lunch with Mike Redmayne on the LSE campus. Since then, I have worked on intermediate criminal verdicts intermittently amidst other projects. I wish Mike had been here to see the research develop, and to advise me in his typical concise and surgical fashion. Somewhat egoistically, during this journey I often wished that I could drop by his office to share with him my doubts. I nonetheless rejoice at the thought that the journey started with Mike, a colleague and a friend who never ceased to be, for me, a source of inspiration.

Over the years, I have presented working papers on intermediate criminal verdicts in several academic venues, including the LSE Law School, the University of Glasgow, the Osgoode Hall Law School, the University of Nottingham, the University of Warwick, the Center for Transnational Legal Studies London, the University of Girona, and the Criminal Law Theory Conference—Online First. I am grateful to those present for their attention and constructive feedback.

James Chalmers, Antony Duff, David Hamer, Jules Holroyd, Fiona Leverick, Dale Nance, Paul Roberts, Mark Spottswood, and my LSE colleagues Richard Bradley, Neil Duxbury, David Kershaw, Niki Lacey, and Michael Lobban read, and commented on, draft chapters. Jonathan Jordan and Silvia Milano advised me on the appendix. I am filled with gratitude towards these colleagues. Their generous contributions to this project are, for me, a reminder of what academic fellowship should involve. I am also grateful to three anonymous OUP reviewers for their encouraging feedback on the book proposal, and to everyone who played a part in the production of the book for their patience and professionalism.

It is for my mum, former judge Giovanna Ichino, that I feel the deepest gratitude. Her help in finding dusty materials on the Italian acquittal *'per insufficienza di prove'* has been invaluable. Had it not been for her unstinting support, I would not have been able to research this intermediate verdict from the comfort of my home in Sheffield. I am also grateful to Stefano Zirulia and Massimo Meccarelli for their kind help in finding some contributions on the *ius commune* criminal process.

The bulk of the book was written between 2020 and 2021. It is, for me, a source of pride to have been able to accomplish this notwithstanding the many disruptions caused by the COVID-19 pandemic, and the time constraints imposed by parenting young children. I thank my family for the overwhelming energy that they have given me in this challenging period.

If there is a place that I am grateful to it is the Peak District, with its fascinating rough rocks. Many of the ideas in the book were formulated while returning home from the crag, after a refreshing climb.

A dear colleague once told me that 'being wrong in interesting and novel ways is about as much as anybody can realistically hope for'. I do hope to have met this standard.

Contents

List of Cases

UNITED KINGDOM

EUROPEAN COURT OF HUMAN RIGHTS

NATIONAL COURTS

Italy

Scotland

United States

Legislative Materials

SCOTLAND

TREATIES, CONVENTIONS, INTERNATIONAL LEGISLATION

Introduction

Criminal trials in England and Wales are characterised by a 'binary' verdict system. The same holds true for many common law and civil law jurisdictions.[1] In a binary system there is a single evidential threshold or standard of proof. If the standard is met, the verdict is 'guilty', the defendant is convicted, and punishment is permitted. If the standard is not met, the verdict is 'not guilty', the defendant is acquitted, and punishment is forbidden. There is no middle ground between the verdict of 'not guilty' and that of 'guilty'.

The binary verdict system is so familiar to us that it may be difficult to conceive of, not to mention take seriously, alternatives to it. Yet alternatives do exist: one is, indeed, implemented in a nearby jurisdiction. Scots law affords the adjudicator the verdict of 'not proven' as an intermediate option between the standard verdicts. As with the binary verdict system, the variable that determines the choice between the options available in the Scottish system is the incriminating evidence. While Scots law does not specify a standard of proof regulating the choice between 'not guilty' and 'not proven', the latter is understood as requiring stronger incriminating evidence than that necessitating the former. When the incriminating evidence is sufficiently strong to meet the reasonable doubt standard, though, the defendant[2] should be convicted. As illustrated by this arrangement, the evidential basis of an intermediate verdict is more robust than the evidential basis of 'not guilty', but less robust than the evidential basis of the 'guilty' verdict. This is the first dimension of the intermediacy of a verdict.

According to Scots law, the legal effects of 'not proven' are the same as those of 'not guilty': they are both instances of acquittal, and neither warrants punishing the defendant. Therefore, 'not proven' is a more favourable outcome for the defendant than the 'guilty' verdict. The intermediate verdict, though, is believed to produce a quantum of social stigma. The stigma is considered to be a result of the verdict's evidential basis: 'not proven' signals the presence of substantial incriminating evidence. Because of the stigma that it is thought to produce, 'not proven' is viewed as

[1] Indeed, while I have not carried out a worldwide survey, I am only aware of two contemporary jurisdictions that do not adopt the binary verdict system. These are Scotland and Israel. I will study the Scottish verdict system in detail in Chapter 1. As for the Israeli verdict system, see Y. Vaki and Y. Rabin, 'Two Kinds of Acquittals—Different Kinds of Doubts' (2021) 32 Criminal Law Forum 97.

[2] Note that, in Scots law, the person charged with committing a crime is referred to as the 'accused', and the alleged victim named in a charge is referred to as the 'complainer'. For consistency across the book, I will use the terms 'defendant' and 'complainant' even when discussing the Scottish verdict system.

Justice In-Between, Federico Picinali, Oxford University Press. © Federico Picinali 2022.
DOI: 10.1093/oso/9780198864592.003.0001

a worse outcome for the defendant than 'not guilty'. Notably, European legal history offers examples of intermediate verdicts that triggered significant detrimental legal consequences for the defendant receiving them. These consequences included fines and surveillance measures, but also severe sanctions such as exile, imprisonment, and corporal punishment. Importantly, though, they were always milder than the punishment warranted by conviction. While the first dimension of the intermediacy of a verdict pertains to its evidential basis, the second pertains to its effect. Insofar as the verdict involves hard treatment—whether merely in the form of causing social stigma,[3] or also in the form of detrimental legal consequences—this treatment is milder than that involved in conviction.

The binary verdict system implements a correspondence between evidence and hard treatment: the latter is warranted if, and only if, the evidence meets a certain sufficiency threshold.[4] Due to the two dimensions of intermediacy, the addition of an intermediate verdict enhances this correspondence. It allows the imposition of hard treatment that is *milder* than that involved in conviction on the basis of *weaker* evidence than that required for conviction. This book is a study of intermediate criminal verdicts and of their justification. In particular, it addresses the question of whether there is a justification for implementing, in the criminal trial, the logic 'weaker evidence, milder hard treatment' just described.[5] Notice that, unlike acquittal and conviction, an intermediate verdict is always a mistake if seen from the perspective of the omniscient observer: either the defendant is guilty and should be convicted and punished, or they are innocent and should be acquitted.

[3] In section 2 below, I elaborate on the claim that the causing of social stigma is a form of hard treatment that may be involved in an intermediate verdict. In Chapter 2, section 2.2.1, I will argue that the social stigma that may be associated with acquittal is not a product—hence, it cannot be seen as a feature—of this verdict. Finally, in Chapter 1, section 1.4, I will point out that the Scottish 'not proven' verdict also includes a significant - but not distinctive - detrimental legal measure.

[4] In fact, this statement is true of the paradigmatic, or central, case of the binary system, where acquittal does not involve any hard treatment whatsoever. One may argue, though, that the English and Welsh verdict system does not fit this paradigm precisely. See Chapter 4, section 4.6, in particular n 69.

[5] This logic may remind some readers of the US doctrine of market share liability in tort law: see the leading case of *Sindell v Abbott Laboratories*, 26 Cal. 3d 588 (1980). In a nutshell, under this doctrine, if harm has been caused by a fungible product, and if it is impossible to identify to the satisfaction of the civil standard of proof who manufactured the particular instance of such product which caused harm, each manufacturer of the product that has been found negligent (say, in the production or the marketing of the product) may be ordered to pay a percentage of the damages, corresponding to the respective share of the market for the product. This doctrine can be read as allowing for a partial payment of damages by the defendant on the ground that there is weaker evidence than that required for a ruling to pay damages in full. It may, therefore, be seen as expression of a similar logic to that mentioned in the text. However—even leaving aside the differences in the respective subject matter, and in the respective forms of remedies/sanctions—there is, at least, a notable dissimilarity between decision-making under the doctrine of market share liability and decision-making under a criminal verdict system including an intermediate verdict. In the case of market share liability, the damages that a manufacturer is ordered to pay are proportional to the respective market share; that is, roughly, to the probability that this manufacturer is, indeed, responsible for producing the instance of the product which caused harm to the plaintiff. An intermediate criminal verdict, instead, need not involve a measure consisting in the sentence that would be warranted by conviction, discounted by the probability of guilt. Indeed, historically intermediate verdicts have not involved measures of this kind.

The question is whether an intermediate verdict can ever be the best course of action from the perspective of an adjudicator, with his or her inevitable epistemic limitations.

1 Why study intermediate criminal verdicts?

The binary verdict system has been called into question already hundreds of years ago, well before the emergence and entrenchment of the 'not proven' verdict in Scotland during the 18th and 19th centuries. The features of the criminal trial of the late Middle Ages in Continental Europe prompted scholars and courts to defend and deploy intermediate criminal verdicts. This development originated a long-lasting debate on the verdict system, which reached a critical phase when the ideals of the French Revolution swept across the Continent, fostering an overhaul of the existing criminal law and procedure. By the second half of the 19th century, the medieval intermediate verdicts had, by and large, disappeared from Continental jurisdictions. Italy represents a case apart. While these verdicts were being abrogated across the Continent, in Italy they morphed into a more benign intermediate verdict that was operative until the last decade of the 20th century.

The Continental debate on the justification of intermediate verdicts seems to have lost traction with the verdicts' demise. Conversely, the issue of whether contemporary jurisdictions featuring a binary system should indeed reject it is attracting increasing attention in the common law literature.[6] This notwithstanding, there remains a widespread dogmatism about this verdict system, as if the reasons for having it were so obvious and persuasive that they do not require academic articulation or testing. In jurisdictions that adopt a binary system—surely in the common law ones—problematising this system is hardly considered part of the academic agenda. This is a mistake.

The mere fact that intermediate criminal verdicts have existed, or still exist, in some jurisdictions raises questions for the legal historian: why is this so? And why didn't, or don't, these verdicts exist in other jurisdictions? Moreover, the mere possibility of an intermediate verdict, as evidenced by legal history rather than just legal theory, raises a question for the legal philosopher: can an intermediate criminal

[6] See A. D. Leipold, 'The Problem of the Innocent, Acquitted Defendant' (2000) 94 Northwestern University Law Review 1297; S. Bray, 'Not Proven: Introducing a Third Verdict' (2005) 72 University of Chicago Law Review 1299; L. Laudan, 'Need Verdicts Come in Pairs?' (2010) 14 International Journal of Evidence and Proof 1; H. Lando, 'The Size of the Sanction Should Depend on the Weight of the Evidence' (2005) 1 Review of Law and Economics 277; T. Fisher, 'Constitutionalism and the Criminal Law: Rethinking Criminal Trial Bifurcation' (2011) 61 University of Toronto Law Journal 811; T. Fisher, 'Conviction without Conviction' (2011) 96 Minnesota Law Review 833; M. Wansley, 'Scaled Punishments' (2013) 16 New Criminal Law Review 309; H. Phalen, 'Overcoming the Opposition to a Third Verdict: A Call for Future Research on Alternative Acquittals' (2018) 50 Arizona State Law Journal 401; and M. Spottswood, 'Continuous Burdens of Proof' (2021) 21 Nevada Law Journal 779.

verdict be justified? Notice that, whether this question is answered affirmatively or not, the result is an interesting one: the answer would overcome the current dogmatism, either through undermining the binary system, or through spelling out a justification for it. Between the historical and the philosophical questions, it is surely the latter that has received less attention in the contemporary literature. While I will address the aetiology of prominent historical and extant intermediate verdicts, my main focus will, indeed, be on the issue of the justification of such decision-making devices. To be more precise, it will be on whether there is a justification for adopting an intermediate verdict in a contemporary criminal justice system such as the English and Welsh one. The study of this issue will start with a reconstruction of the rich and intriguing debates that have concerned and accompanied historical and extant intermediate verdicts. Finding these debates instructive, but ultimately inconclusive, I will put forward a novel case for an intermediate verdict.

My interest in the question of the justification of intermediate criminal verdicts does not result exclusively from learning about historical and extant examples of such verdicts. It was also aroused by the consideration that decision-making in everyday life—at least, my decision-making in my everyday life—is often non-binary even when, similarly to criminal adjudication, it hinges on the probability of a particular fact.. Given this, why could criminal adjudication not be non-binary as well? Consider the following examples, loosely drawn from my personal experience.

1—*Cycling to university*. Federico likes to cycle to university. At the same time, he does not like to be rained on. Besides studying the sky, he usually checks his weather app to find out what is the probability that it will rain during his commute to university. His default option is to cycle in his standard cycling clothes—jersey and shorts. If, however, it rains when he is about to set off from home, or if the chances of rain during the commute are very high (say, above 90 per cent) he takes public transport. In the event of mid to high chances of rain, he cycles wearing waterproof garments instead. Should it rain, wearing the garments would prevent him from getting wet and significantly improve the quality of his commute, compared to the default option. Should it not rain, wearing the garments would only marginally hamper his ride.

2—*Doggy day care*. Jules owns a dog called Otis. Every morning on her way to work she drops Otis at a day-care centre. While Jules is generally pleased with the service given at the centre, there is a carer—Mark—who often forgets to feed the dogs their lunch. When Mark is in charge, Jules always suspects that he failed to feed Otis. Consider that Otis invariably behaves in a ravenous manner, such that it is impossible to tell from his demeanour whether or not he was fed. Because of this situation of doubt, rather than giving Otis his evening meal plus an extra full meal—as Jules would do if she were sure that Mark had failed to feed Otis—or his evening meal only—as Jules would do if she were sure that Mark had fed Otis—Jules gives Otis the equivalent of one and a half meals for dinner. Otis being a big and active dog, if Mark indeed failed to feed him, giving the extra half portion would be important for his sustenance; if, instead, Mark fed him, the extra half portion would upset Otis's stomach only slightly, if at all.

3—*Parenting and cookies*. Robert and Ray are a couple and have a child, Leon, and a dog, Luna. Ray is a keen cook, and he often prepares cookies. The obvious rule in Robert's and Ray's household is that Leon should not take any of the freshly baked cookies left on the counter to cool down. One day, after leaving the steaming cookies on the counter, Ray goes out to meet a friend. Leon and Luna are at home, looked after by Robert. At one point, Robert goes into the kitchen and notices that two cookies are missing from the tray. He also notices some crumbs on the floor. The crumbs make him suspect that the 'thief' is Leon, given that Luna rarely fails to hoover up edible items. On the other hand, Robert has the impression that Leon did not leave his room during the time when the mischief happened. Now, if Robert was sure that Leon had taken the cookies—as he would be had he caught Leon in flagrante—he would reprimand him and impose a 'cookie ban' until the end of the week. If, instead, Robert was sure that Leon had not taken the cookies—as he would be had he caught Luna in flagrante—he would say nothing to Leon and impose no such ban. Robert, however, doubts whether Leon took the cookies. In this situation, it seems to him that the most sensible course of action is to approach Leon, to tell him about the missing cookies, and—unless Leon confesses to the mischief—to give him a short, non-accusatory speech on the importance of respecting the household rules. If Leon is the thief, this speech will serve as an important opportunity to reconsider and, possibly, repent his actions; if Leon is not the thief, it will do little or no harm to him if his activities are briefly disrupted for the sake of hearing a few instructive words from his parent.

In criminal adjudication, decision-making hinges on the probability of a particular fact: the defendant's guilt. In each of these three examples, too, decision-making hinges on the probability of a particular fact—rain, Marks' failure to feed Otis, and Leon's responsibility, respectively. And yet, in these examples, decision-making is non-binary. There is an option between acting as if the relevant fact were false and acting as if the relevant fact were true. This intermediate option is taken when the probability of this fact is such that the decision-maker experiences significant doubt about its occurrence. Notice that this short series of examples gradually approaches the kind of decision-making that takes place in a criminal trial. Unlike *Cycling to university*, the examples of *Doggy day care* and *Parenting and cookies* involve fact-finding that is backward-looking. Moreover, unlike *Cycling to university*, the examples of *Doggy day care* and *Parenting and cookies* involve fact-finding that concerns the agency of individuals—Mark and Leon, respectively. Finally, unlike in *Cycling to university* and *Doggy day care*, decision-making in *Parenting and cookies* is aimed at determining the appropriate response to an individual, as a function of how strongly they are believed to have breached a relevant rule of conduct.

As said earlier, these examples are loosely drawn from my personal experience. I cannot derive from them any generalisation to the effect that people often decide in such a non-binary fashion, nor have I gathered data that would support this generalisation. Still, the approach of the decision-makers in these examples strikes me as rational and prudent. This is, in particular, because of a feature of the intermediate options involved: the distinctive differential impact that such options have between the scenarios of the truth and of the falsity of the relevant fact. Let me clarify: notice that in each example the intermediate option is designed to perform the same function as that which acting as if the relevant fact were true is designed to perform – even if, when this fact is indeed true, the intermediate option would perform this function to a lesser extent than so acting. These functions are, respectively, to protect Federico from the rain during his commute, to provide suitable nourishment to an underfed Otis, and to respond adequately to misbehaviour. Thus, if the fact at issue in each example is, indeed, true—that is, respectively, if it rains, if Mark failed to feed Otis, and if Leon took the cookie—the intermediate option produces significant benefit. If such a fact is, instead, false, in all examples the intermediate option causes only mild inconvenience, if it causes any inconvenience at all. In other words, if the fact at issue is, indeed, true, the intermediate option produces more good than it produces harm if such a fact is false: the intermediate option is more beneficial in the former case than it is detrimental in the latter.[7] Because of this differential impact,[8] in cases of doubt about the relevant fact the intermediate option has an intuitive appeal, from the perspective of the decision-makers involved: if the relevant fact is true, this option will produce significant benefit by performing—albeit to a limited extent—the function of acting as if such a fact were true; if the relevant fact is, instead, false, the detriment caused by this option will not be as significant.[9]

[7] The benefit and the harm produced by the intermediate option are calculated by comparison with the state of affairs at the time of the decision, or with a default option, if there is one.

[8] However, see n 10 below for another factor that, arguably, contributes to the intuitive appeal of the intermediate option, but that is not, in my view, sufficient to justify the adoption of a non-binary set-up.

[9] Notice that *Doggy day care* can easily be restated such that the relevant fact is not whether Mark failed to feed Otis, but whether Otis was fed (by Mark or, indeed, by anyone else). With this restatement, the intermediate option would be designed to perform the same function as that which acting as if the relevant fact were *false* is designed to perform. I have construed the relevant fact as Mark's omission, to make the treatment of the examples easier. It allows me to describe all three examples as cases in which the intermediate option is designed to perform the same function as that which acting as if the relevant fact were true is designed to perform. Nothing of substance hinges on the choice of this construal, though. Under both construals, the intermediate option has a differential impact between the scenarios of the truth and the falsity of the relevant fact. It does not matter whether it is more beneficial in the former or in the latter scenario. What seems to matter for the rationality of taking the intermediate option, in cases of doubt, is that it does have such differential impact: it is more beneficial in one scenario than it is detrimental in the other.

Now, I am not arguing that this differential impact is what justifies adopting a non-binary set-up in every decision problem in which an intermediate option with such an impact can be designed. I have merely reported my intuition that it is this impact which justifies—or, more plausibly, contributes to justifying[10]—adopting a non-binary set-up in the three examples above. The intuition would have to be tested with a more careful analysis of these decision problems,[11] but I cannot undertake such an analysis in this study. However, I will argue that incorporating an intermediate criminal verdict into the verdict system is justified when the verdict has a differential impact that is comparable to that just discussed. To get a flavour of the conclusion that I will reach, imagine a criminal case tried with a binary verdict system. The case is a close one: the probability of guilt is somewhere in the proximity of the standard of proof for conviction. I will argue that, in this epistemic situation, issuing an intermediate verdict would be justified insofar as the verdict is more similar to conviction when the defendant receiving it is guilty than when they are innocent. More precisely, the verdict must consist in, or involve, a measure such that, if the defendant receiving it is guilty, they will experience harder treatment than if they are innocent. Drawing inspiration from an intermediate verdict that originated in continental Europe in the late Middle Ages, I will devise an intermediate verdict that satisfies this requirement.

While the book concerns the issue of the justification of intermediate criminal verdicts, it also contributes to the academic discussion of questions in evidence law theory, and in criminal law theory, that exist and are significant independently of this issue. Among these is the much-debated question of the meaning and justification of the presumption of innocence. It is often asserted—rarely with the support of an argument—that intermediate verdicts are incompatible with the presumption. In order to test this claim, I will present a novel normative theory of the presumption of innocence, which develops my previous work on the issue.[12]

[10] Arguably, the error costs of the intermediate options involved in the three examples are more limited than the error costs of the respective extreme options. From the perspective of the omniscient observer, an intermediate option is always an error. If the relevant fact is true, the agent should act as if such a fact were true; if the relevant fact is false, the agent should act as if such a fact were false. Still, in the examples given, whether the relevant fact is true or false, the intermediate option is a lesser error than acting as if such fact were false when it is indeed true, or acting as if such fact were true when it is indeed false. This, too, is a relevant consideration in favour of taking the intermediate option in cases of doubt. Consider, though, that the greater error cost of an extreme option may be overridden by the value of getting it right by choosing this option, such that the extreme option may still be preferable to the intermediate option in cases of doubt. I suspect that the differential impact described can, under particular epistemic circumstances, contribute to the expected value of the intermediate option, so as to make this the preferred choice.

[11] By this, I mean a decision-theoretic analysis. In other words, the question is whether the differential impact characterising the intermediate option makes it the case that there is a probability range such that when the probability of the relevant fact falls within that range the intermediate option maximises expected value. I will employ such an analysis in Chapter 4 with respect to the decision problem of criminal adjudication.

[12] See F. Picinali, 'The Presumption of Innocence: A Deflationary Account' (2021) 84 Modern Law Review 708.

The book also contributes to the debate on the choice of the standard of proof in a binary system. I will argue that this choice should not exclusively concern the evidence law theorist. Theorists of punishment, too, should devote attention to it. That a theory of punishment should be concerned with adjudication follows from the fact that the State frequently—and paradigmatically—administers punishment as a result of the trial. A theory that is about the justification of State punishment should, therefore, identify the conditions for the State to be justified in resorting to punishment as a result of the trial. Since adjudication is inevitably characterised by uncertainty with respect to the defendant's guilt, a theory of punishment should include an account of how strong the incriminating evidence needs to be for conviction—and, hence, punishment—to be justified; that is, an account of the standard of proof. The book advances a justification of intermediate verdicts that is based on a particular argument for the selection of the standard of proof in the binary system. I will show that this argument—and, hence, my justification of intermediate verdicts—conforms with a wide range of theories of punishment. As the book evidences, then, the study of intermediate criminal verdicts prompts the researcher to confront questions that have implications well beyond the project of justifying a non-binary verdict system. Because of this, it should be seen as a useful study even by those who would reject outright the proposal of adopting an intermediate verdict.

2 A terminological note: what is a criminal verdict and what do I mean by it?

A criminal verdict is a phrase. The giving of it is a speech act;[13] that is, it is an utterance[14] through which one or more actions are performed. These actions include asserting a proposition about facts that pertain to, or constitute, guilt and declaring that the defendant has a certain legal status.[15] The giving of a 'guilty' verdict declares the defendant guilty; that is, it convicts them, making them liable to punishment. The giving of a 'not guilty' verdict declares the defendant not guilty; that is, it acquits them. The assertive component of giving a 'guilty' verdict, in particular, raises a series of questions that have been the subject of recent debate in evidence law theory. Should the speech act assert the defendant's guilt? Should it, instead, assert the probability of their guilt measured by the adjudicator? Or should it assert

[13] For a detailed speech act analysis of verdict giving, see H. L. Ho, *A Philosophy of Evidence Law. Justice in the Search for Truth* (OUP 2008), at 12–32.

[14] A speech act may be performed without uttering words, but this is beside the point here. See M. Green, 'Speech Acts' in E. N. Zalta (ed.), Stanford Encyclopedia of Philosophy (2020), at 4.

[15] The giving of the 'guilty' verdict can also be seen as expressing to the defendant condemnation, criticism, blame for the action they have allegedly committed. See Ho (n 13), at 28–31. This component of said speech act is crucial to expressive and communicative theories of punishment.

that the standard of proof for conviction has been satisfied?[16] What propositional attitude should the adjudicator have towards what is asserted for the relevant assertion to be warranted? Is it acceptance? Belief? Justified belief? True and justified belief? Or knowledge?[17]

Whatever is asserted when giving a 'guilty' verdict, giving an intermediate verdict cannot possibly constitute an assertion of the defendant's guilt. Nor can it constitute an assertion of their innocence, since the verdict presupposes a significant quantum of incriminating evidence. Rather, giving an intermediate verdict may constitute an assertion to the effect that the standard of proof the satisfaction of which warrants the verdict, has indeed been satisfied, whereas the standard of proof for conviction has not. Or the assertion of a probability of guilt that meets the former standard, but not the latter. In this respect, the intermediate verdict is not dissimilar from the 'not guilty' verdict of a typical binary system; that is, a system with a high standard of proof for conviction. The giving of the latter verdict clearly does not assert guilt, but it cannot plausibly assert innocence either, precisely because, due to the high standard, the 'not guilty' verdict may be legitimately issued notwithstanding the presence of substantial incriminating evidence.[18] If anything, giving a 'not guilty' verdict asserts a probability of guilt that is not sufficient to meet the standard for conviction, or it asserts that this standard has not been satisfied.[19] The fact that giving an intermediate verdict or a 'not guilty' verdict asserts neither innocence nor guilt does not settle the question as to which propositional attitude warrants the assertion that may be made. Arguably, given the hypothesised assertions of these two speech acts, all of the above attitudes are plausible candidates.[20] As far as the declaratory component of the speech act is concerned, giving an intermediate verdict may be understood as declaring the defendant liable to whatever detrimental legal consequence the verdict might involve. Or, should the verdict not involve any detrimental legal consequence whatsoever, giving it may amount to a declaration that the defendant is not liable to any such consequence.

[16] For discussion, see B. S. Jackson, 'Truth or Proof? The Criminal Verdict' (1998) 11 The International Journal of the Semiotics of Law 227 and Ho, (n 13), at 121–124.

[17] For discussion, see J. Ferrer Beltrán, 'Legal Proof and Fact Finders' Beliefs' (2006) 12 Legal Theory 293; A. Duff and others, *The Trial on Trial. Vol. III. Towards a Normative Theory of the Criminal Trial* (Hart 2007), at 87–91; Ho, (n 13), ch 3; M. S. Pardo, 'The Gettier Problem and Legal Proof' (2010) 16 Legal Theory 37; D. A. Nance, 'Truth, Justification, and Knowledge in the Epistemology of Adjudication' in B. Zhang and S. Tong (eds.), *Proceedings of the International Conference on Facts and Evidence* (China University of Political Science and Law Press 2018); S. Moss, *Probabilistic Knowledge* (OUP 2018), at 208–216; and S. Moss, 'Knowledge and Legal Proof' in T. S. Gendler and others (eds.), *Oxford Studies in Epistemology. Vol. VII* (OUP forthcoming 2022).

[18] The same holds true for a 'not guilty' verdict in a system including an intermediate verdict, unless the standard of proof, the satisfaction of which warrants the intermediate verdict, is so low that failure to satisfy it warrants an assertion of innocence.

[19] See A. Duff and others, *The Trial on Trial. Vol. I. Truth and Due Process* (Hart 2004), stating at 19 that 'surely "not guilty" cannot amount to an assertion of the defendant's innocence, but must rather be read as asserting that he has not been proved to be guilty'.

[20] See, in particular, Moss, *Probabilistic Knowledge* (n 17), defending the view that someone can believe, assert and know 'probabilistic contents'.

I will not discuss further the—admittedly interesting and important—issues raised by a speech act analysis of verdict-giving. The essential treatment above is sufficient to clarify the concept of a 'verdict' that I will employ in the book. Unless stated otherwise, when using the term 'verdict' I will not refer exclusively to the phrase the giving of which is a speech act with an assertive and a declaratory component. I will refer, instead, to the overall response of the criminal justice system—or of the State—to a particular fact-finding result. To clarify, this response does include the speech act, but it also includes any hard treatment that the system may impose on the defendant.[21] As I will use the term, then, a verdict is a comprehensive course of action taken by the criminal justice system towards the defendant as a function of the outcome of the fact-finding enterprise. Thus, an intermediate verdict is not exclusively the formula that the adjudicator may utter in court in virtue of such outcome; it is also the uttering of it, as well as any hard treatment that the system may inflict in virtue of such utterance. In the book, I will use the terms 'acquittal' and 'conviction' to refer to verdicts so construed.

Earlier, I referred to the causing of social stigma as a form of hard treatment that may be *involved* in an intermediate verdict. This understanding presupposes that social stigma can occur as a result of particular epilogues of adjudication, this being an empirical question that I will touch upon in the course of the book. Causing social stigma is sullying one's reputation. That sullying one's reputation is a form of hard treatment is not in doubt: it surely consists in, and promotes, treatment that is burdensome, harmful, or even painful.[22] Insofar as social stigma is an intended or expected consequence of the speech act of verdict-giving, or of the legal measures that accompany such an act (for example, a term of imprisonment), it seems correct to view the causing of social stigma as part of the course of action taken by the criminal justice system in response to a particular fact-finding outcome: hence, as constitutive of the verdict broadly construed. In this case, the causing of social stigma can be said to be involved in the verdict. If, instead, social stigma is neither intended nor expected by the system, it may be viewed merely as a result, rather than as a component, of the verdict broadly construed. Either way, as debates on the justification of extant and historical intermediate verdicts show, the fact that an intermediate verdict *involves* the causing of social stigma or simply *causes* social stigma is generally treated as a relevant consideration in the assessment of the verdict's justification.

[21] As I will point out in Chapter 4, one may consider that the expression of condemnation through the speech act of giving a 'guilty' verdict is itself a form of hard treatment.

[22] On how the stigma produced by conviction can affect individual well-being, in particular in US society, see W. Logan, 'Informal Collateral Consequences' (2013) 88 Washington Law Review 1103, at 1105–1109. Notably, social stigma has become a more significant phenomenon in the age of the Internet. See S. E. Lageson and S. Maruna, 'Digital Degradation: Stigma Management in the Internet Age' (2018) 20 Punishment and Society 113; and A. Corda and S. E. Lageson, 'Disordered Punishment: Workaround Technologies of Criminal Records Disclosure and the Rise of a New Penal Entrepreneurialism' (2019) 60 British Journal of Criminology 245.

3 An overview of the book

Chapter 1 shows that intermediate verdicts are not a fanciful construct, produced by the mind of an armchair academic. They have been employed by many criminal jurisdictions for centuries. In this chapter, I study, in turn, the intermediate verdicts featuring in the *ius commune* criminal trial of Continental Europe during the late Middle Ages and early modern period; the acquittal '*per insufficienza di prove*', an intermediate verdict provided by the code that regulated Italian criminal procedure for most of the 20th century; and the Scottish 'not proven' verdict. In particular, the chapter reconstructs, and engages with, the lively academic—and, especially in the case of Scotland, also public—debates that have concerned and accompanied these intermediate verdicts. It analyses a series of arguments in favour of, or against, intermediate verdicts advanced in these debates, ultimately finding each of these arguments inconclusive.

In fact, the study of these debates is carried over into Chapter 2. This chapter is fully dedicated to the argument against intermediate verdicts that has played the most prominent role in the Italian and Scottish debates. This is the argument according to which such verdicts are incompatible with the presumption of innocence. In this chapter, I advance a theory of the meaning, and of the justification, of the presumption. The upshot of this theory is that the presumption includes a rule imposing on the criminal justice authorities the burden of giving sufficient reasons for any infringement of the defendant's enjoyment of the rights to which all members of the polity are prima facie entitled, and a rule making impermissible all infringements for which sufficient reasons have not been given. If these reasons are given, instead, the permissibility of the infringement follows from such reason-giving effort. Importantly, though, I argue that the presumption of innocence fully defers to the law—that is, law other than the presumption itself—for the determination of which kinds of infringement are permissible in the abstract, as well as for the determination of which reasons are sufficient for the adjudicator to permissibly agree to a given infringement in a concrete case. The rule on the burden of proof and the rule of treatment included in the presumption of innocence are merely rules of rationality that govern argumentation and adjudication in any particular case, given the law's determinations on permissibility and sufficiency. Within this framework, there can be no such thing as an infringing measure that is not compatible with the presumption of innocence. Any kind of infringing measure can be made to coexist peacefully with the presumption simply by legal fiat; that is, simply by enacting law that makes the infringement permissible when certain reasons are given. If one follows this theory, then, there is no room left to argue that intermediate criminal verdicts are incompatible with the presumption of innocence. Of course, this conclusion is not in itself sufficient to justify the adoption of an intermediate verdict by the criminal justice system. This justification needs to be provided.

In the concluding sections of the chapter, I briefly present an alternative theory of the presumption. According to this theory, the presumption includes a rule on the burden of proof and a rule of treatment that are nominally the same as those mentioned in the previous paragraph. However, the relevant notion of 'sufficiency' in these alternative rules is that of moral, rather than purely legal, sufficiency. I show that the incompatibility between the presumption of innocence and intermediate criminal verdicts is not a necessary implication of this alternative theory.

Chapter 3 lays the foundations for my later attempt to justify intermediate verdicts relying on decision theory, a theory of decision-making enjoining the agent to choose the course of action that maximises expected value. The focus in this chapter is on the binary verdict system. Given decision theory's insistence on the maximisation of expected value, it is often understood as a decision-making tool for the consequentialist only. I argue that this view is mistaken. More precisely, I argue that, in the decision problem of adjudication, both consequentialists and deontologists about punishment can rely on decision theory without relinquishing any tenet of their respective theories of punishment. In a binary system, this decision problem concerns the question of whether to convict—and, hence, to punish—or to acquit—and, hence, not to punish—a defendant whose guilt is uncertain. This question is intimately related to that of setting the standard of proof for conviction. I argue that both consequentialists and deontologists about punishment can—indeed, should—rely on decision theory in order to set their respective standards of proof.

While deontologists about punishment endorse norms that require or permit certain actions even if these do not maximise value, I show that, in the decision problem of adjudication, following the principle of maximising expected value gives the same answer as that given by following these norms, whenever they apply. This means that deontologists about punishment can rely on decision theory without fearing a departure from the norms that define their approach to the justification of punishment. Importantly, though, the upshot of this discussion is not the indistinguishability of theories of punishment in the context of adjudication. While all theories can subscribe to the principle of maximising expected value, they can also differ in what they value, and in how they value it. This can have profound implications for the stringency of the standard of proof for conviction endorsed by each theory and, consequently, for the verdict that each theory would require in any given case.

Showing that, in adjudication, maximising expected value serves the goals of both consequentialist and deontological theories of punishment is important: it allows for justifying intermediate criminal verdicts on decision-theoretic grounds without incurring the objection that, at best, this justification can persuade the consequentialist only. Indeed, especially considering that I will not defend any particular theory of punishment, my goal is for the justification to be as inclusive as possible.

Chapter 4 studies the circumstances under which issuing an intermediate verdict maximises expected value and is, therefore, justified under decision theory. The chapter starts by presenting the well-known decision-theoretic argument for the selection of the standard of proof in a binary verdict system. On the basis of this argument, I identify the condition for the superiority of an intermediate verdict with respect to acquittal and conviction—or the 'superiority condition'. To clarify, I argue that if, and only if, the intermediate verdict satisfies this condition, there is a probability range such that issuing the verdict when the probability of guilt falls within this range yields higher expected value than acquitting and convicting. I then draw from the superiority condition—which is a simple mathematical formula—a heuristic for the identification of a concrete intermediate verdict that is 'superior' in the sense just described. According to this heuristic, an intermediate verdict maximises expected value within a certain range of the probability of guilt if, and only if, it consists in harder treatment when the defendant receiving it is guilty than when they are innocent: notice here the differential impact mentioned earlier. The next step in the chapter is to identify an intermediate verdict that satisfies this heuristic requirement. I show that the requirement is satisfied by a verdict that consists in allowing for a retrial in the presence of new incriminating evidence with substantial probative value. I call this intermediate verdict 'conditional acquittal', and I argue that it has the potential for being justified under both consequentialist and deontological theories of punishment, although I leave it to interested theorists of punishment to give a full answer to this question. I also argue that, from the perspective of the arguments supporting the double jeopardy rule, adopting such an intermediate verdict is preferable to allowing for the retrial of the acquitted, as the current English and Welsh law does. In the conclusion to the chapter, I briefly consider whether historical and extant intermediate verdicts meet the above heuristic requirement.

While not implemented in current or historical legal practice, one can surely conceive of a verdict system featuring a ladder of two or more intermediate verdicts. In such a system, each intermediate verdict constituting a step of the ladder would correspond to a distinct standard of proof, and involve a quantum of hard treatment, both of which gradually increase as the steps approach conviction.[23] The chapter briefly discusses the possibility—indeed, the challenges—of justifying on decision-theoretic grounds a verdict system of this kind.

Finally, Chapter 5 addresses a battery of objections. Some of these are objections to intermediate verdicts *simpliciter*. They build on, and enrich, the debates analysed in Chapter 1. Others are objections to the decision-theoretic case for intermediate verdicts made in the previous chapter.

[23] As we will see, the *ius commune* criminal trial featured more than one intermediate verdict. However, these verdicts were warranted by the satisfaction of the same standard of proof, such that they were alternative options for cases in which this standard was satisfied.

The focus of Chapters 3 and 4 on decision theory suggests that I am committed to a normative account of juridical fact-finding, according to which this enterprise should conform with Bayesian epistemology, to the extent that this is practically viable. To clarify, the essential desiderata of this account are that the fact-finder's degree of belief in the hypothesis of guilt[24] be such that it can be represented with a probability that obeys the axioms of the probability calculus and changes, in conformity with Bayes' theorem, as new evidence is considered; and that the fact-finder reaches their conclusion by assessing their degree of belief in guilt, so understood, against a probability threshold representing the standard of proof. To be sure, as I will stress in Chapter 5, none of the arguments that I offer in the book commit me to the problematic and unpopular view that fact-finders should employ—or, for that matter, that they should be encouraged to employ—Bayes' theorem, likelihood ratios, or, indeed, any mathematical formula whatsoever. In fact, the normative account just outlined does not entail this commitment, insofar as it acknowledges the practical limitations of juridical fact-finding. I am, however, committed to the view that standards of proof should be understood as probability thresholds. Indeed, if they were not so understood, they could not be derived using decision-theory as illustrated in Chapter 4. I am also committed to the view that, irrespective of the techniques employed by fact-finders to update their degrees of belief in guilt in the light of new evidence, they should ultimately reach their conclusions by assessing such degrees of belief against such probabilistic standards of proof. In Chapter 5, I will briefly elaborate on these commitments, showing that they do not undermine the plausibility of a decision-theoretic defence of intermediate verdicts.

Now, the Bayesian approach to fact-finding, and to theorising about fact-finding, has a longstanding pedigree in the academic literature: it has enjoyed, and still enjoys, considerable support. However, it has not gone unchallenged.[25] A defence of the normative account above lies beyond the scope of this work. Any study must take something for granted, and this account—including its decision-theoretic

[24] While the focus is on the fact-finder's degree of belief in the hypothesis of guilt, the fact-finder is, without doubt, under an obligation to heed the evidence made available at trial, and to assess it reasonably. By doing so, the fact-finder should ensure that their degree of belief in—or 'subjective probability' about—guilt is aligned with the relevant 'epistemic probability'; that is, the degree of belief in guilt that is justified, given the evidence. This point invites more elaboration than I can offer here. For further discussion of the notion of 'epistemic probability', and of its relevance for juridical fact finding, see D. A. Nance, *The Burdens of Proof: Discriminatory Power, Weight of Evidence, and Tenacity of Belief* (CUP 2015), at 42–57. See also Ho (n 13), at 110–121.

[25] Consider, in particular, L. J. Cohen, *The Probable and the Provable* (OUP 1977); L. J. Cohen, 'The Role of Evidential Weight in Criminal Proof' in P. Tillers and E. D. Green (eds.), *Probability and Inference in the Law of Evidence: The Uses and Limits of Bayesianism* (Kluwer Academic Publishers 1988); R. J. Allen, 'The Nature of Juridical Proof' (1991) 13 Cardozo Law Review 373; R. J. Allen and M. S. Pardo, 'Relative Plausibility and Its Critics' (2019) 23 International Journal of Evidence and Proof 5; R. J. Allen and M. S. Pardo, 'Inference to the Best Explanation, Relative Plausibility, and Probability' in C. Dahlman and others (eds.), *Philosophical Foundations of Evidence Law* (OUP 2021); and M. Clermont, *Standards of Decision in Law: Psychological and Logical Bases for the Standard of Proof, Here and Abroad* (Carolina Academic Press 2013).

underpinnings—has already been defended persuasively by others.[26] Here, I allow myself to stand on their shoulders. Moreover, I hope that the book will stimulate those who reject this account to consider whether an intermediate verdict could be justified under their respective normative theories. Notwithstanding our fundamental disagreement, their analysis of this question would undoubtedly be a valuable contribution to the study of the verdict system.

With this book, I put the issue of the justification of intermediate verdicts on the table. I show that there is value in addressing the question of whether criminal justice can be pursued through an in-between option. 'Justice in-between' is an unconventional idea, but surely not a new one. Is it possible to present it in a novel and more compelling light? I will show that it is.

[26] For a recent defence, see Nance, 'The Burdens of Proof' (n 24), ch 2. Amongst the earlier defences, see D. A. Nance, 'Naturalized Epistemology and the Critique of Evidence Theory' (2001) 87 Virginia Law Review 1551; R. D. Friedman, 'Answering the Bayesioskeptical Challenge' (1997) 1 International Journal of Evidence and Proof 276; D. H. Kaye, 'The Laws of Probability and the Laws of the Land' (1979) 47 University of Chicago Law Review 34; R. Lempert, 'The New Evidence Scholarship: Analyzing the Process of Proof' in Tillers and Green (n 25); and R. Eggleston, *Evidence, Proof and Probability* (2nd edn, Butterworths 1983). See also F. Picinali, 'Structuring Inferential Reasoning in Criminal Fact Finding: An Analogical Theory' (2012) 11 Law, Probability and Risk 197.

1
Intermediate Verdicts are not a Fanciful Construct

1.1 Introduction

In this chapter, I present three examples of historical or existing verdict systems featuring one or more intermediate verdicts. Many readers will be familiar with the Scottish verdict system and its intermediate 'not proven' verdict. Few, however, may know that intermediate verdicts were part of the *ius commune* trial in Continental Europe during the Late Middle Ages and early modern period, and featured in the Italian criminal justice system of the 19th and 20th centuries.[1] That intermediate verdicts belong to the past, as well as to the present, of the practice of law contributes to legitimising the task that I undertake with this book. It indicates that legislators, practitioners, and scholars in not-too-distant times and not-too-distant countries believed, or still believe, in the existence of reasons for providing the adjudicator with a richer set of options than that characterising the binary system of verdicts. In fact, even criminal justice systems with a long-standing binary tradition have flirted with the logic of 'weaker evidence, milder hard treatment', which informs the concept of an intermediate verdict. This logic was, indeed, prominent in trials at the Old Bailey prior to the emergence of the reasonable doubt standard, a development that took place in the second half of the 18th century.[2]

The conjunction of these experiences is enough to make one suspicious of the dogmatism about the binary verdict system, or the obliviousness about the question of the justification of intermediate verdicts, displayed by many practitioners and scholars of criminal justice systems with no middle ground between acquittal and conviction. Of course, that intermediate verdicts are, or were, justified—or simply believed to be justified—in some legal systems, does not show that they are justified *hic et nunc*. At least, though, it invites consideration of the question whether an intermediate verdict could be justified *today* in *this* legal system, be it the English and Welsh system, or any other system with a binary set-up.

[1] Note that Israeli law also features an intermediate criminal verdict: more precisely, a verdict of 'doubt-based acquittal' that is intermediate between 'full' acquittal and conviction. See Y. Vaki and Y. Rabin, 'Two Kinds of Acquittals—Different Kinds of Doubts' (2021) 32 Criminal Law Forum 97. I will not discuss the Israeli verdict system in the book.

[2] See J. H. Langbein, *The Origins of Adversary Criminal Trial* (OUP 2003), at 261–266.

Justice In-Between, Federico Picinali, Oxford University Press. © Federico Picinali 2022.
DOI: 10.1093/oso/9780198864592.003.0002

In the following sections, I will provide a concise description of the three non-binary verdict systems mentioned earlier, giving an account of the reasons that led to the emergence and—for two of these systems, the demise—of the respective intermediate verdicts. I will reproduce, and critically engage with, the debates about the justification of intermediate verdicts that accompanied each of these legal experiences. The analysis of these debates, in fact, will only be completed in the next chapter. There, I will assess an argument that has featured prominently in the Scottish and Italian debates, and, indeed, was responsible for the repeal of the Italian intermediate verdict. It is the argument according to which intermediate verdicts are not compatible with the presumption of innocence. The upshot of my analysis is that, while these debates do not offer satisfactory arguments against introducing an intermediate verdict in a contemporary binary system like the English and Welsh one, they do not offer satisfactory arguments in favour of doing so either. The inconclusiveness of these debates—at least if referred to such a system—is what motivates the justification of intermediate verdicts that I will offer in later chapters.

1.2 Intermediate verdicts in the *ius commune* criminal trial

The phrase '*ius commune*' is used to refer to a mixture of Roman and canon law that represented the backbone of European legal systems in the period between the rediscovery and initial study of Justinian's Digest in the 11th and 12th centuries and the national codifications of the 19th century. Extraordinary punishment and the suspension of res judicata are two intermediate verdicts that emerged in the *ius commune* criminal trial of the Late Middle Ages, and were a prominent feature of criminal trials in Continental Europe until the French Revolution.[3] In fact, in some European jurisdictions these verdicts were still recognised for a good part of the 19th century. In section 1.2.1, I discuss the origins of these institutions and their significance. In section 1.2.2, I give an account of their decline and subsequent disappearance from European jurisdictions. Finally, in section 1.2.3, I conclude my study of these intermediate verdicts by offering the reader a taste of the debate that took place around them in the 19th century, just prior to their demise.

[3] These do not exhaust the list of intermediate verdicts that were available, but arguably they are the most significant. Another example of *ius commune* intermediate verdict was the *cautio de non offendendo*, essentially a caution not to break the law imposed by the judge on a party upon request by another. While the *cautio* could be issued independently of the criminal process, a judge could also impose it on the defendant as an epilogue of the process itself, for instance if torture was not successful in producing a confession. See M. Meccarelli, 'Tortura e Processo nei Sistemi Giuridici dei Territori della Chiesa: Il punto di Vista Dottrinale (Secolo XVI)' in B. Durand (ed), *La Torture Judiciaire: Approches Historiques et Juridiques, vol II* (Centre d'Historie Judiciaire 2002), at 702–706.

1.2.1 Extraordinary punishment and the suspension of res judicata

The *ius commune* included rigid proof rules inspired by the idea that criminal conviction required evidence that is brighter than sunlight—*probationes luce meridiana clariores*.[4] According to these rules—which I will refer to as the Roman-canon proof rules—conviction could only occur in the presence of full proof—*probatio plena*, and full proof required a confession or two concordant eyewitness testimonies.[5] Importantly, circumstantial evidence—*indicium/indicia*—and the inferences based on it were not normally[6] deemed sufficient for conviction.[7]

There is disagreement among legal historians as to the reasons for the emergence of the Roman-canon proof rules. A prominent account views the origin of these rules as strictly linked to the abolition of ordeals, which resulted from the decision of the Fourth Lateran Council in 1215 to prohibit the clergy from participating in such proceedings.[8] With this development, the connection between criminal justice and the divine was severed, and criminal justice came to be understood as a matter of human decision-making. According to this account, though, the times were characterised by profound distrust in human judgement. This meant that the fundamental change in the administration of criminal justice caused by the abolition of ordeals put the legitimacy of criminal justice at risk. The Roman-canon proof rules were, thus, created in order to cabin, if not exclude, human judgement, by trying to render judicial reasoning superfluous: all that the judge had to do, according to these rules, was to ascertain whether the required items of evidence

[4] G. Alessi Palazzolo, *Prova Legale e Pena: La Crisi del Sistema Tra Evo Medio e Moderno* (Jovene Editore 1979), at 3–4 and M. Meccarelli, *Arbitrium: Un Aspetto Sistematico degli Ordinamenti Giuridici in Età di Diritto Comune* (Giuffrè Editore 1998), at 241.

[5] See Alessi Palazzolo (n 4), at 13; Meccarelli, *Arbitrium* (n 4), at 241–242; J. H. Langbein, *Torture and the Law of Proof: Europe and England in the Ancien Régime* (The University of Chicago Press 1977), at 4. See n 48 below.

[6] See Alessi Palazzolo (n 4), at 25, pointing out that for a series of crimes considered difficult to prove, such as *lèse-majesté*, forgery, and contraband, circumstantial evidence could provide full proof. See also *id.*, at 59, discussing the *Tractatus de Tormentis*, the first medieval treatise specifically dedicated to criminal law, probably written at the end of the 13th century, and of uncertain authorship. The *Tractatus* allowed for conviction to ordinary punishment (ie that statutorily prescribed) in the presence of *indicia indubitata*; that is, unquestionable circumstantial evidence. Finally, see *id.*, at 60–64, discussing the very influential *Tractatus de Maleficiis,* written by Albertus Gandinus around 1287, according to which *indicia indubitata* could justify conviction to ordinary punishment only insofar as they founded a *presumptio juris et de jure*. Failing this, in Gandinus's view, they could only justify conviction to pay a fine.

[7] See Meccarelli, *Arbitrium* (n 4), at 242; Alessi Palazzolo (n 4), ch 2; and Langbein, *Torture and the law of proof* (n 5), at 4.

[8] On the demise of ordeals, see F. McCauley, 'Canon Law and the End of the Ordeal' (2006) 26 Oxford Journal of Legal Studies 473, arguing that while its immediate cause was Pope Innocent III's programme of modernisation of ecclesiastical criminal procedure aimed at increasing crime control, its deeper cause was Pope Gregory VII's programme of spiritual renewal of the clergy, which fostered their withdrawal from secular affairs.

were present. The overarching goal of this regime was to foster public confidence in the system and its decisions.[9]

An alternative account[10] states that the *ius commune* law of proof—understood as the combination of the Roman-canon proof rules and exceptions to them—originated, instead, from the tension between three main factors. The first two factors favoured the emergence of the Roman-canon proof rules. These were, first, the centralisation and bureaucratisation of criminal justice, taking place from the 11th century onwards, and the related need to keep lower courts in check through strict rules of straightforward implementation; and, second, the aim of protecting judges from the damnation of their souls that may result from judicial error,[11] an aim that was pursued by limiting the judges' decision-making powers, in an (illusory) attempt to turn them into a mere instrument of the law. The third factor instead pushed against the use of rigid and demanding decision rules, and was largely responsible for the extraordinary or exceptional doctrines that developed throughout the period studied here. This factor was the harsh criminal policy developing from the 13th century onwards, which resulted from the increasing involvement of the Church in secular matters such as criminal justice, driven by a resolution to enforce core Christian values. This harsh criminal policy was manifestly at odds with proof rules, such as the Roman-canon rules, that hindered the punishment of the guilty.

The alternative account has greater explanatory capacity, in that it contributes to explaining why *ius commune* judges, far from being—and being considered—mechanical enforcers of the law, as the first account suggests, enjoyed a remarkable discretionary power, referred to as *arbitrium iudicis*. *Arbitrium* is a complex concept and a complex power, which had a vast array of manifestations, and was put at the service of a variety of systemic values and public goods.[12] For instance,

[9] See Langbein, *Torture and the law of proof* (n 5), at 6–7. For critical discussion of this account, see McCauley (n 8), at 508–509; R. M. Fraher, 'Conviction According to Conscience: The Medieval Jurists' Debate Concerning Judicial Discretion and the Law of Proof' (1989) 7 Law and History Review 23, at 27–29, 56–58; and M. Damaška, *Evaluation of Evidence: Pre-Modern and Modern Approaches* (CUP 2019), at 16–19. See also F. M. Pagano, *Principj del Codice Penale e Logica de' Probabili per Servire di Teoria alle Pruove nei Giudizi Criminali. Opera Postuma con Alcune Note* (Da' Torchi di Raffaello di Napoli 1828). The anonymous editor of this edition of Pagano's work added a series of explanatory notes, including a note at 84–85 that is relevant to our discussion. In this note, the editor states their view that the rule prohibiting conviction on the basis of circumstantial evidence ultimately originated from the 'barbaric' logic of the ordeals, according to which knowledge could not be obtained by the use of reason, but only by the use of force. With the abolition of the ordeals, the use of force was supplanted by the use of the senses (the direct perception of a confession or of an eyewitness testimony) as the source of knowledge. Reasoning, though, was still not trusted to produce knowledge.

[10] The account is defended by Damaška, *Evaluation of Evidence* (n 9), at 19–26.

[11] Punishment often involved death or maiming. According to Christian theology, imposing blood punishment or being involved in the proceedings that led to such a sentence could constitute a mortal sin, if the judgment was mistaken. For a discussion of how Christian theology addressed the issues of killing in war, and of criminal adjudication involving blood punishment, see J. Q. Whitman, *The Origins of Reasonable Doubt: Theological Roots of the Criminal Trial* (Yale University Press 2008), ch 2.

[12] For a detailed study, see Meccarelli, *Arbitrium* (n 4). See also Fraher (n 9); and M. Meccarelli, 'Criminal Law: Before a State Monopoly' in H. Pihlajamäki and others (eds), *The Oxford Handbook of European Legal History* (OUP 2018), at 646–648.

we find it at play in the law of torture, as an exercise of personal judgement about the strength of the incriminating evidence. Torture was employed as a tool for obtaining the confession needed for conviction, effectively making the requirement of full proof less demanding for the system. Recourse to torture was justified by half-proof—*probatio semiplena*—a phrase that originally designated one eyewitness testimony, but also came to encompass unquestionable circumstantial evidence—*indicia indubitata*.[13] Notwithstanding that scholars had elaborated detailed—even pedantic—taxonomies and exemplifications of *indicia*, especially with an eye to identifying those that could justify torture,[14] the concrete evaluation of circumstantial evidence for the purposes of determining the permissibility of torture necessarily required careful personal assessment on the part of the judge.[15]

More importantly, for our purposes, *arbitrium iudicis* played a role in addressing the system's urge to secure the guilty to justice, described earlier as a force that pulled in the opposite direction of adopting rigid and demanding proof rules for conviction. Key instantiations of *arbitrium* in this role were the *poena extraordinaria* or, indeed, *arbitraria*—that is, extraordinary punishment—and the *absolutio ab instantia*.[16] I refer to the latter institution with the more accessible name 'suspension of res judicata', which makes explicit that this intermediate verdict did not produce res judicata: its nature was precisely to allow for the reopening of the proceedings with the discovery of new incriminating evidence. I start with the study of extraordinary punishment.

The phrase 'extraordinary punishment' meant punishment that completed, or departed from, statutory norms: in particular, punishment that departed from that statutorily prescribed for the given crime. The latter was referred to as 'ordinary' punishment and, for serious crimes, consisted in execution or maiming. The forms of extraordinary punishment were much more varied than the ordinary forms. They could range from a fine to execution, including a vast array of options in-between: different types of corporal punishment and, in the early modern period, the galley, the workhouse, or imprisonment.[17] Extraordinary punishment was a multifaceted institution that judges resorted to in order to develop both the substantive criminal law and the law of evidence. For example, as far as the substantive law is concerned, extraordinary punishment was used to punish crimes for

[13] See Langbein, *Torture and the law of proof* (n 5), at 4–5 and Damaška, *Evaluation of Evidence* (n 9), at 71.

[14] See J. Franklin, *The Science of Conjecture: Evidence and Probability Before Pascal* (John Hopkins University Press 2001), at 15–20, 24–28; and Damaška, *Evaluation of Evidence* (n 9), at 71–72.

[15] See Damaška, *Evaluation of Evidence* (n 9), at 73–74.

[16] For a treatment of these institutions as expression of *arbitrium judicis*, see Meccarelli, *Arbitrium* (n 4), at 195–254; and M. Meccarelli, 'Le Categorie Dottrinali della Procedura e l'Effettività della Giustizia Penale nel Tardo Medioevo' in J. Chiffoleau and others (eds), *Pratiques Sociales et Politiques Judiciaires dans les Villes de l'Occident à la Fin du Moyen Âge* (Ècole Française de Rome 2007), also available at <https://books.openedition.org/efr/1842?lang=it> accessed 3 September 2021. See, in particular, paras 30–39.

[17] See Meccarelli, Arbitrium (n 4), at 212–224; and Langbein, *Torture and the law of proof* (n 5), ch 2.

which the statute did not provide a particular form of punishment, or for which the statute invited the judge to exercise their *arbitrium* in punishing; it was used to criminalise and punish conduct that was not already criminalised by statute; finally, the varied punitive options falling under the umbrella of extraordinary punishment gave the judge the opportunity to adjust the sentence so as to recognise different levels of culpability, as well as circumstances that mitigated or aggravated the crime.[18] What interests us, though, is the role that extraordinary punishment played in the development of a decision rule that sat alongside the Roman-canon proof rules seen earlier. Conviction to ordinary punishment required the satisfaction of such rules. However, failing full proof, and provided that a less demanding evidentiary requirement was satisfied, judges were permitted to convict to a form of (extraordinary) punishment that was less severe than the (ordinary) punishment statutorily prescribed. In other words, extraordinary punishment offered the option of an intermediate verdict.

The idea that judges could impose extraordinary punishment in the absence of full proof has its roots in a passage from a legal commentary written by Pope Innocent IV, dating back to 1250. In this passage, Innocent IV—who was indeed a well-respected legal scholar—countenanced the possibility that, even in the absence of full proof, the judge could impose punishment, although milder than that warranted by such proof.[19] This maxim had significant influence on the subsequent scholarship and, possibly as early as the end of the 13th century, it was acted upon by secular courts in northern Italy, later followed by courts in France, and beyond.[20] In most jurisdictions, the evidential requirement for extraordinary punishment was the same as that for torture; that is, half-proof: one eyewitness testimony or *indicia indubitata*.[21] This meant that, when this evidential requirement was satisfied,

[18] For a detailed discussion of these uses, see Meccarelli, *Arbitrium* (n 4), at 200–240.

[19] See Alessi Palazzolo (n 4), at 51–52.

[20] See Damaška, *Evaluation of Evidence* (n 9), at 106 and Alessi Palazzolo (n 4), at 19–25, 53–54, 79–80, 82–83, 88–95. Langbein claims that extraordinary punishment in the event of evidence falling short of full proof was rarely used until the 16th and 17th centuries, but that starting from this period it effectively supplanted the rigid Roman-canon proof rules, and the related law of torture, allowing judges to convict on the basis of their free evaluation of the evidence. See Langbein, *Torture and the law of proof* (n 5), at 11, 55–60. This view is criticised by Meccarelli, *Arbitrium* (n 4), at 251–254, arguing that extraordinary punishment was an integral part of the *ius commune*, which coexisted with the requirement of full proof rather than supplanting it, and effectively represented its flipside; Damaška, *Evaluation of Evidence* (n 9), at 109–110, arguing that in some countries the requirement of full proof continued to operate until the 19th century with respect to some serious crimes, and pointing out that the institution of extraordinary punishment did not usher in a regime of free evaluation of the evidence, since judges were still bound by the evidentiary rules set for this kind of punishment; and Alessi Palazzolo (n 4), at 32–33, fn 38, pointing out that the institution of extraordinary punishment on the basis of evidence falling short of full proof did not represent the emergence of an alternative system of proof, since it had the same theoretical and epistemological underpinnings of the requirement of full proof, and operated in the same procedural setting.

[21] See Damaška, *Evaluation of Evidence* (n 9), at 106–108, arguing that, according to legal doctrine, the evidence had to produce in the judge the belief that the defendant was guilty, but pointing out that this additional requirement was not strictly observed, and judges often convicted to extraordinary punishment even if they merely suspected guilt. See n 48 below.

the judge enjoyed some discretion—precisely, *arbitrium*—in choosing how to deal with the case. They might acquit, impose extraordinary punishment, opt for torture, and impose ordinary punishment in the event of confession; or opt for torture and impose extraordinary punishment if no confession was obtained and the existing incriminating evidence was not invalidated—'purged'—by the defendant's resistance to the painful interrogation.[22]

The possibility of convicting to punishment lesser than the ordinary punishment, in the presence of weaker evidence of guilt than full proof, was endorsed as an essential tool to circumvent the Roman-canon proof rules, alongside the law of torture. It was especially welcomed by judges. Being on the front line of the administration of criminal justice, they needed practical solutions to give effectiveness to the system, in spite of such demanding decision rules. Extraordinary punishment gave them the opportunity to contain the risk of the guilty escaping punishment, and to target the dangerous, hence fostering public confidence and public safety.[23] To be sure, the use of extraordinary punishment as an intermediate verdict did encounter some reservations amongst the more theoretically oriented scholars, who—mindful of the Roman notion of *onus probandi*—lamented that guilt and the relative burden of proof could not be 'divided', and that, therefore, if full proof of guilt was not obtained, no punishment could be meted out.[24] In fact, it is worth pointing out that 'half- proof' was not, at the time, understood as meaning 'half-truth'. The latter concept is, indeed, dubious, if assessed from an epistemological point of view.[25] Moreover, if deployed in criminal fact-finding as a decision rule of sorts, it may reasonably be seen as conflicting with the core idea that the *probandum* of the process is the defendant's guilt, not a mere part of it. Half-proof was, instead, understood as an evidential, or probability, threshold.[26] Now, the revered Roman maxim *ei incumbit probatio qui dicit, non qui negat* is not subverted by allowing that the satisfaction of different evidential thresholds warrants different consequences for the defendant. This practice does not reallocate the burden of proof, nor does it change or 'divide' the facts that need proving. In section 1.2.3 below, I will address in greater detail two arguments against intermediate verdicts advanced in the later scholarship and based, respectively, on the burden of proof and the notion of guilt.

The suspension of res judicata is another intermediate verdict characterising the *ius commune* trial. It was first elaborated by Italian jurists, and was widely used in the European Continent by the 14th century.[27] It could be issued in the presence of

[22] See Alessi Palazzolo (n 4), at 33–34.

[23] See ibid, at 25, 30; Meccarelli, *Arbitrium* (n 4), at 243–245; and Damaška, *Evaluation of Evidence* (n 9), at 108.

[24] See Alessi Palazzolo (n 4), at 29–30.

[25] Can there be such a thing as a half-true fact? cf K. M. Clermont, *Standards of Decision in Law: Psychological and Logical Bases for the Standard of Proof, Here and Abroad* (Carolina Academic Press 2013), at 151, and ch 5 more generally, countenancing the existence of 'partial truths'.

[26] See Damaška, *Evaluation of Evidence* (n 9), at 33–34, 106–107.

[27] See ibid, at 111.

indicia indubitata. Because this evidential requirement also justified torture and extraordinary punishment, the suspension of res judicata was a valid alternative to these measures. However, as with extraordinary punishment, it could also be issued after torture, if no confession was produced and the *indicia* were not considered purged by the defendant's resistance.[28] As pointed out earlier, the verdict meant that the judgment did not produce res judicata, therefore making it possible to resume criminal prosecution against the defendant if new incriminating evidence was discovered. The defendant was effectively kept in a limbo, with the possibility that further proceedings and severe punishment would materialise at some point in the future. What is more, the defendant could be placed under surveillance and could be the target of measures that limited their activities, including travel restrictions.[29] The suspension of res judicata was, therefore, a helpful instrument in the toolbox of the *ius commune* judge. It could be employed to afflict those who, despite the lack of full proof, were believed to be guilty, with the hope that this proof would later emerge. In particular, the verdict and its restrictive appendages were useful to control those who were perceived as a threat to society.[30]

In the eyes of a contemporary scholar, extraordinary punishment and the suspension of res judicata may not seem truly intermediate options between acquittal and conviction. More precisely, a contemporary scholar may question the claim that the evidential requirement for these measures—in particular, *indicia indubitata*—is epistemically lower than the Roman-canon proof rules. While it may be true that there is still a lingering distrust in circumstantial evidence, we generally accept that evidence of this kind can be sufficiently strong to meet our standard of proof for conviction. Indeed, we recognise that whether evidence is direct or circumstantial with respect to the fact that we aim to prove—for instance, where the issue is identity, whether the evidence is the testimony of an eyewitness identifying the defendant as the perpetrator, or the match between a tyre track found at the scene of the crime and the tyres of the defendant's car—the process of extracting its significance always involves drawing inferences from a known fact to an unknown fact.[31] We might, therefore, think that there is nothing necessarily weaker in *indicia indubitata*, if compared to two eyewitness testimonies or a confession. In fact, research has shown that eyewitness testimony is fraught with

[28] See Meccarelli, 'Tortura' (n 3), at 700–701.

[29] See Damaška, *Evaluation of Evidence* (n 9), at 111–112; and C. G. A. Mittermaier, *Teoria della Prova nel Processo Penale* (Libreria di Francesco Sanvito 1858, translated into Italian by F. Ambrosoli) at 537–538.

[30] See Meccarelli, *Arbitrium* (n 4), at 250, fn 57.

[31] To clarify, the significance of the direct evidence of a witness depends on an assessment of the reliability of such evidence, which involves inferences concerning perception and honesty, among others. See D. A. Schum, *The Evidential Foundations of Probabilistic Reasoning* (Northwestern University Press 1994), at 117–119.

epistemic dangers,[32] and the reliability of confessions is hardly beyond doubt, especially if they are obtained through oppressive or suggestive interviewing techniques.[33] This superimposition of our modern sensibility on the workings of the *ius commune* trial is beside the point, though. What matters here is that, for many scholars and judges of the time, extraordinary punishment and the suspension of res judicata were intermediate verdicts, not only because of their more limited afflictive consequences with respect to ordinary punishment, but also because they were founded on evidence that was considered weaker than the standard warranting this punishment.[34] While not unchallenged,[35] the view that circumstantial evidence could not produce full proof was widespread. However, it was due to lose much of its strength as the experience of the *ius commune* trial progressed through the early modern period.

1.2.2 The decline and demise of the *ius commune* intermediate verdicts

In the 16th and 17th centuries, the European legal scholarship became increasingly critical of the rigid Roman-canon proof rules, but also of the pragmatic solutions that had been devised to circumvent them.[36] On the one hand, some scholars exalted inferential reasoning and argumentation as sources of knowledge, thus criticising the traditional view that circumstantial evidence could not warrant conviction to ordinary punishment.[37] In general, the early modern scholars were less interested than their predecessors in elaborating meticulous hierarchies of evidence types, or in offering pedantic exemplifications of *indicia*; instead, they recognised a central role in the evidential process for the judge's own confidence in guilt.[38] On the other hand, early modern scholars frequently criticised

[32] The literature is vast. For an overview of the empirical research on factors that may affect the reliability of eyewitness testimony, see D. Simon, *In Doubt: The Psychology of the Criminal Justice Process* (Harvard University Press 2012), ch 3.

[33] The literature is vast. For two representative studies of the issue of false confessions—in particular, police-induced false confessions—see S. Drizin and R. Leo, 'The Problem of False Confessions in the Post-DNA World' (2004) 82 North Carolina Law Review 891; and S. M. Kassin and others, 'Police-Induced Confessions: Risk Factors and Recommendations' (2010) 34 Law and Human Behavior 3.

[34] A particularly analytical application of the logic 'weaker evidence, milder hard treatment' is found in the *Malleus Maleficarum,* written by the inquisitors Kramer and Sprenger in 1487. As described in Franklin (n 14), at 52, the *Malleus* provided a detailed correspondence between grades of suspicion/proof and verdicts.

[35] See n 6 above.

[36] See Alessi Palazzolo (n 4), at 131.

[37] See, in particular, the work of Anton Matthes, discussed in ibid, at 167–169. Alessi Palazzolo also describes an instance of Neapolitan legislation from 1621 that allowed judges to convict to ordinary punishment exclusively on the basis of unquestionable circumstantial evidence, which was defined as evidence capable of producing conviction in the judge's mind (ibid, at 192–193). The author, however, points out that this legislation had little practical impact (ibid, at 198).

[38] See ibid, at 133–134.

intermediate verdicts because of a fundamental disagreement with the ideas that there could be an intermediate option between acquittal and conviction, and that weaker evidence than that required for conviction could justify milder punishment than that warranted by conviction.[39]

The Roman-canon proof rules, though, were still very much used in European courts during this period, and were incorporated in important legislative documents such as the German *Constitutio Criminalis Carolina* of 1532.[40] The enduring widespread application of these rules was still chiefly due to their being valued as a device to limit the power of, and to exercise control over, lower courts, thus fostering uniformity in the administration of criminal justice.[41] At the same time, though, intermediate verdicts were viewed by the courts as a necessary expedient to avoid the impunity that the strict application of the standard of full proof would produce; and as an equitable expedient at that, if compared to convicting to ordinary punishment—which was still often execution—on the basis of evidence that most still did not perceive as sufficiently strong to satisfy this standard.[42] Indeed, intermediate verdicts were the subject of legislation across Europe in the 17th century and, especially, the 18th century.[43] Their popularity, however, was to decline within the following century, also as a result of the gradual demise of the demanding decision rules that had made them necessary.

For scholars operating within the Age of Enlightenment, the strictures of the Roman-canon proof rules were intolerable. The dominant view recognised the futility of any attempt to predetermine by normative fiat the epistemic value of types and items of evidence,[44] and expressed confidence in human reasoning, hence in

39 See ibid, at 119–121, 122–124, 159, 170–171.

40 See ibid, at 100–101.

41 See ibid, at 175–176. See also M. Nobili, *Il Principio del Libero Convincimento del Giudice* (Giuffrè Editore 1974), at 107–110.

42 See Alessi Palazzolo (n 4), at 139.

43 For extraordinary punishment, see, in particular, the Grand Duchy of Tuscany's Codice Leopoldino of 1786. Whilst abolishing torture (art XXXIII), the Codice authorised extraordinary punishment up to the severity of exile or confinement, in the event of sufficient circumstantial evidence ('*sufficienti indizi*'), and up to the severity of hard labour, if the defendant was tried for homicide and there was compelling circumstantial evidence ('*indizi urgentissimi*') against them (art CX). For further examples, see Mittermaier (n 29), at 557–561 and accompanying notes, and Langbein, *Torture and the law of proof* (n 5), at 50–55 and accompanying notes. For the suspension of res judicata, see F. Ambrosoli, 'Delle Sentenze Dubitative nei Processi Criminali' (1852) Giornale per le Scienze Politico-Legali, Tomo III, Fascicolo 4, at 257–259, 277–278 and Mittermaier (n 29), at 537–548 and accompanying notes. In some jurisdictions there was a time limit after which the process could not be resumed. Also, jurisdictions differed depending on the restrictive conditions that they imposed on the defendant as part of this intermediate verdict.

44 Amongst the Enlightenment thinkers, Voltaire was particularly critical of the hierarchies and arithmetic of proof elaborated by the *ius commune* tradition. For a telling passage, see his *Commentaire sur le Livre 'Des Délits et Des Peines'* (1767), s XXII, at 63–64, available at <https://gallica.bnf.fr/ark:/12148/bpt6k65400223> accessed 3 September 2021. However, he was also wary of the principle of 'intime conviction', fearing that the good conscience and common sense of adjudicators—on which the principle was premised—may lose their way. See Nobili (n 41), at 122–126.

the capability of a judge to undertake a personal assessment of the evidence before them.[45] Circumstantial evidence was no longer seen as incapable of producing the sort of conviction that warranted punishment in full. It was, therefore, felt that a judge should be left free to convict to ordinary punishment on the exclusive basis of this evidence. It says much about the evolution of legal thought on the matter that the Italian jurist Mario Francesco Pagano, writing in the second half of the 18th century, supported this conclusion by pointing out that all forms of evidence are circumstantial in that they all involve inferential reasoning.[46] Unsurprisingly, scholars of the Enlightenment were also critical of the centuries-old practical solutions devised to circumvent the rigid Roman-canon decision rules. These solutions were seen as unnecessary, insofar as circumstantial evidence was deemed sufficient to warrant conviction to ordinary punishment. Moreover, these scholars attacked the indiscriminate and repressive application that unscrupulous judges had often made of such solutions.[47]

In 1791, two years after the French Revolution, the French National Constituent Assembly legislated that the newly instituted jury should decide criminal cases on the basis of their 'intime conviction'; that is, of an evaluation of the evidence free from the interference of the law. This development unshackled evidential reasoning from a regime of proof rules, and from the underlying legally sanctioned hierarchies of evidence types that had constrained, yet not

[45] This renewed confidence in judicial decision-making is often imputed to the scientific and philosophical developments of the time. See *id.*, at 91–92.

[46] See Pagano (n 9), at 83–84.

[47] See Alessi Palazzolo (n 4), at 207; and Nobili (n 41), at 117, fn 61. Gaetano Filangieri's influential work *La Scienza della Legislazione* offers an interesting example of theory of proof 'in transition' between the *ius commune* law of proof and the principle of free evaluation of the evidence. See G. Filangieri, *La Scienza della Legislazione. Edizione Integrale* (Grimaldi & C. Editori 2003), vol III, ch XIII–XV, at 151–158. The third volume of the work, dedicated to criminal procedure and criminal law, was published in 1783. According to Filangieri, conviction should require the satisfaction of a bipartite decision rule. First, the adjudicator should be morally certain of guilt. Filangieri defined moral certainty as 'that state in which the mind is sure of the truth of a proposition concerning the existence of a fact that we have not witnessed with our eyes' (at 153, my translation). Second, there should be full, or 'legal', proof. Indeed, Filangieri defended a series of rules dictating the kind of evidence that could count as full proof. His notion of full proof, though, was markedly different from that of the *ius commune*. For instance, according to Filangieri a confession was not sufficient for full proof, whereas circumstantial evidence could be sufficient, depending on its characteristics. The requirement of full proof was considered by Filangieri to be a necessary safeguard against the 'idiosyncrasy, corruption, or stupidity' (at 158, my translation) of some judges: in a vein of legal realism *ante litteram*, Filangieri remarked on how 'a good or bad digestion can make [a judge] more or less credulous', hence more or less prone to feel morally certain (at 153, my translation). If neither limb of the decision rule was satisfied, according to Filangieri the adjudicator should acquit. If only one limb was satisfied, instead, the adjudicator should issue the suspension of res judicata, which could not involve a loss of personal freedom, but would carry with it the loss of some political rights (vol III, ch XXI, at 182–184). Filangieri was, instead, critical of extraordinary punishment (for instance, at 154).

neutralised,[48] it for centuries.[49] The emergence of the principle of 'intime conviction' eroded the foundations of the synergic structure made of the standard of full proof, the law of torture, and intermediate verdicts: with the standard gone, the *raison d'être* of the devices for circumventing it subsided. The whole edifice was due to crumble to the ground. This (r)evolution, however, did not happen with the same speed across the European Continent.[50] Extraordinary punishment and the suspension of res judicata were recognised in some jurisdictions well into the 19th century. In the first half of that century, the judicial evaluation of the evidence was still constrained in criminal justice systems retaining an inquisitorial framework. In particular, these systems were still clinging to the long-standing principle that circumstantial evidence could not warrant conviction to ordinary punishment.[51] Indeed, extraordinary punishment on the basis of circumstantial evidence was prescribed in a few European jurisdictions until the middle of the 19th century.[52] The suspension of res judicata had marginally greater longevity; as of 1858 it was still employed by some criminal justice systems in Europe.[53] But it disappeared soon after:[54] more precisely, it morphed into intermediate verdicts such as the Italian '*formula dubitativa*' (doubting formula), which I will discuss in due course.

[48] See Damaška, *Evaluation of Evidence* (n 9). The main theory advanced in Damaška's book is that the Roman-canon proof rules did not have the positive effect of mandating conviction in the presence of full proof. Conviction also required that the judge believe in the accuracy of the two testimonies or the confession: hence, the judge was expected to engage in an assessment of this evidence. According to Damaška, the standard of full proof only had the negative effect of prohibiting conviction to ordinary punishment in the absence of the requisite evidence.

[49] See L. Ferrajoli, *Diritto e Ragione. Teoria del Garantismo Penale* (Editori Laterza 2008), at 115–120, pointing out that 'intime conviction' is not a decision rule or a 'positive' directive on how evidence should be evaluated, but merely a 'negative principle' consisting in the rejection of the Roman-canon proof rules and of the legally sanctioned hierarchies of evidence underlying them. Ferrajoli argues that this principle must, therefore, be complemented with an epistemological—rather than a legal—theory of inferential reasoning and of evidential sufficiency. In his view, the failure to do so on the part of Enlightenment and post-Enlightenment jurists is responsible for many a case of arbitrary administration of criminal justice. See also Nobili (n 41), at 5–10.

[50] See Nobili (n 41), at 113–143, discussing the gradual adoption of the principle of free evaluation of the evidence in parts of the Continent.

[51] See Mittermaier (n 29), at 483–487, referring to the Austrian and German jurisdictions. Until the 1838 reform of the Grand Duchy of Tuscany's Codice Leopoldino of 1786, it was forbidden in the Grand Duchy to convict to ordinary punishment on the basis of circumstantial evidence alone. See n 43 above; G. Carmignani, *Teoria delle Leggi della Sicurezza Sociale* (Fratelli Nistri e co 1832) at 256–280; and G. Brugnoli, *Della Certezza e Prova Criminale: Col Confronto di Varie Legislazioni d'Europa ed in Specie d'Italia* (Tipografia di Carlo Vincenzi 1846) at 53, 80. For extensive treatment of the 1838 reform, see A. Ademollo, *Giudizio Criminale in Toscana Secondo la Riforma Leopoldina dell'Anno 1838. Cenni Teorici Pratici* (Tipografia di Sansone Coen 1840).

[52] See Mittermaier (n 29), at 566, stating that in 1846 the Prussian jurisdiction was the last German jurisdiction to abolish extraordinary punishment; Brugnoli (n 51), at 66, writing, in 1846, that extraordinary punishment had been abolished in almost all European jurisdictions; and, finally, Ambrosoli (n 43), at 274, claiming, in 1852, not to know of any legislation that was still providing extraordinary punishment.

[53] See Ambrosoli (n 43), at 257–259, 277–278; and Mittermaier (n 29), at 546–547. Ambrosoli's work was published in 1852, Mittermaier's in 1858. They both mention the Kingdom of the Two Sicilies and Austria as jurisdictions still featuring the suspension of res judicata.

[54] See Damaška, *Evaluation of Evidence* (n 9), at 112.

1.2.3 A taste of the 19th-century debate on intermediate verdicts

To conclude this account of the intermediate verdicts produced by the medieval legal tradition, I offer a brief critical analysis of a selection of arguments for and against the logic according to which weaker evidence than that required for conviction to ordinary punishment still warranted hard treatment, although milder treatment than such ordinary punishment. These are restatements of arguments advanced by European scholars writing around the middle of the 19th century. The debate is particularly significant since it occurred at a critical time for the survival on the Continent of extraordinary punishment and of the suspension of res judicata. While, by then, most viewed these devices as vestiges of a primitive system of proof, and as objectionable instruments of repression, a few scholars tenaciously defended their rationality and saw value in the system retaining them.

I must start from an obvious argument against the *ius commune* intermediate verdicts that I already hinted at. As seen earlier, extraordinary punishment and the suspension of res judicata were made necessary by the prohibition to convict to ordinary punishment on the basis of anything less than full proof and, in particular, on circumstantial evidence alone. A strong argument against them, then, consisted in pointing out the fallacy of this prohibition. If circumstantial evidence can, indeed, produce in the adjudicator's mind the degree of confidence that is sufficient to warrant ordinary punishment, the argument goes, then the reason for having these intermediate verdicts ceases to exist.[55] This argument may have little importance for the project of justifying an intermediate verdict in a contemporary criminal justice system. After all, given the current dominant sentiments about evidential reasoning, nowadays one could hardly defend the issuing of an intermediate verdict on the basis of circumstantial evidence by claiming that this evidence can never be sufficient for conviction. Arguably, though, the argument played a crucial role in eradicating extraordinary punishment and the suspension of res judicata in the 19th century.

[55] See Mittermaier (n 29), at 541, 557–559, and especially 563. As Pagano had already done in the previous century, Mittermaier recognised that inferential reasoning is also involved in the case of direct evidence (see *id.*, at 157–159). See also Brugnoli (n 51), at 32–33, 81–88, arguing in favour of convicting to ordinary punishment on the basis of circumstantial evidence, and arguing that punishment can only track the severity of the crime, not the strength of the evidence. For a contemporaneous work in stark contrast with Mittermaier's and Brugnoli's works, see Carmignani (n 51), at 176–198, offering a passionate and colourful criticism of circumstantial evidence, alongside a defence of the Roman-canon standard of full proof. Writing about the difficulty of articulating and rationalising circumstantial evidence and the inferences based on it, Carmignani says that, unlike a witness who is disincentivised from lying by their moral compass, and by the threat of the law, 'circumstantial evidence threatens but cannot be threatened; it injures without fear of being injured ... if it plummets on the head of the innocent, circumstantial evidence is like a cleaver handled by an invisible hand, for which no one can be held accountable' (Carmignani (n 51) at 189, my translation). In a later passage, Carmignani argues that, contrary to the widespread sentiment at the time, extraordinary punishment justified by circumstantial evidence is not an instrument of repression: rather, it is more defendant-friendly than allowing conviction to ordinary punishment on the basis of such evidence (see Carmignani (n 51) at 226–228).

A second argument against intermediate verdicts concerns the burden of proof. If the burden of proving guilt is on the prosecution, the argument goes, then a failure to prove guilt means that the defendant should not suffer any negative treatment on the part of the system. Either the burden is discharged and the defendant is convicted, or the burden is not discharged and the defendant is acquitted. There is no room for an in-between option.[56] Evidently, this argument is question-begging. It assumes that there is only one standard of proof, the satisfaction of which warrants imposing hard treatment on the defendant. This may be true, but it cannot be taken for granted. If it were true, it would, indeed, follow that the prosecution's failure to discharge the burden of proof—that is, to meet that unique standard—would necessitate an acquittal. If it were not true, instead, the prosecution's failure to satisfy the standard of proof for conviction would not entail that an intermediate verdict could not be justified. It could, indeed, be justified if there was a standard of proof, lower than that for conviction, the satisfaction of which warranted that intermediate verdict. Notice that, as pointed out earlier, the availability of an intermediate verdict does not alter the allocation of the burden of proof. It would still be for the prosecution to satisfy any standard of proof that warranted a verdict other than acquittal. Whether there is a standard of proof lower than that for conviction, the satisfaction of which warrants an intermediate verdict, is a question that I will pick up again in Chapter 4.

According to a third argument against intermediate verdicts, the logic 'weaker evidence, milder hard treatment' exposes the system's acceptance of an unacceptable risk of harming the innocent, even if to a lesser degree than with the infliction of ordinary punishment. Indeed, 'by distinguishing between ordinary and extraordinary punishment, the State [that issues an intermediate verdict] confesses that it did not dare inflict full punishment, since the certainty of guilt was not full either; as a consequence, the State distinguishes between the punishment that should strike the guilty ... and that which is issued against someone whose guilt is in doubt'.[57] The argument concludes that, by making explicit that it is taking too risky a gamble with the innocents' lives, the criminal justice system is likely to lose legitimacy in the eyes of the public.[58] A stern advocate of extraordinary punishment offered an alternative view. His argument, with Beccarian overtones, was that by increasing the certainty of punishment, this intermediate verdict 'secures the moral force of punishment on the souls'.[59] I read this as a claim that intermediate

[56] See Mittermaier (n 29), at 539–540. The author formulates this argument with reference to the suspension of res judicata, but I see no reason why the argument should not also apply to extraordinary punishment.

[57] ibid, at 561 (my translation).

[58] ibid.

[59] Carmignani (n 51), at 232–233 (my translation). Consider that, while Beccaria argued that the certainty of punishment has greater deterrent effect than its 'cruelty', he seemed critical of extraordinary punishment. See C. Beccaria, *Dei Delitti e Delle Pene* (Einaudi 1965), ch XXVII, at 59–61; and n 61 below.

verdicts increase deterrence: making hard treatment more likely, they enhance the capacity of the criminal law to direct conduct, and, by so doing, they foster the law-abiding person's confidence in the system, hence the system's legitimacy. In Chapter 5, section 5.3, I will address both the argument that intermediate verdicts increase deterrence, and the argument that they affect—and, in particular, undermine—the system's legitimacy. I will show that both arguments are weak, and that the latter argument does not impair the justification of intermediate verdicts that I offer in this book. The reason for postponing the assessment of these arguments is that they both present new and interesting aspects when considered in light of my defence of intermediate verdicts; moreover, my assessment of them will be informed, in part, by such defence.

A fourth argument against intermediate verdicts is encapsulated in this passage: '[p]unishment and guilt form a composite concept, like two terms corresponding to each other, whereby it is not possible to conceive of half-proof, as it is not possible to conceive of half-guilt, since the judge cannot speak of guilt unless it is fully proven according to the law. Certainty does not come in degrees. When certainty is not reached, we are in the domain of doubt, and no punishment can correspond to a situation of doubt.'[60] The starting point of the argument is that someone is either guilty or they are not, which does not deny that guilt, when it does exist, admits of gradations. The argument then considers that inflicting hard treatment on the basis of evidence that falls short of the standard of proof for conviction—allegedly, certainty—is akin to deeming the defendant half-guilty, or guilty to the extent of some other fraction. But this, the argument contends, is nonsense, precisely because there is no such thing as half-guilt.[61] Therefore, the conclusion is that intermediate verdicts are at odds with the notion of guilt—or criminal responsibility—that represents the cornerstone of the criminal justice system. The fallacy of this argument can be exposed by moving from the realisation that whatever the standard of proof for conviction is, it can hardly consist in certainty, if certainty is understood as a probability of one that something is the case.[62]

[60] Mittermaier (n 29), at 564 (my translation).

[61] See Beccaria (n 59), ch XXXI, at 76, where, in passing, Beccaria criticises the concepts of quasi-proof and half-proof on the grounds that someone cannot be 'half-innocent or half-guilty, that is, half-punishable and half-acquittable' (my translation). Contrast Beccaria's view with a passage from Foucault's discussion of torture and criminal fact finding in the *Ancien Régime*: 'Guilt did not begin when all the evidence was gathered together; piece by piece, it was constituted by each of the elements that made it possible to recognise a guilty person. Thus a semi-proof did not leave the suspect innocent until such time as it was completed; it made him semi-guilty; slight evidence of a serious crime marked someone as slightly criminal. In short, penal demonstration did not obey a dualistic system: true or false; but a principle of continuous gradation; a degree reached in the demonstration already formed a degree of guilt': see M. Foucault, *Discipline and Punish: The Birth of the Prison* (Penguin Books 1991), at 42.

[62] Indeed, Mittermaier himself does not understand in these terms the 'certainty' he requires for conviction. In his view, certainty is that state of confidence in a hypothesis produced by the falsification of all other possible hypotheses—importantly, with the exclusion of 'extraordinary' ones. He acknowledges that requiring 'absolute certainty' for conviction would render the administration of criminal justice impossible. See Mittermaier (n 29), at 72–74.

Any criminal justice system that wants to have a chance of convicting criminals must content itself with requiring proof falling short of certainty.[63] Accordingly, when the adjudicator finds the defendant guilty in such a system, they are merely stating that there is a given probability, short of one, that the defendant is guilty. This notwithstanding, a conviction is not the assertion that the defendant's behaviour instantiates a certain fraction of guilt corresponding to the probability of guilt resulting from the assessment of the evidence. The same is true of an intermediate verdict. In this case, the standard of proof is lower than that for conviction. Issuing the verdict, therefore, involves recognising that there is a lower probability of guilt than that warranting conviction. But, again, this is not a statement to the effect that the defendant is, for example, one-third or two-thirds guilty. Probabilities concern facts. Facts either occurred or did not occur.[64] That the most that we can say of a given fact, for example guilt, is that it took place with a probability falling short of certainty, does not deny that we recognise that this fact either did or did not occur. In other words, while a probabilistic assertion is the expression of a degree of belief in a particular fact, the fact is not turned into a matter of degrees by being probabilistically asserted.

The fifth and final argument that I survey was formulated with exclusive regard to the suspension of res judicata. In a public trial, the argument goes, there is little reason for having this intermediate verdict. An interested party can attend the proceedings, have first-hand experience of the incriminating evidence and, thus, 'be able to attribute the right value to an acquittal, and distinguish between the truly innocent and the defendant who re-joins society burdened by a suspicion that was not dispelled'.[65] In other words, if the main reason for this verdict is to point out to the public those defendants against whom there is substantial incriminating evidence, even if not sufficient for conviction, the verdict is unnecessary. The publicity of the trial is sufficient to give interested parties the opportunity to know the strength of the case against the defendant who is not convicted, so as to use this information in order to decide which comportment to take towards them.[66] Against this argument it was objected that if the system is, indeed, interested in delivering to the public information about the strength of the case against the non-convicted, then the system should do so clearly through a verdict. Even assuming that trial publicity is effective and that interested parties can gather the relevant information

[63] See F. Picinali, 'Can the Reasonable Doubt Standard be Justified? A Reconstructed Dialogue' (2018) 31 Canadian Journal of Law and Jurisprudence 365, at 373–375.

[64] This may not be true in the domain of quantum physics, but this is beside the point here. See C. Rovelli, *Helgoland* (Adelphi 2020).

[65] See Mittermaier (n 29), at 541 (my translation).

[66] Mittermaier focuses, in particular, on instances of suspension of res judicata that involve the restrictive condition of barring the defendant from running in an election. He argues that, rather than adopting such a verdict, it is preferable to rely on the fact that electors can, through the public trial, gather the information they need in order to decide whether or not to vote for this individual. See ibid, at 542.

if they wish to do so, the objection contends that it is reckless of the system to rely on these parties' ability to interpret this information correctly. Moreover, it is an abdication, on the part of the system, of its responsibility to 'ensure the complete manifestation of judicial truth'.[67] The system, the objection concludes, should not issue an 'incomplete verdict'—that of acquittal—giving to the public 'the power to complete it' as they see fit.[68] My view with respect to the above argument against the suspension of res judicata is that it misconceives this verdict as being chiefly about delivering information to the public about the strength of the case. Surely an important (the most important?) aspect of this verdict is that it affords the possibility of reopening the proceedings against the defendant if new incriminating evidence emerges. The argument has nothing to say against this aspect,[69] not to mention other significant restrictive conditions that were sometimes included in the verdict.[70] As for the objection, it suffices to point out that the value of delivering clear information to the public cannot be sufficient to justify an intermediate verdict such as the suspension of res judicata. This is, again, because this verdict is more than just a vehicle of information on the strength of the case. Be that as it may, later in the chapter I will consider closely an argument from information similar to the objection at issue here, which has been advanced in defence of the Scottish 'not proven' verdict. There, I will tackle head-on the claim that the availability of an intermediate verdict produces a desirable informational gain.

1.3 The Italian acquittal '*per insufficienza di prove*' in the 1930 Code of Criminal Procedure

The 1807 Code of Criminal Procedure of the short-lived Napoleonic Kingdom of Italy included the suspension of res judicata, with the possibility of significant restrictions on the defendant's liberty. A milder form of this intermediate verdict was provided by the 1819 Code of Criminal Procedure of the Kingdom of the Two Sicilies.[71] Fast-forward fifty years: Italy has finally become a unified country. The

[67] See Ambrosoli (n 43), at 296 (my translation).
[68] See ibid, at 296–297 (my translation).
[69] Consider, though, that Mittermaier also attacked the suspension of res judicata on the basis of the argument from the burden of proof seen earlier, and that—relying on this argument—he criticised the legal and social consequences that affected those who received this verdict. See Mittermaier (n 29), at 539–541.
[70] In some 19th-century jurisdictions these conditions included surveillance measures, travel restrictions, and also custodial measures. See Ambrosoli (n 43), at 260. In fact, Mittermaier—who put forward the argument discussed here—countenanced exceptional cases in which restrictions of this sort could be applied to defendants who had been acquitted of—but were still suspected of having committed—crimes that represented particularly serious attacks on public safety: see Mittermaier (n 29), at 542. Notice also that Ambrosoli only defended a form of suspension of res judicata without additional restrictive conditions for the defendant: see Ambrosoli (n 43), at 277–280.
[71] See Ambrosoli (n 43), at 259–261, 277–278.

1865 Code of Criminal Procedure of the new Kingdom of Italy featured an intermediate verdict that shared with the suspension of res judicata the expression of doubt about the innocence of the defendant. However, the Code allowed criminal proceedings to be resumed with the discovery of new incriminating evidence only if the intermediate verdict had already been issued at the conclusion of the pre-trial phase (*istruzione*).[72] If, instead, the verdict was the epilogue of the trial (*dibattimento*), once the time limit for appealing it had expired, it became res judicata and the prosecution could not be resumed.[73] With the Code of Criminal Procedure of 1913, the formula '*insufficienza di prove*' (insufficiency of evidence) made its first appearance in Italian law.[74] It was constitutive of an intermediate verdict—precisely, acquittal '*per insufficienza di prove*'—[75]available at the conclusion of both the pre-trial and trial phases.[76] In an interesting twist, with regard to the pre-trial phase, the 1913 Code allowed the reopening of the proceedings with the discovery of new incriminating evidence not only when this phase terminated in the intermediate verdict, but also if it ended with 'full' acquittal.[77] Not so for the trial phase: irrespective of the type of acquittal, the verdict became res judicata with the expiration of the time limit for appealing, and the prosecution could not be resumed.[78] The same solutions were followed by the 1930 Code of Criminal Procedure,[79] a code that regulated the Italian criminal process until the reform of 1988, which gave Italy its current code. The acquittal '*per insufficienza di prove*' was provided by article 378(2) for the pre-trial phase, and article 479(3) for the trial. While the essential trait of the suspension of res judicata—that of allowing criminal proceedings to be reopened with the discovery of new incriminating

[72] NB while this will be obvious to many, it is worth pointing out that, in the pre-trial phase, the adjudicator could not convict the defendant but, at most, send them to face trial. For all the codes that I mention in this paragraph, then, the 'verdict system' for the pre-trial phase features this option instead of conviction.

[73] See, in particular, arts 250, 266, 393, 445, and 518 of the 1865 Code of Criminal Procedure. For a critical analysis of this verdict system, and of the debate about it occurring while the 1865 Code was in force, see M. N. Miletti, 'Ombre Sull'Innocenza. La Formula Dubitativa nel Processo Penale dell'Italia Liberale' (2020) 2 Quaderno di Storia del Penale e della Giustizia 177. See also G. A. Anca, 'Insufficienza di Prove' (1993) 7 Digesto delle Discipline Penalistiche 147, at 152–153. In 1879, a young Enrico Ferri argued in favour of introducing the suspension of res judicata in the then-existing trial by jury. In Ferri's view—which was criticised by Arturo Rocco, among others—this verdict did not clash with any 'fundamental legal precept'. See Miletti, ibid, at 185–191 (my translation).

[74] See arts 274(2) and 421(2) of the 1913 Code of Criminal Procedure. See Anca (n 73), at 153.

[75] I am using the term 'acquittal' as a translation of '*proscioglimento*', a term generally used to refer to both the '*sentenza di non luogo a procedere*' issued at the end of the pre-trial phase and the '*sentenza di assoluzione*' issued at the end of the trial.

[76] For a critical analysis of the 1913 reform of the verdict system see Miletti (n 73), at 200–206; and F. Morelli, *Le Formule di Proscioglimento: Radici Storiche e Funzioni Attuali* (Giappichelli 2014), in particular at 118–131.

[77] See art 295(1) of the 1913 Code.

[78] See art 435 of the 1913 Code.

[79] See, in particular, arts 199, 402, and 576 of the 1930 Code of Criminal Procedure.

evidence—was not a distinctive feature of the 1930 intermediate verdict,[80] it is widely recognised in the scholarship that the acquittal '*per insufficienza di prove*' was, ultimately, rooted in the intermediate options elaborated by the *ius commune*.[81] This is evident if one considers the punitive and preventative effects produced by the verdict.

Especially when it was issued at the end of the trial, the acquittal '*per insufficienza di prove*' of the 1930 Code triggered a series of detrimental legal consequences for the individual who received it:[82] it produced a criminal record and could be disclosed to interested parties; it could be taken into consideration for sentencing purposes in separate proceedings; it could be taken into consideration when assessing the individual's dangerousness in separate proceedings; it was often relied upon as a reason to reject an individual's application to have their criminal record cleared of previous convictions; and it could contribute to justifying inflicting, on an individual, measures designed to prevent the commission of crimes on their part, for example surveillance measures or the seizure of assets. There were also a host of laws providing for detrimental effects of the intermediate verdict concerning disciplinary proceedings against, and the related administrative leave of, civil servants and State employees. In addition, it was generally recognised in the literature that the acquittal '*per insufficienza di prove*' affected the social standing of the defendant. The lingering doubt on their guilt left by the verdict, as well as the abovementioned legal consequences, were said to foster social stigma, hindering the defendant's personal and business relationships.[83] A leading scholar remarked that 'words do matter in social life and, in this respect, the acquittal "per insufficienza

[80] As just pointed out, the 1930 Code followed the solutions of the 1913 Code: the intermediate verdict did not allow the reopening of the proceedings if it was issued at the end of the trial phase, whereas any type of acquittal in the pre-trial phase allowed such a measure.

[81] See Anca (n 73), at 151–153; A. Ghiara, 'Presunzione di Innocenza, Presunzione di "Non Colpevolezza" e Formula Dubitativa, anche alla Luce degli Interventi della Corte Costituzionale' (1974) Rivista Italiana di Diritto e Procedura Penale 72, at 99, in particular fn 66, drawing a connection between the acquittal '*per insufficienza di prove*' and extraordinary punishment; V. Manzini, *Trattato di Diritto Processuale Penale Italiano, vol IV* (5th edn, UTET 1956), at 432–433, fn 2, drawing a connection between the acquittal '*per insufficienza di prove*' and the suspension of res judicata; M. Pisani, *Introduzione al Processo Penale* (Giuffrè Editore 1988), at 68–69, pointing out that the legal consequences accompanying the acquittal '*per insufficienza di prove*' are reminiscent of extraordinary punishment, while the possibility of relying on the acquittal '*per insufficienza di prove*' as evidence against the defendant in separate proceedings—see below—is reminiscent of the suspension of res judicata; and G. C. Gebbie and others, '"Not Proven" as a Juridical Fact in Scotland, Norway and Italy' (1999) 7 European Journal of Crime, Criminal Law, and Criminal Justice 262, at 271–272.

[82] See G. Conso, 'È da Rivedere, non da Eliminare l'Assoluzione per Insufficienza di Prove' (1967) 4 Giurisprudenza Italiana 101, at 109–113; G. Conso, 'L'Assoluzione per Insufficienza di Prove: Prospettive "De Iure Condendo"' in *La Frode in Assicurazione. L'Assoluzione per Insufficienza di Prove. Atti del Convegno di Studi Giuridici a Cura della Camera Penale di Trieste, 22–25 Aprile 1967* (CEDAM 1968), at 273–280; and Pisani (n 81), at 60–66.

[83] See Conso, 'È da Rivedere' (n 82), at 108–109; E. Marzaduri, 'Commento all'Art. 530—Sentenza di Assoluzione' in M. Chiavario (ed), *Commento al Nuovo Codice di Procedura Penale, vol 5* (UTET 1989), at 520–521; Gebbie and others (n 81), at 272; Anca (n 73), at 154, 170; Pisani (n 81), at 64; and Ghiara (n 81), at 101.

di prove" is considered a disqualification of sorts'.[84] Finally, the fact that the law allowed the defendant to appeal an acquittal '*per insufficienza di prove*'[85] was taken as implicit recognition on the part of the system that this verdict had some of the attributes of conviction.[86]

In the absence of clear statutory prescriptions concerning the standards of proof to be applied in the trial phase—standards regulating the choice between full acquittal and the intermediate verdict, and the choice between the latter and conviction—scholars endeavoured to identify these evidential thresholds.[87] The resulting dominant view, which was also endorsed in the case law,[88] was as follows: full acquittal was required in the event of a total lack of incriminating evidence, or when the exculpatory evidence made the judge morally certain of innocence; acquittal '*per insufficienza di prove*' was required when the judge's mind was in a state of doubt, due to the fact that the incriminating evidence was incomplete or equivocal, or due to a balance between incriminating and exculpatory evidence; conviction was required when the incriminating evidence made the judge morally certain of guilt.[89]

[84] F. Cordero, *Procedura Penale* (2nd edn, Giuffrè Editore 1971), at 642.

[85] Consider that, under both the 1913 Code and the 1930 Code, the defendant who received the intermediate verdict at the end of the pre-trial phase could request that this phase be reopened, adducing new exculpatory evidence (see art 295(2) of the 1913 Code, and art 402(2) of the 1930 Code), and the defendant who received the verdict at the end of the trial phase could appeal it (see arts 477 and 478 of the 1913 Code, and arts 512 and 513 of the 1930 Code).

[86] See Pisani (n 81), at 61. Notice that the Code of Criminal Procedure of 1930 (NB the following considerations also apply to the current Code) demanded that when the judge fully acquitted, they should express acquittal with one of several formulas succinctly conveying the substantive reasons for the decision. A fully acquitted defendant could appeal against acquittal, seeking to obtain a change of the formula, especially for the purposes of avoiding a civil lawsuit for damages, which, for example, could be brought if the formula stated that they were not culpable, but not if it stated that no *actus reus* took place. See G. D. Pisapia, *Compendio di Procedura Penale* (CEDAM 1975), at 368, 389–390 (with respect to the current Code, see, eg *Corte di Cassazione Penale* no. 26109/2016). Having said this, the acquittal '*per insufficienza di prove*' was subject to further grounds of appeal, provided, in particular, by arts 512 and 513 of the 1930 Code.

[87] Rough indications about the first evidential threshold were provided by art 479(2) of the 1930 Code. Notice that the first evidential threshold was generally spelt out in similar terms to those I am about to mention, also for what concerns the pre-trial phase. As one would expect, this was not the case for the second evidential threshold, considering that, in the pre-trial phase, the defendant could not be convicted but, at most, could be sent to face trial with a '*sentenza di rinvio a giudizio*'. Evidence was deemed sufficient for such a decision when the judge considered it capable of leading to conviction at trial. See G. Leone, *Lineamenti di Diritto Processuale Penale* (4th edn, Jovene 1956), at 348–350.

[88] See, for instance, *Corte Costituzionale* no. 124/1972; *Corte di Cassazione Penale* no. 8265/1988; and *Corte di Cassazione Penale* no. 5771/1988. These decisions highlight the standard regulating the choice between full acquittal and acquittal '*per insufficienza di prove*'. On the standard for conviction (ie that of moral certainty), see, among others, *Corte di Cassazione Penale* no. 12713/1978; *Corte di Cassazione Penale* no. 8224/1983; and *Corte di Cassazione Penale* no. 12508/1986.

[89] See Anca (n 73), at 155–156; Cordero (n 84), at 642; Pisapia (n 86), at 365–366. See also G. Bettiol, *Istituzioni di Diritto e Procedura Penale* (CEDAM 1966), at 217, arguing that the intermediate verdict should be issued when the facts are 'uncertain'; and Leone (n 87), at 430, mentioning as an evidential condition for the intermediate verdict only the case of a balance between incriminating and exculpatory evidence. For a reference to moral certainty as the standard for conviction, see V. Manzini, *Trattato di Diritto Processuale Penale Italiano, vol I* (6th edn, UTET 1967, with updates by G. Conso and G. D. Pisapia), at 234. On moral certainty, see also the case law in the previous note. Consider that the reasonable doubt standard became operative in Italy only at a later stage: first, through the case law of the Corte

The acquittal '*per insufficienza di prove*' has always been a controversial verdict. The consultations on the preliminary draft of the 1930 Code reveal a wide range of opinions on the retention of this verdict. While some participants even suggested adding a further verdict between full acquittal and acquittal '*per insufficienza di prove*',[90] somewhat unsurprisingly a bar association advocated in favour of the elimination of the verdict, due to its supposed stigmatising effect.[91] Also, the Corte di Cassazione del Regno lamented that the verdict produced too many defence appeals under the 1913 Code. It, therefore, suggested that the formula of the verdict be changed into a more defendant-friendly formula, while at the same time removing the defendant's right to appeal.[92] Presenting the draft code in parliament, the Minister of Justice Alfredo Rocco defended the intermediate verdict, arguing that, without it, judges might convict more often in the event of doubt, possibly producing an increase in the rate of false convictions, and that the verdict was a useful tool to target forms of criminality that were difficult to prove.[93] In the end, of course, the acquittal '*per insufficienza di prove*' found a new home in the 1930 Code. But the debate on its merits was far from over.

1.3.1 A taste of the debate on the acquittal '*per insufficienza di prove*'

As a result of the coming into force of the Italian Constitution in 1948, and especially of the European Convention on Human Rights, which Italy ratified in 1955, an argument against the acquittal '*per insufficienza di prove*' came to the fore. This was the argument according to which the intermediate verdict is not compatible

di Cassazione Penale (see, eg no. 30328/2002, no. 25678/2004, no. 33748/2005); and, subsequently, through the law no. 46/2006, which added this standard of proof to art 533(1) of the current Code of Criminal Procedure.

[90] See Ministero della Giustizia e degli Affari di Culto, *Lavori Preparatori del Codice Penale e del Codice di Procedura Penale. Vol IX, Osservazioni e Proposte sul Progetto Preliminare di un Nuovo Codice di Procedura Penale, Parte III* (Tipografia delle Mantellate 1930), at 427–428; and Ministero della Giustizia e degli Affari di Culto, *Lavori Preparatori del Codice Penale e del Codice di Procedura Penale. Vol IX, Osservazioni e Proposte sul Progetto Preliminare di un Nuovo Codice di Procedura Penale, Parte IV* (Tipografia delle Mantellate 1930), at 235.

[91] See Ministero della Giustizia e degli Affari di Culto, *Lavori Preparatori. Parte III* (n 90), at 429.

[92] See Ministero della Giustizia e degli Affari di Culto, *Lavori Preparatori. Parte IV* (n 90), at 234. Interestingly, the alternative formula suggested by the Corte di Cassazione del Regno was '*non provata reità*' (guilt not proven), a formula which, according to the court, has no stigmatising effect. As we will see, this is in contrast with a prominent view in the debate on the Scottish intermediate verdict.

[93] See R. Mangini and others (eds), *Codice di Procedura Penale. Illustrato con i Lavori Preparatori* (Tipografia della Camera dei Deputati 1930), at 278–279, 343. To be sure, the Minister of Justice did not mention explicitly the worry about an increase in the rate of *false* convictions. But this worry seems integral to his concern about a possible increase in convictions in cases characterised by doubt. For a similar view—although expressed when the Code had already been into force for more than thirty years—see Bettiol (n 89), at 217 and Cordero (n 84), at 643.

with the presumption of innocence.[94] According to one version of the argument, the presumption only admits of acquittal and conviction as possible epilogues of the trial: *tertium non datur.* According to a second—but not alternative—version, the presumption does not allow the imposition of detrimental consequences, be these social stigma or specific legal restrictions, on someone who has not been convicted. I will address this argument in the next chapter, which is fully dedicated to the question of the compatibility between the presumption of innocence and intermediate verdicts.[95] Here, it is worth pointing out that, in a much-debated decision, the Italian Constitutional Court ruled that there was no incompatibility.[96] However, during the period in which the 1930 Code was in force, formal proposals to reform the Code were put forward on more than one occasion, and these proposals invariably suggested scrapping the acquittal *'per insufficienza di prove'* precisely on the basis of an alleged incompatibility between the verdict and the presumption of innocence.[97] More importantly, this argument is, arguably, the reason that led the legislator of 1988 to abandon the intermediate verdict.[98] According to article 530(2) of the current Code, the insufficiency of the evidence now warrants a full acquittal.

[94] Notably, the presumption of innocence was already stated in art 9 of the French Déclaration des Droits de l'Homme et du Citoyen of 1789. This notwithstanding, in the early/mid-19th century literature that I have studied, I have not found any argument in favour or against intermediate verdicts that relies on the presumption. The argument from incompatibility, though, was put forward in the debate accompanying the 1865 Code and the 1913 Code, with reference to the respective intermediate verdicts. See Miletti (n 73); and Morelli (n 76), at 118–131.

[95] Note that art 27(2) of the Italian Constitution states: *'L'imputato non è considerato colpevole sino alla condanna definitiva'* ('The defendant should not be considered guilty until a definitive conviction'). The question whether this *'presunzione di non colpevolezza'* ('presumption of non-guilt') is equivalent to the presumption of innocence in art 6(2) of the European Convention on Human Rights (ECHR) has been debated in the Italian scholarship. See, among others, Pisani (n 81), at 70–72; G. Illuminati, *La Presunzione d'Innocenza dell'Imputato* (Zanichelli 1979), at 22–28; G. Illuminati, 'Presunzione di Non Colpevolezza' in *Enciclopedia Giuridica, vol XXVII* (Treccani 1991), at 1–2; Conso, 'È da Rivedere' (n 82), at 107; Ghiara (n 81), at 82–86; and M. Chiavario, 'Case note: *Corte Costituzionale* n.124/1972' (1972) Giurisprudenza Costituzionale 1325, at 1332–1333. The claim of equivalence seems to have prevailed. Be that as it may, Italian law includes the presumption of innocence by virtue of incorporating art 6(2) ECHR.

[96] See *Corte Costituzionale* (n 88). While the court was mainly concerned with the compatibility between the intermediate verdict and art 27(2) of the Italian Constitution, it did argue, in passing, that the intermediate verdict is also compatible with art 6(2) ECHR; indeed, that the two norms are substantially equivalent. See the preceding note.

[97] See Pisani (n 81), at 55, referring to a reform proposal from 1965; and G. D. Pisapia, *Compendio di Procedura Penale* (4th edn, CEDAM 1985), at 414, referring to a draft for a new code, produced in 1978.

[98] See Marzaduri (n 83), at 516–517, 520–521, also stating that the elimination of the intermediate verdict was one of the most-publicised aspects of the reform. Interestingly, though, the elimination of the acquittal *'per insufficienza di prove'* is barely mentioned in the preparatory works for, and the ministerial notes accompanying, the 1988 Code, as reported in G. Conso and others, *Il Nuovo Codice di Procedura Penale. Dalle Leggi Delega ai Decreti Delegati. Vol IV. Il Progetto Preliminare del 1988* (CEDAM 1990), at 99, 1167–1170 and G. Conso and others, *Il Nuovo Codice di Procedura Penale. Dalle Leggi Delega ai Decreti Delegati. Vol. V. Il Progetto Definitivo e il Testo Definitivo del Codice* (CEDAM 1990), at 54–55, 898–899. This suggests that, by that time, the debate on whether the intermediate verdict had to be retained was over, and that the option to scrap the verdict, already implemented in the draft code produced in 1978, was basically taken for granted.

The debate on the acquittal '*per insufficienza di prove*' was particularly lively during the twenty-five years preceding its demise. Already in the early seventies, this debate was perceived as having a clear political, rather than merely academic, dimension;[99] it captivated a broader community than that of legal insiders. In the remainder of this section, I restate and critically assess three arguments that featured in this debate. Although not as prominent as the argument on the incompatibility between the presumption of innocence and the acquittal '*per insufficienza di prove*', these arguments do shed light on the range of values that the participants in the debate felt were at stake in the choice between retaining or scrapping the verdict.

According to a first argument, the acquittal '*per insufficienza di prove*' should be retained, since it expresses and implements the long-honoured principle *in dubio pro reo*. More precisely, this intermediate verdict is seen as a guarantee for the defendant, because its availability effectively amounts to a prohibition on the judge convicting in the presence of doubt about the question of guilt.[100] Notice that this argument was advanced at a time when the reasonable doubt standard was not yet entrenched in Italian law.[101] Given this, one might agree with the proponents of the argument that, at the time, there was value in directing the judge not to convict in the event of doubt about guilt; and, possibly, that the intermediate verdict was, indeed, a vehicle of this directive. Still, the argument appears weak. To begin with, in a bemused rejoinder, a scholar for the abolition of the acquittal '*per insufficienza di prove*' pointed out that the social disqualification and the detrimental legal effects produced by the verdict can hardly be seen as consequences *pro reo*.[102] More importantly, if the proponents of the argument are right in interpreting the principle *in dubio pro reo* as requiring that, in the event of doubt about guilt, the adjudicator should, amongst the available options, take that which is most favourable to the defendant—[103] by implication, that the adjudicator should not convict—it is not at all clear why, when guilt is in doubt, the principle cannot be implemented 'merely' by issuing full acquittal. In other words, why create an intermediate option if the standard options, coupled with the appropriate decision rule, are sufficient to stay true to the principle?[104] In addition, consider that the proponents of the argument understand the principle *in dubio pro reo* not only as setting a decision rule for cases of doubt, but also as allocating the burden of proof to the prosecution.[105]

99 See Chiavario (n 95), at 1327.
100 See Bettiol (n 89), at 216–217 and Leone (n 87), at 429.
101 See n 89 above for information on the introduction of the standard in the Italian system.
102 See Pisani (n 81), at 65.
103 To be sure, I am not convinced that this is the correct interpretation of the principle *in dubio pro reo*, when implemented in the context of fact-finding. Rather than requiring the option *pro reo* in case of doubt *about* guilt, so as to effectively set the overcoming of doubt as the standard of proof for conviction, in my view the principle requires the option *pro reo* in case of doubt *about which option to choose*, whatever the standard of proof for conviction is. For clarification, see Chapter 4, n 12 and accompanying text.
104 cf Pisani (n 81), at 65–66.
105 See, in particular, Bettiol (n 89), at 216–217.

Even if such a construal were correct, it would not follow that the intermediate verdict is an expression or an implication of the alleged second feature of the principle and that it is, on this ground, justified. Indeed, we saw that scholars from the 19th century put forward the opposite argument that intermediate verdicts conflict with the rule allocating the burden of proof to the prosecution. To restate a point made earlier, the fact that the burden of proof is, and should be, on the prosecution says nothing about the justification of intermediate verdicts. This justification depends on whether there is a standard of proof lower than that for conviction, the satisfaction of which warrants issuing such a verdict. I will address this question in Chapter 4.

A second argument in favour of the acquittal *'per insufficienza di prove'* has marked Cartesian overtones. It stems from the consideration that an intermediate verdict reflects the experience of doubting, an experience that is profoundly human, and which characterises many instances of decision-making that we routinely undertake, including in the domain of criminal adjudication. The argument contends that the facade of binary categorical verdicts obliterates the dimension of doubt, doing a disservice to the administration of justice. In particular, the binary straitjacket may alienate adjudicators who, in the event of doubt about whether the defendant is guilty or innocent, would be unable accurately to convey through the verdict the outcome of their evidential reasoning: an epistemic position that lies between confidence in innocence and confidence in guilt. The system would force upon them an unnatural image of themselves as unwavering and assertive fact-finders. In the eyes of the law, then, they would not be recognised and valued as human beings involved in the very human—hence, irremediably uncertain and fallible—enterprise of judging their peers.[106] What is puzzling about this argument is that it was put forward from within a system that requires reasoned verdicts. Let us assume that there is value in allowing the adjudicator to express their doubts about whether the defendant is guilty or innocent, when they do harbour such doubts.[107] Surely the adjudicator can already do so effectively through the report of their reasoning accompanying a decision to acquit the defendant. This report can accurately convey an analysis of the incriminating evidence and of why this

[106] See G. D. Pisapia, 'Relazione di Sintesi al Convegno' in *La Frode in Assicurazione. L'Assoluzione per Insufficienza di Prove* (n 82), at 430, 434–435, 437–438. See also Mangini and others (n 93), at 344, showing that this argument, or components of it, may have played a role in the drafting of the 1930 Code; and Miletti (n 73), at 202–203, reporting a similar argument made in the course of the parliamentary debate about the 1913 Code. Finally, see *Corte Costituzionale* (n 88), para 3, defending the acquittal *'per insufficienza di prove'* on the ground that it represents an outlet for the adjudicator's doubt, where doubt is seen as an 'expression of rationality and ineliminable aspect of our thought' (my translation).

[107] My view is that, if there is value in allowing this, it is not so much because the opportunity to express doubt enhances—if, indeed, it does so—the adjudicator's own experience of judging; rather, it is because the expression of doubt may deliver to interested parties useful information about the defendant. Later in the chapter, though, I will consider and confute an argument advanced in favour of the Scottish 'not proven' verdict, which hinges precisely on an alleged gain in the delivery of information, produced by adopting an intermediate verdict.

evidence, while significant, falls short of the standard for conviction; it can, thus, reflect the doubting mind of the adjudicator, showing that, like the defendant, they are a human being, limited and fallible. With reasoned verdicts in place, then, the intermediate verdict is hardly needed as an additional outlet for the adjudicator's doubts. Admittedly, the argument considered here may be stronger if referred to a system that does not require, or allow, reasoned verdicts. But the enhancement of the adjudicator's own experience of judging, allegedly produced by the opportunity to express doubt, would still fall well short of providing a justification for having an intermediate verdict in such a system. After all, the availability of this verdict is likely to affect not only those who deliver criminal justice, but also, crucially, the recipients of criminal justice, in particular, the defendant. The position of the recipients would need careful consideration in any plausible justificatory attempt.

A final argument, this time advanced against the acquittal '*per insufficienza di prove*' is that intermediate verdicts are not compatible with the adversarial model, this being the model that Italy shifted towards with the 1988 reform.[108] As understood by the argument, the adversarial model is chiefly concerned with settling a dispute between opposing parties, rather than with truth-seeking. And the dispute is settled by identifying a winner, which is the task of an impartial adjudicator with no investigative powers, and deciding exclusively on the basis of the evidence adduced by the parties. According to the argument, the intermediate verdict is problematic if incorporated in such a model, because it does not attribute victory to either party; it does not settle the dispute, effectively leaving the matter at issue in doubt. The verdict, the argument continues, makes more sense in the inquisitorial model, where the role of the investigator and that of the adjudicator are merged and, importantly, truth-seeking is the pre-eminent goal of the process. In such a model, the adoption of an intermediate verdict allows for a more accurate reflection of the result of the epistemological inquiry of the investigator/adjudicator. That this verdict is issued means that the result of the enquiry was, admittedly, inconclusive; but insofar as this result is adherent to the evidence, it nonetheless represents the degree of belief that one is warranted to entertain on the matter at issue. Indeed, the argument contends, it is not due to chance that intermediate verdicts originated in a criminal trial that was markedly inquisitorial: the *ius commune* trial.[109] I mentioned earlier that the 1988 reform of criminal procedure realised a significant shift towards the adversarial model: the current Italian system is best characterised as a balanced mixture of adversarial and inquisitorial features. As an interesting aside in support of the argument considered here, it was pointed out that in the years preceding the reform, the number of those opposing the acquittal

[108] See Anca (n 73), at 149–151. Mine is a re-elaboration of the argument that is succinctly advanced there. Consider that Anca was writing after the 1988 Code had already come into force, but her contribution refers to views expressed prior to that development.

[109] cf Meccarelli, 'Criminal Law' (n 12), at 641–642, describing adversarial aspects of the *ius commune* trial.

'per insufficienza di prove' seemed to grow at the same rate as the number of those favouring the shift towards adversarialism.[110]

I disagree with this argument on a series of counts. For a start, in the 19th century, intermediate verdicts already featured in systems with marked adversarial traits.[111] And an intermediate verdict currently features in the adversarial Scottish system, which I will consider in the next section. This indicates that the alleged incompatibility is not as strong as the argument would have us believe. Relatedly, and more importantly, the argument caricatures and misconceives the adversarial model—or, at least, concrete instantiations of it—in assuming that this model is not concerned with the search for truth, but merely with identifying the winner in the fray.[112] Surely the powers afforded to the judge in the fact-finding process of the current Italian system are a strong indication that truth-seeking is still held as a crucial value, notwithstanding that the system has embraced some adversarial features.[113] Even the English and Welsh system, which does not afford such extensive powers, obviously recognises the importance of truth-seeking,[114] and, indeed, does give the court a set of tools to prevent false convictions.[115] This means that, insofar as the value of the intermediate verdict rests on its epistemic significance, there is no reason to see the verdict as a foreign body if situated into the organism of an adversarial system. In fact, though, since an intermediate verdict may not merely be the expression of the outcome of an epistemological inquiry—for example, it might impose hard treatment in the form of stigma and/or of a legal measure—an assessment of such a verdict cannot be limited to its epistemic significance. And I do not see why other possible components of the verdict may be valuable in the inquisitorial model, but not in the adversarial one. For instance, if the verdict does impose hard treatment, issuing such a verdict in an adversarial system may count as a marginal win for the prosecution, or as a lesser defeat than

110 See Anca (n 73), at 150.

111 See Ambrosoli (n 43), at 259, 266–267, giving examples of adversarial systems including the suspension of res judicata and, relatedly, stressing the importance of truth-seeking in adversarial systems with public prosecution.

112 This is not to deny that, historically, the adversarial system had a 'truth deficit'. See Langbein, *The Origins of Adversary Criminal Trial* (n 2), at 306–310, 331–343. For an account of the increase in judicial activism in Anglo-American adversarial systems, often with the aim of enhancing the accuracy of the outcome, see M. R. Damaška, *Evidence Law Adrift* (Yale University Press 1997), at 134–142.

113 Consider, for instance, the judicial power to appoint an expert witness (art 224 of the 1988 Code of Criminal Procedure), the judicial power to admit evidence that is not put forward by the parties (arts 422 and 507 of the Code), or the judicial power to order the prosecutor to carry out further investigation (art 421 *bis* of the Code).

114 Consider, for instance, that s 1.1.(2)(a) of the Criminal Procedure Rules 2020 mentions 'acquitting the innocent and convicting the guilty', ie reaching a true outcome, as a component of the 'overriding objective' of dealing with criminal cases 'justly'. Also consider ss 3 and 7A of the Criminal Procedure and Investigations Act 1996, imposing on the prosecution a duty to disclose to the accused any material that 'might reasonably be considered capable of undermining the case for the prosecution against the accused or of assisting the case for the accused'.

115 To give just a couple of examples, consider the duty of the court to stop a weak case from going to trial, as per *R v Galbraith* [1981] 1 WLR 1039, and the duty of the court to warn the jury about the frailties of eyewitness identification evidence, as per *R v Turnbull* [1977] QB 224.

an acquittal, depending on the specific nature of the verdict. Even assuming that adversarialism is chiefly about settling a dispute by identifying the winner, then, the intermediate verdict may well serve this goal. Finally, competitive contests that end in a draw—that is, that have no winner—are certainly not unheard of. Because of this, were it true that the intermediate verdict does not identify the winner in the adjudicative contest, to argue that the competitive, partisan nature of the adversarial trial is what undermines the intermediate verdict does not take the case against the verdict very far.

1.4 The Scottish 'not proven' verdict

Unlike the Italian acquittal '*per insufficienza di prove*', the Scottish 'not proven' verdict does not originate in the *ius commune* tradition. The appearance of the 'bastard verdict'—as Sir Walter Scott once referred to it—[116] is considered 'a pure historical accident'.[117] Here is how the Scottish three-verdict system came into existence.

Up until the beginning of the 17th century, indictments in Scotland were framed in general terms, without a precise exposition of the facts alleged to have taken place. The jury was in charge of deciding whether the defendant was guilty or not guilty, and was not given detailed guidance as to which facts had to be established before a verdict of 'guilty' could be issued.[118] In the 17th century, a custom developed of producing long and complex indictments, containing a thorough list of facts alleged to have occurred. This made it necessary for judges to give the jury special directions—'interlocutors'—detailing, for each charge, the facts that they needed to consider proven before the defendant could be convicted of that charge.[119] As a result, it became the practice for juries to construct their verdicts on the model of these directions, and to return only 'special verdicts'; that is, verdicts stating, for each factual allegation constituting the charge, whether it was 'proven'

[116] See N. Gow, 'The Case for Not Proven' (1993) 143 New Law Journal 753, at 753. In 1827, Scott, who was also an advocate and sheriff in Selkirk, attended the trial of one Mary Smith for poisoning a servant girl. The trial resulted in a 'not proven' verdict. He wrote in his diary: 'Waited to see the poisoning woman. She is clearly guilty, but as one or two witnesses said the poor wench hinted an intention to poison herself, the jury gave that bastard verdict, not proven. I hate that Caledonian medium quid. One who is not proven guilty is innocent in the eyes of the law.' See ibid.

[117] I. D. Willock, *The Origins and Development of the Jury in Scotland* (The Stair Society 1966), at 217.

[118] See ibid; J. M. Barbato, 'Scotland's Bastard Verdict: Intermediacy and the Unique Three-Verdict System' (2005) 15 Indiana International and Comparative Law Review 543, at 547; and Scottish Office, *Juries and Verdicts: Improving the Delivery of Justice in Scotland* (1994), at 26. The verdict of innocence was expressed with phrases such as 'made qwyt', 'deliuerit innocent', 'clangit', or 'clene and sakles'; in the early 17th century, it was also expressed with the threefold verdict 'clene, innocent and acquit'. The verdict of guilt, instead, was expressed with phrases such as 'convictus', 'convicit', 'fylit', 'in wrang', or 'had done wrangis'; in the early 17th century, it was also expressed with the threefold verdict 'fylet, culpable and convict'. There were, however, variations of terminology between different courts: '[I]t is not until well into the eighteenth century ... that the modern forms "guilty" and "not guilty" firmly established themselves.' See Willock (n 117), at 217–218.

[119] See Willock (n 117), at 218–219, and Scottish Office (n 118), at 26.

or 'not proven'.[120] It would then be for the judge to decide whether the defendant was 'guilty' or 'not guilty' of the charge, on the basis of the findings of the jury.[121] It is possible that this development was encouraged by a deliberate policy on the part of Crown authorities to strip juries of their power to decide the question of guilt. This policy may have resulted from the fact that, during the period between the 1660 Restoration and the 1688 Glorious Revolution, juries were often reluctant to convict under unpopular and repressive statutes targeting Presbyterian Covenanters.[122]

The 1726 trial of Samuel Hale and, especially, the 1728 trial of Carnegie of Finhaven are credited with being the occasions on which the jury regained its right to deliver the verdicts of 'guilty' and 'not guilty'.[123] This was not a return to the original position, though: the 'not proven' verdict did not disappear from the scene. Consider that special verdicts were still used in the 18th century, after the above trials.[124] More importantly, in the 19th century 'not proven' started to be used as a third option, alongside 'guilty' and 'not guilty'. The verdict had, by then, lost its original function of signalling that a particular factual allegation had not been proven; instead, it had become a form of acquittal, signalling that the case against the defendant, considered as a whole, had not been established. A plausible hypothesis is that, in the period in question, juries returned a 'not proven' verdict when they considered the evidence insufficient for conviction, but nonetheless were suspicious about the defendant and wished to convey their disapproval of the defendant and of their behaviour.[125] Also, juries might have used 'not proven' as an opportunity for nullification; in particular, they probably resorted to this verdict when they felt sympathy for a defendant that they considered guilty, and wanted to spare

[120] See Willock (n 117), at 219, pointing out that special verdicts 'related the facts found proved, often at considerable length, and likewise the facts found not proved'.

[121] ibid.

[122] See ibid; Gow (n 116); and Barbato (n 118), at 547–548.

[123] See Willock (n 117), at 220–221. Hale was charged with homicide and Carnegie of Finhaven was charged with murder. They were both found 'not guilty'. Carnegie of Finhaven's lawyer strongly encouraged jurors to reclaim their power to use this verdict. See also Barbato (n 118), at 548, fn 46.

[124] See Willock (n 117), at 221. Apparently, they had become obsolete by the 1830s.

[125] See Barbato (n 118), at 549. See also C. Passarella, 'From Scotland to Italy and Back: Enrico Ferri, the Verdict of Not Proven and its Consequences on the Accused' (2020) Forum Historiae Iuris, available at <https://forhistiur.net/2020-11-passarella/> accessed 5 May 2021, paras 13–40, offering a detailed description of four high-profile 19th-century murder cases (those of Mary Smith (1827), Christina Gilmour (1844), Madeleine Smith (1857), and Alfred John Monson (1893)), in which, arguably, the juries involved returned 'not proven' verdicts due to an unwillingness to convict on circumstantial evidence alone. In a recent work, Hannah Phalen has argued that one of the merits of 'not proven' is that it allows the jury 'to express moral condemnation without the legal ramifications that come with a guilty verdict'. According to Phalen, the intermediate verdict 'gives the jury a venue to clarify an acquittal. This is particularly important in cases where the jury believes the defendant is culpable but that the prosecution has not met its burden of proof'. See H. Phalen, 'Overcoming the Opposition to a Third Verdict: A Call for Future Research on Alternative Acquittals' (2018) 50 Arizona State Law Journal 401, at 402, 417–419.

them the rigour of the law, especially the death penalty.[126] If these hypotheses are sound, they show that, while the Scottish three-verdict system is far from being the result of careful design on the part of a lawmaker with a criminal justice agenda,[127] the origins and especially the entrenchment of the system may not be accidental after all. It seems, instead, that adjudicators studiously resorted to 'not proven' because they considered it capable of performing functions that the 'guilty' and 'not guilty' verdicts could not perform: an in-between role of expressing disapproval and imposing stigma, without, however, producing the harsh consequences of conviction. The use of 'not proven' as an intermediate option between the standard verdicts has continued to this day.

The law considers 'not proven' as a form of acquittal. In terms of legal consequences, it is, indeed, undistinguishable from a 'not guilty' verdict. The standard direction on verdicts by the Judicial Institute for Scotland is clear on this point. It recites, 'There are three verdicts you can return on any charge: guilty, not guilty, or not proven. Not guilty and not proven are verdicts of acquittal and have the same effect. An accused acquitted of a charge cannot be prosecuted again on that charge, save in exceptional circumstances, and it makes no difference whether the acquittal verdict is not guilty or not proven.'[128] As hinted at in the direction, 'not proven'—like 'not guilty'—does not produce a criminal record.[129] The 'exceptional circumstances' under which both the fully acquitted and the defendant receiving 'not proven' can be retried have been introduced by the Double Jeopardy (Scotland) Act 2011. In particular, according to section 4 of the Act, in both cases of acquittal, the defendant may be retried if new incriminating evidence is found. This undoubtedly represents a detrimental legal feature of the 'not proven' verdict, but not one that is exclusive to the intermediate verdict. As I will suggest at the end of Chapter 4, this recently introduced feature of 'not proven' may play a significant role in the verdict's justification.

A notable aspect of the verdict's operation is that neither the statutory law nor the case law prescribes a standard of proof regulating the choice between 'not guilty' and 'not proven', whereas the prescribed standard of proof for conviction is proof beyond reasonable doubt. In other words, the law does not specify the epistemic circumstances that warrant issuing 'not proven' instead of 'not guilty'. Hence, the law does not provide a clear definition of the meaning of the intermediate verdict,

[126] See Barbato (n 118), at 549–550, citing as evidence of this use of 'not proven' the 1844 murder trial of Christina Gilmour, the 1845 murder trial of Isabella Rae, and the 1857 murder trial of Madeleine Smith; and Passarella (n 125), para 18.

[127] See Willock (n 117), at 217, stating that 'if ['not proven'] is to be regarded as an institution to be valued, it can scarcely be claimed as a manifestation of the genius of Scottish criminal jurisprudence'.

[128] See Judicial Institute for Scotland, *Jury Manual* (2021), at 114.2.

[129] However, information about both 'not proven' and 'not guilty' verdicts may be disclosed to a prospective employer as part of a Protecting Vulnerable Groups (PVG) background check. See R. Ormston and others, *Scottish Jury Research: Findings from a Large-Scale Mock Jury Study* (Scottish Government, Social Research Series 2019), at 48–49.

leaving it to the adjudicator—be it the jury or the judge—to interpret and apply 'not proven' as they see fit, with the only obvious limitation that they should not issue this verdict if the reasonable doubt standard is satisfied. Indeed, judges are actively discouraged from attempting to explain to the jury the verdict's meaning, in particular by comparing it to 'not guilty'.[130] The lack of legal definition of the verdict has attracted criticism.[131] This state of affairs, though, has not prevented the emergence of a generally accepted understanding of the difference between 'not guilty' and 'not proven': the former is taken to signify that the adjudicator believes that the defendant did not commit the crime charged; the latter, instead, is read as indication that the adjudicator, while possibly believing that the defendant is guilty, considers the evidence insufficient to meet the reasonable doubt standard.[132] Recent empirical research shows that mock jurors interpret the difference in similar terms.[133]

During the 20th century, there was substantial disagreement in the Scottish legal profession over the merits of 'not proven', with some prominent figures viewing the verdict as theoretically indefensible, and others considering it a valuable feature of Scottish criminal procedure.[134] While the question whether the verdict should be scrapped was formally considered already in 1975 by the Thomson Committee,[135] it was in the nineties that 'not proven' was thrust into the limelight. This occurred

[130] See Judicial Institute for Scotland (n 128), at 110.1, stating that 'It is dangerous to attempt to explain any difference between the not proven and not guilty verdicts. It is a misdirection to tell the jury that not proven is appropriate in circumstances where the Crown has not established guilt, whereas not guilty may be appropriate where the jury believes the accused has exculpated himself. However, it has been held not to be a misdirection that a jury might return a not proven verdict where the Crown have not established guilt beyond reasonable doubt but where there are still "lingering doubts" as to the accused's guilt, or where the words "not guilty" would "stick in their throats"' (citing *Larkin v HM Advocate*, 1993 SCCR 715). See also *Sweeney v HM Advocate*, 2002 SCCR 131 and Scottish Office (n 118), at 29–30.

[131] See *id.*, at 36; S. A. Bennett, 'Not Proven: The Verdict' (2002) 12 Scots Law Times 97; and M. McMahon MSP, *Public Consultation on a Proposal for a Bill to Replace the Current System of Three Verdicts in Criminal Trials with Two, and to Increase the Majority Required for Conviction*, 28 June 2012, at 10–12.

[132] See P. Duff, 'The Not Proven Verdict: Jury Mythology and "Moral Panics"' (1996) 41 Juridical Review 1, at 6; Scottish Office (n 118), at 29; and J. Chalmers and others, 'A Modern History of the Not Proven Verdict' (2021) 25 Edinburgh Law Review 151, at 161–163. In his *Commentaries on the Law of Scotland, Respecting Crimes, vol II*, David Hume offers a similar understanding of the difference between 'not proven' and 'not guilty'. He writes that '[n]ot uncommonly, the phrase *not proven* has been employed to mark a deficiency only of lawful evidence to convict the pannel; and that of not guilty, to convey the jury's opinion of his innocence of the charge'. The passage is reported in Willock (n 117), at 221. Chalmers and others (ibid) favour a 'contextual' interpretation of the use of the intermediate verdict—already suggested by A. V. Dicey—according to which the decision of the adjudicator to issue 'not proven' may have different meanings, depending on the circumstances of the case.

[133] See Ormston and others (n 129), at x, 40, 52–55. Notice, though, that some mock jurors justified their choice of 'not guilty' on the basis of their belief that one or more prosecution witnesses were lying, rather than on the basis of a belief in the defendant's innocence; and that some mock jurors justified their choice of 'not proven' on the basis of a difficulty to decide between the truthfulness of the accounts of, respectively, prosecution and defence witnesses, rather than by referring to the fact that they entertained a reasonable doubt about guilt. See ibid, at 52.

[134] See Gow (n 116).

[135] See Duff (n 132), at 7 and Barbato (n 118), at 552–554.

as a result of three highly publicised murder cases in which the juries returned the intermediate verdict.[136] The parents of one of the victims, together with their constituency MP, harnessed the public dissatisfaction with the outcomes of these cases and spearheaded a political campaign for the abolition of 'not proven'. The pressure on the Scottish Office was such that it agreed to include the question whether to scrap 'not proven' in a review of the criminal justice system that had been independently planned, and was originally aimed at reducing costs and increasing efficiency.[137] In 1994 the Scottish Office produced four consultation papers, one of which was mainly devoted to discussing the future of the intermediate verdict, alongside other issues concerning the jury.[138] Following the consultation process, the Scottish Office published a White Paper containing a series of reform proposals.[139] The abolition of 'not proven' was not one of them. With reference to the intermediate verdict, the White Paper states: 'a considerable weight of informed opinion against the three-verdict system would be necessary to justify its abolition. Such weight of opinion does not appear to exist at present.'[140] This was not the end of the public and political controversy surrounding the 'not proven' verdict. Not long after the White Paper was published, the House of Commons voted to retain the verdict, following a strongly polarised debate.[141] Further high-profile cases contributed to keeping public focus on the issue.[142] And, in 2016, a bill to abolish 'not proven' was discussed and ultimately rejected by the Scottish Parliament.[143]

In recent years, the domain of sexual offences—rape and attempted rape, in particular—has provided the principal battleground for the debate on 'not proven'. Official statistics for 2019–2020 show that 1 per cent of all court proceedings in Scotland resulted in 'not proven', and that this verdict accounted for 20 per cent of acquittals. These figures rise to 13 per cent and 38 per cent, respectively, when considering exclusively trials for sexual assault, and to 25 per cent and 44 per cent, respectively, when considering exclusively trials for rape and attempted rape. Notably, for all other offences the percentage of court proceedings resulting in 'not proven', ie the first figure, is significantly lower.[144] Statistics from previous years paint a similar picture; in fact, the figures concerning the use of 'not proven' in

[136] See Duff (n 132), at 7 and Gow (n 116).
[137] See Duff (n 132), at 7–10.
[138] See Scottish Office (n 118).
[139] See Scottish Office, *Firm and Fair. Improving the Delivery of Justice in Scotland* (1994).
[140] ibid, at 19.
[141] See Barbato (n 118), at 563–566.
[142] ibid, at 570–571.
[143] See <https://www.parliament.scot/parliamentarybusiness/Bills/70453.aspx> accessed 12 May 2021. The Criminal Verdicts (Scotland) Bill was introduced by M. McMahon MSP on 27 November 2013, after a consultation process led by him. See McMahon (n 131) and M. McMahon MSP, *Summary of Consultation Responses*, 29 October 2013. The bill was defeated on 25 February 2016.
[144] See Scottish Government, *Criminal Proceedings in Scotland, 2019–2020* (2021), at 52. Even in homicide cases, where 'not proven' accounts for 38% of acquittals, the percentage of court proceedings resulting in 'not proven' is significantly lower than in sexual assault and, especially, in rape and attempted rape cases (6%).

proceedings for rape and attempted rape have increased steadily between 2016 and 2020.[145] The substantially higher rate of 'not proven' verdicts in proceedings for sexual assault, rape, and attempted rape invites an explanation. Here is a plausible hypothesis. Consider that Scots law features the doctrine of corroboration, which essentially requires that for conviction there must be two separate sources of evidence for each element of the offence.[146] Corroboration may be difficult to provide in trials for sexual offences, in particular as regards the element of lack of consent, with respect to which there may be little to no evidence besides the conflicting versions of the complainant and of the defendant. Against this backdrop, it was argued that the availability of 'not proven' gives the jury the opportunity to acquit when it finds that the complainant's testimony is credible but not sufficiently corroborated, and to do so without sending to the complainant the heartbreaking message that they were not believed, and that their evidence was consequently rejected—a message that, arguably, would be sent by the 'not guilty' verdict.[147] Insofar as this argument captures how juries negotiate the tension created by the difficulty of satisfying the requirement of corroboration in 'one person's words against another's' scenarios, and by the particular vulnerability and emotional stress affecting complainants in proceedings for sexual offences, the argument may contribute to explaining the higher rate of 'not proven' verdicts in such proceedings.[148] This

[145] In 2018–2019, 1% of all court proceedings resulted in 'not proven', and the verdict accounted for 19% of acquittals. These figures rise to 11% and 29%, respectively, when exclusively considering proceedings for sexual assault and to 21% and 40%, respectively, when exclusively considering proceedings for rape and attempted rape. See Scottish Government, *Criminal Proceedings in Scotland, 2018–2019* (2020), at 55. In 2017–2018, 1% of all court proceedings resulted in 'not proven' and the verdict accounted for 17% of acquittals. These figures rise to 11% and 33%, respectively, when exclusively considering proceedings for sexual assault, and to 19% and 35%, respectively, when exclusively considering proceedings for rape and attempted rape. See Scottish Government, *Criminal Proceedings in Scotland, 2017–2018* (2019), at 53. In 2016–2017, 1% of all court proceedings resulted in 'not proven', and the verdict accounted for 17% of acquittals. These figures rise to 11% and 32%, respectively, when exclusively considering proceedings for sexual assault, and to 17% and 28%, respectively, when exclusively considering proceedings for rape and attempted rape. See Scottish Government, *Criminal Proceedings in Scotland, 2016–2017* (2018), at 51. While juries use 'not proven' more frequently than judges do (see n 148 below), Chalmers and others have shown that, from the mid-nineteenth century onwards, there has been a gradual decrease in the proportion of 'not proven' verdicts amongst jury acquittals, and they have advanced tentative explanations for this phenomenon. See Chalmers and others, 'A Modern History of the Not Proven Verdict' (n 132), at 154–157.

[146] For a discussion of the doctrine, and a critical assessment of the recent recommendation by the Carloway Review to abolish it, see J. Chalmers and F. Leverick, '"Substantial and Radical Change": A New Dawn for Scottish Criminal Procedure?' (2012) 75 Modern Law Review 837, at 849–855. See, in particular, 850–851 for doctrines that marginally ease the burden of corroboration in cases involving sexual offences.

[147] See Barbato (n 118), at 568–569; Scottish Office (n 118), at 33–34; Lord McCluskey, 'Not Proven: A Reply' (2002) 17 Scots Law Times 148, at 149; and Chalmers and others, 'A Modern History of the Not Proven Verdict' (n 132), at 153, 167–168. Indeed, as these sources indicate, this interpretation of the role of not proven in trials for sexual offences has been used to defend the verdict, especially in the nineties.

[148] There are probably other contributing causes of this phenomenon. First, the rate of 'not guilty' verdicts, too, is significantly higher in rape/attempted rape and sexual assault cases than in the proceedings for most of the other crimes (see Scottish Government (n 144), at 52). This indicates a general reluctance to convict in these cases, rather than just an increased propensity to resort to 'not proven'. A second consideration applies exclusively to trials for rape and attempted rape. In Scotland, all such trials take place in the High Court, and are, therefore, jury trials (see Criminal Procedure (Scotland)

notwithstanding, the reality is that many complainants interpret 'not proven' precisely as an indication that they were not believed by the jury, or as offering the jury an opportunity for 'copping out' of its responsibility to deliver justice.[149] On these grounds, a new campaign to abolish 'not proven' has recently been launched.[150]

To conclude this brief account of the controversies surrounding 'not proven' in the last thirty years, it is interesting to point out that, while the intermediate verdict was being attacked and scrutinised in its homeland, there have been academic calls for introducing 'not proven' in the US system.[151]

1.4.1 A taste of the debate on 'not proven'

Amongst the arguments advanced in the ongoing debate on the merits of 'not proven', one is that the intermediate verdict is incompatible with the presumption of innocence. This argument was formulated in both of the versions that already appeared in the Italian debate on the acquittal '*per insufficienza di prove*'. As seen earlier, according to one version, the presumption only admits of acquittal and conviction as possible epilogues of the trial: there is no room for a third option. According to a second, but not alternative, version, the presumption does not allow

Act 1995, s 3(6)). Importantly, there is evidence that juries are significantly more likely than judges to use 'not proven'. See <https://www.gov.scot/publications/foi-202100199803/> accessed 4 August 2021, showing that the rate of 'not proven' in solemn proceedings (where the jury is used) is significantly higher than the rate of 'not proven' in summary proceedings (where the jury is not used).

149 See <https://www.rapecrisisscotland.org.uk/campaigns-end-not-proven/> last accessed 2 September 2021. An anonymous complainant writes: 'The not proven verdict came as a blow and I felt I wasn't believed . . . I feel like the jury took the "easy way out"'. Another complainant, Clare, writes: 'The not proven verdict makes victims feel they are not believed, I felt I wasn't believed and I was absolutely devastated when I got that verdict'. Another complainant, Natalie, writes: 'It's a cop out . . . leaves no sense of justice. It leaves survivors like me with no closure . . . a feeling of being disbelieved'. See also the empirical research conducted by Vanessa Munro in *Piecing Together Puzzles: Complainers' Experiences of the Not Proven Verdict* (2020), available at <http://wrap.warwick.ac.uk/137857/> accessed 7 April 2021. Bearing in mind the small sample size, the research shows that, insofar as complainants interpreted not proven as an indication that the adjudicator believed their account, they experienced disappointment and mistrust towards a system that 'on the one hand tokened belief that an assault took place against them, but on the other nonetheless failed to hold an attacker accountable' (at 8). Also, complainants involved in the research understood 'not proven' as allowing jurors to abdicate their responsibility to make a decision (at 9). For further discussion of this research, see J. Chalmers and others, 'Beyond Doubt: The Case Against "Not Proven"' (2021) Modern Law Review, DOI: 10.1111/1468-2230.12707, at 12–14.

150 See <https://www.rapecrisisscotland.org.uk/campaigns-end-not-proven/> accessed 2 September 2021. See also <https://www.theguardian.com/law/2018/nov/13/call-for-abolition-of-not-proven-verdict-in-scottish-law> accessed 2 September 2021. Interestingly, a popular view amongst contemporary Scottish legal practitioners is that 'not guilty' should be abolished, rather than 'not proven'. See Chalmers and others, 'Beyond Doubt' (n 149), at 30.

151 See S. Bray, 'Not Proven: Introducing a Third Verdict' (2005) 72 University of Chicago Law Review 1299; and Phalen (n 125), mentioning, at 405, some isolated US cases in which 'not proven' was used, as well as two attempts at passing legislation in California that would have introduced 'not proven'. On the sporadic use, and the perception of, 'not proven' in the US system, see also Barbato (n 118), at 572–577.

the imposition of detrimental consequences—in the case of 'not proven', the focus has been on social stigma—[152] on someone who has not been convicted. I will address both versions of the argument in the next chapter. Here, I briefly consider other arguments that have featured in the debate on 'not proven', in Scotland and overseas.

With reference to the controversy surrounding 'not proven' that occurred in the nineties in Scotland, it was remarked that 'it took place in the absence of any substantial information about the alleged problem which was causing concern; it was based on anecdotal evidence and preconception'.[153] To a large extent this was due to the obstacles that the law places on conducting research involving actual jurors: hence, on understanding how juries actually conceive of, and apply, the intermediate verdict. However, the important symbolic role that the jury plays in the public perception and imagination of criminal justice may have played a part as well: because of this role the 'impressions which people have of the institution are more significant than what it actually does in practice. This results in the fact that concern about the jury can be manufactured quickly and easily, by the media and others, without much in the way of firm evidence to suggest that there is indeed a genuine problem.'[154] In recent years, though, some significant developments have partially lifted the veil of ignorance shrouding the workings of the Scottish jury. Four empirical studies have been conducted on how mock jurors understand and apply 'not proven',[155] with the latest—by far the most extensive and realistic—being commissioned by the Scottish Government.[156] Even accounting for the inevitable limitations of these studies—above all, the fact that the materials with which participants were primed cannot reproduce the same atmosphere of a real trial, and the fact that these materials cannot represent the full variety of cases that the criminal justice system deals with—one can reasonably say that our knowledge of how 'not proven' operates has increased substantially.[157]

[152] On the claim that 'not proven' produces social stigma, see, in particular, Scottish Office (n 118), at 35–36, McMahon (n 131), at 10, 14–15; Barbato (n 118), at 563–564, 573–575, and Chalmers and others, 'Beyond Doubt' (n 149), at 21–23. See also n 175 below.

[153] Duff (n 132), at 6.

[154] ibid, at 4.

[155] See M. Smithson and others, 'Guilty, Not Guilty, or … ? Multiple Options in Jury Verdict Choices' (2007) 20 Journal of Behavioral Decision Making 481; L. Hope and others, 'A Third Verdict Option: Exploring the Impact of Not Proven on Mock Juror Decision Making' (2008) 32 Law and Human Behavior 241; L. J. Curley and others, 'The Bastard Verdict and its Influence on Jurors' (2019) 59 Medicine, Science and the Law 26; and Ormston and others, (n 129). The authors of this last study offer a succinct treatment of it in J. Chalmers and others, 'Three Distinctive Features, but what is the Difference? Key Findings from the Scottish Jury Project' (2020) 11 Criminal Law Review 1012.

[156] See Ormston and others (n 129).

[157] I mention here a few empirical findings that will not be discussed in the text, but that contribute to the understanding of how 'not proven' is likely to operate in practice. First, mock jurors that are given the option of 'not proven' express greater confidence in their decision, irrespective of the verdict chosen (see Hope and others (n 155), at 248. For a similar finding see Ormston and others, (n 129), at 38). Second, the availability of 'not proven' does not affect the length of deliberation, the extent of juror participation, the number of evidential issues discussed, or the extent and the accuracy of the discussion of legal issues (see *id.*, at 29–37). Third, the availability of 'not proven' is 'associated with slightly

For example, a long-standing claim in the debate about 'not proven' has been that the availability of the verdict decreases the likelihood of conviction. Complainants and the families of deceased victims, left disgruntled by a 'not proven' outcome, often relied on this claim to attack the verdict;[158] others relied on it to defend 'not proven', arguing that the intermediate verdict enhances the protection of the defendant against false conviction.[159] This claim has now received some empirical backing: by and large, experimental research has shown that 'not proven' lures jurors away from both the 'not guilty' and 'guilty' verdicts.[160] This confirmation of the claim may not help advance the debate, since the opposing parties do not argue about the veracity of the claim, but about whether the decrease in the likelihood of conviction is, indeed, a good or a bad thing. However, the confirmation does uncover something interesting about the operation of 'not proven'. Considering that, in the studies at issue, the cases with which mock jurors were primed, and the standard of proof for conviction, were the same for the group of participants who could only choose between the standard verdicts, and for the group of participants also given the option of 'not proven', one could argue that the decrease in the rate of conviction detected in the latter group signals decision-making inconsistency.[161] To clarify, other things being equal, if the defendant is considered guilty beyond a reasonable doubt when the option of the intermediate verdict is not available, they should also be considered guilty beyond a reasonable doubt when the

lower levels of dissatisfaction (although not with significantly higher levels of satisfaction) with the experience of serving on a jury' (see *id.*, at viii, 58. For critical discussion of this finding, see Chalmers and others, 'Beyond Doubt' (n 149), at 26–28). Finally, some mock jurors mistakenly believe that 'not proven' and 'not guilty' produce different legal effects, in particular with respect to the possibility of a retrial (see Ormston and others, (n 129), at 45–48).

[158] See Duff (n 132), at 8. More recently, such an attack has been made by McMahon (n 131), at 10, 12–14.

[159] See Chalmers and others, 'A Modern History of the Not Proven Verdict' (n 132), at 166; Scottish Office (n 118), at 33; and Chalmers and others, 'Beyond Doubt' (n 149), at 24–26. That some consider 'not proven' as a valuable safeguard for the defendant is also evidenced by the fact that a possible switch to a binary system is sometimes said to necessitate an increase of the majority required for conviction in the Scottish jury: currently, this is a simple majority of 8 out of 15 jurors. See McMahon (n 131), at 17–19; and Chalmers and others, 'A Modern History of the Not Proven Verdict' (n 132), at 167.

[160] See Ormston and others (n 129), at viii, 20–22, pointing out that, while the move away from 'not guilty' when 'not proven' is available was detected both at the juror level and at the jury level, the move away from conviction was detected only at the juror level. At v, though, the researchers write that, unlike the number of jurors involved (863), the number of juries (64) was 'relatively small, making it unlikely that anything other than large differences in verdicts between juries would be picked up statistically'. In other words, the sample of juries may have been too small to safely conclude that the availability of 'not proven' makes no difference to the rate of conviction at the jury level. See also Hope and others (n 155), at 245, 248, pointing out that the availability of 'not proven' decreases the conviction rate only when the evidence is of 'moderate' strength. cf Curley and others (n 155), at 32, finding that, when 'not proven' was available, the move away from 'not guilty' was statistically significant, whereas the move away from 'guilty' was not; and Smithson and others (n 155), at 486, 492, finding that 'the hypothesis that the Not Proven option attracts jurors away from returning a conviction has been flatly contradicted ... in Study 1, where Not Proven drew participants away from full acquittals [ie the 'not guilty' verdict] to a greater extent'.

[161] See Hope and others (n 155), at 249–250.

option is available.[162] Be that as it may, in Chapter 4 I will show that, according to the decision-theoretic justification of intermediate verdicts, once such a verdict is adopted by the system, the standard of proof for conviction increases with respect to the standard of the binary system. If so, the likely decrease in the rate of convictions produced by the availability of an intermediate verdict would be the natural result of implementing the decision-theoretic model, not an inconsistency in decision-making.

An argument often advanced against 'not proven' is that the intermediate verdict offers the adjudicator—the jury, in particular—a 'cop-out'; in other words, a convenient escape route from a difficult decision problem, which is seized by the adjudicator in close cases as an opportunity to avoid fuller deliberation and confrontation in the jury room.[163] I briefly mentioned this argument earlier, when discussing the relatively high rate of intermediate verdicts in proceedings for sexual assault, rape, and attempted rape. Now, there is evidence that some mock jurors see 'not proven' in this way or, at least, as enabling a compromise that overcomes disagreement within the jury.[164] However, scholars have pointed out that, while the decisional difficulty—or closeness—of a case is shown to increase the propensity of mock jurors to choose 'not proven', this need not mean that the intermediate verdict is used as a 'decision-avoidant option'. Rather, it may simply mean that this verdict is chosen precisely to reflect the closeness of the case, in particular the uncertainty as to whether the standard of proof for conviction is met.[165] In other words, in close cases 'not proven' may be issued not out of laziness or faint-heartedness, but because it is the option that, after careful consideration, is seen to best fit the evidence:[166] the adjudicator considers that there is substantial incriminating evidence,

[162] It is interesting that, in a similar vein to the argument from *in dubio pro reo* featuring in the Italian debate on the acquittal *'per insufficienza di prove'*, some have argued in favour of 'not proven' on the ground that 'it provides an additional outlet for reasonable doubt. Notwithstanding the clear principle (which is explained to juries in each solemn case) that a case must be proved beyond reasonable doubt, there is a risk ... that some would in fact decide on a basis which is closer to the balance of probabilities ... In such circumstances ... the existence of the not proven verdict is a safeguard which allows judges and juries to express their reasonable doubts in a manner acceptable to them'. See Scottish Office (n 118), at 33. cf Ormston and others, (n 129), at 29, 31–32, finding that mock juries who were not given the 'not proven' option were more likely to discuss the meaning of the reasonable doubt standard during deliberation, and that the definitions they reached were often more demanding than that given in the instruction they received on the standard of proof. Importantly, whether it is true or not that, in practice, 'not proven' reinforces the message of an instruction on the reasonable doubt standard, there is no reason to accept that the stringency of this particular standard *should* change when the intermediate verdict is introduced.

[163] See Barbato (n 118), at 569, 574; Scottish Office (n 118), at 32; Bray (n 151), at 1314–1320; and Chalmers and others, 'Beyond Doubt' (n 149), at 30. See also n 149.

[164] See Ormston and others (n 129), at 40, 48; and Chalmers and others, 'Beyond Doubt' (n 149), at 17–18, 27–28.

[165] See Smithson and others (n 155), at 493; and Ormston and others (n 129), at 44–45. See also Bray (n 151), at 1314–1320.

[166] See Gebbie and others (n 81), at 275; and Curley and others (n 155), at 28, 32–33, both arguing, in favour of 'not proven', that it allows the adjudicator to express their assessment of the evidence more accurately than the standard verdicts allow for, this being a point that we have already encountered in the context of the debate on the acquittal *'per insufficienza di prove'*.

but they are not confident that it is sufficient to convict, nor do they think that it is sufficiently weak to issue a 'not guilty' verdict. Far from being a non-decision, then, 'not proven' may be seen and employed as the option that fills the grey decisional area between the 'standard' verdicts. Notice that this view, and this use, of 'not proven', conform with the generally accepted understanding of the verdict, discussed earlier. In Chapter 5, section 5.6, I will give and confute an argument against intermediate verdicts in general, which is modelled after the argument against 'not proven' just considered.

Against 'not proven', it was pointed out that it is dissatisfactory for victims, 'who are left hanging in the air of frustration and mystery that comes at the end of a trial when a not proven verdict is handed down'.[167] In response to this argument, the Scottish Office said that 'it is difficult to imagine that a not guilty verdict, which would be the logical alternative, would be less hurtful'.[168] A first possibility is that the victims' dissatisfaction with 'not proven' is due to the belief that the availability of this intermediate verdict reduced the likelihood of conviction: a belief that, as mentioned earlier, has support from the empirical research. If so, however, the dissatisfaction is not so much with the particular verdict that was handed down in the case; it is really with the system which, by adopting 'not proven', affords yet another protection to the defendant, further steepening the slope of the prosecution's uphill task. I have already pointed out that, for some, the merit of 'not proven' resides precisely in its being an additional safeguard against false conviction. This stand-off concerning the value of the decrease in the likelihood of conviction produced by the availability of the intermediate verdict can only be overcome through a comprehensive assessment of the relevant interests. The interests of the victims are important, of course, but surely they are not the only interests at stake.[169] A second, but not alternative, possibility is that the dissatisfaction of victims receiving a 'not proven' verdict is due to the defendant not being *in fact* convicted and/or to the victims' feeling of not being believed by the adjudicator.[170] If so, this dissatisfaction is also likely to be experienced—and possibly more acutely—in the case of a 'not guilty' verdict. If, however, it is not a reason to scrap 'not guilty'—and surely it is not—how could it be a reason to scrap 'not proven'? In this respect, the Scottish Office's rejoinder seems an apt one.

One last argument worth surveying features in the literature from overseas, and echoes an argument concerning the suspension of res judicata, considered earlier in the chapter. Notably, it was advanced as an argument in favour of introducing 'not proven' in the US, not as an argument in favour of retaining 'not proven' in

[167] These words were uttered in 1995 by George Robertson, then MP for Hamilton South. See Barbato (n 118), at 564. See also ibid, at 570–571, 578; and McMahon (n 131), at 14, stating that '[v]ictims and relatives sometimes also find this outcome unsatisfactory, as it denies them a sense of closure'.

[168] Scottish Office (n 118), at 37.

[169] For further discussion, see Chalmers and others, 'Beyond Doubt' (n 149), at 24–26.

[170] See n 149 above.

Scotland.[171] According to this argument, the availability of this intermediate verdict allows the adjudicator to convey, to the public, more precise information about the strength of the case against acquitted defendants than the information which the adjudicator could convey in a typical binary system of verdicts. To clarify, in a binary system with a high standard of proof for conviction, 'not guilty' is consistent with the presence of scant evidence of guilt, but also of substantial incriminating evidence. As a result of this ambivalence, the public is left in doubt about whether the acquitted defendant is guilty or not, this being an epistemic position that may have repercussions on the ability of interested parties to decide how to relate to the defendant—for instance, whether to befriend or employ them.[172] Of course, any interested party may gather information on the incriminating evidence available against the defendant by taking advantage of the publicity of trials—assuming that the trial is ongoing, or that it received particular media attention such that data about it are easily accessible after its conclusion. However, the argument contends that delivering this information through a verdict—precisely by adopting 'not proven'—would be more effective. With a 'not proven' verdict in place, the system clearly differentiates between the acquitted defendants who are likely to be innocent, ie those who received a 'not guilty' verdict, and the acquitted defendants who are likely to be guilty, ie those who received a 'not proven' verdict. In drawing this distinction, the argument contends, the system renders an important service to individuals who are considering whether to establish a personal or professional relationship with the defendant, and possibly also to public institutions that are called to make decisions concerning the defendant—for example whether the defendant should be allowed to adopt a child—and would benefit from information on the probability of their guilt.

Let us assume, for the sake of argument, that the public wants, information about the probability that an acquitted defendant is guilty, and that it is true that the adoption of 'not proven' represents a more effective way of delivering such information than simply relying on trial publicity.[173] The issue is whether this increased effectiveness in data delivery is sufficient to justify the intermediate verdict. I doubt

[171] What follows is the restatement of an argument presented in Bray (n 151), at 1307–1314. See also F. Picinali, 'Do Theories of Punishment Necessarily Deliver a Binary System of Verdicts? An Exploratory Essay' (2018) 12 Criminal Law and Philosophy 555, at 560–561. In fact, a similar argument is discussed in a recent work concerning the Scottish verdict system: see Chalmers and others, 'Beyond Doubt' (n 149), at 14–20. The authors point out that the communicative role that 'not proven' allegedly plays, according to the argument, is actually hindered by the lack of clarity as to the verdict's meaning.

[172] See L. Laudan, 'Need Verdicts Come in Pairs?' (2010) 14 International Journal of Evidence and Proof 1; and A. D. Leipold, 'The Problem of the Innocent, Acquitted Defendant' (2000) 94 Northwestern University Law Review 1297, both criticising a binary system of verdicts with a high standard of proof on the ground that acquittal in such a system is not sufficiently exonerating, since it leaves room for considerable doubt about the innocence of the defendant.

[173] This second assumption itself presupposes that, whether or not 'not proven' goes on the criminal record, the fact that someone received this verdict is made readily accessible to interested parties. cf n 129 and accompanying text, for the Scots law on this point.

that this is the case. Notice that, if the information is indeed delivered through the verdict system, and is relied upon by interested parties, two effects are produced.[174] On the one hand, the 'not guilty' verdict acquires greater exonerating force than the force it possesses under a binary system, because it signals that the adjudicator considered the defendant innocent, or likely to be such. On the other hand, the recipients of the 'not proven' verdict should be expected to experience greater stigma than they would have experienced had they been acquitted in a binary system, since 'not proven' unequivocally signals that there is substantial incriminating evidence against them.[175] The question is whether these effects of the data-delivering service allegedly rendered to the public by adopting 'not proven' are, overall, a good or a bad thing. The answer depends on the distribution of the trial outcomes produced in a system featuring 'not proven'. In particular, it hinges on how the 'not guilty' and 'not proven' verdicts are distributed among innocent and guilty defendants. Thus, it depends on the rate of innocent defendants that are exonerated by 'not guilty' (a positive outcome), on the rate of guilty defendants that are also exonerated by 'not guilty' (a negative outcome), on the rate of innocent defendants that are stigmatised by 'not proven' (another negative outcome), and on the rate of guilty defendants that are also stigmatised by 'not proven' (another positive outcome). Calculating the distribution of such positive and negative outcomes, and assessing its overall value,[176] are both necessary operations for determining whether the delivery of additional information through the use of 'not proven' does, indeed, justify introducing this verdict.[177] In Chapter 5, section 5.3.2, I will argue that calculating the distribution of the trial outcomes of an existing, and especially of a hypothetical, criminal justice system is beyond our current cognitive capabilities.

[174] These effects are clearly acknowledged by Bray. See Bray (n 151), at 1320–1326, stating at 1326 that '[n]o legal system can simultaneously have a high standard of proof, exoneration for the innocent, and no stigma for those acquitted because of insufficient evidence. One aim must be sacrificed. Not proven is a choice to accept greater stigma in the middle category as the cost of exoneration for others. Not proven is the better path because the innocent deserve exoneration more than the likely-guilty deserve lessened stigma'. This passage begs the question of how the 'not guilty' and the 'not proven' verdicts will be distributed among the innocent and the guilty, an important question for which no precise answer seems possible. See below.

[175] cf Phalen (n 125), at 414, making the surprising suggestion that 'not proven' produces the same quantum of stigma as that associated with 'not guilty' in a binary system of verdicts. Phalen's suggestion is countered by the widespread perception that 'not proven' produces substantial stigma (see the views reported in Scottish Office (n 118), at 35–36). This perception has also been detected through empirical research (see Ormston and others (n 129), at 51–52 and Hope and others (n 155), at 249–250). Moreover, Phalen's comparative assessment is countered by the fact that the abolition of 'not proven'—that is, significantly, the institution of a system with 'not guilty' as the only form of acquittal—has often been defended precisely by claiming that the intermediate verdict stigmatises the defendant unfairly: see, among others, McMahon (n 131), at 10, 14–15; and Barbato (n 118), at 563–564, 573–575.

[176] By this, I mean the aggregate value of all the outcomes involved, given their distribution.

[177] In fact, these operations are not sufficient. As explained in Chapter 5, the strategy of justifying an intermediate verdict by looking at distributions of trial outcomes requires that one calculates the overall distributions of outcomes of both the binary and the non-binary systems, and then compares their respective values: that is, the aggregate values of all the outcomes produced by each verdict system, given their respective distributions.

If I am right in this, it follows that 'not proven' cannot be justified on the ground that it conveys useful information to the public: what appears to be a service to the public may well be a greater disservice to the innocent and, more generally, to the delivery of criminal justice. Of course, someone could make a guess of the likely distribution of outcomes. However, that the public wants information on evidence incriminating the acquitted, and that the availability of 'not proven' allows to deliver this information better than trial publicity already does, are also, by and large, guesses. Three guesses do not make a solid argument.

1.5 Concluding remarks

Intermediate criminal verdicts have featured in several legal systems. Their content has varied considerably, ranging from serious forms of extraordinary punishment to the relatively benign Scottish 'not proven'. Their justification has always been a source of controversy. In this chapter, I have offered an account of the most prominent and captivating arguments in favour or against intermediate verdicts that have appeared in the debates surrounding the *ius commune* extraordinary punishment and suspension of res judicata, the Italian acquittal '*per insufficienza di prove*', and the Scottish 'not proven'. Considering the watershed role played by the Enlightenment with respect to ideas pertaining to the administration of criminal justice, it is perhaps unsurprising that arguments advanced two hundred years ago rely on concepts and values that are still central to the contemporary criminal justice discourse. Indeed, an echo of these arguments is clearly audible in the more recent debates on intermediate verdicts.

None of the arguments surveyed provides a conclusive case in favour or against intermediate verdicts. In fact, some of these arguments are just wrong. My assessment of the debates reproduced in this chapter, though, is still incomplete. The analysis of the argument from legitimacy, and of that from deterrence—which featured in the 19th-century debate on the *ius commune* intermediate verdicts—is postponed until Chapter 5. Moreover, in Chapter 5 I will have more to say about the argument that intermediate verdicts offer a 'cop-out' to the adjudicator, advanced in the Scottish debate. Finally, I have yet to address the popular argument according to which intermediate verdicts are not compatible with the presumption of innocence. The next chapter is dedicated to this task.

2

The Presumption of Innocence

A Decisive Objection to Intermediate Verdicts?

2.1 Introduction

As mentioned in the previous chapter, a recurrent argument in the debates accompanying the Scottish 'not proven' and the Italian acquittal '*per insufficienza di prove*' is that these intermediate verdicts are not compatible with the presumption of innocence. In fact, the argument is often cast in terms of intermediate verdicts in general: it is the intermediate nature of the verdict, described in the Introduction to the book, that is allegedly incompatible with the presumption. The presumption of innocence is unanimously viewed as a fundamental requirement for criminal justice. In other words, it is considered a norm of such importance that, if we were to relinquish it, we could not see ourselves as doing justice in the criminal law domain. The norm has a common law pedigree;[1] it is enshrined in Article 6(2) of the European Convention on Human Rights (ECHR), and in other international law instruments.[2] It follows that, if the presumption of innocence were indeed incompatible with intermediate verdicts, the possibility of justifying one such verdict may well be fundamentally undermined.

In this chapter, I consider whether an intermediate verdict can be compatible with the presumption of innocence. There are two reasons for addressing this question in a separate chapter. The first reason is that answering the question of compatibility requires considerable groundwork concerning the nature of the presumption of innocence. In earlier work, I have formulated a comprehensive theory of the presumption.[3] There is no need for me to rehearse this theory in full here. I will only engage with the aspects of the presumption that are relevant to the question of compatibility. Notice that, with respect to these aspects only, the view that I defend here diverges in part from my earlier theorisation. The second reason is

[1] The classic reference is *Woolmington v DPP* [1935] AC 462 (HL). For a recent analysis of this case see L. Farmer, 'Innocence, the Burden of Proof and Fairness in the Criminal Trial: Revisiting *Woolmington v DPP* (1935)' in J. D. Jackson and S. J. Summers (eds), *Obstacles to Fairness in Criminal Proceedings: Individual Rights and Institutional Reforms* (Hart 2018), at 57.

[2] See Art 11(1) of the Universal Declaration of Human Rights and Art 48 of the Charter of Fundamental Rights of the European Union.

[3] See F. Picinali, 'The Presumption of Innocence: A Deflationary Account' (2021) 84 Modern Law Review 708. See also F. Picinali, 'Innocence and Burdens of Proof in English Criminal Law' (2014) 13 Law, Probability & Risk 243.

Justice In-Between, Federico Picinali, Oxford University Press. © Federico Picinali 2022.
DOI: 10.1093/oso/9780198864592.003.0003

that the argument that intermediate verdicts are incompatible with the presumption of innocence is substantially more popular than the arguments against such verdicts addressed in the previous chapter. It is, therefore, sensible to give special visibility to its assessment.

A quick terminological note is in order. In this chapter, I use the term 'defendant' to refer not just to the individual who has been charged with a criminal offence, but also to the suspect during the investigative phase. While this terminology is imprecise, I adopt it for the sake of simplicity. In any case, it will be clear from the context whether I am dealing with any specific part of the process.

2.2 The argument for incompatibility

The argument that intermediate verdicts are incompatible with the presumption of innocence has been given different formulations in the literature.[4] Moreover, the incompatibility is often asserted without explanation, as if it were a self-evident truth. I offer, below, a restatement of the argument for incompatibility, which provides a reasonable synthesis of the different versions of it to be found in the literature, and spells out the steps of the argument that are often left implicit. With this restatement, I aim to put the argument in its best light. Undoubtedly, someone could formulate other versions of the argument for incompatibility. Besides not being featured in the literature, though, the other versions that I could conceive of are not as promising as the one I am about to set out.[5]

[4] The argument features in the following contributions: G. Conso, 'È da Rivedere, non da Eliminare l'Assoluzione per Insufficienza di Prove' (1967) 4 Giurisprudenza Italiana 101, at 107–108; M. Pisani, *Introduzione al Processo Penale* (Giuffrè 1988), at 70–72; A. Ghiara, 'Presunzione di Innocenza, Presunzione di "Non Colpevolezza" e Formula Dubitativa, anche alla Luce degli Interventi della Corte Costituzionale' (1974) Rivista Italiana di Diritto e Procedura Penale 72, at 90–101; G. Illuminati, 'Presunzione di Non Colpevolezza' in *Enciclopedia Giuridica, vol XXVII* (Treccani 1991), at 7; E. Marzaduri, 'Commento all'Art. 530—Sentenza di Assoluzione' in M. Chiavario (ed), *Commento al Nuovo Codice di Procedura Penale, vol 5* (UTET 1989), at 520–521; F. Morelli, *Le Formule di Proscioglimento: Radici Storiche e Funzioni Attuali* (Giappichelli 2014), at 118–131, 158–166; J. M. Barbato, 'Scotland's Bastard Verdict: Intermediacy and the Unique Three-Verdict System' (2005) 15 Indiana International and Comparative Law Review 543, at 563, 564, 573–575; M. McMahon MSP, 'Consultation Paper: Reform of Criminal Verdicts (Scotland) Bill', 28 June 2012, at 10, 14–15; M. McMahon MSP, 'Summary of Consultation Responses', 29 October 2013, at 4–5; Scottish Office, *Juries and Verdicts: Improving the Delivery of Justice in Scotland* (1994), at 35–36; L. J. Curley and others, 'The Bastard Verdict and its Influence on Jurors' (2019) 59 Medicine, Science and the Law 26, at 29. Consider also M. Damaška, *Evaluation of Evidence: Pre-Modern and Modern Approaches* (CUP 2019), at 112, arguing for the incompatibility between the presumption of innocence and the intermediate verdicts provided in the *ius commune* trial. Finally, see J. Chalmers and others, 'Beyond Doubt: The Case Against "Not Proven"' (2021) Modern Law Review, DOI: 10.1111/1468-2230.12707, at 21–23, recognising a tension between the Scottish 'not proven' verdict and the presumption of innocence, but stating that, especially because of the verdict's ambiguous meaning, 'not proven' is unlikely to be found to contravene Art 6(2) ECHR.

[5] Consider three possible arguments for incompatibility built, respectively: (1) on the view that the presumption of innocence includes a rule allocating to the prosecution the burden of proving guilt at trial; (2) on the view that it includes a rule imposing on the adjudicator a particular way of regarding the defendant at the start of the trial; and (3) on the view that the presumption includes the reasonable

The argument is premised on the claim that the presumption of innocence includes a rule of conduct according to which the criminal justice authorities should treat the defendant as innocent until they prove the defendant guilty. Here is how the argument reads the rule of conduct into the presumption, and understands this rule. The presumption of innocence is conceptualised as positing the innocence of the defendant as the status quo characterising the beginning of the criminal process. This status quo consists in the defendant's enjoyment of those rights to which all members of the polity are prima facie entitled. These include the rights to liberty, to privacy, to property, and to reputation. The rule of conduct embedded in the presumption says that this status quo can be altered only if the prosecution provides proof of the defendant's guilt, where 'proof of guilt' is evidence of guilt that the adjudicator considers sufficient to satisfy the standard of proof for conviction. Nothing short of proof of guilt can justify a change in the status quo. Without such proof, then, the criminal justice authorities cannot infringe upon the defendant's enjoyment of the rights characterising the status quo. They must treat the defendant as innocent; that is, as entitled to enjoying those rights. Now, the argument correctly points out that intermediate verdicts cannot possibly be premised on proving guilt, lest they lose their intermediate nature and effectively become undistinguishable from conviction. We saw in the Introduction to the book that the evidential basis of an intermediate verdict is less robust than the evidential basis of the 'guilty' verdict. Hence, for issuing an intermediate verdict it must be sufficient to satisfy a standard of proof that is lower than that warranting conviction. From this, the argument concludes that, insofar as intermediate verdicts infringe upon the

doubt standard as the standard of proof for conviction. On (1), as already remarked in the previous chapter, a rule allocating to the prosecution the burden of proving guilt at trial is hardly at odds with intermediate verdicts. The presence of an intermediate verdict does not deny the rule: the prosecution would still bear the burden of proving guilt for the purposes of conviction and, in conformity with this arrangement, it would also bear the burden of introducing enough evidence of guilt to justify an intermediate verdict. On (2), in Picinali, 'The Presumption of Innocence' (n 3), at 20–24, I argued against the view that the presumption includes a rule imposing on the adjudicator a particular way of regarding the defendant at the start of the trial. Be that as it may, this rule would not conflict with intermediate verdicts. While the rule concerns the start of the trial, these verdicts are adopted at the end of it, and require a quantum of evidence of guilt. When this evidence is present, it is correct for the adjudicator no longer to regard the defendant as the alleged rule would require. Therefore, there would be no inconsistency between this rule and a hypothetical intermediate verdict that involved regarding the defendant differently from what the rule would require. On (3), in ibid, at 18–20, I also argued against the view that the presumption of innocence sets the reasonable doubt standard as the standard of proof for conviction. However, even if it were true that the presumption requires the satisfaction of this standard for the purposes of conviction, it would not follow from this fact that intermediate verdicts are incompatible with the presumption. Arguably, they would be incompatible with the presumption if they required such a standard as well. This is because, requiring the same standard of proof as that required by the presumption for conviction, they would lose their intermediate nature in a system where the presumption is operative. But why should every intermediate verdict require proof beyond a reasonable doubt? I cannot think of a plausible argument that would support such a view. Indeed, under the decision-theoretic framework that I will adopt in Chapter 4, the standard of proof warranting a given verdict depends, among other things, on the severity of the verdict. Given that intermediate verdicts can vary in severity, their respective standards of proof can vary as well. On the variability of standards of proof depending on the particulars of the case see Chapter 5, section 5.2.

defendant's enjoyment of the rights to which all members of the polity are prima facie entitled, they are not compatible with the presumption of innocence, because they violate the rule of conduct embedded in it: they produce a change in the status quo in the absence of proof of guilt.

2.2.1 Some interpretive remarks about the argument

There are some important interpretive remarks to make with regard to the argument for incompatibility. The first, and most significant, remark concerns the rule of conduct on which the argument is premised. Consider that, for a criminal justice system to function—or, at least, to function effectively—it must be possible, in some circumstances, for the criminal justice authorities to infringe upon the rights of a defendant who has not been proven guilty. In other words, it must be possible to alter the status quo even in the absence of proof of guilt. For example, intrusive surveillance techniques may have to be used in order to prevent and detect crime; forensic and biometric samples may have to be collected from the defendant without their consent for the purposes of testing whether these samples match samples found at the crime scene;[6] also, the defendant may have to be arrested and, possibly, remanded in custody to prevent them from causing harm to others, from committing other offences, from perverting the course of justice by interfering with witnesses, from avoiding justice by fleeing, etc.[7] These infringing measures cannot be viewed as incompatible with the presumption of innocence *just because* they are taken in the absence of proof of guilt. After all, they can be—and routinely are—justified without appealing to proof of guilt. What is more, at least some of these measures are, ultimately, instruments for obtaining such proof;[8] it would be perverse to require proof of guilt for their justification. And yet, the argument for incompatibility seems to treat these measures as incompatible with the presumption—hence, impermissible—precisely because they alter the status quo in the absence of proof of guilt. This renders the argument highly implausible.

To prevent the argument from foundering at the starting gates, a restatement of it is needed. The source of the implausibility is the premise of the argument, according to which the presumption of innocence includes a rule of conduct to the

[6] Here, I am not suggesting that this operation is always justified. The justification of non-consensual collection depends, among other things, on the nature of the sample (ie whether it is intimate or not), and on the amount of force required to collect it.

[7] For critical discussion of these measures, see L. Campbell and others, *The Criminal Process* (5th edn, OUP 2019), at 91–94, 106–111, 123–129, 236–266. Another clear interference with the status quo is the use of stop-and-search (see ibid, at 84–91). The necessity of this measure, though, is a hotly debated issue.

[8] Besides the use of surveillance techniques, and of forensic samples, which are clearly instrumental to proving guilt, consider an arrest performed in order to have the opportunity to interview the suspect, or a remand in custody aimed at preventing the defendant from intimidating witnesses.

effect that, in the absence of proof of guilt, the criminal justice authorities must not infringe upon the rights of the defendant characterising the status quo. The restated argument should, therefore, be premised on the presumption including a different rule of conduct. More precisely, this should be a rule that meets the following desiderata: it must render intermediate verdicts impermissible, insofar as they infringe upon the status quo, and it must not treat proof of guilt as a necessary condition for every infringement, lest the above restrictive measures be ruled out. As an example of a rule of this kind, consider a rule that, on the one hand, authorises infringements of the status quo occurring prior to, or during, the trial, as long as they are supported by sufficient reasons, and, on the other hand, treats proof of guilt as necessary only for infringements occurring as an epilogue of the trial, thus ruling out intermediate verdicts that infringe upon the status quo. To be sure, there is no need to flesh out the argument for incompatibility further, by articulating a plausible rule that meets the above desiderata, and that can be read into the presumption of innocence. Stating these desiderata is sufficient to assess whether they can be met, and hence, whether the argument for incompatibility can succeed.

The second interpretive remark concerns the reach of the argument for incompatibility. Notice that the argument only targets *infringing* intermediate verdicts; that is, intermediate verdicts that infringe upon the defendant's enjoyment of the rights to which all members of the polity are prima facie entitled. However, someone could question the distinction between infringing and non-infringing intermediate verdicts, arguing instead that all intermediate verdicts are of the former kind, and hence, that they are all incompatible with the presumption of innocence, if indeed the argument for incompatibility is sound. This extensive interpretation of the argument can be defended by reasoning that, inevitably, intermediate verdicts leave the question whether the defendant is innocent or guilty in doubt, since they are intermediate between the categorical verdicts of 'not guilty' and 'guilty', and that the doubt expressed by the intermediate verdict infringes upon the right to reputation of the defendant, which is considered part of the status quo of innocence.[9] Accordingly, even if the verdict does not include infringing measures such as a penalty, it does alter this status quo.

Consider two objections to this extensive interpretation of the argument for incompatibility. First, it might be objected that, in a binary system with a high standard of proof, such as that of England and Wales, a defendant may be acquitted even in the presence of substantial evidence of guilt. Therefore, acquittal leaves room for considerable doubt about the innocence of the defendant,[10] this being a

[9] See Conso (n 4), at 108; Ghiara (n 4), at 101; McMahon, 'Consultation Paper' (n 4), at 14–15; Barbato (n 4), at 563, 564; Scottish Office (n 4), at 35–36.

[10] Larry Laudan and Andrew Leipold have both argued in favour of a verdict system involving more than two verdicts and, in particular, a verdict of 'innocence'. They have done so precisely on the ground that acquittal in the binary system is not sufficiently exonerating, since it leaves room for considerable doubt about the innocence of the defendant. See L. Laudan, 'Need Verdicts Come in Pairs?' (2010) 14 International Journal of Evidence and Proof 1; and A. D. Leipold, 'The Problem of the Innocent,

claim that we have already encountered when studying the debate on the Scottish 'not proven' verdict. Notwithstanding that acquittal expresses such doubt, though, it is not, in these binary systems, considered incompatible with the presumption of innocence. Hence, contrary to what the extensive interpretation of the argument presupposes, an incompatibility with the presumption is unlikely to depend exclusively on the fact that a verdict expresses doubt about innocence. A second objection is that whether a verdict expresses doubt about the innocence of the defendant, and, if so, how much doubt it expresses, both depend on how high the range of the probability of guilt corresponding to the verdict is. If the verdict, be it intermediate or not, is issued only when the probability of guilt falls within a sufficiently low range, the doubt expressed by the verdict is negligible. To clarify, according to this second objection it is not the intermediate nature of the verdict per se that is responsible for the expression of doubt and the consequent infringement of the right to reputation. Whether doubt is expressed, and the right is infringed, does not depend on the fact that the range of the probability of guilt corresponding to an intermediate verdict is higher than that corresponding to 'not guilty' and lower than that corresponding to the 'guilty' verdict. It depends, instead, on where the probability range corresponding to the intermediate verdict lies on the probability spectrum. Contrary to what is presupposed by the extensive interpretation of the argument for incompatibility, this second objection contends that it would be possible to have an intermediate verdict that expresses insignificant doubt and does not, therefore, infringe on the right to reputation.

Now, let us assume that the right to reputation is, indeed, part of the status quo of innocence, as the argument for incompatibility contends. I am not convinced by the claim—which lies at the basis of the extensive interpretation of the argument for incompatibility, and is echoed in the two objections to it—that the right to reputation, and hence the status quo, is infringed by the mere expression of doubt in the verdict. If anything, the infringement lies in the uptake, by the polity, of the

Acquitted Defendant' (2000) 94 Northwestern University Law Review 1297. In virtue of the fact that the non-binary systems they propose each include an option with a stronger exonerating effect than that of acquittal in the binary system, Laudan and Leipold both argue that their systems enforce the presumption of innocence, rather than undermining it. Laudan writes that '[t]here is nothing in this way of structuring the trial that undermines the spirit or the letter of the presumption of innocence, properly parsed. On the contrary, it is much more compatible with that principle than existing matrices of outcomes are because it makes available a genuinely exculpatory verdict' (Laudan, ibid, at 15). Leipold, in particular, defends a system where, after a finding of 'not-guilty', the jury would be asked to decide whether the defendant is 'innocent', this being the third available verdict. He argues that '[p]roviding a chance at vindication might shore up the presumption of innocence. Asking the jury to debate the defendant's [innocence] ... should remind jurors that the presumption is more than a legal fiction, and would remind the rest of us that sometimes innocent people do pass through the pre-trial filtering process.' (Leipold, ibid, at 1352). Unlike the system that I defend in this book, Laudan's and Leipold's systems do not involve the introduction of an intermediate verdict between acquittal and conviction. Rather, they involve the introduction of a verdict that is more extreme than acquittal, it being a verdict that presupposes a finding of innocence (in fact, the system envisaged by Laudan is more complex than this, involving a total of four possible verdicts).

doubt expressed in the verdict. Indeed, someone's reputation is damaged only if they suffer a quantum of social stigma as a result of the verdict; that is, if they are perceived by the polity as being possibly, or probably, guilty of the crime charged.[11] So, the questions we need to attend to are whether, and when, an intermediate verdict produces social stigma; the fact that it does express doubt about the defendant's innocence cannot be viewed as sufficient to make it an infringing verdict.

While it is true that the extent of doubt expressed by a verdict depends on where the probability range corresponding to the verdict lies on the probability spectrum, I am not persuaded that social stigma, too, depends on this variable. Hence—and contrary to the second objection considered earlier—I am not persuaded that it is this variable that determines whether an intermediate verdict infringes the right to reputation. For social stigma to depend on how high the probability range corresponding to a verdict is, the polity—at least, a significant portion of it—would have to be tuned in to the rules of adjudication to an extent that is probably unrealistic. More precisely, they would need to have a fairly accurate understanding of which probability range corresponds to the verdict in question, for this range to actually influence their perception of the defendant. To be sure, whether social stigma is so tied to the probability range corresponding to a verdict is an interesting question that warrants empirical investigation. Here, I tentatively endorse the view that *if* an intermediate verdict does indeed produce social stigma, this is because of the intermediate nature of the verdict, because of its name and the related formula uttered in court to issue the verdict, and because of the infringing measures that are included in the verdict, if any. Since the verdict, by its very nature, sits between the two standard options, it must convey a quantum of doubt about the issue of guilt. The name and the formula of the verdict, too, may convey such doubt. Think of the Italian acquittal '*per insufficienza di prove*'. The phrase in inverted commas, which was used both to refer to the verdict and to issue it in court, clearly alludes to the presence of incriminating evidence, even if insufficient for conviction. Finally, any infringing measure included in the verdict—think, for example, of extraordinary punishment—singles out the defendant as someone who does not have good standing in the community. The intermediate nature of a verdict, its name and formula, and the possible infringing measures included in it are obviously more visible and comprehensible aspects of adjudication than the epistemic conditions that warrant that verdict; that is, the probability range to which the verdict

[11] See *Axel Springer AG v Germany*, application no 39954/08, ECtHR (Grand Chamber), 7 February 2012. Reflecting on the relationship between Art 10 (freedom of expression) and Art. 8 (right to respect for private life, which includes the right to reputation) of the European Convention on Human Rights, the Court wrote that: 'In order for Article 8 to come into play, however, an attack on a person's reputation must attain a certain level of seriousness and in a manner causing prejudice to personal enjoyment of the right to respect for private life' (para 83).

corresponds. Accordingly, it is reasonable to expect the polity to be more tuned in to these aspects than to such conditions.[12]

With respect to the question of the compatibility between acquittal and the presumption of innocence, hinted at by the first objection, my tentative view is that acquittal does not *produce* social stigma, and cannot, therefore, infringe the right to reputation. To clarify, if acquittal is indeed correlated with social stigma, this is not a result of the doubt about the defendant's innocence expressed by this verdict; that is, the correlation does not result from facts about the range of the probability of guilt corresponding to acquittal; it does not depend on where the standard of proof regulating the choice between this and the immediately harsher verdict lies. Rather, the correlation between acquittal and stigma results from the fact that the acquitted has previously been charged, tried publicly, and possibly arrested and remanded in custody.[13] If anything, the verdict of acquittal can be criticised for failing to neutralise the stigma produced by these earlier measures.[14] If, indeed, stigma is not a product of acquittal, in the sense just clarified, the question of the compatibility between acquittal and the presumption of innocence does not arise.[15] The

[12] Having said this, I recognise that the Scottish 'not proven' verdict is perceived as producing social stigma, both in the public opinion and by mock jurors in experimental studies (see the works on the Scottish verdict system referenced in n 4. For the empirical research, see R. Ormston and others, *Scottish Jury Research: Findings from a Large-Scale Mock Jury Study* (Scottish Government, Social Research Series 2019), at 51–52; and L. Hope and others, 'A Third Verdict Option: Exploring the Impact of Not Proven on Mock Juror Decision Making' (2008) 32 Law and Human Behavior 241, at 249–250), and that, even though the epistemic conditions that warrant the verdict are not identified by the law, mock jurors appear to share the rough understanding of these conditions that is prevalent in the literature. According to this understanding, 'not proven' is issued when the adjudicator, while possibly believing that the defendant is guilty, considers the evidence insufficient to meet the reasonable doubt standard (see Chapter 1, section 1.4). While such an understanding may be responsible for the perception of the verdict as producing social stigma, it is plausible to argue that the understanding itself ultimately depends on the name and formula of the verdict and, especially, on its intermediate nature. In this regard, consider Bernard Jackson's account of the pragmatics of 'not proven'. Jackson starts by arguing that the lay person—as opposed to the legal professional—understands 'not guilty' in ontological, rather than in cognitive terms. In other words, they take 'not guilty' to mean 'innocent' rather than 'not proven guilty'. He then argues that 'not proven' is understood by the lay person both in cognitive and in ontological terms: (given its name and formula) it is taken to mean that there was not sufficient evidence for conviction, but (given its intermediate nature) it is also taken to mean that the defendant was indeed 'guilty'. 'This is because a "not proven" verdict... excludes a "not guilty" verdict. Since [the defendant] has not been found "not guilty", the thought process goes, he cannot really be innocent.' See B. S. Jackson, 'Truth or Proof? The Criminal Verdict' (1998) 11 International Journal for the Semiotics of Law 227, at 242.

[13] See Leipold (n 10), at 1305–1311; H. Phalen, 'Overcoming the Opposition to a Third Verdict: A Call for Future Research on Alternative Acquittals' (2018) 50 Arizona State Law Journal 401, at 413–414; N. W. D. Litt, 'Curiosities of Criminal Justice' (1975) 48 Police Journal 5, at 9–10. For an empirical study evidencing the social stigma associated with acquittal, see R. D. Schwartz and J. H. Skolnick, 'Two Studies on Legal Stigma' (1962) 10 Social Problems 133, in particular at 136–137.

[14] This stigma produced by infringing measures may be reduced, at least in some cases, by educating the polity about the fact that these measures can be, and often are, adopted with respect to innocent individuals.

[15] There is, of course, a question concerning the compatibility between the presumption of innocence and infringing measures such as arrest and remand in custody. I will address this question later in the chapter.

first objection is, therefore, misguided in analogising the case of acquittal and that of an intermediate verdict.

Having rejected the objections to the extensive interpretation of the argument for incompatibility, I am, nonetheless, persuaded that the argument should not be interpreted as targeting every intermediate verdict. The distinction between infringing and non-infringing intermediate verdicts is a valid one to draw, and the argument for incompatibility should only refer to the former. This is because whether a particular intermediate verdict—not including infringing measures such as a penalty—does indeed infringe upon the status quo, as this is construed by the argument for incompatibility, ultimately depends on the empirical question whether the verdict produces social stigma, thus infringing the right to reputation. And an answer to this question requires appropriate investigation.[16] Should it turn out that it does not produce social stigma, then the verdict at issue would not affect the status quo. Caution, therefore, invites us not to treat, a priori, all intermediate verdicts as infringing.[17]

The third and final interpretive remark about the argument for incompatibility concerns the relationship between this argument and a claim of 'logical' incompatibility between the presumption of innocence and intermediate verdicts, which is frequently advanced in the literature as if it were a self-evident truth. The claim is that, '[a]s a matter of logic—given [that] one is presumed to be innocent unless and until one is proved ... guilty—there can only be two possible verdicts'.[18] Now, if the presumption of innocence stated that someone should be (fully) acquitted if they are not proved guilty, it would be true, and self-evidently so, that the presumption would be logically incompatible with a verdict that is intermediate between acquittal and conviction. The presumption would countenance two verdicts only: *tertium non datur*. But the presumption does not state any such rule.[19] It says, instead, that until someone is proved guilty, they should be *presumed innocent*; hence, if at the end of the trial they are not proved guilty, they should be presumed innocent.

[16] See J. Chalmers and others, 'A Modern History of the Not Proven Verdict' (2021) 25 Edinburgh Law Review 151, at 165. With regard to the Scottish 'not proven' verdict and the debate around it, the authors remark on the need for empirical evidence on the issue of stigma, and point out that arguments about stigma are still largely anecdotal. See also n 12.

[17] In the Introduction to the book, I spoke in terms of verdicts involving, or causing, 'hard treatment'. As I will point out again later, I take the imposition of hard treatment to mean an infringement of the status quo of innocence.

[18] McMahon, 'Consultation Paper' (n 4), at 14, quoting from an article by H. McLachlan that appeared in the *Scotsman* newspaper on 3 April 2007. A similar argument is found in Pisani (n 4) at 71, and in Morelli (n 4), at 127–128, 162–163. Pisani's view is quoted with approval in Marzaduri (n 4), at 520. More than just a trace of this argument is found in Arturo Rocco's criticism of the suspension of res judicata in the early 20th century. See M. N. Miletti, 'Ombre Sull'Innocenza. La Formula Dubitativa nel Processo Penale dell'Italia Liberale' (2020) 2 Quaderno di Storia del Penale e della Giustizia 177, at 188.

[19] cf Damaška (n 4), at 112. Arguing for the incompatibility between the presumption of innocence and the intermediate verdicts of the *ius commune*, he states that '[a]bsent legal legerdemain, the presumption demands that the defendant be acquitted whenever his or her guilt has not been proven.' I hope not to be accused of legal trickery as a result of the arguments to follow.

The above claim of logical incompatibility assumes that acquittal is the only epilogue of the trial that is compatible with presuming the defendant innocent. This, however, is not a self-evident or analytical truth. It is an assertion that must be defended, starting with a definition of what it means to 'presume someone innocent'. It may mean to allocate the burden of proof in a particular way, and/or to treat the defendant in a particular way, and/or to regard the defendant in a particular way, and/or to set a particular standard of proof for conviction, etc. Depending on how the question is answered, it may be possible to argue that, in the absence of proof of guilt, acquittal is the only option logically compatible with the presumption. But, again, an argument is needed here, and I cannot think of anything more promising than an argument premised on a rule of treatment supposedly embedded in the presumption, such as the argument for incompatibility given earlier.[20] To assert without argument that there is a logical implication between the presumption of innocence and a binary system of verdicts, then, is to be wilfully blind about the meaning of the presumption, and to fail to engage at all with the question of its compatibility with intermediate verdicts.

2.3 The presumption of innocence and the allocation of the burden of proof

The success of the argument for incompatibility depends on whether the presumption of innocence includes a rule of conduct that renders intermediate verdicts impermissible, insofar as they infringe upon the rights to which any member of the polity is prima facie entitled, but does not treat proof of guilt as a necessary condition for interfering with these rights. As seen earlier, treating proof of guilt as such a condition produces the implausible result of ruling out a host of measures that are generally accepted, often implemented, and, arguably, crucial to the functioning of the criminal justice system. To be in the position to assess if and how the presumption contributes to regulating the conduct of the criminal justice authorities vis-à-vis the defendant, it is necessary to introduce a rule of evidence that virtually everyone reads into the presumption of innocence, and, especially, to elucidate the justification for this rule. I am referring here to the rule allocating to the prosecution the burden of proving the defendant's guilt at trial. From the study of this rule, and of its justification, it will emerge that, in fact, the presumption of innocence includes a more general rule allocating to the criminal justice authorities the burden of justifying not just conviction and punishment, but also interferences with the defendant's rights taking place before and during the trial. Moreover, as I will show,

[20] For other possible, but implausible, arguments for incompatibility, see n 5 above.

the rationale for the allocation of this general burden of proof has important implications for the regulation of the conduct of the criminal justice authorities.

2.3.1 The allocation of the burden of proof at trial and its traditional justification

It is generally accepted that the presumption of innocence is not a 'legal presumption of fact'.[21] This phrase is used to refer to evidentiary devices that require or authorise the inference of a fact that may not, or could not, be inferred on the basis of the available evidence. For example, under section 76 of the English and Welsh Sexual Offences Act 2003, the fact-finder is required to infer the complainant's lack of consent to a sexual act if it is proven that the defendant 'intentionally induced the complainant to consent ... by impersonating a person known personally to the complainant'. The presumption of innocence does not trigger any inference whatsoever.

One might object that the presumption demands that the adjudicator *infers* that the defendant has not committed the crime charged if, at the end of the trial, the prosecution has not proven guilt. However, especially in a system characterised by a high standard of proof for conviction, it would be unreasonable to demand that the adjudicator infer lack of responsibility on the mere basis of a failure to meet such a standard. Instead of triggering an inference of innocence as the epilogue of an unsuccessful prosecution, the presumption recognises innocence as the starting point of the criminal process, allocating the burden of proof to the party that wants to alter this starting point. I will argue, though, that the 'innocence' constituting such starting point is not an assertion to the effect that the defendant has not committed the crime charged; it is, instead, the defendant's enjoyment of the rights to which all members of the polity are prima facie entitled.

The rule according to which, at trial, the prosecution bears the burden of proving the defendant's criminal responsibility is generally viewed as the core component of the presumption of innocence. Besides being widely acknowledged in the literature,[22] this rule has a solid basis in the conception of the presumption defended by

[21] See P. Roberts and A. Zuckerman, *Criminal Evidence* (OUP 2010), at 231; P. Roberts, 'Presumptuous or Pluralistic Presumptions of Innocence? Methodological Diagnosis towards Conceptual Reinvigoration' (2021) 198 Synthese 8901, at 8921; R. Glover, *Murphy on Evidence* (14th edn, OUP 2015), at 738–739; R. Munday, *Cross and Tapper on Evidence* (13th edn, OUP 2018), at 134–135; and P. R. Ferguson, 'The Presumption of Innocence and its Role in the Criminal Process' (2016) 27 Criminal Law Forum 131, at 135–137. See also J. B. Thayer, 'Presumption of Innocence in Criminal Cases' (1897) 6 Yale Law Journal 185, at 211–212, arguing passionately that the presumption of innocence is not evidence; that it does not have probative value.

[22] See, among others, A. Ashworth, 'Four Threats to the Presumption of Innocence' (2006) 10 International Journal of Evidence and Proof 241, at 243; Roberts and Zuckerman, (n 21), at 244; A. Stumer, *The Presumption of Innocence: Evidential and Human Rights Perspectives'* (Hart 2010), at xxxviii; A. Duff, 'Presuming Innocence' in L. Zedner and J. V. Roberts (eds), *Principles and Values in Criminal Law and Criminal Justice* (OUP 2012); J. D. Jackson and S. J. Summers, *The Internationalisation of*

the European Court of Human Rights (ECtHR),[23] and by the English and Welsh case law.[24] It is traditionally justified by appealing to the value of protecting the innocent from conviction: more precisely, of protecting the liberty, privacy, dignity, and reputation of the innocent, all fundamental rights that would be undermined by conviction. Indeed, the usual argument in support of the rule is that fact-finding is fallible, and that—precisely because of the costs that conviction has for the innocent in terms of curtailment of fundamental rights—the risk of an adverse false outcome should be allocated unevenly between the parties, so that most of it is borne by the prosecution.[25]

Consider the justification for the rule on the burden of proof offered in a recent work by Richard Lippke.[26] While bearing distinctive features, this justification, by and large, fits the traditional account, since it focuses on protecting the fundamental rights of the defendant that are at stake in adjudication. According to Lippke, the rule allocating to the prosecution the burden of proof is an essential building block of an articulated 'proof structure', which also includes the standard of proof, as well as a directive about how the adjudicator should regard the defendant at the outset of the trial.[27] In Lippke's view, each of these components of the proof structure contributes to ensure—and to assure the polity—that when a fellow citizen is convicted, this is done justifiably. But why should we insist on such justification? Lippke's answer is that we should do so because of the fundamental rights that punishment typically curtails: the rights to liberty, privacy, and

Criminal Evidence: Beyond the Common Law and Civil Law Traditions (CUP 2012), at 200; L. Campbell, 'Criminal Labels, the European Convention on Human Rights and the Presumption of Innocence' (2013) 76 Modern Law Review 681, at 682–683; I. Dennis, *The Law of Evidence* (7th edn, Sweet and Maxwell 2020), at 445. This component of the presumption is also recognised by academics focusing on legal systems other than the English and Welsh system. See P. J. Schwikkard, *Presumption of Innocence* (Juta and Co 1999), at 29; J. H. Wigmore, *A Treatise on the Anglo-American System of Evidence in Trials at Common Law, vol 9* (3rd edn, Little Brown 1940), at 407; L. Laudan, *Truth, Error, and Criminal Law: An Essay in Legal Epistemology* (CUP 2006), at 93–96.

[23] See S. Trechsel, *Human Rights in Criminal Proceedings* (OUP 2005), at 167–174.

[24] See *Woolmington* (n 1), where the rule according to which the burden of proving guilt is on the prosecution is seen as a component of the 'golden thread' of English criminal law, the other component being the standard of proof beyond a reasonable doubt.

[25] See Ashworth (n 22), at 246–251, stressing the justificatory role of the 'fundamental right not to be wrongly convicted'; Stumer (n 22), at 28–37, seeing the protection of the innocent from false conviction as the 'most obvious reason' for having the presumption; Roberts and Zuckerman (n 21), at 244–247, stressing the justificatory role of 'the fundamental right not to be subjected to the profound harm of wrongful conviction and punishment'; Campbell (n 22), at 683, stating that the rule on the burden of proof is underpinned by 'the need to avoid wrongful convictions'; Dennis (n 22), at 445–448, stating as a reason for the rule on the burden of proof that it 'is constructed so as to minimise the risk of [wrongful conviction]'. Other related reasons that are often offered in support of the rule on the burden of proof are the fact that the prosecution has an opportunity for advance preparation, and the imbalance of resources between the prosecution and the defence. See, among others, P. Roberts, 'Taking the Burden of Proof Seriously' [1995] 10 Criminal Law Review 783, at 786–787.

[26] See R. L. Lippke, *Taming the Presumption of Innocence* (OUP 2016), at 97–99 and ch 5.

[27] Ibid, at 81–82, 97. Lippke conceptualises the presumption of innocence as consisting only of this last component of the proof structure. I have criticised this component in Picinali, 'The Presumption of Innocence' (n 3), at 20–24.

autonomy. Such 'basic moral rights', he argues, 'are not supposed to be curtailed easily or else their considerable moral weight is not given its proper due ... [I]t is widely accepted that basic moral rights are strongly constraining considerations in the design of social, political, and legal institutions and practices. It follows that we should be cautious about setting up institutions that have the potential to curtail rights'.[28] In Lippke's view, then, the *raison d'être* for the proof structure—hence, for the rule on the burden of proof—is the protection of the fundamental rights that conviction and punishment curtail. His 'moral assurance account'[29] provides protection through insisting on the justification of any infringement of these rights: no defendant should suffer an infringement if appropriate reasons for it are not given.[30]

While I agree that the presumption of innocence includes a rule allocating to the prosecution the burden of proving criminal responsibility at trial, I disagree with the traditional justification of this component. To clarify, I recognise that the value of giving protection to the fundamental rights of the defendant that are at stake in adjudication is a reason for having this rule. There is, however, a reason that takes priority over this value, and that alone is sufficient to justify the rule. This reason is the principle of inertia in argumentation.

2.3.2 An alternative justification: the principle of inertia in argumentation

The principle of inertia in argumentation has been theorised, first by Chaim Perelman and Lucie Olbrechts-Tyteca, and, later, by Robert Alexy. Their accounts of the principle, though, are rather terse, and discuss its role in legal argumentation generally. While what follows builds on these accounts, it develops them significantly. This is done in order to clarify the connection between the principle and rationality, and, especially, to explain the functioning of the principle in the specific context of the criminal process.

According to the principle of inertia, in the absence of sufficient reasons to the contrary, the status quo should be preserved.[31] The phrase 'status quo' is used here

[28] See Lippke (n 26), at 110.

[29] See ibid.

[30] See ibid, ch 5, in particular 110–113.

[31] See C. Perelman and L. Olbrechts-Tyteca, *Traité de l'Argumentation: La Nouvelle Rhétorique* (2nd edn, Editions de l'Institut de Sociologie de l'Université Libre de Bruxelles 1970), at 140–148. At 142 the authors write, 'Le plus souvent ... l'orateur ne peut tabler, pour ses présomptions, que sur l'inertie psychique et sociale, qui, dans les consciences et dans les sociétés, fait pendant à l'inertie en physique. On peut présumer, jusqu'à prevue du contraire, que l'attitude adoptée antérieurement—opinion exprimée, conduit préférée—se continuera dans l'avenir ... Le changement, par contre, doit être justifié; une decision, une fois prise, ne peut être renversée que pour des raisons suffisantes.' See also R. Alexy, *A Theory of Legal Argumentation: The Theory of Rational Discourse as Theory of Legal Justification* (Ruth Adler and Neil MacCormick trs, OUP 1989), at 171–173, 195–197. At 171 Alexy writes, '[t]he principle of inertia states that an opinion which has been accepted in the past may not be abandoned again

to refer to any state of affairs that has previously been decided by the parties involved in an argumentative exchange. It may be a practical status quo—that is, a communal plan of action—or an epistemic status quo—that is, a shared view of the world. The principle implies that, if a party wants the status quo to change, they have to give others sufficient reasons for the change they seek:[32] they have to discharge a burden of proof. I will soon discuss this implication—indeed, the nature of the principle—in greater detail. It is worth illustrating, first, how the principle operates.

Consider, for example, a group of friends who have decided to meet at someone's house, and to watch a particular movie. If a member of the group has a change of mind and wants the group to watch a different movie, according to the principle of inertia they will have to advance sufficient reasons to persuade the group to change the communal plan. Absent such reason-giving effort, the principle says that the plan should not change.[33] Consider, now, the argumentation taking place in the criminal trial. The relevant status quo for the purposes of this argumentation is the defendant's innocence; that is, their enjoyment of those rights to which all members of the polity are prima facie entitled. These may include the right to liberty, to privacy, to property, to reputation etc. Of course, by the time of the trial, some of the defendant's rights may have already been restricted: in particular, the defendant may have been arrested and remanded in custody. I will consider this possibility in section 2.3.3 below. As in the argument for incompatibility presented earlier, the status quo of innocence is not understood here as a cognitive attitude about, or an assertion of, the fact that the defendant is innocent of the crime

without sufficient reason'. At 195 he gives a slightly different enunciation of the principle: the 'principle of inertia stipulates that a view or practice which has once been accepted should not be abandoned without some reason'. As Alexy points out, the principle of inertia 'has the character of a rule allocating the ... burden of proof: the appeal to an existing practice does not require justification, "change only must be justified"' (Alexy, ibid, at 171–172, quoting from C. Perelman, *Justice* (Random House 1967), at 10. A similar claim is made in Alexy, ibid, at 268). According to Perelman, Olbrechts-Tyteca, and Alexy, the principle of inertia performs further roles in addition to allocating the burden of proof in an argumentative exchange: 'It underlies the appeal to precedent and to accepted norms in both legal science and ethics' and, more generally, 'it makes argument actually possible' by allowing for presuppositions without which no argumentation could begin (Alexy, ibid, at 172. See also Perelman and Olbrechts-Tyteca, ibid, at 144). Perelman and Olbrechts-Tyteca also view the principle as the foundation of the 'rule of justice', according to which like cases should be treated alike (Perelman and Olbrechts-Tyteca, ibid, at 294).

32 Of course, a party might not succeed in providing sufficient reasons for the change that they seek, but the reasons provided might be sufficient for a less radical change. It still remains the case that whatever the change to the status quo, it should not take place in the absence of sufficient reasons *for it*, and that, in the absence of sufficient reasons for any change, the status quo should be preserved.

33 I will point out later that it is possible that a sufficient number of members of the group who have initially supported the status quo will independently change their minds, and that this will prompt the group to revise the status quo without an argumentative exchange actually taking place. The point made here, though, is that, insofar as this does not happen, ie insofar as the status quo stands, then the status quo should not change unless those who argue for a given change produce sufficient reasons for it.

charged.[34] It is not an epistemic status quo. It is, instead, a practical status quo consisting in the communal plan to afford the defendant, as a member of the polity, the enjoyment of the rights to which all members are prima facie entitled. This plan results from a decision made by the polity through the appropriate institutional mechanisms: above all, legislation. A conviction, with the accompanying sentence, constitutes an infringement of some of the defendant's rights characterising the status quo; it constitutes a change in the status quo. Therefore, the principle of inertia implies that the prosecution—which argues for such a change—bears the burden of proving to the polity that there are sufficient reasons for the change. This is done by producing evidence that proves, to the satisfaction of the standard of proof for conviction, that the defendant is guilty of a crime.[35] The presumption of innocence enforces the principle of inertia in the criminal trial. It reminds us that the defendant's unfettered enjoyment of the prerogatives of their membership in the polity is the relevant status quo: the state of affairs that the polity has previously decided. Implementing the principle, the presumption provides that the prosecution has to justify the change of the status quo that it argues for, by proving that the defendant is responsible for a crime. In the absence of such proof, the status quo should be preserved.[36]

As the above examples indicate, the principle of inertia concerns the dynamics of the argumentation, not its content. To clarify, it allocates the burden of proof, but says nothing about what the status quo is or should be, or how it might change. Importantly, it says nothing about what an individual or institution should consider to be sufficient reasons for a given change:[37] in particular, about where the

[34] In Picinali, 'The Presumption of Innocence' (n 3), at 20–24, I show that the presumption of innocence does not impose a cognitive attitude as the point of departure of the adjudicator's task.

[35] Notice that, besides affording the defendant the enjoyment of relevant rights, the communal plan of action constituting the status quo of innocence can be conceptualised as including also the provision for, and the regulation of, cases in which these rights can be infringed upon by the State (eg it may describe the kind of behaviour on the part of a member of the polity that warrants an infringement of their rights). It is, indeed, reasonable to consider these matters the necessary subject of a polity-level agreement on the relationship between State and individual. However, the status quo cannot include the *hic et nunc* infringement of such rights, lest it is self-contradictory. This means that infringements of the rights enjoyed by the defendant are alterations of the status quo, even if they have been anticipated and regulated in it. And the criminal justice authorities seeking such infringements have to provide sufficient reasons for them, showing that the conditions for interfering set in the status quo (eg that the defendant behaved in a particular way) have been met.

[36] One might argue that the principle of inertia does not make any original contribution to the debate on the presumption of innocence since it replicates the honoured Roman maxim *'ei incumbit probatio qui dicit, non qui negat'*. While I do not deny that the implications of this maxim for the allocation of the burden of proof at trial may be the same as the implications of the principle (see Picinali, 'The Presumption of Innocence' (n 3), at 12–18), the two are not equivalent. If anything, the role of the principle is to *justify* a rule such as that stated in the maxim. The principle *is not* such a rule.

[37] cf Alexy, 'A Theory of Legal Argumentation' (n 31), stating, at 173, that the principle of inertia 'says nothing about when [the status quo] is to be doubted and about how the matter should be decided in cases of doubt'. Setting these criteria is left 'to the reasonableness of those participating in discussion'. As I will soon point out, the principle does not include a standard of moral or epistemological sufficiency. However, the principle does include a threshold of sufficiency of sorts: for a change of the status quo to occur rationally, it requires the giving of reasons that are *in fact* sufficient to rationally change the mind of one's interlocutors. The reason-giving effort that is needed to meet this threshold of 'factual'

criminal standard of proof should lie. These matters define the argumentative context, and may vary significantly from one context to another. The principle of inertia, instead, invariably applies in each context. Indeed, the principle is operative both in the case of the group of friends planning to watch a movie, and in the case of the criminal trial; but the relevant status quo, the change to it that is possible and is sought, and the relevant standard of moral or epistemological sufficiency, differ markedly in the two argumentative contexts. The previous paragraph identified the status quo, and the proposed change thereof, for the argumentative context of the criminal trial. These are, innocence and conviction, respectively. As pointed out, the reasons for such a change are the incriminating evidence presented at trial. The assessment of sufficiency of these reasons, then, presupposes the identification of the facts that constitute criminal responsibility, and of the standard of proof that needs satisfying in order to consider these facts established. Even if the principle of inertia itself is silent on these matters, the questions remain as to what facts the prosecution must prove to obtain the change of the status quo represented by conviction, and as to whether a standard of proof for conviction can, nonetheless, be read into the presumption of innocence. I have addressed these questions elsewhere.[38] Being irrelevant to the assessment of the argument for incompatibility, I will not address them again here.

Notice that respect for the principle of inertia can be regarded as a requirement of rationality in argumentation,[39] at least if we assume the rationality of the parties involved. Rationality consists in the validity of reasoning; that is, in its 'formal correctness'.[40] Accordingly, an instance of reasoning is rational insofar as its conclusion is correctly inferred from its premises, whether or not the premises and the conclusion are morally and epistemically sound.[41] Imagine, for instance, that the

sufficiency is likely to vary from one argumentative context to another. See n 44 below, and accompanying text.

[38] See Picinali, 'The Presumption of Innocence' (n 3), at 12–20. In those pages, I also addressed the question of the legitimacy of reverse burdens. In a nutshell, I argued, first, that the facts that the prosecution must prove to obtain a change of the status quo are the 'constitutive facts' for the crime charged, these being the facts that the legislator and the interpreter identify as necessary for someone to be responsible for such crime. The principle of inertia has nothing to say about what these facts should be. I then argued that the principle of inertia requires that the prosecution bears both the evidential and legal burdens of proof on all constitutive facts; hence, that reverse burdens on such facts—or on facts that 'overlap' with these—are illegitimate. Their illegitimacy is due to their being in conflict with the principle of inertia; that is, to their irrationality.

[39] This is how it is regarded by Alexy, 'A Theory of Legal Argumentation' (n 31), who includes the principle in his 'theory of rational discourse'.

[40] See G. H. von Wright, 'Images of Science and Forms of Rationality' in G. H. von Wright, *The Tree of Knowledge and Other Essays* (E. J. Brill 1993), at 173.

[41] See ibid, at 172, 173 (stating that '[a]n argument can be rational but its premisses and conclusions may be unreasonable'). See also the conceptions of rationality endorsed in F. Picinali, 'Two Meanings of "Reasonableness": Dispelling the "Floating" Reasonable Doubt' (2013) 76 Modern Law Review 845, at 855–856; W. M. Sibley, 'The Rational Versus the Reasonable' (1953) 62 The Philosophical Review 554, at 555–557; C. Perelman, *The New Rhetoric and the Humanities: Essays on Rhetoric and its Applications* (W. Kluback tr, D. Reidel Publishing Company 1979), at 117–118; J. Rawls, *Political Liberalism* (Columbia

legislator intends to enhance the truth-finding role of the criminal process, and believes that the use of oppressive and suggestive interviewing techniques by the police is a means to achieve this goal. Given these premises, it is rational for the legislator to encourage the police to adopt such techniques. This decision, indeed, correctly follows from the premises.[42]

Now, consider a group of rational individuals—that is, of individuals capable of rational reasoning—which has chosen a communal plan of action, or accepted a view of the world. Irrespective of the decision rule applied—be it relative majority, absolute majority, supermajority, or unanimity—and irrespective of whether group members participate directly in the decision or do so through representatives, the rational individuals participating in the decision who have supported the communal plan or view will have done so because the considerations that they recognise as reasons for or against that plan or view—in short, the recognised reasons—warrant an inference to that plan or view. In other words, they will have done so because that plan or view is correctly inferred from the recognised reasons. As a matter of rationality, then, these individuals should not change their opinion unless they come to recognise reasons that are sufficient for them to disregard the inference previously drawn; that is, reasons that make it the case that the plan or view of the world previously decided is not correctly inferred from the reasons that they *now* recognise. Failing this, such plan or view continues to be the conclusion of a correct inference from the recognised reasons. Rationality, thus, demands that these individuals continue supporting the status quo and, consequently, that the group decision be upheld. If, through private enquiries, a sufficient number of supporters of the status quo involved in the decision come to recognise sufficient reasons against inferring the status quo, then the group will be called to decide again, and the status quo will be rationally altered without an argumentative exchange actually taking place. But insofar as this does not happen—that is, insofar as the status quo stands—the status quo should not change unless those who argue for change make enough supporters of the status quo recognise sufficient reasons to change their mind. The implication of the principle of inertia, then, is that, given a status quo, the party in the group who argues for a change of it has to discharge a burden of proof: this is a necessary means for the status quo to change rationally.[43]

University Press 1993), at 50, 51; and R. Alexy, 'The Reasonableness of the Law' in G. Bongiovanni and others (eds), *Reasonableness and Law* (Springer 2009), at 5–7.

[42] More precisely, the conclusion is linked to the premises by a correct motivational means-end connection. On the role of means-end connections in practical inference, see R. Audi, *Practical Reasoning* (Routledge 1989) 95–102; G. E. M. Anscombe, 'Practical Inference' in M. Geach and L. Gormally (eds), *Human Life, Action and Ethics: Essays by G. E. M. Anscombe* (Imprint Academic 2005).

[43] It is generally the case that the necessary means to persuade someone who would not persuade themselves through private enquiry is to give them sufficient reasons. However, in the case of group deliberation with a status quo, the failure to persuade—that is, to discharge a burden of proof—means that the status quo stands, and that it continues to bind the party that fails. I will come back to this point in section 2.4.2.

Notice that with the phrase 'sufficient reasons' I am not referring to a standard of moral or epistemological sufficiency: the principle of inertia does not incorporate any such standard. I refer, instead, to reasons that are *in fact* sufficient to rationally change the mind of one's interlocutor.[44] It may be that this person would rationally change their mind even if given reasons that are weaker than the reasons that morality or epistemology would require for the inference of the status quo to be disregarded. Or it may be that they would not rationally change their mind unless given reasons that are stronger than the reasons that would be sufficient from a moral or epistemological point of view. Be that as it may, unless this person is given reasons that are sufficient to make it the case that the reasons that they recognise no longer support a correct inference of the status quo, they will be rationally bound to draw this inference and, hence, to support the status quo.

The model presented in the previous paragraph is intended to show that the principle of inertia is a requirement of rationality, and that it implies the allocation of the burden of proof. To adapt the model to the particular institutional context of the criminal trial, and of criminal justice more generally, the status quo of innocence may be conceptualised as resulting from a hypothetical social contract or, more concretely, from the deliberation of a constituent assembly or of an ordinary legislative body. Assuming the rationality of those involved, the communal plan is warranted by a correct inference from the reasons that they recognise. Qua representatives of the polity, those in charge of adjudication endorse the inference previously drawn by the (representatives of the) polity, and sanctioned through the means just mentioned; hence, they need to be given sufficient reasons to disregard this inference and, thereby, to change the status quo.

There is a significant difference between argumentation in an informal context, such as that of the group of friends planning to watch a movie, and argumentation in the context of the criminal trial: the institutional nature of the latter. The adjudicator, who is called on to decide whether the status quo of innocence should be altered through conviction, is an institution: its composition and its operation are governed by the law, so that the adjudicator, being a representative of the polity, can act in conformity with the polity's judgement. In particular, the determinations of

[44] Consider that the reason-giving effort that is needed to satisfy this threshold of 'factual' sufficiency is likely to vary from one argumentative context to another. Depending on the argumentative context, the inference of the status quo drawn by each rational individual may be supported by stronger or weaker reasons; that is, the balance of reasons may tip in favour of the status quo to varying degrees. Therefore, the strength of the reasons needed for the inference from recognised reasons to status quo to be disregarded by such individual may vary from one context to another. For instance, in the context of the group of friends interested in watching a movie, someone's support for a certain movie may not be based on particularly strong reasons. Hence a change of status quo may be achieved relatively easily by whoever in the group argues for it. Arguably, things are different in the context of the criminal trial. Because the reasons that the polity has for affording the defendant certain rights are strong—that is, because the stakes involved in changing the status quo through adjudication are high—for the polity to agree to an interference with such rights a substantially greater reason-giving effort is needed: the satisfaction of a demanding standard of proof.

which changes of the status quo are permissible in the abstract, of which behaviour on the part of the defendant warrants which change, and of the standard of proof that needs to be satisfied, with reference to such behaviour, for the adjudicator to conclude in a concrete case that there are sufficient reasons for a given change, are all determinations made by the law, as expression of the polity's judgement: [45] they are not left to the sensibility of the individual, or the individuals, who perform the function of adjudicating. By setting the standard of proof for conviction, the law determines that, when a certain reason-giving effort is made by the prosecution, the adjudicator will find that the reasons given are sufficient for conviction and will, therefore, agree to such change of the status quo. When, conversely, the prosecution falls short of making that reason-giving effort, the law determines that the adjudicator will find that the reasons given are not sufficient, and will not agree to the change. The principle of inertia is operative even if argumentation is institutional, in the sense just described. Moreover, it is irrelevant that the standard of proof chosen by the law may be utterly inadequate: the principle of inertia operates even if the standard is higher or lower than is morally justified, given the stakes. Once a standard of proof for conviction is chosen in a binary verdict system, the fact that the standard is not met means that the reasons that the polity—and, hence, the adjudicator as the polity's representative—recognise still warrant inferring the status quo and that, therefore, rationality demands that the status quo not be changed. For the status quo to change rationally, the prosecution has to give sufficient reasons to satisfy the standard of proof for conviction. This reason-giving effort is the necessary means for the prosecution to bring about the intended change: if, and only if, reasons sufficient to satisfy the standard of proof are given, will the polity—and, hence, the adjudicator as the polity's representative—recognise reasons such that the inference of the status quo is no longer warranted by the reasons that they recognise. The principle of inertia, then, does not allocate to the prosecution the burden of showing that conviction is morally justified, but merely the burden of showing that it is justified according to the law; that is, according to the polity. The standard of proof chosen may well be inadequate, but it identifies the reason-giving effort that will, *in fact*, make the polity and, hence, the adjudicator, rationally change their minds; moreover, it identifies the reason-giving effort without which the polity and, hence, the adjudicator, will not, *in fact*, rationally change their minds. Of course, these considerations presuppose that the law is informed by rationality. In particular, they presuppose that the determinations with which the law directs the workings of the adjudicator reflect the rational—even if not necessarily morally justified—judgement of the polity, as this is channelled through the legislative process.

[45] The communal plan of action constituting the status quo of innocence can be conceptualised as already including these determinations. See n 35 above. On the choice whether to delegate to the adjudicator the selection of the standard of proof for conviction see Chapter 4, section 4.2.

Considering the argumentative context of the criminal trial, then, the claim advanced here is that the rule allocating to the prosecution the burden of proving criminal responsibility is not justified by the value of protecting the fundamental rights of the defendant which are enjoyed in the status quo and encroached upon in the event of conviction; rather, it is justified by the consideration that—irrespective of what these rights are, and of their importance—it is rational to allocate the burden of proof as the rule demands, since this allocation follows from the principle of inertia. This claim, though, needs careful explanation.

Since respect for the principle of inertia is a requirement of rationality, I argue that, in the justification of the rule on the burden of proof, the principle takes priority over the reason normally advanced in the literature and just rehearsed. How so? First, consider that following this reason in the allocation of the burden of proof may well be a requirement of reasonableness, but it is not demanded by rationality itself. Reasonableness consists in more than mere formal correctness of reasoning. In particular, it also involves respect for the moral values that are relevant to a given instance of decision-making.[46] Hence, the decision of the legislator in the example described earlier may be unreasonable, insofar as encouraging the use of oppressive and suggestive interviewing techniques disrespects the value of protecting the defendant's rights, and insofar as this is, indeed, a value that should be acted upon, in particular, in deciding on the regulation of evidence-gathering. However, as previously shown, that decision is rational because it originates from an inference that is formally correct. Protecting the defendant's rights is not a requirement for the formal correctness of reasoning.[47]

Second, as the above characterisations of rationality, and of reasonableness, make clear, while rationality does not presuppose reasonableness, rationality is a necessary condition for reasonableness.[48] The conceptual point advanced here

[46] The connection between reasonableness and morality is generally accepted in the literature. See Sibley (n 41); Perelman, *The New Rhetoric and the Humanities* (n 41), at 124–133; J. Finnis, *Natural Law and Natural Rights* (Clarendon Press 1980), at 100–133; Rawls, *Political Liberalism* (n 41), at 48–54; von Wright (n 40), at 173; M. Moore, 'On Reasonableness' (1996) 13 Journal of Applied Philosophy 167, at 175–177; J. Rawls, *Justice as Fairness: A Restatement* (Erin Kelly (ed), Belknap Press 2001), at 7; M. Moran, *Rethinking the Reasonable Person: An Egalitarian Reconstruction of the Objective Standard* (OUP 2003), at 286–316; A. Wierzbicka, *English: Meaning and Culture* (OUP 2006), at 131, 136; N. MacCormick, *Practical Reason in Law and Morality* (OUP 2008), at 156–161; T. A. Spragens, Jr, 'Democratic Reasonableness' in S. P. Young (ed), *Reasonableness in Liberal Political Philosophy* (Routledge 2009), at 91–93; Alexy, 'The Reasonableness of the Law' (n 41), at 5, 6; G. Sartor, 'A Sufficientist Approach to Reasonableness in Legal Decision-Making and Judicial Review' in Bongiovanni and others (n 41), at 17–19.

[47] Of course, in specific instances of reasoning, the premises may warrant a decision to protect the defendant's rights, such that it would be irrational to decide otherwise. This, however, does not make the protection of such rights a requirement of rationality. Rationality, instead, requires respecting the formal correctness of reasoning which, in such specific instances, would demand a decision to protect these rights.

[48] As already pointed out, rationality is not a sufficient condition for reasonableness. The latter also requires that the premises of an instance of reasoning be morally (and epistemically) sound. On the distinction between reasonableness and rationality, see Picinali, 'Two Meanings of "Reasonableness"' (n 41), at 855–862. See also Alexy, 'The Reasonableness of the Law' (n 41); Sartor (n 46); Sibley (n 41); Perelman, *The New Rhetoric and the Humanities* (n 41), ch 11; Rawls, *Political Liberalism* (n 41), at

conforms with the common-sense intuition that a decision, an action, a plan, etc cannot be reasonable if it is irrational. Consider someone who has a goal *A*, believes that *B* is not a means to achieve *A*, and nonetheless decides to perform *B* in order to achieve *A*. This instance of decision-making would be unreasonable even if *A* and *B* were morally appropriate, and even if the belief that *B* is not a means to achieve *A* were accurate. The unreasonableness of this line of reasoning derives from its being an invalid inference; that is, from its irrationality. Similarly, changing the status quo in the presence of reasons for change that are insufficient for such a change would be unreasonable, even if such reasons were morally appropriate. The unreasonableness of this behaviour derives from the fact that, in such instances, rationality demands that the status quo be maintained, since it is still warranted by the correct inferences of its supporters.

The upshot of this discussion is that requirements of rationality, such as the respect for the principle of inertia, are also requirements of reasonableness. Instead, *other* requirements of reasonableness—as the protection of the defendants' rights may well be—are just requirements of reasonableness, full stop. Requirements of the former kind are, therefore, more basic than requirements of the latter kind. On this ground, they can be taken to enjoy priority. In the justification of the rule allocating the burden of proof at trial, then, the principle of inertia can be taken to enjoy priority over the reason normally advanced in the literature. In fact, in addition to being of secondary importance, this reason is not even necessary to achieve such justification. As shown earlier, the principle of inertia can achieve it by itself. To clarify, the point here is not that the value of protecting the defendant's rights that are at stake in adjudication is not a reason for allocating the burden of proof to the prosecution at trial. Rather, the point is that this is not a necessary reason, and that it takes the back seat with respect to the principle of inertia. Of course, this holds only if we value rationality and reasonableness as principles informing the criminal process. If we did not so value them, the relationship of priority defended earlier would be irrelevant in this context, and the principle of inertia would have little or no normative power therein. I doubt, though, that anyone would argue that we should not thus value these qualities of reasoning.

At this juncture, one might object that I have not shown that the principle of inertia is necessary to justify the rule on the allocation of the burden of proof at trial. This is correct, but there is no need to do so. By showing that the principle of inertia is sufficient for this justification, I have also shown that the justification available in the literature is not necessary. And by showing that the principle of inertia takes priority over such justification, I have also shown that, as things stand, it gives us the strongest justification for the rule.

48–54; and A. Aarnio, *The Rational as Reasonable: A Treatise on Legal Justification* (D Reidel Publishing Company 1987).

Before moving forward, I want to reassure the sceptical reader that my reliance on rationality, rather than reasonableness, to justify the rule allocating the burden of proof at trial is not at all a denial of the claim that reasonableness, in particular as exercised in political morality, plays a fundamental role in regulating the context of trial argumentation. I explained earlier that the principle of inertia is silent with respect to what the status quo is or should be, how it might change, and what an individual or institution should consider to be sufficient reasons for changing it. Indeed, these matters vary from one argumentative context to another, whereas the principle invariably applies in all contexts. Now, I accept that the rights to liberty, to privacy, to reputation etc, and, more fundamentally, an underlying theory of the appropriate relationship between State and individual play a role in defining these matters; that is, in defining that to which an individual is prima facie entitled, how such state can be altered if they are shown to have committed a crime, what facts constitute criminal responsibility, and what the applicable standard of proof should be. For instance, in Chapters 3 and 4 I argue that the standard of proof hinges on how one evaluates the possible outcomes of the trial. Such evaluation cannot be just a matter of rationality:[49] it depends also on moral considerations, such as the above rights and the above theory. In this section, I have simply denied that moral considerations play a necessary role in allocating the burden of proof at trial.

2.3.3 Reconsidering the rule allocating the burden of proof

In the previous section, I argued that the rule according to which the prosecution must bear the burden of proving guilt at trial is justified by a requirement of rationality: the principle of inertia in argumentation. Because—as is unanimously recognised—this rule is entrenched in the presumption of innocence, the presumption can be understood as the vehicle through which the principle of inertia is implemented in the criminal process.

Notice, though, that, according to Article 6(2) ECHR, the presumption of innocence applies from the time when the defendant is charged with an offence. In other words, it also applies before the start of the trial. In fact, it is important to consider that the ECtHR adopts an interpretation of the term 'charge' that is autonomous from, and more extensive than, the domestic notion. The defendant is deemed charged for the purposes of the presumption of innocence even if no formal charge has been brought against them.[50] Commenting on the Court's case

[49] It is widely recognised that there are rationality constraints on one's preferences over outcomes. For discussion, see M. Peterson, *An Introduction to Decision Theory* (2nd edn, CUP 2017), at 174–194.

[50] See Trechsel (n 23), at 31–36, and 155–156. It is interesting to note that, in earlier drafts of the Convention, the presumption was afforded to 'any person' or 'everyone', without mentioning the need to be charged with an offence. See ibid, at 154.

law, Stefan Trechsel argues that Article 6 'applies to all procedural steps which are directly relevant to the decision as to the guilt or innocence of the accused', beginning with the investigative phase.[51]

This broad understanding of the sphere of application of the presumption is in line with the role of the presumption as the vehicle for the principle of inertia. Given that this principle is a requirement of rationality, we should want it to be respected throughout the criminal process, understood as the series of phases starting with the investigation and ending with the determination of the question of guilt. Hence, the norm that implements the principle in the criminal process should be given application in all such phases. Remember that the status quo on which the presumption of innocence is premised is the defendant's enjoyment of the rights to which all members of the polity are prima facie entitled, and that the principle of inertia implies that those who seek to infringe upon such enjoyment need to give sufficient reasons for the infringement. Now, because an infringement may well occur before or during the trial—again, think of the examples of surveillance measures, of the non-consensual collection of forensic biometric samples, of arrest, and of remand in custody—the presumption should be understood as allocating to the authorities not just the burden of giving sufficient reasons for a particular epilogue of the trial by proving guilt in court, but also the burden of giving sufficient reasons for any earlier infringement.

What this means, then, is that the presumption of innocence does not merely include a rule allocating to the prosecution the burden of proving the defendant's guilt at trial. It includes a broader rule—of which the former is a specific implication—allocating to the criminal justice authorities the burden of giving sufficient reasons for any infringement of the status quo of innocence. True, the process of proof at trial—hence, the giving of reasons for conviction, and their assessment—is significantly more regulated than the process of proof pertaining to other infringements upon the status quo. This can be justified by the fact that conviction represents the most serious infringement, and the one to which earlier infringements are instrumental. However, the giving of sufficient reasons by the criminal justice authorities should be necessary for the adoption of any measure that infringes upon the defendant's enjoyment of rights characterising the status quo. The principle of inertia and, therefore, the presumption of innocence so demand.

Notice that I am not alone in arguing that the presumption of innocence imposes on the criminal justice authorities the burden of justifying infringements of the status quo of innocence occurring prior to conviction.[52] However, those who have argued for this broad rule on the burden of proof have done so by appealing to political morality, in particular to a notion of the appropriate relationship

[51] See ibid, at 32.
[52] See Ashworth (n 22), at 249; and Jackson and Summers (n 22), at 206.

between State and individual. As stated earlier, my view is that political morality is relevant to setting the status quo; that is, to choosing what rights a member of the polity is prima facie entitled to; also, it is relevant to determining which reasons should be deemed sufficient for a particular change of the status quo. However, the allocation of the burden to provide sufficient reasons is a matter of rationality, prior to being a matter of political morality. Earlier, I pointed out that, in the institutional context of the criminal trial, it is the law that sets the standard of proof for conviction, reflecting the polity's rational judgement. The standard identifies the reasons that are necessary and sufficient for the polity—and, hence, the adjudicator as the polity's representative—to rationally agree to such a change of the status quo. The same holds true for those infringements of the status quo, occurring prior to conviction, that the law provides. The law may not require an argumentative exchange in which the criminal justice authorities effectively give reasons, for the particular infringement they seek, to an adjudicator representing the polity.[53] However, the law does identify the reasons that justify each infringement, such that, when these reasons are detected by the criminal justice authorities, the polity can be taken to have rationally agreed to the infringement.[54] The principle of inertia requires that sufficient reasons be given for an infringement to occur, but it does not incorporate a threshold of moral or epistemological sufficiency, and it operates irrespective of whether the choice of the applicable standard(s) made through the law is reasonable or not. Even if the law were to set an unreasonably high standard of sufficiency for a given pre-trial infringement, it would still be the case that, until the standard is satisfied, the reasons that the polity recognises warrant a correct inference of the status quo. Rationality would, therefore, demand that the status quo be preserved. For the infringement to be a rational outcome, the criminal justice authorities have to give sufficient reasons to satisfy such an unreasonably high standard. To restate a point made earlier, then, under my construal of the presumption of innocence, this norm does not place on the criminal justice authorities the burden of providing the moral justification for any infringement of the status quo that they seek prior to conviction. The burden placed, by the presumption, on the criminal justice authorities is, instead, that of showing that such an infringement is justified according to the applicable legal standard of sufficiency; that is, according to the polity's rational judgement.

[53] In England and Wales, an argumentative exchange is required for a remand in custody. See the English and Welsh Bail Act 1976, in particular sch 1, pt 1, para 2.

[54] For example, see s 61 of the English and Welsh Police and Criminal Evidence Act 1984 for the non-consensual collection of fingerprints, and s 24 of the English and Welsh Police and Criminal Evidence Act 1984 for arrest without warrant.

2.4 The presumption of innocence and the treatment of the defendant

As seen earlier, the argument for the incompatibility between the presumption of innocence and intermediate verdicts rests on the premise that the presumption includes a rule on how the criminal justice authorities should treat the defendant. I have pointed out that, for the argument to succeed, it must be possible to identify, as part of the presumption, a rule of conduct that renders impermissible intermediate verdicts of the infringing kind, without treating proof of guilt as the necessary condition for an infringement of the status quo. If proof of guilt were so treated, in fact, infringing measures such as the use of surveillance techniques, the non-consensual collection of forensic biometric samples, arrest, and remand in custody would be at odds with the rule. Considering that these measures are important for, if not crucial to, the effective functioning of the criminal justice system, ruling them out would be implausible. In sections 2.4.1 and 2.4.2, I identify the rule of treatment included in the presumption. In section 2.5, I assess whether this rule satisfies the desiderata just stated.

Given the formulation of the presumption in Article 6(2) ECHR, one may be wary of interpreting it as including a rule on how to treat the defendant. If anything, to say that someone should be '*presumed* innocent until proved guilty' is to demand a particular way of viewing, rather than treating, this individual. As I have shown in previous work,[55] though, notwithstanding the formulation of Article 6(2) ECHR, it is doubtful whether the presumption imposes any particular way of viewing the defendant. If this is correct, one should not rely on the formulation as a conclusive argument that the presumption does not impose a rule of conduct.

Indeed, it is widely accepted by academics and courts alike that the presumption includes the rule according to which, throughout the criminal process, the criminal justice authorities[56] should treat the defendant as innocent until they are proved guilty of the crime charged.[57] Some authors even argue that this rule is a 'logical consequence' of the rule concerning the allocation of the burden of proof

[55] See Picinali, 'The Presumption of Innocence' (n 3), section 2.3, where I criticise Laudan's and Lippke's views on the matter.

[56] The norm may be extended to target the behaviour of all State authorities, insofar as this behaviour is related to the allegations against the defendant. There are differing views as to whether the rule should also extend to agents other than State authorities. Compare A. Duff, 'Who Must Presume Whom to be Innocent of What' (2013) 42 Netherlands Journal of Legal Philosophy 170, at 180–182 with T. Weigend, 'Assuming that the Defendant is Not Guilty: The Presumption of Innocence in the German System of Criminal Justice' (2014) 8 Criminal Law and Philosophy 285, at 288–290. See also D. A. Nance, 'Civility and the Burden of Proof' (1994) 17 Harvard Journal of Law and Public Policy 647, at 647–655, although Nance's focus is on the presumption as a way of regarding, rather than treating, an individual. This debate is irrelevant for my purposes, given that my focus is on conduct that is the prerogative of State (in particular, criminal justice) authorities; that is, issuing (intermediate) verdicts.

[57] Ashworth (n 22), at 243–244; Ferguson (n 21); H. Stewart, 'The Right to Be Presumed Innocent' (2014) 8 Criminal Law and Philosophy 407; Weigend (n 56). The rule of treatment is also read into the presumption by the ECtHR. See Trechsel (n 23), at 163–164, 178–191.

at trial. According to these authors, if a 'guilty' verdict is authorised only when the prosecution has proven its case, it follows that, up to that point, the defendant should be treated as innocent of the crime charged.[58] Later, I will reconsider this claim of logical relation.

What does it mean, though, that the defendant should be treated *as innocent*? To address this question, it is useful to introduce the distinction between actual—or material—innocence, and legal—or probatory—innocence.[59] The former is the state of affairs consisting in not having committed the crime charged; the latter is the state of affairs consisting in not having been proven guilty of the crime charged through the criminal process. Let us consider, first, a rule according to which the criminal justice authorities should treat the defendant as *actually* innocent until they are proved guilty of the crime charged. Is this rule part of the presumption?

2.4.1 Treating the defendant as an 'actually' innocent person

Of course, the supposed rule stating that criminal justice authorities should treat the defendant as actually innocent, etc is not premised on the assertion that the defendant is actually innocent, this being a fact that not even the criminal process is designed to establish. Rather, the rule hypothesises that the defendant is actually innocent, and invites the authorities to treat them according to this hypothesis until they are proved guilty. The rule should, therefore, be understood as requiring the criminal justice authorities to treat the defendant *as the authorities should treat the defendant if the defendant were actually innocent.*

Notice that this formulation of the rule is still elliptical. Consider that our agency is governed by our beliefs about the relevant matters, rather than by the actuality of the relevant matters, the latter being a state of affairs that we may not—possibly cannot—have access to.[60] If, for instance, we do not want to make friends with cruel and selfish people, and we believe that a particular individual is cruel and selfish, we will not make friends with them, even if they are actually kind and generous. It follows that demanding that the criminal justice authorities treat the defendant as the authorities should treat the defendant if the defendant were actually innocent is making an empty demand. How the authorities should behave vis-à-vis the defendant cannot depend on whether the defendant is actually innocent or not. The authorities have no access to this state of affairs, thus no opportunity to regulate

[58] See Schwikkard (n 22), at 36. cf Jackson and Summers (n 22), at 205.

[59] On this distinction, see Laudan, *Truth, Error, and Criminal Law* (n 22), at 12, 96–106, and Lippke (n 26), at 14–16. See also H. L. Packer, *The Limits of the Criminal Sanction* (Stanford University Press 1968), at 166–167, discussing the importance of the notion of legal innocence for the 'due process model' of adjudication.

[60] Of course, this is not to deny that the actuality of the relevant matters can (and probably most often does) influence our beliefs about them.

their conduct accordingly. How the authorities should behave depends, instead, on their beliefs on the relevant matters, including on whether the defendant is innocent (which is not to deny that the authorities have a duty to ensure that their beliefs reflect the available evidence on this issue).[61] However, any belief on whether the defendant is innocent—and on any other relevant fact, for that matter—is compatible with the state of affairs consisting in the actual innocence of the defendant. As a result, the hypothetical fact relied upon by the rule in order to provide a criterion for appropriate conduct, ie actual innocence, does not have any constraining effect on the authorities' behaviour.

To properly constrain the behaviour of the authorities towards the defendant, we need to formulate the rule so as to refer to the hypothesis that the authorities believe in actual innocence, rather than to the hypothesis of actual innocence itself. Thus, the rule should be expressed as directing criminal justice authorities to treat the defendant *as the authorities should treat the defendant if they believed that the defendant is actually innocent*.[62] However, once the rule is spelt out as suggested, it becomes evident that it is an unreasonable rule to impose on criminal justice authorities. Arguably, if the police believed that an individual is actually innocent, as a matter of both law and morality the police should not investigate them, interview them, arrest them, invite them to take part in an identification procedure, take bodily samples from them, etc. Similarly, if the prosecution believed that an individual is actually innocent, as a matter of both law and morality it should not bring charges against them and present a case at trial seeking their conviction. It follows that, if a criminal justice authority had to treat the defendant as the authority should treat the defendant—whether under the law or under morality—if they believed that the defendant was actually innocent, none of the above actions should ever be performed. Since these actions are vital to the criminal process, under this rule the criminal process would simply become impossible. This shows that the rule is highly implausible and should be rejected.[63]

[61] If the authorities have breached this duty by culpably ignoring any relevant evidence, it is arguable that how they should behave vis-à-vis the defendant depends on the belief that they would have had, had they not ignored such evidence.

[62] Another possibility is a rule providing that the criminal justice authorities should treat the defendant as the authorities *would* treat the defendant if they believed that the defendant was actually innocent. How the authorities would treat the defendant under this hypothetical is an empirical, rather than a normative, question. The answer to this question may depend on variables other than the applicable rules of treatment. These variables may include, for instance, whether the operating officers are honest individuals. Moreover, it is a question that has no univocal answer: similarly situated defendants may be treated differently based on these variables, even if such differential treatment is unwarranted. As a result, this alternative rule does not posit an appropriate, or a stable, criterion for conduct, and should be rejected on these grounds.

[63] Would it be sensible to argue that the presumption of innocence requires the particular treatment consisting in declaring 'actually innocent' those who are not found guilty through the proceedings? Without dramatically altering the nature of the criminal process, it would not. The criminal process in jurisdictions such as England and Wales is not designed to produce claims about actual innocence. The fact that, at the end of the process, someone is not found guilty surely does not warrant the claim that they are actually innocent. Since the standard of proof for conviction is considerably high, a failure to meet this standard is compatible with the presence of substantial evidence of guilt. Might the

2.4.2 From treating the defendant as a 'legally' innocent person to no infringement without sufficient reasons

Let us now consider the alternative rule, according to which the criminal justice authorities should treat the defendant as *legally* innocent until they are proved guilty of the crime charged. Notice that, unlike the rule studied previously, this rule does not consist in hypothesising a state of affairs and demanding that the authorities act as they should do if such a state of affairs were true. Indeed, until the defendant is proved guilty, they *are* legally innocent. Thus, if valid, the rule would constrain the authorities' behaviour only with regard to a defendant who is *in fact* legally innocent.

The precept of the rule is, however, unclear: what does treating someone as legally innocent mean? A possible answer is that it means *not treating them as they should be treated if they had been found guilty*, ie if they were not legally innocent. Reformulated in light of this answer, the rule would provide that, until the defendant is proved guilty, the criminal justice authorities should not treat the defendant as such authorities should treat the defendant if the defendant had been found guilty of the crime charged.[64] The problem with a rule so formulated is that there are ways of treating a person that, arguably, the authorities should endorse—whether under the law or under morality—both when engaging with someone who has been found guilty, and when engaging with someone who has not been found guilty. These include, for instance, respecting the person's dignity and physical integrity. The rule, however, denies this: at a close look, one sees that it presents the treatment required for the legally innocent as being alternative to the treatment required for those who have been found guilty.

This problem is avoided by giving a different answer to the question at the start of the previous paragraph: treating the defendant as legally innocent means not treating them in ways that can only be justified in the presence of proof of guilt; that is, evidence of guilt that an adjudicator considered sufficient to satisfy the standard of proof for conviction. In light of this answer, the rule can be reformulated as stating that, until the defendant is proved guilty, the criminal justice authorities should not treat the defendant in ways that can only be justified in the presence of proof of guilt. This rule appears to convey effectively the idea that the defendant should be treated as legally innocent: if legal innocence is the absence of

presumption of innocence require, instead, that those who are not found guilty through the proceedings be declared legally innocent? A requirement of this kind would be nugatory. Since legal innocence is the state of not having been found guilty through the criminal process, if the defendant is not found guilty, then a declaration of legal innocence is *in re ipsa*.

[64] Another possibility would be a rule providing that the criminal justice authorities should not treat the defendant as the authorities *would* treat the defendant if they were found guilty. For a criticism of a rule of this kind, see n 62 above.

proof of guilt, treating someone as legally innocent should mean treating them in any way that can be justified in the absence of such proof. Notice, then, that the rule does not prohibit measures such as collecting a forensic biometric sample without the defendant's consent, arresting the defendant, and remanding them in custody awaiting trial, since, arguably, these measures can be justified by appealing exclusively to considerations other than the presence of proof of guilt. For instance—and with some simplification—the non-consensual collection of fingerprints may be justified by the need to test whether the defendant's fingerprint matches a fingerprint found at the crime scene, by the consideration that the collection is not a particularly intrusive measure, and by the seriousness of the offence;[65] an arrest may be justified by reasonable grounds for suspecting the defendant's involvement in an offence, and by the need to prevent the defendant from causing physical injury to another person;[66] a remand in custody may be justified by the expectation that, if granted bail, the defendant would interfere with witnesses or otherwise obstruct the course of justice.[67] Which are, instead, the impermissible ways of treating the defendant who has not been proven guilty? Arguably, it is impermissible for the criminal justice authorities to refer to the defendant as 'guilty' of the crime charged in any official communication,[68] or to impose on the defendant a sentence that would only be justified in the event of conviction.[69] This is because proof of guilt is necessary to justify both official assertions of guilt on the part of the authorities and conviction; that is, the imposition of such a sentence.

In previous work,[70] I argued that the rule that, until the defendant is proved guilty, the criminal justice authorities should not treat the defendant in ways that can only be justified in the presence of proof of guilt is a necessary normative implication, if not an essential defining feature, of the institution of the criminal process itself; to be more precise, of any criminal process that attaches distinctive

[65] cf s 61 of the English and Welsh Police and Criminal Evidence Act 1984. Under English and Welsh law, the collection of intimate samples, such as samples of blood or semen, requires consent. See s 62 of the Act.

[66] cf s 24, in particular (5)(c)(i), of the English and Welsh Police and Criminal Evidence Act 1984.

[67] cf the English and Welsh Bail Act 1976, sch 1, pt 1, para. 2(1)(c).

[68] The idea that the presumption of innocence protects the legally innocent defendant from assertions of guilt on the part of the criminal justice authorities—indeed, any State authorities—is well entrenched in the ECtHR case law, and endorsed by the scholarship. See Trechsel (n 23), at 164, 178–179; Campbell (n 22); and Weigend (n 56), at 294–295. This idea has also been endorsed in the EU Directive 2016/343 'on the strengthening of certain aspects of the presumption of innocence and of the right to be present at the trial in criminal proceedings'. Art 4.1 of the directive states: 'Member States shall take the necessary measures to ensure that, for as long as a suspect or an accused person has not been proved guilty according to law, public statements made by public authorities, and judicial decisions, other than those on guilt, do not refer to that person as being guilty.' Notably, while the European Union has not yet acceded to the ECHR, Art 48 of the Charter of Fundamental Rights of the European Union states the presumption of innocence in terms that are roughly the same as those of Art 6(2) ECHR, and the latter article is explicitly mentioned in the recital of the directive just discussed.

[69] There is no attempt here to give a comprehensive account of the measures that would be forbidden by the rule, in the absence of proof of guilt.

[70] See Picinali, 'The Presumption of Innocence' (n 3), at 27–28.

significance to the proof of guilt. In such a criminal process, I noted, only if an individual is proved guilty to the satisfaction of the relevant standard is it justified to treat them in certain ways. Therefore, I considered it contradictory to adopt a criminal process so designed if, even in the absence of proof of guilt, the authorities were allowed to treat an individual in ways that, according to the design of the process, required such proof. For this criminal process to be meaningful, I concluded, the rule at issue here must be part of it.

This argument led me to the view that the rule of treatment protecting legal innocence is not part of the presumption of innocence. Since the rule has solid normative grounding in the institution of any criminal process attaching distinctive significance to the finding of guilt, I argued that the rule would be justified and operative even if the system did not include the presumption. I supported this view with the consideration that the presumption of innocence, as formulated in Article 6(2) ECHR, presupposes the existence of the criminal process, and that this confirms that the process is a more fundamental normative entity than the presumption itself, and is therefore capable of providing a deeper justification for the rule at issue.

My previous argument contains two related mistakes. First, I was wrong in arguing that the rule of treatment protecting legal innocence is a necessary normative implication of the criminal process itself. Notice that, as I have understood this rule in previous work—and as I have understood it so far in this section, which draws on such work—the rule incorporates a standard of moral, rather than purely legal, justification. Therefore, in the above paragraphs, when discussing the permissibility of certain infringements under the rule, it is their moral justification that I was concerned with. To make the standard apparent, the rule should be formulated as stating that, until the defendant is proved guilty, the criminal justice authorities should not treat the defendant in ways that are *morally* justified only in the presence of proof of guilt. Now, by attaching distinctive significance to the proof of guilt, the criminal process sets such proof as a standard of legal justification: according to the law, certain infringements of the status quo are justified if, and only if, proof of guilt is achieved. While desirable, it is not an essential feature of such a criminal process that, in the absence of proof of guilt, the process prohibits infringements that are morally justified only when proof of guilt is achieved. In other words, the process may well authorise infringements that are morally justified only when proof of guilt is achieved, without, however, requiring that such proof be present. After all, legal justification should, but need not, track moral justification. This means that a process attaching distinctive significance to the proof of guilt may well fall foul of the above rule of treatment without incurring any contradiction. A rule of treatment that is, indeed, a normative implication of such a criminal process is the rule stating that, until the defendant is proved guilty, the criminal justice authorities should not treat the defendant in ways that are *legally* justified only in the presence of proof of guilt. Authorising departures from this rule would be inconsistent with a criminal process that attaches distinctive significance to the proof of guilt.

My second mistake was to deny that the presumption of innocence includes a rule protecting legal innocence. The presumption, indeed, includes such a rule, albeit only the version of the rule that treats proof of guilt as a standard of legal justification. It is true that, as I have just shown, this rule is a normative implication of the institution of a criminal process attaching distinctive significance to proof of guilt. However, the rule is implied by such a process *because* it is an implication of a normative entity that is more fundamental than the process itself: the principle of inertia. If this is correct, though, given that the presumption of innocence is the vehicle through which the principle is implemented in the criminal process, the rule should be understood as being part of the presumption. After all, if the presumption includes a rule that is implied by the principle—that is, the rule allocating the burden of proof—why should it not be construed as also including a distinct rule that is implied by the principle as well, and is, indeed, operative in the criminal process? Let me explain more carefully the relationship between the principle of inertia and the rule protecting legal innocence.

The principle of inertia says that in the absence of sufficient reasons to the contrary, the status quo should be preserved. An implication of the principle, studied earlier, is that the party in an argumentative exchange who intends to change the status quo bears the burden of providing sufficient reasons for the change sought. Notice that a second implication of the principle is that, if the status quo is a communal plan of action—that is, a practical arrangement that the parties involved understand as binding—[71] any conduct by a party which conflicts with this plan, and for which sufficient reasons have not been given, is impermissible, as far as the communal plan in force is concerned. In other words, a party seeking an alteration of the communal plan is bound by this plan if they do not give sufficient reasons for such alteration (assuming that sufficient reasons for change are not given by any other party, of course). This is what it means to preserve the status quo in the absence of sufficient reasons for a change thereof. Consider that the impermissibility of behaviour that is inconsistent with the communal plan of action is, ultimately, determined by the parties' understanding of this arrangement as binding, but the continued existence of the original plan and, hence, its continued capacity to bind the parties involved, depend on whether sufficient reasons for changing the plan are given. Therefore, the impermissibility of inconsistent behaviour follows from the failure to give sufficient reasons for change; that is, for such behaviour. In other words, if sufficient reasons for inconsistent behaviour are not given, the original communal plan should, as a matter of rationality, be upheld; but if such plan is

[71] For a discussion of the normative nature of both individual and shared plans, see S. J. Shapiro, *Legality* (Harvard University Press 2011), ch. 5, building on M. E. Bratman, *Intention, Plans, and Practical Reason* (Harvard University Press 1987).

upheld, inconsistent behaviour is impermissible. I must stress that the impermissibility at issue here is impermissibility from the perspective of the content of the communal plan. Whether it is also moral impermissibility depends on the moral soundness of such content. The rule that, until the defendant is proved guilty, the criminal justice authorities should not treat the defendant in ways that are legally justified only in the presence of proof of guilt is expression of this second implication of the principle of inertia. Remember that the relevant status quo in the context of the criminal process is the polity's communal plan to afford the defendant the enjoyment of those rights to which all members of the polity are prima facie entitled. I pointed out earlier that, in the institutional context of the criminal process, it is the law that, reflecting the rational judgement of the polity, determines which changes of the status quo are permissible in the abstract, and which reason-giving effort is necessary for the polity—and, hence, the adjudicator as the polity's representative—to conclude that there are sufficient reasons for a given change in the concrete case. If certain infringements of the rights included in the status quo are legally justified only in the presence of proof of guilt, as is the case in a criminal process that attaches distinctive significance to such proof, then, absent proof of guilt, there are not sufficient reasons for bringing about these particular alterations of the status quo. Hence, they are impermissible, as far as the law is concerned.

In fact, the second implication of the principle of inertia entails a broader rule of treatment than that protecting legal innocence. This rule is the flip side of the rule, discussed earlier, that allocates to the criminal justice authorities the burden of giving sufficient reasons for any infringement of the status quo, ranging from pre-trial infringements to conviction. The rule of treatment says that the criminal justice authorities should not treat the defendant in any way for which they have not provided sufficient reasons: more precisely, that they should not infringe upon the defendant's enjoyment of those rights characterising the status quo if they have not satisfied the legal standard of sufficiency for the specific infringement that they wish to bring about. This means that—assuming that the status quo includes the right to liberty—it is impermissible for the authorities to arrest the defendant if they have not given sufficient reasons for arresting, according to the applicable standard; it is impermissible for the authorities to remand the defendant in custody if they have not given sufficient reasons for a remand, according to the applicable standard; and—as the rule protecting legal innocence provides—it is impermissible for the authorities to treat the defendant in ways that are legally justified only in the presence of proof of guilt, if the defendant has not been proven guilty. The presumption of innocence being the vehicle of the principle of inertia in the criminal process, it includes this broader rule on the permissibility of the authorities' actions. The relevant notion of permissibility here is that of legal permissibility, of course. Not only is permissibility assessed from the perspective of the communal plan of action constituting the status quo—that is, from the perspective of a legal norm—but also, it is the law that sets the applicable standard of sufficiency for any infringement it provides. Finally, consider that the presumption of innocence, which enforces the communal plan of action and the standards of sufficiency, is itself a legal norm. For this reason alone, the rule of treatment included in the presumption must concern what is permissible according to the law.

I said earlier that for some authors the rule stating that the defendant should be treated as innocent until proven guilty is a logical consequence of the rule allocating to the prosecution the burden of proving guilt at trial. I have shown that the rule on the burden of proof included in the presumption is broader than the rule allocating to the prosecution the burden of proving guilt at trial, and that the rule of treatment included in the presumption is broader than the rule to treat the defendant as legally innocent until proved guilty. I have shown that there is, indeed, a logical relationship between the two broad rules that I have identified: they are both entailed by the principle of inertia in argumentation, as this applies to the criminal process.

2.5 Reassessing the argument for incompatibility

The study of the presumption of innocence undertaken in the previous sections allows for a better understanding of the argument for incompatibility, and of the conditions under which it succeeds. Remember from section 2.2.1 that the argument is premised on reading into the presumption of innocence a rule making impermissible intermediate verdicts of the infringing kind, without ruling out infringing measures such as the use of surveillance techniques, the non-consensual collection of forensic biometric samples, arrest, and remand in custody. As explained earlier, this means that the rule cannot treat proof of guilt as a necessary condition for interfering with the status quo. Now, is such a rule part of the presumption?

The argument for incompatibility misconstrues the presumption of innocence by understanding it as a norm that can prescribe the content of the status quo of innocence (for example, the right to reputation), that can incorporate a standard of sufficiency for a given infringement of the status quo (for example, proof of guilt), and a norm that can directly take a stance against a particular kind of infringement (for example, infringing intermediate verdicts). If, however, the presumption is merely a norm that enforces the principle of inertia in the criminal process, it cannot do any of these things. As seen in the previous section, the presumption of innocence does not rule out, a priori, any particular infringement upon the defendant's enjoyment of those rights characterising the status quo. All that it says is that those seeking a particular infringement through the criminal process—that is, the criminal justice authorities—must give sufficient reasons for it, and that if sufficient reasons for a particular infringement are not given, it is impermissible for these authorities to put it into practice. In the argumentative context of the criminal process, it is the law—that is, law other than the presumption itself—that, reflecting the rational judgement of the polity, determines the kinds of infringement of the status quo that are permissible in the abstract, and determines which reason-giving effort is necessary for the polity—and, hence, the adjudicator as the polity's representative—to conclude that there are sufficient reasons for a given infringement in the concrete case. The presumption of innocence operates on the basis of the law: it defers fully to the determinations that the law has made concerning which infringements are permissible given which reason-giving efforts. Given these determinations, the presumption merely enforces rules of rationality that govern argumentation and adjudication in any particular case: precisely, the rule on the burden of proof and the rule of treatment.

According to the latter rule, an infringement is impermissible if the reasons that the law deems sufficient for it are not given. If, however, these legally sufficient reasons are given, permissibility rationally follows from such reason-giving effort. The upshot is that, as far as the presumption of innocence is concerned, the giving of reasons that are sufficient to satisfy the applicable legal standard is a necessary—but also a sufficient—condition for the permissibility of an infringement of the status quo of innocence. Assuming that the law reflects the rational judgement of the polity, the fact that these reasons are not given means that the reasons that the polity—and, hence, the adjudicator as the polity's representative—recognise still warrant the inference of the status quo representing the starting point of the argumentative exchange, such that rationality, via the presumption of innocence, demands that the status quo not be changed.

Within this framework, there can be no such thing as an infringing measure that is not compatible with the presumption of innocence. Any kind of infringing measure can be made to coexist peacefully with the presumption simply by legal fiat; that is, simply by enacting law that makes the infringement permissible when certain reasons are given. This is true for measures such as the use of surveillance techniques, the non-consensual collection of forensic biometric samples, arrest, and remand in custody. But it is also true for infringing intermediate verdicts. If, as argued here, the presumption of innocence merely enforces rules of rationality, and if, therefore, it fully defers to the law, as expression of the polity's rational judgement, with regard to whether a particular alteration of the status quo is permissible given a particular reason-giving effort, it follows that the presumption does not offer a standpoint from which to declare legally impermissible the kinds of infringement that the law provides, or to critically assess the reason-giving effort that, according to the law, is sufficient to warrant such kinds of infringement.[72]

[72] Of course, I am always assuming that the law reflects the rational, even if not necessarily reasonable, judgement of the polity. If, for instance, due to the inadequacy of the legislative process, the standard of sufficiency set by the law for a given infringement were lower than the standard of sufficiency that the polity would want to be satisfied for it to agree to the infringement, according to the presumption of innocence the infringement would be impermissible should only the former standard be satisfied. Failure to satisfy the latter standard means that there are not sufficient reasons for the polity to agree to change the status quo through the infringement. Moreover, a failure of the law to set a clear standard of sufficiency for a given infringement may be problematic from the perspective of the presumption of innocence, insofar as such vagueness about the standard does not reflect the polity's judgement about

The presumption of innocence has nothing to say against infringing intermediate verdicts—or any other infringing measure, for that matter. Once the issue of compatibility dissolves, the question to attend to is whether there are sufficient reasons—this time, reasons that are *morally* sufficient—for the law to provide an infringing intermediate verdict. In other words, it is the question whether a moral justification can be given for the law—that is, the polity—to adopt one such verdict. Should there be such a justification, and should the law consequently include an infringing intermediate verdict in the verdict system, the presumption of innocence would not be in conflict with this decision-making device. It would simply say that using this device is impermissible if the sufficient reasons for issuing it, set by the law reflecting the polity's rational judgement, have not been given.

Consider now an alternative theory of the presumption of innocence, according to which the presumption incorporates a standard of moral justification. Under this theory, the presumption includes a rule on the burden of proof, and a rule of treatment, that are nominally the same as those discussed earlier. To recapitulate, the first rule states that those seeking a particular infringement through the criminal process—that is, the criminal justice authorities—must give sufficient reasons for it; and the second rule states that, if sufficient reasons for a particular infringement are not given, it is impermissible for these authorities to put it into practice. However, according to this alternative theory, the relevant notion of 'sufficiency' is that of moral, rather than purely legal, sufficiency. Notice that the presumption, so understood, would still concern and enforce legal permissibility: the presumption, after all, is a legal norm. Legal permissibility, though, would be aligned with moral permissibility. It would not depend exclusively on the rationality of an infringement, given the status quo of innocence and the legal determinations about which infringements are permissible given which reason-giving efforts. It would depend on the reasonableness of the infringement; that is, on whether a moral justification for it is provided. Understood in these terms, the presumption of innocence would offer a standpoint from which to declare legally impermissible the kinds of infringement that the law provides, or other hypothetical kinds of infringing measures; moreover, it would offer a standpoint from which to critically assess the reason-giving effort that, according to the law, is sufficient to warrant such kinds of infringement. This is the standpoint of morality.[73] According to

where it should lie. Perhaps, it is on this ground that the Scottish 'not proven' verdict and the Italian acquittal '*per insufficienza di prove*' (more precisely, the law regulating these verdicts) may be deemed in breach of the presumption. cf Chalmers and others, 'Beyond Doubt' (n 4), at 21–23. Consider also that, according to the presumption, the law could not provide an infringing measure while not requiring any reason-giving effort for the measure to be implemented. This would contradict the status quo of innocence. See n 35 above.

[73] This theory of the presumption of innocence seems to be endorsed by Ashworth (n 22), at 249, stating, with reference to the role of the presumption in the criminal process as a whole, that 'in relation to the several preliminaries to conviction which may require the exercise of power over a suspect, the proper approach is to require the state to provide *acceptable* reasons for exercising such power—notably, in relation to detention for questioning, reasonable grounds for suspecting involvement in the particular crime ... So also, public prosecutors should not charge a person with an offence unless they

the presumption, so understood, the satisfaction of the applicable legal standard of sufficiency may not be sufficient for the permissibility of a particular infringement of the status quo, since it may not provide a moral justification for such infringement. Moreover, infringements of a kind that can never be morally justified would be incompatible with the presumption: putting them into practice would never be legally permissible. Notice that the argument for incompatibility is premised on this theory of the presumption of innocence. It is by understanding the presumption as incorporating a standard of moral justification that the argument can claim that there is an incompatibility between infringing intermediate verdicts and the presumption of innocence.

I will not engage here in a thorough comparative assessment of the two theories I have presented.[74] It suffices to point out a reason to reject the theory that the presumption incorporates a standard of moral justification: this theory produces an unnecessary duplication of roles. Indeed, the rights included in the status quo of innocence already establish the relevant moral constraints on the kinds of infringement that the law could provide, and on the reason-giving effort that the law should require for such infringements to be morally justified in the particular case.[75] Importantly, not only do these right-based constraints operate in the process of lawmaking, but they can also be used to reinterpret or censure existing legal norms that disrespect them, as happens under the Human Rights Act 1998 and the ECHR. Given this, is it not unnecessary to interpret the presumption as including these very constraints? If, instead, the presumption is understood as enforcing only a principle of rationality and the rules that the principle implies, the presumption and the rights included in the status quo perform distinct roles. These rights promote the justice, or the reasonableness, of an infringing decision by ensuring that it respects the relevant moral values. The presumption of innocence, instead, promotes the justice, or the reasonableness, of an infringing decision, by ensuring that the decision is rational. No doubt someone will object that the theory of the

are satisfied that there is sufficient evidence ... The presumption of innocence is a moral and political principle, based on a widely shared conception of how a free society ... should exercise the power to punish' (italics added). See also Jackson and Summers (n 22), at 206.

[74] Consider that someone who endorses the theory according to which the presumption incorporates a standard of moral justification can still hold that the rule on the burden of proof is justified by the principle of inertia. They can still understand this rule as an implication of the principle: if indeed the applicable legal standard identifies the reason-giving effort that is necessary and sufficient for the polity—and, hence, the adjudicator as a representative of the polity—to agree to an infringement, satisfying the standard is, for the criminal justice authorities, a necessary means to obtain the infringement sought. However, according to the theory considered here, the presumption of innocence would also require that the standard be morally justified, given the infringement at issue. In other words, the presumption would require an alignment between legal and moral sufficiency. This is not a requirement of the presumption of innocence, under the alternative theory that I endorse.

[75] See Lippke (n 26), at 113, stating that 'the more the authorities seek to intrude upon or interfere with the basic rights of citizens, the stronger the reasons they must give in order to justify doing so', and arguing (at 146–147) that these 'progressive justificatory burdens' do not derive from the presumption of innocence itself; rather, they derive from the rights at issue.

presumption that I endorse renders this norm nugatory, given the norm's deference to the legal determinations on permissibility and sufficiency. This objection, though, would be too fast. Consider that, under the theory of the presumption that I endorse, this norm includes the rule that is generally regarded as the core component of the presumption by the competing theories: the rule allocating the burden of proof to the criminal justice authorities and, especially, allocating the burden of proving guilt at trial to the prosecution. Moreover, the rule of treatment that the presumption includes under the theory that I endorse does not merely replicate the legal determinations on permissibility and sufficiency. The rule, and its rationale, show that a failure to stay true to these determinations, in any given case, does not just warrant a charge of unfairness: it warrants the harsher charge of irrationality.

Be that as it may, if one were to endorse the theory according to which the presumption of innocence includes a standard of moral justification, it would not necessarily follow that the presumption would be incompatible with infringing intermediate verdicts. Under such theory, the presumption would not necessarily say that these verdicts should not be issued by the adjudicator; it would say that they should not be issued without giving a moral justification for so doing. This begs the question of whether such justification can ever be given. If the answer is no, infringing intermediate verdicts would be categorically forbidden by the presumption: they would be incompatible with it, such that a binary system of verdicts should be enforced.[76] If the answer is, instead, yes, an infringing intermediate verdict would be compatible with the presumption, and issuing it in the specific case would be permissible insofar as the criminal justice authorities discharge their burden of providing a justification for doing so in such a case. The upshot is that, under the theory according to which the presumption incorporates a standard of moral justification, the question of the compatibility between the presumption and infringing intermediate verdicts would boil down to the question of the moral justification of the latter. In other words, whether the rule of treatment included in the presumption of innocence would, indeed, be the rule of treatment that the argument for incompatibility requires in order to be successful would depend on the possibility of giving a moral justification for issuing an infringing intermediate verdict. If such a justification could never be given, the two rules would coincide, and the argument would succeed. More precisely, the rule of treatment included in the presumption would meet the desiderata discussed in section 2.2.1. It would categorically rule out infringing intermediate verdicts; and it would do so without treating proof of guilt as a necessary condition for infringements of the status quo posited by the argument. To clarify, if, indeed, issuing an infringing intermediate verdict could never be morally justified, this could not possibly be because proof of guilt is such a condition according to morality. Indeed, proof of guilt is not such

[76] Or an intermediate verdict could be adopted if non-infringing, assuming that there is any such thing. See above, section 2.2.1, and n 82 below.

a condition, as far as moral justification is concerned: as argued in section 2.4.2, infringing measures such as the non-consensual collection of forensic biometric samples, arrest, and remand in custody can be justified on moral grounds in the absence of such proof.

2.6 Concluding remarks

The assessment of the argument for incompatibility was an opportunity to revisit the meaning and justification of the presumption of innocence. In this chapter, I defended the view that the presumption is the vehicle through which the principle of inertia in argumentation is implemented in the criminal process. This means that the presumption includes a rule imposing on the criminal justice authorities the burden of giving sufficient reasons for any infringement of the defendant's enjoyment of the rights to which all members of the polity are prima facie entitled; it also means that the presumption includes a rule making impermissible all infringements for which sufficient reasons have not been given. I have explained that the presumption fully defers to the law—that is, law other than the presumption itself—for the determination of which infringements of the status quo are permissible given which reason-giving efforts. Given the law's determinations, the presumption merely enforces rules of rationality that govern argumentation and adjudication in any particular case. Therefore, the presumption does not offer a standpoint from which to declare legally impermissible the kinds of infringement of the status quo of innocence that the law provides. Under this conception of the presumption of innocence, there can be no such thing as a kind of infringement that is incompatible with the presumption. Any kind of infringing measure can be made to coexist peacefully with the presumption simply by legal fiat. If one follows this theory, then, there is no room left to argue that infringing intermediate verdicts are incompatible with the presumption of innocence. Of course, this conclusion is not, in itself, sufficient to justify the adoption of an intermediate verdict by the criminal justice system. This justification needs to be provided.

I believe that the above two rules exhaust the meaning of the presumption of innocence. While I have not defended this view here, it is the upshot of my work on the presumption. I have argued elsewhere[77] that the presumption of innocence does not include the reasonable doubt standard as the standard of proof for conviction, nor does it include a rule defining an epistemic point of departure for the adjudicator's task; that is, a way of regarding the defendant at the start of the trial. In previous work[78] I have also discussed the implications of the principle of inertia

[77] See Picinali, 'The Presumption of innocence' (n 3).
[78] See ibid, at 12–18.

for the legitimacy of reverse burdens of proof, thus giving more flesh to the rule allocating to the prosecution the burden of proving guilt at trial.[79] All of these issues were irrelevant to the assessment of the argument for the incompatibility between intermediate verdicts and the presumption of innocence and have, therefore, been left aside.[80]

In the previous section, I presented an alternative theory, according to which the presumption of innocence incorporates a standard of moral justification. So understood, the presumption of innocence would offer a standpoint from which to declare legally impermissible the kinds of infringement that the law provides, or other hypothetical kinds of infringing measures. However, the presumption would not necessarily rule out infringing intermediate verdicts. The question of the compatibility between the presumption of innocence and infringing intermediate verdicts would boil down to the question whether issuing such verdicts can ever be morally justified.

Whichever of these two theories of the presumption one accepts, in order to justify the adoption of an infringing intermediate verdict as an in-between option for the adjudicator, one has to show that there are conditions under which issuing an infringing intermediate verdict is morally justified. In the Introduction to the book, I wrote that this work addresses the issue of whether there is a justification—by which I mean a moral justification—for implementing, in the criminal trial, the logic 'weaker evidence, milder hard treatment', which is reflected in the concept of an intermediate verdict.[81] I take the imposition of hard treatment, that is, of treatment that is burdensome, harmful, or even painful, to be an infringement of the particular status quo of innocence accepted by our polity, for which the presumption of innocence—however it is interpreted—demands that sufficient reasons be given.[82] This understanding does not presuppose anything controversial about the

[79] For a sketch of my arguments on this point, see n 38.

[80] See n 5 above.

[81] As stated in the Introduction to the book, according to the logic, *insofar as* the intermediate verdict involves hard treatment, this treatment is milder than that involved in conviction. Accordingly, the logic leaves room for the possibility of non-infringing intermediate verdicts, should there be any. See the following note.

[82] Assuming that there is such a thing as a non-infringing intermediate verdict (see above, section 2.2.1), would the issuing of such a verdict require a reason-giving effort, even if such an effort is not demanded by the presumption of innocence? Presumably so. While issuing the hypothesised verdict does not infringe upon the rights included in the status quo of innocence, it may be understood as altering another status quo: that consisting in the binary verdict system. Notice that this status quo may well be conceptualised as part of the status quo of innocence itself, insofar as it contributes to setting the conditions for the legal permissibility of infringements of the rights characterising the status quo of innocence (see n 35 above). As pointed out in the Introduction to the book, though, the supposed status quo setting the binary verdict system is 'opaque', in that the reasons for such a system are not apparent, and its justification is seldom discussed in the current scholarship. I am, therefore, reluctant to treat the binary verdict system as a communal plan of action actually endorsed by the polity. The need to give reasons for non-infringing intermediate verdicts, then, may be understood simply as following from a party's goal to persuade others to establish, rather than alter, a status quo: precisely, an agreed-upon verdict system. The reason-giving effort is, for this party, a necessary means of achieving their goal of status quo-building.

content of such status quo. In fact, one can define hard treatment by contrasting it with the rights characterising the status quo of innocence, whatever these rights are: it is burdensome or harmful treatment precisely because it infringes upon these rights. In Chapter 4, I will advance a justification for issuing intermediate verdicts that involve hard treatment.

3

Acquittal vs Conviction

We can all be Expected-Value Maximisers in this Choice

3.1 Introduction

In the previous chapter, I have argued for understanding the presumption of innocence as a norm that enforces merely rules of rationality. Given such understanding, there can be no incompatibility between the presumption and infringing intermediate verdicts. This conclusion, of course, is not in itself sufficient to justify the adoption of an intermediate verdict by the criminal justice system. This justification needs to be provided. In Chapter 4, I will give an argument that identifies the conditions under which issuing an infringing intermediate verdict is justified. I will also defend the claim that such conditions are met in the case of a specific intermediate verdict, which I call 'conditional acquittal'. The task of the present chapter, instead, is to lay the groundwork for these forthcoming arguments: I will set out the premises that one needs to accept to endorse the arguments, and will show that acceptance of these premises is—or should be—widespread. Let me clarify.

Theories of punishment are often classified as consequentialist or deontological. Under a consequentialist theory, the permissibility of punishment depends exclusively on the value of the consequences of punishing. Under a deontological theory, instead, the permissibility of punishment depends also on reasons other than the value of such consequences. My justification of intermediate verdicts in Chapter 4 is based on applying decision theory to the problem of criminal adjudication. In a binary verdict system, this is the problem of deciding whether to convict—hence to punish—the defendant, or to acquit—hence not to punish—them.[1] Now, decision theory is a theory of decision-making that enjoins the agent to follow the principle of maximising expected value.[2] Because of its insistence on expected-value maximisation, decision theory is generally understood as a decision-making tool for the consequentialist only. In this chapter, I argue that this decision-making tool is also for the deontologist about punishment: they, too, can be an expected-value maximiser with respect to the problem of adjudication, without relinquishing any

[1] In the next section, I clarify the relationship between the choices whether or not to punish, and whether to convict or acquit. In other words, I clarify in what sense a theory of punishment is also a theory about the latter choice.

[2] This is true of 'normative' decision theory. 'Descriptive' decision theory, instead, aims at explaining and predicting how people actually make decisions. See M. Peterson, *An Introduction to Decision Theory* (2nd edn, CUP 2017), at 3.

DOI: 10.1093/oso/9780198864592.003.0004

tenets of their theory of punishment. If my argument succeeds, I will have shown that my forthcoming justification of intermediate verdicts can be accepted both by consequentialists and deontologists about punishment. Indeed, especially considering that I will not defend any theory of punishment, my goal is for this decision-theoretic justification to be as inclusive as possible.

The goal of formulating an inclusive justification drives a particular terminological choice. Consider that decision theorists typically talk in terms of expected 'utility' rather than expected 'value'. I choose the latter term in order not to alienate, from the outset, deontologically minded readers, who may otherwise understand my project as that of persuading them that they are utilitarians at heart. There is nothing substantial, though, in this terminological switch. I interpret the notion of 'value' as decision theorists generally interpret that of 'utility'.[3] It is essentially a measure of preference: to say that, in a decision problem, an outcome has greater value than another is to say that the decision-maker prefers the former to the latter.[4]

The focus in this chapter is on the binary system of verdicts; therefore, on a system according to which adjudication involves the choice between acquittal and conviction only. The principle of maximising expected value is a practical directive requiring that an individual who is deciding how to act chooses the course of action with highest expected value. According to the principle, the adjudicator should convict if, and only if, the expected value of convicting is higher than, or equal to, that of acquitting; otherwise, they should acquit. In the next chapter, I will explain in detail how the principle of maximising expected value operates with regard to the choice of the adjudicator, but it is necessary that I quickly clarify the notion of 'expected value' at this stage. The expected value of an action is the sum of the expected values of the action's possible outcomes. Therefore, since the possible outcomes of convicting are the conviction of the innocent (or false conviction) and the conviction of the guilty (or true conviction), the expected value of convicting is the sum of the expected values of these two outcomes; and since the possible outcomes of acquitting are the acquittal of the innocent (or true acquittal) and the acquittal of the guilty (or false acquittal), the expected value of acquitting is the sum of the expected values of these two outcomes. The expected value of an outcome is the product of the outcome's value and of the probability of the outcome occurring, given the relevant act (ie convicting or acquitting). It follows that the expected value of convicting the innocent is the product of the value of this outcome and of the probability of the defendant being innocent; the expected value of convicting

[3] See ibid, ch 5 and R. Briggs, 'Normative Theories of Rational Choice: Expected Utility' in E. N. Zalta (ed), *Stanford Encyclopedia of Philosophy* (2017), at 9–11.

[4] Of course, this understanding of value does not deny that there are facts of the world that inform one's preferences and, hence, the outcomes' values. Also consider that, 'there is nothing in the formalism of expected utility theory that requires us to use subjective rather than objective values' (Briggs (n 3), at 11). Accordingly, the reader who dislikes a definition of 'value' in terms of the decision-maker's preference is free to adopt a more objective definition. To be sure, I work with the assumption that, in the problem of adjudication, the decision-maker's preferences are informed by the theory of punishment that they endorse.

the guilty is the product of the value of this outcome and of the probability of the defendant being guilty, and so on.

To give a quick example of the operation of the principle with arbitrary numbers, assume that the value of convicting the innocent is 1, the value of convicting the guilty is 4, the value of acquitting the innocent is 3, and the value of acquitting the guilty is 2. Assume also that the probability of guilt is 0.8, hence that the probability of innocence is 1 - 0.8 = 0.2. In this case, the expected value of convicting is 3.4 (ie, 0.8 × 4 + 0.2 × 1), whereas that of acquitting is 2.2 (ie, 0.8 × 2 + 0.2 × 3). Therefore, the principle of maximising expected value enjoins the adjudicator to convict. No doubt, some readers will be taken aback by the implied requirement that the outcomes' values be expressed in numbers. I will deal with this worry in Chapter 5. However, neither the arguments in the present chapter nor those in the next require that I express numerically the outcomes' values. Notice that the principle of *maximising value* is a special normative implication of the general principle of *maximising expected value*: the former applies when the agent is certain about which outcome will result from which act, such that the probability of the outcome given the act is one, and the expected value of the act is the value of this outcome.

It is important to consider that decision theory does not place any constraint on which value an outcome should have; indeed, it does not place any constraint on which reasons should be taken into account in the assessment of an outcome's value. As explained in section 3.6 below, which reasons are considered in the context of criminal adjudication will depend on the theory of punishment endorsed by the decision-maker. Let me explain. For the principle of maximising expected value to operate as described above, it is necessary to create a value function corresponding to the decision problem at issue. For our purposes, this means creating a numerical scale where the four trial outcomes are arranged as a function of their value.[5] Obviously, the value function is likely to vary from one theory of punishment to another, because different theories, whether consequentialist or deontological, justify punishment in different ways. In other words, they differ in their views about the reasons that affect the values of punishing and of not punishing; hence, the values of trial outcomes. In section 3.6, I will show how features that are deemed central to prominent theories of punishment can be accounted for in the process of creating their respective value function. The upshot of my analysis is that, in the context of adjudication, what distinguishes theories of punishment is not whether they adhere to the principle of maximising expected value: they all do. Rather, these theories differ in how they assess the values of trial outcomes; hence, in the respective value function upon which the principle is applied.

[5] As I will point out later, what is required is an interval scale. This is a numerical scale that accurately reflects the differences between the values of outcomes, rather than the ratios between these values. On this concept, see Peterson (n 2), at 25–26. For an exemplification of how to assign numerical values to outcomes so as to construct an interval scale, see ibid, at 101–104, applying the strategy developed by J. von Neumann and O. Morgenstern in their seminal work *Theory of Games and Economic Behavior* (2nd edn, Princeton University Press 1947).

Now, following the principle of maximising expected value in the choice between conviction and acquittal entails understanding the standard of proof as a decision rule devised to maximise expected value; that is, as a decision-theoretic standard of proof. The standard of proof sets the epistemic conditions for conviction. If it is the case that the adjudicator should convict if, and only if, doing so maximises expected value, then the epistemic conditions set by the standard of proof should be such that convicting in their presence maximises expected value. This simple insight is important for the argument that I will advance in the next chapter in support of intermediate verdicts. My justification of intermediate verdicts, indeed, is based on the well-known decision-theoretic argument for the identification of the standard of proof in a binary system. If I succeed in showing that both consequentialists and deontologists about punishment can rely on decision theory in adjudication, I will also have shown that it is open to both to understand the standard of proof as an expected-value maximising rule; hence, to endorse the decision-theoretic argument for the standard's identification. In fact, I will show that both consequentialists and deontologists about punishment *should* understand the standard of proof in these terms.

'But why'—a reader may ask at this point—'should theories of punishment be concerned with the problem of setting the standard of proof for conviction, or with the problem of adjudication, for that matter?' That a theory of punishment should be concerned with adjudication[6] follows from the fact that the State frequently—and paradigmatically—administers punishment as a result of the trial.[7] A theory that is about the justification of (State) punishment should, therefore, identify the conditions for the State to be justified in resorting to punishment as a result of the trial. Now, theories of punishment concern choices of action, in particular choices about how to treat individuals. Accordingly, they should include an account of how to deal with a fundamental variable affecting human decision-making: the uncertainty about the facts relevant to our acting. In the case of punishment, the preeminent relevant fact is the defendant's responsibility.[8] Or, at least, this is the fact that adjudication is mostly concerned with. How probable should the defendant's responsibility be for conviction and punishment to be justified under a given theory? This question, ie the question of the standard of proof, is rarely regarded as

[6] See S. R. Galoob, 'Retributivism and Criminal Procedure' (2017) 20 New Criminal Law Review 465, at 467, claiming, with particular focus on retributivism, that theorists of punishment should explore the implications that their theories have for criminal procedure.

[7] As is well known, most criminal cases are dealt with by means of a guilty plea. In England and Wales, the guilty plea rate for cases dealt with at the Crown court between July and September 2020 was 79% (with 65% of these pleas being entered prior to trial). See Ministry of Justice, *Criminal Court Statistics Quarterly, England and Wales, July to September 2020*, 17 December 2020, at 9. While this rate represents an increase with respect to the previous trend, possibly due to the influence of the COVID-19 pandemic, earlier rates were, nonetheless, high. See L. Campbell and others, *The Criminal Process* (5th edn, OUP 2019), at 319.

[8] For a defence of the claim that the uncertainty about other facts that are relevant to the permissibility of punishment under retributivism (eg that proportionate punishment is possible, or that it is appropriate to make offenders suffer) may undermine a retributivist justification of punishment, see A. J. Kolber, 'Punishment and Moral Risk' (2018) 2018 University of Illinois Law Review 487.

part of the agenda of theorists of punishment,[9] who often work under the assumption of certainty about the defendant's responsibility. Surely plenty of important work on the justification of punishment has been done by bracketing off the question of the standard of proof, hence assuming innocence or guilt. However, since adjudication does not—or, at least, is unlikely to—reach certainty about responsibility, no theory of punishment can claim to have effective guiding force until it removes the assumption and addresses the question. This chapter provides a framework for answering the question of the standard of proof, that works for both consequentialists and deontologists about punishment.

A final introductory note: while, in this chapter, I treat the adjudicator as the decision-maker, in Chapter 4 I will argue that the construction of the value function and, consequently, the setting of the standard of proof, are, in fact, tasks for the legislator.

3.2 A clarification of the claim and an overview of my defence

The claim that I defend in this chapter can be stated in these terms: in the context of the decision problem whether to convict or acquit, the adjudicator can follow the principle of maximising expected value without thereby relinquishing any tenets of their theory of punishment, whether this is consequentialist or deontological. Below, I make four clarificatory remarks about this claim. Then, I explain how I intend to defend it.

First, theories of punishment are about the choice whether or not to punish, rather than the choice whether or not to convict. It is, therefore, reasonable to ask whether what a theory of punishment says about the former choice, for example that the innocent should not be punished, can be read as a claim that the theory makes about the latter, for example that the innocent should not be convicted. In the Introduction to the book, I explained that I construe 'conviction' and 'acquittal' as referring to verdicts in the broad sense. This means that they do not refer exclusively to the speech acts of giving 'guilty' and 'not guilty' verdicts, respectively. They refer to the overall response of the criminal justice system to a particular fact-finding result. So understood, conviction typically involves punishment,[10]

[9] A notable exception is A. Walen, 'Proof Beyond a Reasonable Doubt: A Balanced Retributive Account' (2015) 76 Louisiana Law Review 355. cf Jeffrey Reiman's contribution in J. Reiman and E. van den Haag, 'On the Common Saying that it is Better that Ten Guilty Persons Escape than that One Innocent Suffer: *Pro* and *Con*' (1990) 7 Social Philosophy and Policy 226. Very brief references to the standard of proof can be found in V. Tadros, *The Ends of Harm: The Moral Foundations of Criminal Law* (OUP 2011), at 327–330. The standard is discussed in other works that deal with the justification of punishment (see, for instance, H.L. Packer, *The Limits of the Criminal Sanction* (Stanford University Press 1968), at 136–139). Often, though, this is done without recognising the need to justify the standard as part of the preferred account of the justification of punishment, as if the standard and the theory of punishment were, effectively, unrelated.

[10] I say 'typically' rather than 'always' because the convicted defendant may be given a pardon or, more likely, an absolute or conditional discharge.

whereas acquittal does not. In the context of adjudication, then, an obligation (or a permission) to punish can be treated as an obligation (or a permission) to convict, whereas an obligation (or a permission) not to punish can be treated as an obligation (or a permission) to acquit. Notice, though, that this conclusion also holds if someone construes 'conviction' and 'acquittal' as referring exclusively to the speech act of verdict-giving. For an expressivist about punishment,[11] conviction, so construed, may well already be a form of punishment. Indeed, it may even be the central form. This is because the speech act of giving a 'guilty' verdict conveys condemnation or censure for wrongdoing. Hence, one would expect that, for the expressivist, prescriptions about whether to convict should correspond to prescriptions about whether to punish. Be that as it may, both expressivists and non-expressivists are likely to understand conviction, narrowly construed, as making the defendant the appropriate target of some form of hard treatment constituting punishment; and acquittal, narrowly construed, as not making the defendant so.[12] Therefore, they are each also likely to concur with the claim that an adjudicator who, according to their respective theories, was under an obligation (or a permission) to impose punishment on the defendant would also be under an obligation (or a permission) to convict; and that an adjudicator who was under an obligation (or a permission) not to impose punishment on the defendant would also be under an obligation (or a permission) to acquit. Such an understanding of the relationship between the choice whether or not to punish and the choice whether or not to convict, then, holds whether 'conviction' and 'acquittal' are construed broadly or narrowly. It shows that a theory of punishment also has something to say about the latter choice. The arguments advanced in this chapter rely on this understanding.

Second, when I talk about the choice whether to convict or acquit, I take the substantive law as fixed. I assume that this law is clear and that the adjudicator will follow it without question, so that the subject matter of the decision is exclusively whether there is enough evidence of guilt to convict for a given crime. Neither the issue of legal interpretation, nor the option of disregarding the rules of conduct, justifications, or excuses constituting the substantive law are accounted for in the decision problem that I address. This is because my interest is in the epistemic, rather than the legal-substantive, conditions for a given adjudicative decision.

Third, to argue that the adjudicator can rely on the principle of maximising expected value in their choice whether to convict or to acquit is not to support a

[11] See J. Feinberg, 'The Expressive Function of Punishment' in J. Feinberg, *Doing and Deserving: Essays in the Theory of Responsibility* (Princeton University Press 1970). See also A. von Hirsch, *Censure and Sanctions* (Clarendon Press 1993); A. Ashworth and A. von Hirsch, *Proportionate Sentencing: Exploring the Principles* (OUP 2005), ch 2; R. A. Duff, *Punishment, Communication, and Community* (OUP 2001), ch 3.

[12] As far as expressive (and communicative) theories of punishment are concerned, von Hirsch and Ashworth, on the one hand, and Duff, on the other, understand hard treatment as a necessary component of punishment, although they do so for different reasons. For details, see the works in the previous note.

theory of the criminal process according to which the whole process should be geared towards maximising the value that the adjudicator's choice can produce. Let me clarify. In the decision problem whether to convict or acquit, value is maximised when a true outcome is produced; that is, the defendant is convicted if guilty, and is acquitted if innocent. This is because, arguably, in any plausible value function, true outcomes are more valuable than false ones; I will have more to say later about the values of trial outcomes, of course. Now, the criminal process includes a complex series of decision problems preceding the adjudicator's choice between conviction and acquittal: in particular, problems that concern the acquisition of the evidence, its admissibility, and its presentation in court. Virtually everyone agrees that these decision problems should not be governed exclusively by the desire to enhance the accuracy of fact-finding; in other words, that they should not be governed exclusively by the desire to increase the probability that the adjudicator's choice between conviction and acquittal produces a true outcome, hence maximising value. Instead, these decision problems are widely regarded as being regulated also by values, rights, and interests that may pull the relevant decision-maker towards actions that decrease the probability of a true trial outcome occurring.[13] The clearest example of this phenomenon is the problem whether to admit reliable and highly probative evidence that has been obtained through a serious violation of a fundamental right of the defendant. An exclusive concern for reaching a true trial outcome would, arguably, lead to the admission of the evidence. However, many believe that the breach of the defendant's right demands that the evidence be excluded.[14] The claim that I defend in this chapter pertains exclusively to the decision problem whether to convict or to acquit, which represents the final stage of the trial. At this stage, the evidence has already been gathered, admitted, and presented, or excluded. The question for the adjudicator is to assess whether it is sufficient for conviction. I contend that both consequentialists and deontologists about punishment can answer this question by following the principle of maximising expected value, without thereby relinquishing any tenets of their respective theories of punishment.

Fourth, one may consider that it is open to a theorist of punishment—presumably a deontologist—to argue that the choice whether to convict or to acquit should be regulated by a standard of proof that, unlike the decision-theoretic

[13] See Campbell and others (n 7), ch 2 and 345–347; A. Duff and others, *The Trial on Trial: Volume 3: Towards a Normative Theory of the Criminal Trial* (Hart 2007); P. Roberts and J. Hunter (eds), *Criminal Evidence and Human Rights: Reimagining Common Law Procedural Traditions* (Hart 2012); R. L. Lippke, 'Fundamental Values of Criminal Procedure' in D. K. Brown and others (eds), *The Oxford Handbook of Criminal Process* (OUP 2019). cf L. Laudan, *Truth, Error, and Criminal Law: An Essay in Legal Epistemology* (CUP 2006), criticising several evidence and procedural rules that promote non-epistemic values for being 'truth-thwarting'.

[14] For a recent extensive treatment of the problem of improperly obtained evidence, see D. Giannoulopoulos, *Improperly Obtained Evidence in Anglo-American and Continental Law* (Hart 2019).

one that we will study in the next chapter, is not identified by considering the values of the possible outcomes of a trial; hence, a standard of proof that is not devised to maximise the expected value of the decision. Rather, this hypothetical standard of proof would be informed exclusively by procedural values—roughly, values that pertain to how the criminal process unfolds, rather than to its possible outcomes—that transcend the logic of expected-value maximisation presented earlier. For instance, one might claim that the reasonable doubt standard is justified by the need to respect the defendant as a reasonable interlocutor in the proceedings. According to this argument, any defendant would be disrespected—silenced, even—if they were the recipient of a categorical verdict of 'guilty' when a reasonable exculpatory account is still standing unchallenged. Hence, all such accounts, ie reasonable doubts, must be eliminated for conviction to be justified.[15] I am suspicious about justificatory strategies of this kind, because I am sceptical about the possibility of justifying a standard of proof independently of the values of the possible outcomes of the decision problem. After all, when deciding how much evidence of someone's guilt we need before convicting them, it is reasonable to consider what is at stake in our choice between acquittal and conviction, for example how serious the mistake of convicting an innocent person, or of acquitting a guilty person, is. Ignoring these stakes for the sake of a procedural value seems unwarranted, especially when these stakes are high. It would be akin to the behaviour of an individual who, not knowing how to recognise edible mushrooms, decides to snack on a mushroom offered by a passer-by, for fear of displaying, in the interaction, a lack of respect, or of gratitude for the gift. Obviously, the claim

[15] I presented a more articulated version of this argument in my article F. Picinali, *Can the Reasonable Doubt Standard Be Justified? A Reconstructed Dialogue* (2018) 31 Canadian Journal of Law and Jurisprudence 365, 388–401. Consider, though, that this argument about respect is just one component of the justification of the reasonable doubt standard that I offered in ibid. Another component consisted in showing that there are means other than lowering the standard of proof that can be relied upon to increase the incidence of true conviction: in particular, devices that enhance the identification of the guilty and the quality of the evidence. I argued that it is because such devices exist that the standard of proof can be identified by appealing to the respect for the defendant. My bipartite justification of the reasonable doubt standard, then, was not completely independent of a consideration of the values of trial outcomes. After all, it rested on the argument that true conviction is desirable, but that tweaking the standard of proof is not necessary to increase its incidence. This argument was prompted by Laudan's criticism that the reasonable doubt standard allows too many instances of false acquittal, and that it should, therefore, be replaced with a lower standard of proof, in order to increase the incidence of true conviction (L. Laudan, 'The Rules of Trial, Political Morality, and the Costs of Error: Or, is Proof Beyond a Reasonable Doubt Doing More Harm than Good?' in L. Green and B. Leiter (eds), *Oxford Studies in Philosophy of Law* (OUP 2011)). I now think, though, that I was wrong in making the leap from the sensible claim that the incidence of true conviction can be increased without lowering the standard of proof to the unreasonable denial that the primary function of a standard of proof is to 'reflect and operationalise' the values of the possible trial outcomes (Picinali, ibid, at 389–390). In the end, what I provided in my article was just a rebuttal to Laudan's attack on the reasonable doubt standard; that is, I provided an argument defending the first of the above claims, thus showing that Laudan did not give sufficient reasons to abandon this standard. I did not, however, give sufficient reasons for having the reasonable doubt standard in the first place. I now think that to do so would have required assessing whether the standard is justified on decision-theoretic grounds.

that I defend in this chapter is premised on the rejection of such a 'proceduralist' account of the standard of proof.

A possible strategy for defending my claim would be to start by arguing that the principle of maximising expected value is a requirement of rationality: an argument that is central to decision theory.[16] I could then argue that both consequentialists and deontologists about punishment must follow this principle in the choice whether to convict or to acquit a defendant, lest their theory is irrational and, consequently, unjustified. The issue with this strategy is not the existence of decision problems—such as the Allais paradox and the Ellsberg paradox—in which a rational answer can be given without following the principle of maximising expected value;[17] nor is it the existence of decision problems—such as the St Petersburg's paradox—in which following this principle gives answers that defy rationality.[18] Indeed, these rather contrived scenarios are nothing like the adjudicator's choice whether to convict or acquit a defendant. Their existence should not call into question the rationality of following the principle of maximising expected value when making this choice. The issue with such strategy, instead, is that a deontologist may argue that the choice between conviction and acquittal is regulated by 'restrictions'; that is, norms that forbid the agent from acting in a particular way, even when so acting maximises value (hence, expected value); and that if this means that, by following the restriction, the adjudicator is acting irrationally, so be it. After all, that such deontological norms have an 'apparent air of irrationality' is not a new insight;[19] but this insight has not stopped deontologists—and deontologists about punishment, in particular—from defending them.

[16] The standard way to prove that the principle of maximising expected value is a requirement of rationality is through a representation theorem. Such theorems show that, if an individual's preferences respect a set of rationality axioms, then these preferences can be represented by a pair of probability and value functions measuring the individual's degrees, respectively, of belief and of desire, such that an action is preferred to another if, and only if, the expected value of performing the former is greater. See R. Bradley, *Decision Theory with a Human Face* (CUP 2017), at 42–43. See also ibid, at 9–13, and ch 2, saying that the principle (which Bradley phrases in terms of 'utility' rather than 'value') expresses both a consistency requirement on the agent's preferences and a requirement connecting preference to choice; and P. Weirich, *Realistic Decision Theory: Rules for Nonideal Agents in Nonideal Circumstances* (OUP 2004), at 20–30, treating compliance with the principle of maximising value (Weirich, too, uses the term 'utility') as a necessary condition for an agent's acting rationally under the idealisation of full information, and then generating, from this principle, that of maximising expected value, to be applied in cases of uncertainty about which outcome will result from which act.

[17] See Peterson (n 2), at 80–84.

[18] See ibid, at 84–88.

[19] The apparent problem with restrictions is that they forbid an action even if acting as forbidden would prevent $1 + n$ instances of that forbidden action. See S. Scheffler, *The Rejection of Consequentialism: A Philosophical Investigation of the Considerations Underlying Rival Moral Conceptions* (OUP 1982), ch 4. The phrase in inverted commas is at 83. Famously, the seeming irrationality of restrictions is discussed by Nozick in his *Anarchy, State and Utopia* (Basic Books 1974), at 30–33. For a criticism of Nozick's defence of restrictions (or 'side-constraints', as he calls them), see D. O. Brink, 'Some Forms and Limits of Consequentialism' in D. Copp (ed), *The Oxford Handbook of Ethical Theory* (OUP 2007), at 395–396.

I must follow a different strategy, then. In section 3.3, I provide definitions of consequentialist and deontological theories of punishment, and show that a consequentialist about punishment is well-served by following the principle of maximising expected value in the decision problem of adjudication. In section 3.4, I assess whether, according to prominent deontological theories of punishment, there is any restriction that is operative in this decision problem. I identify two such restrictions: one enjoying widespread support amongst deontologists about punishment, the other supported by an unpopular strain of retributivism. Notably, deontological morality also justifies departures from the principle of maximising value by appealing to 'permissions'; that is, norms that allow, rather than require, such a departure. I identify a permission that, according to a different strain of retributivism, is operative in the adjudicator's decision problem. In section 3.5, I show that following the principle of maximising expected value in this decision problem yields the same answer as that given by following any of the three deontological norms that I have identified, whenever any of them applies. I also argue that, when no restriction or permission applies, the principle of maximising expected value is the only decision rule left to the deontologist. I thus conclude that a deontologist about punishment can follow the principle of maximising expected value without fearing a departure from any of their deontological commitments.[20] As pointed out already in the Introduction, section 3.6 is dedicated to explaining how the value function for the decision problem of adjudication may differ depending on the theory of punishment endorsed. Notice that I will not treat the way in which a theory of punishment builds its value function as being determinative of whether the theory is consequentialist or deontological. The distinction that I am about to draw between these families of theories relies on other considerations. As I will clarify later, though, the defence of my claim does not hinge on this definitional choice.

[20] With a steady series of recent articles, Seth Lazar is attempting to elaborate a version of decision theory that can serve deontological morality in scenarios characterised by empirical uncertainty. See S. Lazar, 'Anton's Game: Deontological Decision Theory for an Iterated Decision Problem' (2016) 29 Utilitas 88; S. Lazar, 'Deontological Decision Theory and Agent-Centered Options' (2017) 127 Ethics 579; S. Lazar, 'In Dubious Battle: Uncertainty and the Ethics of Killing' (2018) 175 Philosophical Studies 859; S. Lazar, 'Limited Aggregation and Risk' (2018) 46 Philosophy and Public Affairs 117; S. Lazar, 'Deontological Decision Theory and the Grounds of Subjective Permissibility' in M. Timmons (ed), *Oxford Studies in Normative Ethics, vol 9* (OUP 2019); S. Lazar and P. A. Graham, 'Deontological Decision Theory and Lesser-Evil Options' (2019) 198 Synthese 6889; and S. Lazar, 'Duty and Doubt' (2020) 8 Journal of Practical Ethics 28. For a similar approach, see H. Spector, 'Decisional Nonconsequentialism and the Risk Sensitivity of Obligation' (2016) 32 Social Philosophy and Policy 91. For criticisms of Lazar's project, see S. Tenenbaum, 'Action, Deontology, and Risk: Against the Multiplicative Model' (2017) 127 Ethics 674. The main challenge of Lazar's project lies in accommodating, in the decision-theoretic model, features that are, in his view, essential to deontological morality. These include, in particular, permissions to act suboptimally, which may or may not be self-favouring for the agent. For further discussion, see nn 55 and 57 below.

3.3 Consequentialist vs deontological theories of punishment

My reason for introducing the distinction between consequentialist and deontological theories of punishment is not to produce a comprehensive taxonomy of existing theories. The following treatment of the distinction will be terse, being limited to the information that is necessary to defend my claim. Moreover, I accept that the distinction may not capture some possible theories of punishment (for instance, a possible theory grounded in virtue ethics). Arguably, though, it captures the most prominent theories available.

According to a consequentialist about punishment, the permissibility of punishment depends exclusively on the values of the consequences—or outcomes—brought about, respectively, by punishing and by not punishing. To clarify, punishing is permissible if, and only if, it produces an outcome with value that is equal to, or higher than, the value of the outcome produced by not punishing; indeed, punishing is obligatory in the latter case. The assessment of outcomes depends on what is considered valuable under the particular consequentialist theory of punishment. A typical consequentialist theory of punishment is concerned with crime reduction and, therefore, values outcomes in virtue of the extent to which they foster a reduction in crime.[21]

According to a deontologist about punishment, instead, the permissibility of punishment does not depend exclusively on the values of the outcomes brought about, respectively, by punishing and not punishing. It also depends on restrictions and permissions.[22] To restate the definition given earlier, a restriction is a norm that *prohibits* an action even if this action maximises value;[23] that is, even if it produces an outcome whose value is the highest amongst the values of the outcomes of the decision that are actually possible. Hence, a restriction might require punishing—that is, it might forbid not punishing—even if not punishing maximises value; or it might forbid punishing, even if punishing maximises value. In the next section, I will offer two examples of such norms. A permission, instead, is a norm that *allows* an action even if value is maximised by acting otherwise. So,

[21] For further discussion of the notion of a consequentialist theory of punishment, see Duff (n 11), at 3–7.

[22] For a discussion of restrictions and permissions as defining features of deontological morality, see Scheffler (n 19), arguing that, unlike permissions (which he calls 'agent-centred prerogatives'), restrictions are difficult to justify. See also D. McNaughton and P. Rawling, 'Deontology' in Copp (n 19), at 425–426; L. Alexander and M. Moore, 'Deontological Ethics' in E. N. Zalta (ed), *Stanford Encyclopedia of Philosophy* (2016), at 5–6; J. Broome, 'The Structure of Good: Decision Theory and Ethics' in M. Bacharach and S. Hurley (eds), *Foundations of Decision Theory* (Basil Blackwell 1991), at 123–128; B. Williams, 'A Critique of Utilitarianism' in J. J. C. Smart and B. Williams, *Utilitarianism: For and Against* (CUP 1973), at 108–118.

[23] Notice that this definition also captures the case of a norm that requires the agent to perform action *A*, even if the alternative *B* maximises value. Indeed, an obligation to perform *A* entails a prohibition on performing *B*. Should there be such a thing as a deontological moral dilemma, whereby the agent is both under an obligation to perform *A* and under an equally strong obligation to perform *B*, this case could, arguably, be dealt with by means of a permission.

a permission might allow punishing even if not punishing maximises value; or it might allow not punishing even if value is maximised by punishing. Needless to say, under a permission, the act that maximises value is allowed as well. In the next section, I will offer an example of permission. Whether a theory of punishment is consequentialist or deontological, then, depends on whether it recognises restrictions on the maximisation of value or permissions not to maximise value.

As the reader will have noticed, I have, in giving these definitions, assumed certainty as to which outcome is produced, respectively, by punishing and by not punishing; hence, I have talked in terms of punishing or not punishing as maximising value, rather than expected value. I have, therefore, assumed certainty about the guilt or innocence of the potential target of punishment, states of the world that determine which outcome will be produced by punishing or not punishing. I now want to assess what consequentialist and deontological theories of punishment say concerning the choice whether or not to punish—that is, to convict—in the context of adjudication, a context characterised by uncertainty about the defendant's responsibility.

I claim that, in adjudication, both consequentialists and deontologists about punishment can follow the principle of maximising expected value without thereby relinquishing any tenets of their respective theory of punishment. In fact, I will show that this would be the case even if the adjudicator could reach certainty about the defendant's responsibility: given certainty, of course, the principle in question can be expressed as that of maximising value *tout court*. The upshot is that, in the context of adjudication, restrictions and permissions are effectively unnecessary for decision-making. This, however, does not mean that the distinction I have drawn between consequentialist and deontological theories of punishment is inadequate. Restrictions and permissions remain the defining features of the latter theories. For instance, a restriction against punishing those who are known to be innocent would determine the different decisions that, a consequentialist and a deontologist endorsing the restriction would, respectively, reach in a thought experiment in which punishing someone who is known to be innocent would avert an arbitrarily high number of crimes, or of instances of punishment of the innocent. By so doing, the restriction highlights not only a commitment of the deontological theory that includes this norm, but also how far this theory is willing to go in order to respect this commitment. While restrictions and permissions about punishment play a decisive normative role in such thought experiments, I argue that they do not provide necessary guidance in the particular context of the adjudicator's decision problem whether to convict or to acquit: following the principle of maximising expected value yields the same answer as that given by following any of these deontological norms, whenever any of them applies.

Let us consider, first, a consequentialist theory of punishment. It seems intuitively right to expect that, under conditions of uncertainty about the responsibility of the defendant, a consequentialist adjudicator would convict if, and only if, doing so maximises expected value. Is this so? There is a debate in moral philosophy about whether moral obligations should be understood as 'objective' or 'subjective';[24] in other words, about whether moral obligations concern what the agent should do, assuming their awareness of all relevant facts, or, instead, what the agent should do given their actual epistemic condition. For a consequentialist about morality, the alternative can be expressed as that between being obligated to perform the act that, in fact, maximises value, and being obligated to perform the act that maximises expected value. One might be excused for thinking that this alternative has no practical significance when working under conditions of uncertainty about which act maximises value. 'Surely'—they might opine—'the best that an agent can do in this situation is to maximise expected value'. However, it is precisely in particular scenarios characterised by uncertainty that the agent's allegiance to objectivism or to subjectivism about moral obligation makes a difference. Indeed, in the event of certainty about which act maximises value, the alternative dissolves. Consider this famous hypothetical from Frank Jackson:

> Jill is a physician who has to decide on the correct treatment for her patient, John, who has a minor but not trivial skin complaint. She has three drugs to choose from: drug *A*, drug *B*, and drug *C*. Careful consideration of the literature has led her to the following opinions. Drug *A* is very likely to relieve the condition but will not completely cure it. One of drugs *B* and *C* will completely cure the skin condition; the other though will kill the patient, and there is no way that she can tell which of the two is the perfect cure and which the killer drug. What should Jill do?[25]

From Jill's epistemic perspective, it is reasonable to view the giving of drug *A* as the act that maximises expected value. This action is very likely to provide a partial cure and, unlike giving drug *B* or *C*, it does not involve a 0.5 probability of killing John. If Jill were a subjectivist about moral obligation, then, she would choose this action. However, Jill believes that giving drug *A* is not the action that maximises value, because she believes that it does not provide a complete cure. If Jill were an objectivist about moral obligation, then, she would not administer drug *A*. In Jackson's view, not only does objectivism give an intuitively wrong answer in Jill's

[24] See, among others, F. Jackson, 'Decision-Theoretic Consequentialism and the Nearest and Dearest Objection' (1991) 101 Ethics 461; F. Feldman, 'Actual Utility, the Objection from Impracticality, and the Move to Expected Utility' (2006) 129 Philosophical Studies 49; M.J. Zimmerman, *Living With Uncertainty: The Moral Significance of Ignorance* (CUP 2008) (Zimmerman defends what he calls the 'prospective view', which he sees as compatible with both consequentialist and deontological moral theories. According to this view, one is to act so as to maximise 'expectable value', where the term 'expectable' reflects both the uncertainty as to whether an outcome will occur, and the uncertainty as to the value of the outcome. See ibid, at 33–42); P.A. Graham, 'In Defense of Objectivism about Moral Obligation' (2010) 121 Ethics 88.

[25] See Jackson (n 24), at 462–463.

case, but it deprives consequentialism of practical guiding force, because 'the fact that an action has in fact the best consequences may be a matter which is obscure to an agent'.[26] Indeed, in Jill's case, allegiance to objectivism would allow her to identify an action as impermissible, but not to single out the action that she should perform.

While I sympathise with Jackson's position,[27] I also think that the debate between objectivism and subjectivism about a consequentialist's moral obligations is, indeed, of no practical significance in the context of the adjudicator's choice whether to convict or acquit. Consider that Jill has three options, and that, while uncertain about which act maximises value, she believes that one of them does not, in fact, maximise value; thus, that it is impermissible for an objectivist.[28] This is why whether she is an objectivist or a subjectivist about moral obligation is relevant to her decision: depending on the approach taken, she will reach a different answer about the permissibility of one of the available options: that is, giving drug *A*. Notice that a similar situation does not arise in the context of adjudication in a binary verdict system. The adjudicator only has two options: acquittal or conviction. If, like Jill, they believed that one option does not, in fact, maximise value, they would also believe that the other option is required; importantly, they would believe so whether they are objectivist or subjectivist about moral obligation. To illustrate, if they believed that conviction does not, in fact, maximise value, in either case they would conclude that they should acquit. Indeed, they would believe that acquittal is the option that, in fact, maximises value: that is, the option to choose if they are objectivist. Therefore, from their epistemic perspective, acquittal would be the option that maximises expected value;[29] that is, the option to choose if they are subjectivist. If, instead, and unlike Jill, they did not have any belief whatsoever

[26] See ibid, at 466–467.

[27] As the reader may have noticed, I revealed my sympathy for subjectivism in Chapter 2, when discussing the hypothetical rule to treat the defendant as an actually innocent person, until they are proven guilty.

[28] Whether this option is, in fact, impermissible under objectivism, rather than merely being believed to be impermissible, is beside the point. What matters here is that being a subjectivist or an objectivist has practical significance, in Jill's problem, since it affects her decision-making. If she believes that giving drug *A* is impermissible for an objectivist, she will not choose that option, if she is an objectivist.

[29] If I believe that an option, in fact, maximises value, I believe that the actual state of the world is such that taking this option will produce the outcome with highest value, given such state of the world. Hence, this is the option that maximises expected value from my epistemic perspective. To illustrate, assume that, in the adjudicator's value function, the four possible outcomes are in the following decreasing order of value: true conviction, true acquittal, false acquittal, and false conviction. Given this value function, if the adjudicator believes that acquittal, in fact, maximises value, they also believe that the defendant is innocent, such that by acquitting they will produce the outcome with highest value, given the state of the world that they believe to be true, ie the defendant's innocence. Acquittal is, therefore, the option that maximises expected value, given their epistemic perspective. For probabilistic interpretations of 'categorical belief', see section 3.5.2 below.

as to which option does or does not, in fact, maximise value, their best chance of maximising value would be to maximise expected value:[30] if objectivist and conscientious, they would behave as the subjectivist would, ie they would be expected-value maximisers.[31] In contrast to Jill's case, then, it would make no difference to the adjudicator whether they endorsed objectivism or subjectivism about moral obligation. They would choose the same action either way: this is the action that maximises expected value. The subjectivist adjudicator would consider this action morally required. The objectivist adjudicator, instead, would consider that they are morally required to perform the action that, in fact, maximises value. However, in trying to live up to their moral obligation, they would maximise expected value. In this sense, being an expected-value maximiser would not, for them, mean relinquishing any tenets of their theory of punishment.

The upshot of this discussion is that a consequentialist adjudicator should understand the standard of proof in decision-theoretic terms; that is, as a decision rule that identifies the epistemic conditions under which conviction maximises expected value, and should, therefore, be chosen. The subjectivist should follow this decision rule, since the rule implements the principle of maximising expected value; the objectivist should follow it when they have no belief as to which option, in fact, maximises value, such that the most sensible directive left to them is the principle of maximising expected value. In any case, whether acting on the basis of said belief—if they have it—or of the principle—hence, the decision-theoretic standard—the objectivist adjudicator would maximise expected value, as shown above. Having said this, I recognise that, given the definition of the 'intermediacy' of a verdict that I will give in the next chapter, intermediate verdicts are never permissible for an objectivist. As we will see, while these verdicts may maximise expected value, they are never the option that, in fact, maximises value: if the defendant is innocent, issuing an intermediate verdict is less valuable than acquitting; if the defendant is guilty, issuing an intermediate verdict is less valuable than convicting. After all, as pointed out in the Introduction to the book, an intermediate verdict is always a mistake if seen from the perspective of the omniscient observer. An objectivist, then, would surely prefer a binary verdict system to the richer system that I will try to justify.

[30] Here, I am not so much relying on the 'long run' argument, according to which maximising expected value leads to the maximisation of value in a long run of cases (for a critical discussion see Peterson (n 2), at 72–75). My point is that, under the hypothesised circumstances, an adjudicator who aims at maximising value *in the individual case* does not seem to have a better practical directive to follow than the principle of maximising expected value.

[31] See Lazar, 'Deontological Decision Theory and Agent-Centered Options' (n 20), at 603–604. cf Feldman (n 24), at 67–69; Graham (n 24), at 97–103.

3.4 Deontological restrictions and permissions about punishment

My analysis of how deontologists should approach the question of punishment under conditions of uncertainty about the defendant's responsibility starts from identifying examples of restrictions to the maximisation of value and permissions not to maximise value that may be part of their theories. I say 'examples', but, in fact, I could not find plausible candidates other than those discussed below.[32]

While my analysis is not confined to retributivist theories, in order to identify plausible deontological norms, it is useful to rely on Alexander and Ferzan's taxonomy of retributivist accounts.[33] As for restrictions, consider what they call 'weak' and 'strong' retributivism. Weak retributivism treats desert as a necessary condition for punishment. This strain of retributivism, therefore, includes a restriction according to which the punishment of the innocent is forbidden, even if punishing maximises value. Strong retributivism, instead, treats desert as a necessary and sufficient condition for punishment, and as a reason that mandates punishment. This strain of retributivism, therefore, includes a restriction according to which the punishment of the guilty is required, even if not punishing maximises value. As for permissions, consider what Alexander and Ferzan call 'moderate' retributivism, according to which desert is a necessary and sufficient condition for punishment, but does not mandate punishment. This strain of retributivism includes a permission—not a requirement—to punish the guilty, even if not punishing maximises value. If it did not allow punishment under such circumstances, it could not understand desert as a sufficient condition for punishment.

In fact, in the way in which I have formulated them, the above norms are unlikely to appeal to any retributivist, or deontologist for that matter. To see this, take, first, the restriction stating that the punishment of the innocent is forbidden. Respecting this norm implies giving up the enterprise of punishment altogether, because no workable criminal justice system can guarantee that no innocent person will be punished in the long run.[34] This apparent problem, which was dubbed the 'fallibility argument',[35] has been denied by claiming that, in fact, the restriction only

[32] Here are the possible restrictions and permissions that I will not consider: a duty to punish the innocent (even if not punishing maximises value); a duty not to punish the guilty (even if punishing maximises value); a permission not to punish the guilty (even if punishing maximises value); a permission to punish the innocent (even if not punishing maximises value); a permission not to punish the innocent (even if punishing maximises value). Indeed, I cannot think of existing theories of punishment that would endorse any of these norms. Unlike the other norms in this list, the last is not implausible. As we will see, though, deontological theories usually endorse a duty, rather than a mere permission, not to punish the innocent.

[33] See L. Alexander and K. Ferzan, *Crime and Culpability: A Theory of Criminal Law* (CUP 2009), at 7–10.

[34] See M. Moore, *Placing Blame: A Theory of the Criminal Law* (OUP 2010), at 156.

[35] D. Dolinko, 'Retributivism, Consequentialism, and the Intrinsic Goodness of Punishment' (1997) 16 Law and Philosophy 507, at 510.

prohibits the punishment of an individual *who is known by the agent to be innocent*[36] (consider that, insofar as punishment is, by its nature, intentional,[37] there is no need to complement the restriction by mentioning the intentionality of the action).[38] Now, setting up or supporting a criminal justice system expecting—or even knowing—that it will produce instances of false conviction in the long run, does not fall foul of the restriction. The innocent people who will be punished are 'mere' statistical lives, from the perspective of the lawmaker, who, by establishing the system, is vicariously punishing them: they are not known to be innocent by the lawmaker. In this second formulation, the restriction appears to have considerable support amongst retributivists[39] and deontologists in general.[40]

Consider, now, the restriction characterising strong retributivism, which requires the punishment of the guilty. Attempting to respect this norm would demand

[36] See Moore (n 34), at 158. See also R. Aboodi and others, 'Deontology, Individualism, and Uncertainty: A Reply to Jackson and Smith' (2008) 105 The Journal of Philosophy 259, at 267. For criticism of Moore's reply to the fallibility argument, see Dolinko (n 35), at 510–513.

[37] See H. L. A. Hart, *Punishment and Responsibility: Essays in the Philosophy of Law* (2nd edn, OUP 2008), at 5.

[38] In fact, the restriction is frequently expressed as forbidding the intentional punishment of the innocent. See the works cited below, in nn 39 and 40. Because punishment is by its nature intentional, though, the seemingly redundant requirement of 'intention' is best understood and expressed as a requirement of knowledge—or, at the very least, of 'categorical belief'—that the individual punished is innocent. After all, many accept that, to do *A* intentionally, one needs to know that she is doing *A* (for a defence of this position, see the classic G. E. M. Anscombe, *Intention* (2nd edn, Harvard University Press 2000), at 11–15, 49–51. For critical discussion, see K. Setiya, 'Intention' in E. N. Zalta (ed), *Stanford Encyclopedia of Philosophy* (2018), at 22–31). If *A* is described as 'punishing the innocent', someone who does *A* intentionally knows that they are punishing an individual, and that this individual is innocent. A problem with the proposed formulation of the restriction is that the norm is factive: because knowledge presupposes a *true* and justified belief, the agent cannot (or, at least, may be unable to) tell whether the norm applies to them, insofar as they do not have access to the truth. For a concise response to this challenge to factive norms, see S. Moss, 'Knowledge and Legal Proof' in T. Szabo Gendler and J. Hawthorne (eds), *Oxford Studies in Epistemology, vol 7* (OUP forthcoming 2022), at 27–29. It suffices to say that what matters for my purposes is the 'belief' component of knowledge. Whether a deontologist formulates the restriction as requiring belief, justified belief, or true and justified belief, etc. is irrelevant to the arguments to follow.

[39] See Moore (n 34), ch 4 (Moore, however, would probably agree to violate the restriction when doing so prevents harm that is greater than a given threshold. See ibid, at 720–726. For criticism of this view, see L. Alexander, 'Deontology at the Threshold' (2000) 37 San Diego Law Review 893); Duff (n 11), at 8 (criticising consequentialism about punishment on the grounds that 'in principle [it] sanction[s] the deliberate "punishment" of those known to have committed no offense'); Alexander and Ferzan (n 33), at 9; Walen, 'Proof Beyond a Reasonable Doubt' (n 9), at 379–381 (but see A. Walen, 'Retributive Justice' in E. N. Zalta (ed), *Stanford Encyclopedia of Philosophy* (2020) at 31, stating that '[i]t is a conceptual, not a deontological, point that one cannot punish another whom one believes to be innocent'). See also D. Husak, 'Retributivism *in Extremis*' (2013) 32 Law and Philosophy 3, at 15–16, countenancing a violation of the restriction when the 'instrumental gain is sufficiently great'.

[40] See Tadros (n 9), ch 6. In Tadros's 'duty view' of punishment, the restriction finds its justification in the 'means principle', according to which one should not use others as means to achieve the good. However, Tadros accepts that the restriction can be departed from for the sake of preventing a much greater harm than the punishment of the innocent (ibid, at 128, 138). See also M. N. Berman, 'Two Kinds of Retributivism' in R. A. Duff and S. Green (eds), *Philosophical Foundations of Criminal Law* (OUP 2011), at 447–449, pointing out that the view that it is impermissible to punish someone who is known to be innocent is widely shared by theorists of punishment, including non-retributivists. cf Hart (n 37), at 11–13, arguing that the punishment of the innocent is at odds with both a retributive and (at least if done openly) a utilitarian 'general justifying aim'.

committing an unreasonable amount of State resources to the investigation of crimes, to the identification of the guilty, to their trial, and their punishment. The costs of this policy, in terms of infringements of privacy and neglect of other crucial obligations of the State vis-à-vis its citizens, would be considerable.[41] And still, it would be unrealistic to expect that the norm would not be violated: many crimes would go unpunished. To make it possible to respect the norm without having to punish everyone—hence, to make this a plausible norm—a similar tweak to that made to the other restriction is needed. Thus, the norm should be read as requiring the punishment of an individual *who is known by the agent to be guilty*.[42] Once evidence is acquired, such that the adjudicator can reasonably claim knowledge of the defendant's guilt, the adjudicator should convict. Considering sufficient something short of knowledge would probably not do. Remember that, here, we are dealing with a restriction: in particular, a norm that requires an action even if an alternative would maximise value.[43] Moreover, a strong retributivist still sees desert as a necessary condition for punishment. It is, therefore, unlikely that they would endorse a norm that requires punishing even when there is a significant risk of punishing the innocent, and when not punishing maximises value. The risk of undeserved punishment should be minimised—or, at least, made acceptable—for punishment to be required even when suboptimal. This is done by limiting the scope of the restriction to cases in which the adjudicator knows that the defendant is guilty. This reformulation of the restriction, after all, draws support from the famous passage of Kant's *The Metaphysics of Morals*, which contributed to him being regarded as the archetypal strong retributivist.[44] When Kant theorised the duty of a dissolving society to execute all murderers up to the last, he referred to a murderer who is in prison.[45] Arguably, then, he had in mind someone who was known to have committed a crime. Even when reformulated as incorporating the agent's knowledge of the defendant's guilt, though, the restriction is hardly popular amongst contemporary retributivists.[46]

Finally, I come to the permission to punish the guilty, characterising moderate retributivism. If the permission is to have practical significance, it should specify

[41] See Alexander and Ferzan (n 33), at 8.

[42] See n 38 above for what concerns the factive nature of this norm. What matters for my purposes is the 'belief' component of knowledge. Whether a deontologist formulates the restriction as requiring belief, justified belief, or true and justified belief, etc. is irrelevant to my argument.

[43] See n 23 above.

[44] But see B. S. Byrd, 'Kant's Theory of Punishment: Deterrence in its Threat, Retribution in its Execution' (1989) 8 Law and Philosophy 151, arguing that deterrence played an important role in Kant's theory of punishment.

[45] See I. Kant, *The Metaphysics of Morals* (M. Gregor ed, CUP 1996), at 106.

[46] See Duff (n 11), at 19; Berman, 'Two Kinds of Retributivism' (n 40), at 450–452; Moore (n 34), at 157. A hint to the restriction is found in Brudner's retributivism. He writes about his 'legal retributivism' that, 'because its reason for punishing is to deny a practical denial of rights that would appear valid were its self-contradictoriness not practically demonstrated, it holds that the state ought generally to punish those who have licensed their coercion ... and so it may ... be called strong'. See A. Brudner, *Punishment and Freedom: A Liberal Theory of Penal Justice* (OUP 2009), at 51.

the epistemic attitude about guilt that the agent must have for punishment to be permissible even when the alternative maximises value. The fact that an individual is actually guilty and that I am, therefore, allowed to punish them is not enough for me to be able to make use of this permission. This is because I may not be aware that they are guilty and, hence, that punishing them is open to me. Notice that this criticism does not apply to the two restrictions considered earlier. Even without reference to the agent's epistemic attitude about guilt, they can guide agency so as to reach the desired goal. If the innocent should not be punished, come what may, then the State could simply not set up a system of punishment; if the guilty must be punished, come what may, then the State could punish everyone. What epistemic attitude about guilt should be read into the permission, then? Again, I do not think that anything short of knowledge would do. A moderate retributivist still considers desert a necessary condition for punishing. Moreover, they do not view desert as a conclusive reason for punishing; rather, they accept that the punishment of the deserving be forgone when the costs of punishing are sufficiently great to render it suboptimal.[47] How, then, could they consider punishment authorised if there is a significant risk of punishing the innocent, and if punishing is not the option that maximises value? The risk of undeserved punishment should be minimised—or, at least, made acceptable—for punishment to be allowed even when suboptimal. For the permission to be a plausible component of moderate retributivism, then, it should require knowledge of guilt on the part of the agent.[48] So reformulated, the permission appears to have some support amongst retributivists.[49]

No one can meaningfully accept all three norms, because the permission cannot be operative if the restriction requiring the punishment of the guilty is endorsed: whoever accepts this restriction is left with only one option in the case in which they know that the defendant is guilty. Whether someone who rejects all three norms can still call themselves a 'retributivist' depends on how retributivism is defined. If, for instance, retributivism merely requires recognising the intrinsic value of deserved punishment—hence, that desert is a reason to punish—and the intrinsic disvalue of undeserved punishment—hence, that lack of desert is a reason not to punish—then this person could be a retributivist.[50] For this credo to be

[47] See Alexander and Ferzan (n 33), at 8–10. cf D. Husak, 'Why Punish the Deserving?' in D. Husak, *The Philosophy of Criminal Law: Selected Essays* (OUP 2010).

[48] See n 38 above about the factive nature of the permission, so formulated. What matters for my purposes is the 'belief' component of knowledge. Whether a deontologist formulates the permission as requiring belief, justified belief, or true and justified belief, etc. is irrelevant to my argument.

[49] Moderate retributivism is endorsed by Alexander and Ferzan (n 33). But see also Walen, 'Retributive Justice' (n 39), at 31, saying that the deontological aspect of retributivism lies in the fact that desert opens up 'an avenue of justification for hard treatment . . . making permissible what might otherwise have been impermissible'.

[50] cf Moore (n 34), at 157, claiming that 'what *is* distinctively retributivist is the view that the guilty receiving their just deserts is an intrinsic good' (italics in the original). Moore's own retributivism, of course, is richer than this condition. For a thicker set of minimal retributivist conditions, see Walen, 'Retributive Justice' (n 39), at 1.

endorsed, desert need not be seen as a necessary or sufficient condition for punishment, even less as a conclusive reason for punishment. To be sure, this issue does not concern me here. What matters, for my purposes, is that, if someone rejects all these norms, they are consequentialists about punishment, whether they are also retributivists or not.[51]

3.5 The role of restrictions and permissions in adjudication

As mentioned in section 3.2, I aim to show that following the principle of maximising expected value in the decision problem of adjudication yields the same answer as that given by following any of the three deontological norms that I have identified, whenever any of them applies. Hence, that it yields an answer that conforms with the tenets of a theory of punishment that endorses any of these norms.

3.5.1 Should they be integrated into the value function?

Notice that, in order to achieve my aim, there is no need for me to integrate the above norms into the decision-theoretic model—in particular, into the value function—of a deontologist about punishment. Let me explain.

As pointed out in the Introduction to this chapter, in order to employ the principle of maximising expected value, the decision-maker needs a value function. A value function is a numerical scale in which the possible outcomes of a decision problem are arranged as a function of their value. Philosophers have remarked on the difficulty of accounting for deontological norms—in particular, restrictions—within a value function for the purposes of implementing the principle of maximising expected value.[52] Imagine a deontological moral theory including a restriction not to kill someone who is, in fact, innocent. To clarify, the hypothetical restriction applies irrespective of the agent's degree of belief in the innocence of the target. Intuitively, the best way to incorporate this restriction into the decision-theoretic model is to assign infinite disvalue to any outcome that consists in the killing of an innocent person. By doing so, irrespective of the values of the other possible outcomes of a decision, the agent is always forbidden from choosing a course of action that may result in the death of an innocent person. Indeed, any action that has a higher than zero probability of resulting in the death of an innocent

[51] That retributivists can be consequentialist is a fact that is accepted by some scholars. See Moore (n 34), at 155–159; Berman, 'Two Kinds of Retributivism' (n 40). cf J. Gardner, 'Introduction' to Hart (n 37), at xvi. For a criticism of this view, see Dolinko (n 35).

[52] See M. Colyvan and others, 'Modelling the Moral Dimension of Decisions' (2010) 44 Nous 503, at 511–519; and F. Jackson and M. Smith, 'Absolutist Moral Theories and Uncertainty' (2006) 103 The Journal of Philosophy 267.

person is forbidden, since it has infinite expected disvalue. The apparent problem with this strategy is that, for all we know, any of our actions has at least a minuscule probability of resulting in the death of an innocent person. Hence, it was argued, every action appears to be prohibited under this model.[53]

On a closer look, one sees that the problem is not with how the strategy just described integrates the restriction into the value function. If the restriction is as hypothesised, ie if it forbids killing the innocent *tout court*, assigning infinite disvalue to outcomes that consist in the killing of an innocent person seems the correct way of reflecting it in the model. The problem, instead, lies with the restriction itself. If we are categorically forbidden from killing the innocent, we may well be categorically forbidden from acting, insofar as any of our actions may result in the death of an innocent person. One can surely hypothesise a deontological moral theory containing such a restriction, but it would be a highly implausible theory indeed. A plausible deontological moral theory may, instead, posit restrictions only on actions that have a thick causal connection with a given result and/or are performed by the agent with a particular mental state.[54] For example, it may prohibit the causing (understood as distinct from the mere allowing, enabling, or accelerating) of an innocent's death or the *intentional* killing of someone who the agent *knows* to be innocent. In either case, it would not be true of every action of ours that it may fall foul of the relevant restriction.

The deontological restrictions identified in section 3.4 concern, precisely, actions performed with a particular mental state regarding a relevant fact (if I am right about the formulation of these norms, then, the deontologist about punishment is a subjectivist about moral obligation since, according to them, what the agent should do depends on the agent's epistemic condition). One of the two restrictions forbids the punishment of someone who is known by the agent to be innocent, rather than forbidding the punishment of the innocent *tout court*. The other requires the punishment of someone who is known by the agent to be guilty, rather than requiring the punishment of the guilty *tout court*. These norms, then, apply only under conditions in which there is no need for the agent to rely on decision theory in order to identify the course of action required. If the agent has the relevant knowledge, the restrictions apply and, thus, give the agent all the guidance they need. Nothing of practical significance would be gained by attempting to build these restrictions into the decision-theoretic model.[55] As seen earlier, the deontological permission

[53] See Colyvan and others (n 52), at 512–513. See also Jackson and Smith (n 52), at 271–272. The restriction considered by Jackson and Smith forbids the *intentional* killing of the innocent, but applies irrespective of the agent's degree of belief in the innocence of the target (cf n 38 above). The authors consider other possible strategies for incorporating restrictions in a decision-theoretic model, and ultimately find them all unsatisfactory.

[54] For discussion, see Alexander and Moore (n 22), at 6–15.

[55] My work concerns the enterprise of criminal adjudication only. It is beyond its scope to assess whether it is possible to build a value function that incorporates the restrictions endorsed by a plausible deontological moral theory. See G. Oddie and P. Milne, 'Act and Value: Expectation and the Representability of Moral Theories' (1991) 57 Theoria 42, arguing that any moral theory can be

about punishment requires knowledge of guilt on the part of the agent. If the agent has such knowledge, the permission applies, and it puts the agent in the position to identify one of the permissible courses of action without resort to decision theory. Decision theory can then be employed independently to identify the course of action that maximises expected value. If different from the course of action already permitted, this would be another permissible act for the agent.[56] Again, nothing of practical significance would be gained by attempting to incorporate the permission into the decision-theoretic model.[57]

What is more important, my goal here is to show that following the principle of maximising expected value in the decision problem of adjudication yields the same answer as that given by following any of the three deontological norms that I have identified, whenever any of them applies. In order to do this, I do not need to prove that deontological restrictions and permissions about punishment can be integrated in the decision-theoretic model, so as to provide the deontologist about punishment with a unique decision-making tool. I only need to show that if the deontologist about punishment relies on decision theory, they are not going to fall foul of any of those three deontological norms.

3.5.2 Decision theory as a safe choice for the deontologist

Consider the scenario in which the adjudicator does not know whether the defendant is guilty or innocent. Since the three norms surveyed presuppose knowledge of guilt or innocence on the part of the adjudicator, they are simply not applicable in such a scenario. Accordingly, what should a deontologist adjudicator do? When deontological restrictions and permissions run out, the only strategy left to a deontologist is to follow the decision rule followed by the consequentialist;

represented through an agent-neutral axiology. See also Lazar, 'Deontological Decision Theory and Agent-Centered Options' (n 20), at 585–586, fn 19 and Lazar, 'Duty and Doubt' (n 20), at 45–46, arguing that the restrictions of a deontological moral theory can be accounted for through the construction of an appropriate value function. Consider, though, that Lazar's deontology is not 'absolutist': he accepts that restrictions can be overridden 'in extremis'. Hence, representing them in the value function would not require assigning infinite disvalue to outcomes consisting in their violation.

56 At least, if the permission allows the act that maximises expected value, rather than just the act that maximises value.

57 My work concerns the enterprise of criminal adjudication only. It is beyond its scope to assess whether it is possible to incorporate into the decision-theoretic model the permissions endorsed by a plausible deontological moral theory. See Lazar, 'Deontological Decision Theory and Agent-Centered Options' (n 20), and Lazar and Graham (n 20). Lazar and Graham—who work with scenarios in which it seems reasonable for a deontologist to make a permission available to the agent even when the agent operates under conditions of ignorance about the relevant facts—account for permissions within the decision-theoretic model by making correctives to the principle of maximising expected value, rather than through incorporating them into the value function.

that is, to maximise expected value.[58] After all, the maximisation of expected value does matter to a deontologist, as long as no norm forbids it. Of course, following the same decision rule does not mean reaching the same decision. As pointed out already, and as explored further in section 3.6, different theories of punishment may have significantly different value functions; therefore, in the very same case, the principle of maximising expected value may enjoin the supporters of different theories of punishment to reach different decisions.

In the event of lack of knowledge about guilt or innocence, then, the deontologist adjudicator should maximise expected value. It is the principle of maximising expected value that tells them when the evidence of guilt is sufficient for conviction to be warranted. In other words—and as I will explain in detail in the next chapter—the principle, together with the relevant value function, sets the epistemic conditions for conviction: it provides a standard of proof. Because cases in which adjudication fails to reach knowledge abound, a deontologist about punishment needs a decision-theoretic account of the standard of proof; that is, they need to identify the standard of proof as a decision rule that promotes the maximisation of expected value.[59]

What about cases in which the adjudicator has the relevant knowledge, such that any of the deontological norms apply? I argue that, in these cases, following the principle of maximising expected value—hence, the decision-theoretic standard of proof—yields the same answer as that given by following this norm. Thus, the adjudicator can follow the former without fearing a departure from the latter.

The starting point of this argument is to consider, briefly, the value function that is likely to be accepted by a deontologist about punishment. Of course, the reference here is to the value function pertaining to the binary choice whether to acquit or convict; hence, a value function with only four entries, each corresponding to a possible outcome of that choice: true conviction, false conviction, true acquittal, and false acquittal. Many deontologists see desert (or, if not retributivist, guilt) as a necessary condition for punishment, thus endorsing the restriction against punishing those who are known to be innocent. Insofar as they do so, and insofar as they factor into their assessment of false conviction its serious detrimental consequences (for the defendant and beyond), they are likely to consider this the least valuable of the outcomes.[60] Insofar as a deontologist also sees desert (or guilt) as a sufficient, and possibly even conclusive, reason for punishment—thus endorsing the permission, or even the duty, to punish those who are known to be guilty—they

[58] See M. S. Moore, 'Patrolling the Border of Consequentialist Justifications: The Scope of Agent-Relative Restrictions' (2008) 27 Law and Philosophy 35.

[59] For a similar view with specific regard to retributivism, see E. H. Atiq, 'What Unconditional Credence in Individual Desert Claims does Retributivism Require?' (2018) University of Illinois Law Review Online 138.

[60] For a retributivist argument to the effect that false conviction is considerably worse than false acquittal, see Walen, 'Proof Beyond a Reasonable Doubt' (n 9), at 432–434.

are likely to consider true conviction the most valuable outcome.[61] One may object that, for the deontologist, true acquittal is more valuable than true conviction; more precisely, that this is the case for a deontologist who understands desert or guilt as a necessary condition for punishment. The objection is based on the consideration that true acquittal avoids the substantial disvalue of punishing the innocent: a disvalue that, in the arithmetic of such a deontologist, may well be greater in magnitude than the value of punishing the guilty. While the argument that I offer in this section also works if true acquittal is the most valuable outcome in the function, and true conviction the second-most valuable, I want to take a brief detour to show that the objection fails, since it involves unwarranted double counting.

Consider that, in order to apply the principle of maximising expected value, the value function must take the form of an interval scale.[62] This is a scale that reflects accurately not just the order of the outcomes as a function of their value (as an ordinal scale would), but also the difference in value between outcomes, such that we can say how much better an outcome is than another for the decision-maker.[63] As I will show in the next chapter, identifying a standard of proof that works as a decision rule for the maximisation of expected value requires that we get right, in particular, the interval between the values of true conviction and false acquittal, and that between the values of true acquittal and false conviction. This second interval is at issue here.

The above argument for regarding true acquittal as the most valuable outcome is wrong in that it counts the absence of the reasons for giving relatively low value to false conviction as the reason to give relatively high value to true acquittal.[64] If, for example, the suffering that punishment imposes on the innocent, or the intrinsic disvalue of undeserved punishment, are already treated as reasons to attribute a certain value to false conviction, avoiding such suffering and disvalue may not *also* be treated as a reason to attribute a certain value to true acquittal. Otherwise, in calculating the difference between the values of these two outcomes—which should be accurately reflected in the interval scale—one would be treating as separate reasons the presence and the absence of the same facts: the former pushing down the value of false conviction, the latter pulling up the value of true acquittal. This is obviously mistaken.[65] This technical point aside, whoever advances the argument that true

[61] This seems true even for a retributivist who does not factor into the assessment of true conviction the beneficial consequences of punishment. See section 3.6.1 below.

[62] See Peterson (n 2), at 101–102; Briggs (n 3), at 14–15; and K. Steele and H. O. Stefánsson, 'Decision Theory' in E. N. Zalta (ed), *Stanford Encyclopedia of Philosophy* (2016), at 9.

[63] On the concept of 'interval scale' and the use of such scales in decision theory, see Peterson (n 2), at 22–28, 101–110. Everyday examples of interval scales are the Fahrenheit and Celsius temperature scales.

[64] See L. Laudan and H. D. Saunders, 'Rethinking the Criminal Standard of Proof: Seeking Consensus about the Utilities of Trial Outcomes' (2009) 7 International Commentary on Evidence 1, at 27–29.

[65] I suspect that Walen's 'simplifying assumptions', which he relies upon to justify factoring only the false outcomes into the decision-theoretic formula for the standard of proof, incur the mistake discussed here. I am referring to his assumptions that the value of false conviction is the negative of the

acquittal is the most valuable outcome fails to appreciate that, while the conviction of a guilty person can generally be treated as a success of the criminal process—is the prospect of true conviction not amongst the main reasons, if it is not the main reason, for having this process?—only under particular circumstances can the acquittal of the innocent be treated this way. These are the cases where an innocent person is brought to trial on no fault of the criminal justice authorities, for example because, unfortunately, there was strong incriminating evidence against them, and there was no other reasonable lead to follow. Under normal circumstances, however, the very fact that an innocent person is brought to trial signals a failure of the process. Acquitting this person is a remedy to such a failure, not a success.[66]

Be that as it may, the value function of a deontologist about punishment is likely to present true conviction and true acquittal as the two most valuable outcomes of adjudication, and false conviction as the least valuable. I doubt that there is anything controversial in this claim. For the purposes of the argument that I present in this section, there is no need to know more about the structure of this value function.

Remember that the three deontological norms surveyed earlier apply when the decision-maker knows about the defendant's guilt or innocence. Knowledge of *p* is generally understood as requiring 'full', 'outright' or 'categorical' belief that *p*. This is something more than having high confidence: it is 'closer to a commitment or a being sure'.[67] The notion of categorical belief lends itself to three main interpretations, in terms of probability.[68] I consider each of these in turn, with the aim of showing, for each interpretation of this notion—hence, also of knowledge—that, when any of the deontological norms applies, according to this interpretation, following the principle of maximising expected value delivers the same answer as following this norm does.

According to the first interpretation, categorical belief is the highest degree of belief in a given proposition, represented by a probability of one that the proposition is true. In other words, to have a categorical belief is to be (absolutely) certain. Given this interpretation, whenever the deontologist adjudicator knows that the defendant is innocent, the expected value of convicting is lower than that of acquitting since, according to the adjudicator, there is a probability of one that conviction

value of true acquittal, and that the value of false acquittal is the negative of the value of true conviction. See Walen, 'Proof Beyond a Reasonable Doubt' (n 9), at 407–408.

[66] Consider Lord Kilbrandon, *Other People's Law: The Hamlyn Lectures, 18th Series* (Stevens & Sons 1966), at 61, stating that 'almost every verdict of acquittal manifests a miscarriage of justice. Either a guilty man has escaped, and the machinery of crime prevention has in that instance broken down, or an innocent man has been wrongly arraigned, to his grievous and undeserved injury'.

[67] See J. J. Ichikawa and M. Steup, 'The Analysis of Knowledge' in E. N. Zalta (ed), *Stanford Encyclopedia of Philosophy* (2018), at 5–6.

[68] Here, I am clearly relying on the 'subjective' notion of probability as degree of belief. But see the Introduction to this book, n 24.

will produce the worst possible outcome, ie false conviction. Instead, whenever the adjudicator knows that the defendant is guilty, the expected value of convicting is higher than that of acquitting, since, according to the adjudicator, there is a probability of one that conviction will produce true conviction, which is either the best possible outcome or the second-best below true acquittal. Needless to say, in this epistemic situation, the probability that acquittal results in true acquittal equals zero for the adjudicator, and, under either version of the value function, false acquittal—which the adjudicator considers certain in the event of acquittal—is worse than true conviction; hence, conviction maximises expected value. The upshot is that, whenever the norm forbidding the punishment of a person who is known to be innocent applies, the principle of maximising expected value demands acquittal; whenever the norm requiring the punishment of a person who is known to be guilty applies, the principle demands conviction; whenever the norm allowing the punishment of a person who is known to be guilty applies, conviction is, indeed, the choice that maximises expected value, such that there is no sub-optimal option left to the adjudicator. If so, a deontologist adjudicator could follow the principle of maximising expected value without fearing a departure from any of the norms surveyed.

In fact, this interpretation of categorical belief lends itself to the objection that, unlike a categorical belief that *p*—that is, a being sure of *p*—absolute certainty may well be an unattainable epistemic state of mind; hence, that the two cannot possibly be equivalent. But the interpretation has also come under attack for another reason.[69] Notice that, if this interpretation were correct, each time we claim to believe categorically that *p*, we should be indifferent between maintaining the status quo and choosing a voucher that sentences us to the status quo if *p* is true, and to a loss of, say, £1 million if *p* is false. Indeed, if a categorical belief corresponds to a probability of one, we should consider the loss impossible. And yet, it does not seem at all incoherent for someone who has a categorical belief that *p* to prefer the status quo to the voucher; in other words, to prefer not to gamble £1 million, for no gain, on *p* being true. This suggests that a categorical belief that *p* need not correspond to a probability of one that *p*. Because of these apparent difficulties, it is worthwhile considering alternative interpretations of categorical belief.

According to a second interpretation, categorical belief corresponds to a very high, but not maximally high, degree of belief. It is, therefore, represented by a probability threshold that is close, but not equal, to one. Notice that this interpretation does not incur the problem raised in the previous paragraph. Someone who categorically believes that *p* under this interpretation, and is faced with the choice between the status quo and the voucher, need not be indifferent between the two, since the probability of the loss materialising—that is, of *p* being false—is

[69] The following argument is taken from M. Kaplan, *Decision Theory as Philosophy* (CUP 1996), at 91–93.

higher than zero. Thus, they would be justified in preferring the status quo. As far as criminal adjudication is concerned, similar considerations to those made with regard to the first interpretation can be made here. Whenever, applying the second interpretation of categorical belief, the deontologist adjudicator knows that the defendant is innocent, the expected value of convicting is lower than that of acquitting since, according to the adjudicator, there is a very high probability that conviction will produce the worst possible outcome—false conviction—and a very low probability that it will produce the best, or second-best outcome—true conviction. Hence, in these epistemic circumstances, acting so as to maximise expected value is equivalent to following the restriction not to punish someone who is known to be innocent: both require acquittal. Similarly, whenever the adjudicator knows that the defendant is guilty, the expected value of convicting is higher than that of acquitting since, according to the adjudicator, there is a very high probability that conviction will produce the best, or the second-best, possible outcome, and a very low probability that it will produce the worst. Hence, in these epistemic circumstances, acting so as to maximise expected value is equivalent to following the duty to punish someone who is known to be guilty: both require conviction. And the permission to punish someone who is known to be guilty is effectively redundant, since convicting is, indeed, the optimal course of action. If this is correct, a deontologist adjudicator could follow the principle of maximising expected value without fearing a departure from the norms at issue.

To be sure, the argument I have just given is rough around the edges. In order to tighten it, it would be necessary to work with a fully fledged numerical value function, to be more precise than I have been with respect to the probability threshold that may correspond to categorical belief under this second interpretation, and then to calculate, in exact terms, the expected values of convicting and acquitting, respectively, for the cases in which the deontological norms apply. Having said this, a failure to tighten the argument may be excused. In fact, while the second interpretation of categorical belief does not have the problematic implication of the first, it does suffer from problems of its own. To see this, suppose that the threshold for categorical belief is 0.9. Suppose, also, that you are confronted with a lottery, such that out of 1,000 tickets, only one will win. The probability of any ticket losing is, thus, 0.999. Therefore, for each ticket, you should have a categorical belief that it will lose. And yet, since you are all but certain that this is a fair lottery, you assign a probability very close to one that one ticket will win. Hence, you should also categorically believe that one of the 1,000 tickets will win. Needless to say, your categorical beliefs are inconsistent: you cannot, at the same time, believe categorically that each ticket will lose, and that not all of them will. And yet, the current interpretation of 'categorical belief' allows for this problematic result.[70] Notice that this

[70] For this, and further criticisms of the second interpretation of categorical belief, see ibid, at 94–98, and H. L. Ho, *A Philosophy of Evidence Law: Justice in the Search for Truth* (OUP 2008), at 133–134.

example can be replicated with probability thresholds that are higher or lower than that chosen to represent categorical belief.

There is a third interpretation of categorical belief that enjoys considerable—and growing—support in the philosophical literature. According to this interpretation, categorical belief is the degree of belief in a proposition that justifies acting as the agent would act if they were certain that the proposition is true, given what is at stake in the decision problem.[71] To illustrate, consider the question whether the adjudicator has a categorical belief in guilt. In order to answer it, we need to assess the stakes; that is, the values of the possible outcomes of the decision problem whether to convict or to acquit. We then need to identify, on the basis of these values, the degree of belief in guilt that justifies acting as the adjudicator would act if they were certain that the defendant is guilty. Of course, since in any plausible value function—and surely in the deontologist's—convicting the guilty is better than acquitting the guilty, we must take it that 'acting as the adjudicator would act if they were certain that the defendant is guilty' means convicting. The question whether the adjudicator has a categorical belief in guilt can, thus, be rephrased as follows: does the adjudicator have a degree of belief in guilt that justifies convicting, given the values of the possible outcomes of the decision problem? The answer to this question is given precisely through identifying a decision-theoretic standard of proof:[72] a probability threshold such that when the probability of guilt is higher[73] than this threshold, conviction maximises expected value, given the relevant value function. Categorical belief in guilt, then, is the degree of belief in guilt represented by a probability of guilt that is higher than the decision-theoretic

[71] This view is tentatively endorsed in R. Nozick, *The Nature of Rationality* (Princeton University Press 1993), at 96–97. cf R. C. Stalnaker, *Inquiry* (MIT Press 1984), at 79–81. For more-recent defences, see B. Weatherson, 'Can we do Without Pragmatic Encroachment?' (2005) 19 Philosophical Perspectives 417, in particular at 434–436, and B. Weatherson, 'Knowledge, Bets, and Interests' in J. Brown and M. Gerken, *Knowledge Ascriptions* (OUP 2012), in particular at 86–90. See also S. Moss, *Probabilistic Knowledge* (OUP 2018), at 58–63, 206, distinguishing between a 'strict' and a 'loose' content of categorical belief, and stating that 'full belief strictly requires certainty, but loosely requires merely having credence that is close enough to certainty for practical purposes'. The third interpretation of categorical belief discussed in this section is expression of the theory of pragmatic encroachment. The most prominent claim of this theory is that the notion of 'knowledge' is 'interest-relative'. This means that the truth conditions for a knowledge utterance are not constituted exclusively by epistemic factors. Whether it is true that someone 'knows that *p*' can depend on the importance that getting the matter right has for the subject, thus on their practical interests involved. See J. Fantl and M. McGrath, 'On Pragmatic Encroachment in Epistemology' (2007) 75 Philosophy and Phenomenological Research 558; J. Stanley, *Knowledge and Practical Interests* (Clarendon Press 2005), 85–96, 179–182. This approach has also been taken towards other epistemic notions, such as 'reason for belief' (see J. Fantl and M. McGrath, 'Pragmatic Encroachment: It's Not Just About Knowledge' (2012) 9 Episteme 27), 'epistemic justification' (see J. Fantl and M. McGrath, 'Evidence, Pragmatics, and Justification' (2002) 111 Philosophical Review 67), and 'belief' itself (see Weatherson's works referenced earlier). And one of its proponents has claimed that 'all epistemic notions are interest-relative' (Stanley, ibid, at 182) in the sense expressed above.

[72] See D. A. Nance, 'Truth, Justification, and Knowledge in the Epistemology of Adjudication' in B. Zhang and S. Tong (eds), *Proceedings of the International Conference on Facts and Evidence* (China University of Political Science and Law Press 2018), at 128–130.

[73] But see the following note.

standard of proof. What about categorical belief in innocence? This is the degree of belief in innocence that justifies acquitting—that is, acting as the adjudicator would act if they were certain that the defendant is innocent—given the values of the possible outcomes of the decision problem. Because the probability of innocence is one minus the probability of guilt—in other words, innocence is the negation of guilt—categorical belief in innocence can be defined as the degree of belief *in guilt* represented by a probability *of guilt* that is lower than the decision-theoretic standard of proof.[74] Under this third interpretation of categorical belief, then, whenever the adjudicator knows that the defendant is guilty, conviction maximises expected value, since, according to the adjudicator, the probability of guilt is higher than the decision-theoretic standard of proof. And whenever the adjudicator knows that the defendant is innocent, acquittal maximises expected value, since, according to the adjudicator, the probability of guilt is lower than the decision-theoretic standard of proof. Similarly to what we have seen with the first interpretation, whenever the norm forbidding the punishment of a person who is known to be innocent applies—given the adjudicator's knowledge of innocence—the principle of maximising expected value demands acquittal; whenever the norm requiring the punishment of a person who is known to be guilty applies—given the adjudicator's knowledge of guilt—the principle demands conviction; whenever the norm allowing the punishment of a person who is known to be guilty applies, conviction is, indeed, the choice that maximises expected value, such that there is no suboptimal option left to the adjudicator. As with the previous two interpretations of categorical belief, according to the third, a deontologist adjudicator can follow the principle of maximising expected value without fearing a departure from the norms surveyed.[75]

In this section, I argued that, when none of the three deontological norms previously identified applies—due to the fact that the adjudicator lacks the relevant knowledge—a deontologist adjudicator *must* follow the principle of maximising

[74] As I will show in Chapter 4, when the probability of guilt equals the standard of proof, the adjudicator is indifferent between acquitting and convicting. Both acts maximise expected value. This means that the adjudicator is justified both in acting as they would act if they were certain that the defendant is guilty, and in acting as they would act if they were certain that the defendant is innocent. Hence, it would seem that, according to the third interpretation of categorical belief, the adjudicator would have both a categorical belief in guilt and a categorical belief in innocence. This is odd. After all, they cannot have a commitment, such as the commitment that is said to characterise categorical belief, to both a proposition and its negation (cf A. Amaya, 'Epistemic Ambivalence in Law' (2021) 31 Philosophical Issues 7). A corrective is, thus, needed to salvage the plausibility of the third interpretation. The corrective simply consists in denying that, when the probability of guilt equals the standard of proof, the adjudicator has a categorical belief in guilt, or in innocence. In such a case, therefore, the adjudicator does not have knowledge of guilt, nor of innocence. It seems hard to find similarly simple correctives to salvage the plausibility of the first two interpretations of categorical belief. A discussion of this point, though, falls beyond the scope of this work. See Chapter 4, n 12 for discussion of the role of the principle *in dubio pro reo* as a tiebreaker for cases in which the probability of guilt equals the standard of proof.

[75] For non-probabilistic interpretations of categorical belief, see Kaplan (n 69), ch 4; and Ho (n 70), at 130–135, 143–151.

expected value in relation to their particular value function, and that, when any of these norms applies, a deontologist adjudicator *can* follow this principle without fearing a departure from such a norm. This shows that, in all cases of uncertainty about the defendant's guilt, a deontologist adjudicator can follow the principle without relinquishing any tenets of their theory of punishment.[76] In fact, as the discussion of the first interpretation of 'categorical belief' indicates, this conclusion is also valid for cases of certainty, if any such cases exist.[77] I have already remarked on the fact that my arguments do not entail dismissing deontological norms as superfluous appendages of a theory of punishment. The role that they can play in thought experiments—such as that sketched in section 3.3, for instance—is, in itself, sufficient to show their importance. Moreover, I acknowledge that, in the decision problem of adjudication, it is these norms that, if applicable, indicate what the right answer[78] is for the adjudicator endorsing them: that the principle of maximising expected value is safe to follow for such adjudicator depends on the fact that the principle gives this answer. In other words, the deontological norms enjoy priority. Relatedly, someone may contend that, even if following these norms produces the same result as that produced by following the principle of maximising expected value, it matters to a deontologist adjudicator to see themselves as reaching this result for a reason, ie the applicable deontological norm, as opposed to another reason, ie the principle. I have no objection to this, other than saying that, given what I have shown, someone may well follow the principle of maximising expected value precisely as a means to stay true to the reasons represented by the deontological norms.

[76] Notice that my conclusions also apply to the case of the threshold deontologist, who accepts that a restriction or permission should be ignored when it requires or makes permissible, respectively, an action that is suboptimal from the perspective of (expected) value maximisation, and when the optimal alternative is sufficiently better than this action, so as to pass a given threshold of (expected) value. Indeed, I have shown that, whenever the restrictions or permissions discussed apply, the action that they, respectively, require or permit is also the optimal course of action. Therefore, the threshold deontologist does not face any choice between optimality and adherence to deontological norms.

[77] Let me elaborate. If the adjudicator were certain of innocence, acquittal would maximise expected value, given the value function of the deontologist. Certainty of innocence means having a categorical belief in innocence under any of the three interpretations of categorical belief surveyed. Hence, if the adjudicator endorsed the restriction against punishing someone who is known to be innocent, this restriction would apply under any of the three interpretations (assuming the other components of knowledge). Following the principle of maximising expected value would yield the same result as that produced by following this restriction. If the adjudicator were certain of guilt, conviction would maximise expected value given the value function of the deontologist. Certainty of guilt means having a categorical belief in guilt under any of the three interpretations surveyed. Hence, if the adjudicator endorsed the norm requiring the punishment of someone who is known to be guilty, this norm would apply under any of the three interpretations (assuming the other components of knowledge). Following the principle of maximising expected value would yield the same result as that produced by following this restriction. Should the adjudicator, instead, endorse the norm permitting the punishment of someone who is known to be guilty, this norm would apply under any of the three interpretations (assuming the other components of knowledge). Besides being permitted by this norm, conviction would also be the optimal option according to the principle of maximising expected value.

[78] In the case of a permission, in fact, there are potentially two right answers.

3.6 Different theories of punishment, different value functions

The upshot of my discussion so far is that a deontologist about punishment needs to conceive of the standard of proof as a decision rule for the maximisation of expected value; more precisely, a decision rule that sets the probability of guilt that must be met or surpassed for conviction to be the choice that maximises expected value.[79] This decision rule is necessary in cases of lack of knowledge about innocence or guilt: in these cases, the deontologist must rely on decision theory. In cases of knowledge about innocence or guilt, instead, the decision-theoretic standard of proof is unnecessary, insofar as the deontological norms already provide a decision rule; however, following the standard—that is, the principle of maximising expected value—yields the same result as that produced by following these norms. In the next chapter, I will show how a decision-theoretic standard of proof is identified.

Arguing that both deontologists and consequentialists about punishment should conceive of the standard of proof in decision-theoretic terms, though, does not mean that they should select the same standard of proof. Not only is it the case that deontologists may select a different standard from that selected by consequentialists; it is also the case that, within these families of theories of punishment, there may be significant variations in the standards of proof adopted by different theories. This is because each theory has its own value function: it may rank trial outcomes differently from other theories or, more likely, it may acknowledge smaller

[79] Someone may argue that I am being too fast here. Some deontologists have put forward justifications of the reasonable doubt standard relying on the values of trial outcomes (in fact, on the value of false conviction), but not on the principle of maximising expected value. See A. Stein, *Foundations of Evidence Law* (OUP 2005), at 172–178; and R. Kitai, 'Protecting the Guilty' (2003) 6 Buffalo Criminal Law Review 1163. Both works draw on R. Dworkin, *A Matter of Principle* (Clarendon Press 1985), ch 3. cf Y. Lee, 'Deontology, Political Morality, and the State' (2011) 8 Ohio State Journal of Criminal Law 385. I cannot do justice to these theories individually. It suffices to say that they each advance a version of the argument that, because false conviction is a serious wrong—to put it as Dworkin does (ibid, at 80), it inflicts a 'moral harm'—the State has a duty to do its best to avoid it, and that endorsing the reasonable doubt standard is required by the State's duty to do its best. It was convincingly shown that this argument cannot succeed. See Laudan, 'The Rules of Trial' (n 15), at 208–218; Walen, 'Proof Beyond a Reasonable Doubt' (n 9), at 376–377, 381–390; and Picinali (n 15), at 373–375. If the State had to do its best to protect the innocent from conviction, a more stringent standard than the reasonable doubt standard should be adopted, eg a standard of proof beyond any doubt, permitting unreasonable doubts to trump conviction. Also, the State should put in place a series of other measures to avoid false conviction, which would render true conviction a very unlikely prospect indeed. At a closer look, then, the 'maximalist' defenders of the reasonable doubt standard are, in fact, accepting that the State does not do its best (to protect the innocent from conviction) for the sake of having a realistic prospect of convicting the guilty. They are, in other words, accepting a trade-off between the possible outcomes of the trial, such that the prospect of producing a valuable outcome (true conviction) justifies the risk of producing a costly one (false conviction). If, however, the selection of the standard of proof is premised on this trade-off, then there is not a more convincing way of performing the trade-off than relying on decision theory and the principle of maximising expected value.

or greater intervals between the values of certain outcomes than those acknowledged by other theories. These differences affect the expected value of acquittal, and of conviction, in a given case, such that the choice that maximises expected value for one theory may not maximise it for another. As it will become clear in the next chapter, they also affect the identification of the probability threshold that indicates which of the two actions maximises expected value; that is, they affect the selection of the standard of proof.

In this section, I want to present three ways in which theories of punishment can differ in how they construct their respective value functions. These differences relate to the reasons that are relied upon by each theory in their assessment of trial outcomes. In presenting these differences, I will account for reasons—be these rights, duties, claims, principles, or values—that are considered central to prominent deontological theories of punishment. Before proceeding, though, I want to stress that these differences are irrelevant to the distinction between consequentialist and deontological theories of punishment, in light of the definitions that I have provided in section 3.3. Someone may well reject these definitions, and argue that what makes a deontological theory of punishment 'deontological' is (or is also) the way in which it assesses the values of outcomes, for example the reasons it relies upon, how it weighs them, and how it deals with conflicts between reasons.[80] This definitional disagreement need not detain us here. The important point, for my purposes, is that such redesigning of the distinction between consequentialist and deontological theories of punishment would not deny the conclusion that I have reached in the previous section: once the value function for any of these theories is built, following the principle of maximising expected value in the decision problem of adjudication does not involve relinquishing any tenets of the theory at issue. This is because the possible features of a theory of punishment that might have justified a departure from the principle of maximising expected value—that is, restrictions and permissions—have been shown not to produce such a departure, and the way in which a theory constructs its value function, even if considered constitutive of the theory's deontological nature, cannot produce such a departure either: the value function is simply the footing on which the principle operates. Consider, though, the caveat in section 3.6.4 below.

[80] See M. N. Berman, 'Punishment and Justification' (2008) 118 Ethics 258, arguing that retributivism is not consequentialist because, in the case of a guilty person, desert justifies punishment by 'cancelling' reasons against punishment (ie the fact that punishment inflicts suffering intentionally), rather than by overriding these reasons. But see Berman, 'Two Kinds of Retributivism' (n 40), arguing that the justification of punishment offered by retributivism has a consequentialist structure. cf Moore (n 34), at 155–156, suggesting that whether a retributivist is a consequentialist or a deontologist depends on whether they accept agent-centred norms that require, or authorise, a departure from the maximisation of value.

3.6.1 Recognising different reasons

To begin with, a theory of punishment may recognise a reason in the evaluation of trial outcomes that other theories do not recognise, such that, for the latter, this reason is irrelevant to the construction of their value functions. The obvious example is desert. In assessing the value of true conviction, a retributivist will factor in the intrinsic value of deserved punishment; in assessing the value of false conviction, they will factor in the intrinsic disvalue of undeserved punishment.[81] Those who do not recognise desert as a reason to punish the guilty,[82] and lack of desert as a reason not to punish the innocent, will not treat desert as a relevant consideration in constructing their value function; in particular, they will not treat its presence or absence as reasons to attribute certain values, respectively, to true and false conviction.[83]

A defender of a communicative theory of punishment may account for respect and/or dignity in the evaluation of true conviction. More precisely, they may consider that amongst the reasons that make true conviction valuable is the fact that it treats wrongdoers with the respect that is owed to them as members of the community; that is, as autonomous individuals who are bound by the community's norms, and must be 'called to account and censured' for their breaches of these norms.[84] Not everyone needs to recognise respect and dignity as reasons to attribute a certain value to true conviction, or to any other outcome, for that matter. To give an extreme example of this, anyone who argues that the sole justification for punishment is crime prevention would value true conviction exclusively as a function of how much crime prevention it produces, whether through deterrence or through incapacitation.

As far as crime prevention is concerned, most are likely to consider it a valuable aspect of true conviction. Some would accept that false conviction, too, is made more valuable by the fact that it contributes to preventing crimes, if indeed it does so contribute. There are, however, retributivists who would not consider crime prevention as a reason to be factored into the assessment of true or of false conviction, since they claim that only the 'immediate' or 'direct' consequences of acquittal or conviction should be taken into account as reasons for or against punishing, lest retributivism becomes consequentialist.[85] Of course, this

[81] Alternatively, the counterparts of these may be factored into the assessment of false acquittal and true acquittal, respectively. I say 'alternatively' because factoring desert into the assessment of both outcomes involving innocence, or of both outcomes involving guilt, would produce the problem of double counting explained in section 3.5.2.

[82] Indeed, most retributivists would also consider desert a necessary condition for punishing. This tenet is reflected in the three versions of retributivism mentioned in section 3.4 of this chapter. See also Walen, 'Retributive Justice' (n 39).

[83] See, eg Tadros (n 9), ch 4.

[84] See Duff (n 11), at 113. See also Ashworth and von Hirsch (n 11), at 18.

[85] See Reiman, in Reiman and van den Haag (n 9), at 231–232. Reiman seems to argue that taking into account non-immediate or indirect consequences would render retributivism consequentialist. I do not share the same understanding of the consequentialist/deontological divide, especially not in the case of theories of punishment, as shown by the distinction drawn in section 3.3.

position begs the questions of distinguishing between consequences that are immediate and consequences that are not,[86] and of explaining why only the former should matter under retributivism and deontological ethics. These issues, though, need not detain us here. A more articulated retributivist approach to the question whether crime prevention should be factored into the assessment of trial outcomes is found in Walen's decision-theoretic justification of the reasonable doubt standard.[87] According to Walen's retributivism, desert is a necessary condition for punishment. If so, the beneficial consequences of punishment, including crime prevention, may be treated as reasons to punish only if desert is present, lest punishing the innocent is condoned when doing so produces sufficient benefit.[88] This means that, for example, crime prevention may contribute to justifying punishing the deserving, but it may never contribute to—not to mention be sufficient to—justifying punishing the non-deserving. To put it in Walen's words, '[d]esert functions like a gate in the normative equivalent of a transistor: until it is switched on, the potentially greater normative force of the instrumental reasons is switched off'.[89] In order to implement the idea that desert is a necessary condition for punishment, Walen argues that desert must also play this transistor-like function in the evaluation of trial outcomes for the purposes of choosing the standard of proof. If it did not play this role, true and false conviction may be assigned high enough values on the basis of their beneficial consequences that convicting would maximise expected value, even in the presence of little evidence of guilt.[90] Thus, the beneficial consequences that punishment may produce should not be treated as reasons to attribute a certain value to true or false conviction; hence, they should be considered irrelevant to the construction of the retributivist's value function. Only once the standard has been identified on the basis of such value function, and once guilt has been proven to its satisfaction, can these consequences be treated as reasons to punish.[91]

Other considerations that not all theories of punishment may recognise as reasons in the evaluation of trial outcomes emerge from a diagnosis of the behaviour of the State when falsely acquitting or falsely convicting. In the case of false acquittal, the State may be seen to breach a duty to protect individuals from victimisation by the falsely acquitted. In the case of false conviction, instead, the State may be seen to breach a duty not to inflict harm on the innocent. A deontologist about morality may contend that, *ceteris paribus*, breaching a duty to prevent harm

[86] cf Broome (n 22), at 123–124.
[87] See Walen, 'Proof Beyond a Reasonable Doubt' (n 9).
[88] See Walen, 'Proof Beyond a Reasonable Doubt' (n 9), at 426–427. See also Husak, 'Why Punish the Deserving?' (n 47).
[89] Walen, 'Proof Beyond a Reasonable Doubt' (n 9), at 427.
[90] ibid.
[91] For a criticism of Walen's approach, see Picinali (n 15), at 385–387.

is not as serious a failure as breaching a duty not to harm. This view can be defended by appealing to a difference in strength between the correlative claims, respectively, to be aided and not to be harmed, the latter being the stronger. A theorist of punishment who is a deontologist about morality, then, may contend that there is a difference in the seriousness of the breaches that the State is responsible for in case of false outcomes, and that this difference should be reflected in the evaluation of false acquittal and false conviction.[92] A theorist of punishment who is a consequentialist about morality is unlikely to recognise this difference, instead focusing exclusively on the magnitude of the harms and benefits produced by the State falsely acquitting and falsely convicting.

3.6.2 Weighing reasons differently

The second way in which theories of punishment may differ in how they build their respective value functions concerns the weighing of reasons. Two theories may both recognise a particular reason in the assessment of trial outcomes, but weigh it differently. An example is offered by Duff's 'three Rs of punishment'. In Duff's communicative theory, punishment censures wrongdoing, but also aims at eliciting a qualified response from the wrongdoer; that is, their repentance, their reform, and their reconciliation with the victim.[93] True conviction promotes the three Rs, and this is clearly relevant in the assessment of this outcome by someone who shares Duff's views. In fact, it may be argued that even false acquittal can promote these goals, albeit less effectively, insofar as having a brush with justice can foster self-reflection and a feeling of guilt. Be that as it may, whoever considers crime prevention to be a reason for punishing is likely to value the promotion of the three Rs as well; hence, to recognise this promotion as a reason in the assessment of true conviction. After all, repentance, reform, and reconciliation mean that the recipient of punishment is less likely to commit a crime in the future. Still, someone who does not embrace the communicative aspect of Duff's theory will not value the

[92] For a discussion of this argument, see Walen, 'Proof Beyond a Reasonable Doubt' (n 9), at 390–394. The argument is patient-centred, in that it focuses on the perspective of those who are affected by the conduct of the State. It is the difference in the claims of these patients that justifies a different evaluation of the respective breaches committed by the State. Walen convincingly shows that a corresponding agent-centred argument relying on the distinction between doing harm and allowing harm could not successfully apply to the State. Under deontological morality, doing harm is considered worse than allowing harm to happen, because an agent has a strong claim not to have to sacrifice themselves for the sake of others. But since the State exists to serve the interests of its citizens, it is doubtful whether it can have such a claim when those at risk of harm are its citizens. Therefore, it is doubtful whether the State's doing harm to a citizen is worse than the State's allowing harm to happen to a citizen; *ceteris paribus*, then, the State's responsibility for failing to protect a citizen by falsely acquitting someone who later victimises this citizen should be similar to the State's responsibility for inflicting harm on an innocent citizen through conviction. For further discussion, see Picinali (n 15), at 377–379.

[93] See Duff (n 11), at 107–112.

promotion of the three Rs as much as Duff does. For Duff, the three Rs represent the means through which the wrongdoer can engage in the communicative enterprise initiated with punishment. They are, in themselves, the realisation of a desired appropriate interaction between the community and the wrongdoer, characterised by mutual respect and inclusion. Therefore, according to Duff's theory, their promotion is valuable beyond the fact that it fosters and foretells a diminution in crime.

3.6.3 Assigning a higher order to certain reasons

The third way in which theories of punishment can differ in how they build their respective value functions concerns the roles that they assign to reasons in the evaluation of trial outcomes. To clarify, two theories might both recognise two competing reasons in the assessment of trial outcomes, but one of the theories might assign orders to reasons, such that the higher-order reason should not be balanced with the lower-order competing reason in the assessment of one or more such outcomes. An example of this phenomenon concerns the problem of aggregation. Faced with the choice whether to save a person's life or to spare an arbitrarily high number of people from a headache that will leave each bedridden for a day, a deontologist about morality is likely to argue that, no matter how many people would be spared the headache, the right course of action is to save the person's life. The idea at the basis of this view is that there are claims (for example, to be spared a headache) that are simply irrelevant in the decision problem because they are too weak compared to the competing claims (for example, to have one's life saved). Therefore, it is not open to the agent to aggregate the former so as to outweigh the latter.[94] A possible way of understanding this notion of relevance is by considering a claim relevant if the bearer of that claim, faced with the choice whether to act in their self-interest or to satisfy the competing claim of another individual, would be morally permitted to do the former.[95] This test is non-aggregative in that it is applied to each claim individually and, once a claim is deemed irrelevant according

[94] See T. M. Scanlon, *What We Owe to Each Other* (Harvard University Press 1998), at 238–241; A. Voorhooeve, 'How Should We Aggregate Competing Claims?' (2014) 125 Ethics 64. In fact, the problem of aggregation does not exclusively concern the weighing of conflicting claims of different strengths coming from different people; it also concerns the weighing of conflicting claims of the same strength, where the number of people with a claim is greater than the number of those with the conflicting claim; and it concerns the weighing of intrapersonal claims. Those opposing aggregation in the second of these three cases maintain that numbers do not count. For discussion see Scanlon, ibid, at 229–241; F. M. Kamm, 'Aggregation and Two Moral Methods' (2005) 17 Utilitas 1; and M. Otsuka, 'Saving Lives, Moral Theory, and the Claims of Individuals' (2006) 34 Philosophy and Public Affairs 109. I doubt that the problems raised by the second and third cases could be relevant to the construction of the value function for adjudication of a theorist of punishment who is a deontologist about morality. But whether they are, indeed, relevant is for such a theorist of punishment to say.

[95] See Voorhooeve (n 94), at 72–73.

to the test, it simply drops out of the picture. Now, the choice whether to acquit or convict is of far greater complexity than the above hypothetical: its outcomes are not as clear-cut, and it is generally characterised by uncertainty as to which outcome will result from which action.[96] Still, in their evaluation of trial outcomes, a theorist of punishment may appeal to the resistance towards aggregation of deontological morality. Consider the value of false conviction. False conviction frustrates the claim of the innocent person not to be punished. Yet, it might satisfy other people's claims, including claims that the theorist in question may deem irrelevant in light of the above test. The victims' claims for closure offer a good example of claims of the irrelevant kind. After all, it is reasonable to argue that it would not be permissible for a victim to 'give themselves closure' at the cost of frustrating the innocent's claim not to be punished. If so, in assessing the value of false conviction, our theorist might want to ignore the fact that this outcome satisfies such competing irrelevant claims. No matter how many claims are satisfied by false conviction, if these claims are irrelevant when compared to the competing claim of the innocent defendant, their satisfaction should not increase the value of this outcome. Notice that, when it comes to assessing true conviction, the competition disappears since, arguably, the guilty defendant does not have a claim not to be punished. Hence the satisfaction of the victims' claims for closure, for instance, can be taken into account. This means that, for the theorist in question, such satisfaction counts as a reason in the construction of the value function—hence, in the decision problem of adjudication—even if it is not relevant to the assessment of a particular outcome: false conviction. Now, a theorist of punishment who is a consequentialist about morality is unlikely to frame the competition between reasons discussed here as a competition between frustrating or satisfying distinct claims or rights; surely, though, they would recognise that false conviction harms the innocent, while it may benefit others, including the victims. However, in the evaluation of false conviction, they would not assign to the harm done to the innocent an exclusionary role with respect to any of the benefits obtained by others. They would allow the benefits to outweigh the harm, if the aggregate of the former is sufficiently great.

Some may argue that what I have just presented (but see also the last paragraph of section 3.6.1 above) is not the example of a difference in the way of constructing the value function that is determined by a difference in the theories of punishment endorsed, respectively, by two decision-makers. Rather, here, the difference in the way of constructing the value function is determined by whether or not the decision-makers have a commitment—in this case, a commitment against aggregation—that can be part of their underlying moral outlook, yet does not contribute to an account of the justification of punishment; in other words, it is not part of a theory of

[96] For an elaborate discussion on how to deal with the problem of aggregation in decision-making under uncertainty, see Lazar, 'Limited Aggregation and Risk' (n 20).

punishment. I think this argument is mistaken. Consider that such a commitment has a bearing on the construction of the value function; the value function is necessary to identify the standard of proof; and the identification of the standard of proof is part of a theory of punishment, given that, as argued already in the Introduction to this chapter, the justification of punishment in any instance of adjudication depends on where the standard lies. It follows that the commitment in question, too, is part of the theory of punishment of whoever endorses it. Indeed, on a close look, a reason to increase or decrease the value of a trial outcome is a reason for or against punishment. There is nothing controversial, then, in holding that a theory of punishment includes any reason that affects its respective value function. One may have grounds to prefer a narrower conception of 'theory of punishment' than this. I believe that the disagreement between us would be nominal, and would not detract from the substantive point advanced here: the value function of two decision-makers may differ depending on the reasons that they rely upon in the evaluation of trial outcomes and on how they rely upon such reasons. Hence, the fact that they are both well-served by the principle of maximising expected value does not mean that they would decide cases in the same way.

3.6.4 A caveat

I have presented three ways in which theories of punishment may differ in their construction of their respective value functions. I do not claim that this is an exhaustive list of opportunities for differentiation. I hope, though, that it shows how it is possible to account for important differences between theories of punishment, even when all these theories effectively adhere to the principle of maximising expected value. The fact that both consequentialists and deontologists about punishment can follow this principle in adjudication surely does not mean that their theories are reduced to one; that if conviction is justified for one theory, then it is for the other; that all theories should choose the same standard of proof. The building of a value function offers plenty of scope for a theory to defend its singularity and further its commitments.[97]

[97] It may be argued that some or all trial outcomes—as bearers of value—are incomparable with one another, say because the values that inform the evaluation of an outcome are themselves incomparable with the values that inform the evaluation of another outcome. That two objects are incomparable means that it is not possible to hold that one is better than, worse than, or equal to the other, not to mention to represent them on a cardinal value function (see R. Chang, 'Introduction' in R. Chang (ed), *Incommensurability, Incomparability, and Practical Reason* (Harvard University Press 1997), at 4–7; and J. Griffin, 'Incommensurability: What's the Problem?' in Chang (ed), ibid, at 35–38). If the argument were sound, the decision-maker's preferences over the outcomes would violate the axiom of completeness, an axiom of rationality at the basis of standard decision theory, according to which the decision-maker must either prefer an object to another, or be indifferent between the two. However, it has been argued that incomparability does not preclude rational choice. See Chang, ibid, at 9; and N. Hsien, 'Is Incomparability a Problem for Anyone?' (2007) 23 Economics and Philosophy 65. Also, decision theorists have devised ways of dealing with incomparability. Whether these are successful is an

There is a caveat to make.[98] As shown in the discussion of Walen's retributive account of the standard of proof, a theory of punishment may treat something as a reason for or against punishing without also treating it as a reason in the construction of the value function; hence, in the problem of adjudication.[99] In Walen's retributivism, for example, crime reduction is a reason for punishing—albeit being 'switched off' until desert is present—but it is not also a reason for attributing a particular value to true or false conviction. Hence, it does not feature in the assessment of trial outcomes. This means that not everything that is of value to this theory of punishment is taken into account in the decision problem whether to convict or to acquit, notwithstanding that this decision problem is precisely about the distribution of punishment. In applying decision theory to address this problem, then, this theory of punishment is not maximising expected value *tout court*; rather, it is maximising the portion of expected value that the theory considers relevant to adjudication. One may call this portion expected *relevant* value. To be sure, that a theory of punishment only aims to maximise expected relevant value in adjudication does not affect my arguments in the remainder of the book. For these arguments to apply to any given theory, it does not matter if the theory leaves out of the value function something that it values about punishing or not punishing (I leave it to the supporters of such a theory to grapple with the potential incoherence of this choice). It only matters that, once the value function is built, the theory aims to maximise, or, at least, is well served by maximising, expected value as defined with exclusive regard to such function.

3.7 Concluding remarks

In this chapter, I have shown that, in the context of the adjudicator's problem whether to convict or acquit, both consequentialists and deontologists about punishment can follow the principle of maximising expected value without relinquishing any tenets of their respective theories. I have acknowledged that deontological restrictions and permissions may apply to this decision problem, but I have argued that, whenever any of them does apply, following the principle of maximising expected value gives the same answer as that given by following this

open question. See Peterson (n 2), at 183–190. It lies beyond the scope of this work to consider whether incomparability between values or concrete bearers of value does exist and, if so, whether it affects criminal adjudication.

[98] I am grateful to Antony Duff for pushing me to consider this point.

[99] To connect this to the point made at the end of the previous section, while any reason that affects the value function is part of the corresponding theory of punishment (it is, indeed, a reason for or against punishing), a theory of punishment may, apparently, recognise reasons for or against punishing without deeming them relevant to the construction of the value function.

deontological norm. I have also argued that, when such norms do not apply, the deontologist has nothing left to follow but the principle of maximising expected value. In drawing these conclusions, I am encouraged by the fact that a leading retributivist has relied on decision theory to identify the standard of proof that can serve the goals of his theory of punishment.[100]

Now, consider this variation on Jackson's hypothetical involving doctor Jill:

> Jill is a physician who has to decide on the correct treatment for her patient, John. John is experiencing symptoms that Jill suspects are being caused by a non-trivial health condition. She has only one medicine for that condition at her disposal. The medicine comes in pills and the maximum dose for an adult is one pill. Careful consideration of the literature has led her to the following conclusions: (a) If John has the condition, not giving him the pill means that the condition will gradually worsen. If he does not have the condition, not giving him the pill will make no difference to him; (b) If John has the condition, giving him the pill will cure him. If he does not have the condition, giving him the pill will cause severe side effects; finally, (c) if John has the condition, giving him half of the pill will substantially relieve the condition, but not cure it completely. If John does not have the condition, giving him half of the pill will cause only mild discomfort. Should Jill give John the pill, not give the pill, or give only half of it?

Obviously, the question cannot be answered without information about the probability that John has the condition. But the hypothetical is sufficient to trigger the intuition that there is a probability range such that, if the probability that John has the condition is above this range, expected value is maximised by giving him the whole pill; if the probability that John has the condition is below this range, expected value is maximised by not giving John the pill; and, crucially, if the probability that John has the condition is within this range, expected value is maximised by giving him only half of the pill. In other words, the intuition is that Jill's epistemic standpoint could be such that she should give John only half of the pill.

What if Jill was, in fact, the adjudicator in a criminal trial; if giving half of the pill and giving the full pill were two instances of hard treatment, the former being milder; if John was a defendant; and if the relevant probability concerned his

[100] See Walen, 'Proof Beyond a Reasonable Doubt' (n 9). Notably, Walen seems to support both the restriction against punishing someone who is known to be innocent and the permission to punish someone who is known to be guilty. See above, nn 39 and 49. He is, therefore, a deontologist about punishment, in light of the definition given earlier.

criminal responsibility? Does this alternative scenario not trigger a similar intuition?[101] In particular, does it not seem true that inflicting the milder hard treatment maximises expected value within a particular—if unspecified—range of the probability of guilt? In the next chapter, I will argue that, under certain conditions, this is, indeed, true.

[101] A notable difference between the scenario of Jill qua doctor and that of Jill qua adjudicator is that Jill's epistemic perspective in the former scenario is effectively the same as John's: at least once the patient has been informed of the probability that he has the relevant condition, of how this probability has been calculated, and of the evidential basis used for this calculus. In the latter scenario, instead, Jill's and John's epistemic perspectives are different in that John knows (possibly is certain of) whether he is responsible for the crime, whereas Jill may not have such knowledge (or certainty, for that matter). Hence, from John's epistemic perspective, the intermediate course of action is, inevitably, mistaken. The difference discussed here, though, is irrelevant for our purposes. In both scenarios, our focus is on the epistemic perspective of the decision-maker.

4
The Decision-Theoretic Case for Intermediate Criminal Verdicts

4.1 Introduction

In the previous chapter, I argued that both consequentialists and deontologists about punishment can employ decision theory to address the problem of adjudication in a binary verdict system, without relinquishing any tenets of their theories of punishment; hence, that it is open to both camps to understand the standard of proof as a decision rule for the maximisation of expected value. Indeed, I argued that both camps should understand the standard of proof in these terms, even though the decision-theoretic standard may be considered redundant by a deontologist if one of the surveyed deontological norms applies, thus giving them sufficient guidance.[1] In this chapter, I show how such a standard of proof is derived from a value function encompassing the possible outcomes of the adjudicator's decision problem. In order to do so, I rely on a decision-theoretic argument for the selection of the standard of proof in a binary system that has enjoyed considerable support within evidence law theory. The innovative contribution of this chapter consists in using this argument as the basis for formulating a decision-theoretic argument in defence of intermediate criminal verdicts. If I am right that both consequentialists and deontologists about punishment can employ the principle of maximising expected value in the context of adjudication, my justification of intermediate verdicts should be immune from a deontologist's complaint that it is consequentialist in nature. This justification should, indeed, be capable of building consensus across the divide between consequentialist and deontological theories of punishment.

According to the principle of maximising expected value, as applied in a binary verdict system, the adjudicator should convict if, and only if, doing so maximises expected value; otherwise, they should acquit. Consider the possibility of introducing an intermediate verdict, such that the adjudicator is required to choose this verdict when the probability of guilt falls within a certain range. This

[1] In fact, the same is true for a consequentialist-objectivist adjudicator when they have a belief as to which act, in fact, maximises value, such that they would choose this act on the basis of said belief without needing the (identical) guidance provided by the decision-theoretic standard of proof. See Chapter 3, section 3.3.

Justice In-Between, Federico Picinali, Oxford University Press. © Federico Picinali 2022.
DOI: 10.1093/oso/9780198864592.003.0005

addition would be justified if, and only if, expected value is indeed maximised by choosing the intermediate verdict when the probability of guilt falls within that range; in other words, it would be justified if, and only if, choosing the intermediate verdict in such epistemic circumstances yields higher expected value than acquitting and convicting. In this chapter, I identify the condition that is necessary and sufficient for it to be the case that there is a probability range such that choosing an intermediate verdict when the probability of guilt falls within that range maximises expected value. I call this the 'superiority condition', precisely because it is the condition at which the intermediate verdict is superior to both acquittal and conviction in terms of expected-value maximisation.[2]

As I explained in the previous chapter, in order to apply the principle of maximising expected value, the decision-maker needs to construct a value function; that is, a numerical scale where outcomes are arranged as a function of their value. More precisely, the value function must take the form of an interval scale.[3] This is a scale that reflects accurately not just the order of the outcomes as a function of their value (as an ordinal scale would), but also the difference in value between outcomes, such that we can say how much better an outcome is than another for the decision-maker.[4] The value function of a binary system of verdicts includes, exclusively, the values of the four standard outcomes: true conviction, false conviction, true acquittal, and false acquittal. With the addition of an intermediate verdict, the value function must also feature the values of the two intermediate outcomes: issuing the intermediate verdict when the defendant is innocent, and issuing the intermediate verdict when the defendant is guilty. The superiority condition concerns the respective positions that the values of the intermediate outcomes should have in the value function relative to the values of the standard outcomes. If, and only if, the values of the intermediate outcomes have the requisite positions, issuing the intermediate verdict maximises expected value when the probability of guilt falls within a particular range.

While I will speak in terms of intermediate verdicts *tout court*, the reader will be aware by now that the main challenge is to justify the issuing—hence, the introduction in the verdict system—of an intermediate verdict that infringes upon the status quo of innocence, this being the kind of intermediate verdict for which the presumption of innocence demands that sufficient reasons be given. As pointed

[2] Interestingly, many years ago Dennis Lindley made brief remarks suggesting that adopting the decision-theoretic approach to criminal fact-finding is conducive to adopting intermediate verdicts. See D. V. Lindley, 'Subjective Probability, Decision Analysis and their Legal Consequences' (1991) 154 Journal of the Royal Statistical Society: Series A (Statistics in Society) 83, at 88–89.

[3] See M. Peterson, *An Introduction to Decision Theory* (2nd edn, CUP 2017), at 101–102; R. Briggs, 'Normative Theories of Rational Choice: Expected Utility' in E. N. Zalta (ed), *Stanford Encyclopedia of Philosophy* (2017), at 14–15; and K. Steele and H. O. Stefánsson, 'Decision Theory' in E. N. Zalta (ed), *Stanford Encyclopedia of Philosophy* (2016), at 9.

[4] On the concept of 'interval scale' and the use of such scales in decision theory, see Peterson (n 3), at 22–28, 101–110. Everyday examples of interval scales are the Fahrenheit and Celsius temperature scales.

out in the conclusion to Chapter 2, I understand a verdict that involves[5] hard treatment to be a verdict that infringes upon the status quo of innocence accepted by our polity.[6] This understanding does not presuppose anything controversial about the content of such status quo. My justification of intermediate verdicts concerns, precisely, those verdicts that involve hard treatment. In particular, I will identify a specific intermediate verdict of this kind that has potential for being justified on decision-theoretic grounds under any theory of punishment to which my argument applies.

A final note to the reader, before proceeding: while understanding the formal arguments that I am about to put forward does not require any advanced mathematical skill, I appreciate that some readers may not have the time or the patience required to digest these arguments properly. These readers can jump directly to section 4.4.1. Needless to say, this choice comes at the cost of a less precise understanding of my justification of intermediate verdicts.

4.2 The decision-theoretic argument for the selection of the standard of proof in a binary system

The basis for my argument in defence of intermediate verdicts is the well-known decision-theoretic argument for the selection of the standard of proof in a binary system. To restate a definition given in the previous chapter, decision theory is a theory of decision-making according to which rationality requires that decision-makers follow the principle of maximising expected value.[7] A decision-theoretic standard of proof, then, is a decision rule such that the decision it prompts maximises expected value. In order to identify this standard of proof, we need to model the decision problem that the adjudicator faces in a binary system. This is done by identifying the acts that are open to the adjudicator in such a system; the relevant states of the world that, combined with the available acts, produce the possible outcomes of the decision problem; and, indeed, the possible outcomes.

A binary system features only the acts of acquitting and convicting. A state of the world is relevant to a decision problem insofar as it affects the decision-maker's preference amongst the available acts. The innocence and the guilt of the defendant

[5] Someone may doubt that a verdict that merely causes, rather than involves, hard treatment could be considered infringing. I will not address the issue here. On this distinction, see section 2 of the Introduction to the book.

[6] According to this understanding, then, a non-infringing intermediate verdict—should there be any such thing—cannot involve any hard treatment, not even in the form of causing social stigma. See chapter 2, section 2.2.1. On the justification of such intermediate verdicts see chapter 2, n 82. On the fact that such verdicts are still captured by the definition of 'intermediate verdict' given in the Introduction to the book, see chapter 2, n 81. See also n 98 below.

[7] This definition applies to 'normative' decision theory. 'Descriptive' decision theory, instead, aims at explaining and predicting how people actually make decisions. See Peterson (n 3), at 3.

are, therefore, relevant states in a reasonable adjudicator's choice whether to convict or acquit. While they are not the only states that are relevant to this choice,[8] the reason for focusing on them is that my goal is to identify the standard of proof. To clarify, it is to find out how the probabilities that these particular states of the world are true—in other words, the probability of guilt and, hence, that of its negation, innocence—should affect the adjudicator's preference amongst the available acts. If innocence and guilt are the salient states, then the possible outcomes of the decision problem are convicting the innocent (or false conviction), convicting the guilty (or true conviction), acquitting the innocent (or true acquittal), and acquitting the guilty (or false acquittal).[9] Matrix 1 illustrates the relationship between the acts, the states of the world, and the outcomes for adjudication in a binary system.

State / Act	Innocence	Guilt
Conviction	*Convicting the innocent (ci)*	*Convicting the guilty (cg)*
Acquittal	*Acquitting the innocent (ai)*	*Acquitting the guilty (ag)*

Matrix 1

The principle of maximising expected value enjoins the decision-maker to choose the act with highest expected value. It is worth repeating here the few bits of information that I gave in the previous chapter concerning the notion of 'expected value'. The expected value of an act is the sum of the expected values of the act's possible outcomes. Thus, the expected value of convicting is the sum of the expected values of convicting the innocent and convicting the guilty; the expected value of acquitting, instead, is the sum of the expected values of acquitting the innocent and acquitting the guilty. The expected value of an outcome is calculated by multiplying

[8] For instance, irrespective of whether the defendant is innocent or guilty, the adjudicator's choice may be affected by whether conviction has a deterrent effect, insofar as the adjudicator values such an effect. These additional relevant states of the world are still featured in the proposed model of the decision problem. Indeed, as seen in the previous chapter, they are factored into the evaluation of trial outcomes. For instance, someone who values deterrence and believes that conviction has a deterrent effect—at least, if it is not known that the defendant is innocent—would consider both convicting the innocent and convicting the guilty more valuable than they would be in the absence of such an effect.

[9] One may understand the outcomes of a decision problem as all-encompassing states of affairs; more precisely, as possible worlds that are equal to one another, except for the distinctive combination of act and state characterising each of them (and the distinctive consequences of such combination). The model of the decision problem only highlights the features of the possible world constituting an outcome that are relevant to the problem. See Peterson (n 3), at 23.

the outcome's value and the probability of the outcome occurring, given the relevant act; that is, the probability of the state of the world that, combined with the relevant act, yields the outcome.[10] For example, the expected value of convicting the innocent is given by multiplying the value of this outcome and the probability of innocence; the expected value of convicting the guilty is given by multiplying the value of this outcome and the probability of guilt, and so on. Once the expected value of each act has been calculated, the decision-maker is in a position to choose between them. The following inequality expresses the condition for conviction to be warranted under decision theory:

$$p \cdot V_{cg} + (1-p) \cdot V_{ci} \geq p \cdot V_{ag} + (1-p) \cdot V_{ai} \qquad (1)$$

where p is the probability of guilt, $1-p$ is the probability of its negation, innocence, V_{cg} is the value of convicting the guilty, V_{ci} is the value of convicting the innocent, V_{ag} is the value of acquitting the guilty, and V_{ai} is the value of acquitting the innocent. Thus, conviction is warranted if, and only if, the expected value of convicting, expressed by the first part of the inequality, is equal to, or higher than, the expected value of acquitting, expressed by the second part.[11] This is the same as saying that the adjudicator is permitted to convict if, and only if, convicting maximises expected value.

I am now able to clarify the notion of 'decision-theoretic standard of proof'. This is the probability of guilt at which the expected value of convicting is equal to the expected value of acquitting, such that both acts are permissible.[12] When

[10] Notice that innocence and guilt, ie the relevant states of the world, are probabilistically dependent on the acts of convicting, and of acquitting. To see this, consider that, insofar as the adjudicator aims at convicting the guilty and acquitting the innocent, and insofar as they decide on the basis of the available evidence rather than haphazardly, their choice to convict is indicative of guilt, while their choice to acquit is indicative of innocence. Whether or not this probabilistic dependence needs to be accounted for in calculating the probability of the states of the world depends on whether one endorses 'evidential' decision theory or 'causal' decision theory. According to the former, for the purposes of decision-making the probability of a state should reflect the fact that the act is evidence of the state, if indeed the act is so. Thus, the probability of the state should consist in the conditional probability of the state, given the act. According to the latter, instead, the probabilistic dependence of the state on the act should matter only if it registers a causal influence between the act and the state. This is the approach that is followed in the decision-theoretic argument for the selection of the standard of proof in a binary system. Since the acts of convicting, and of acquitting, do not cause the state of innocence or the state of guilt, a causal decision theorist would not reflect said probabilistic dependence in their assessment of the probability of these states. See Peterson (n 3), ch 9; P. Weirich, *Realistic Decision Theory: Rules for Nonideal Agents in Nonideal Circumstances* (OUP 2004), at 28–30, 208–210; and Briggs (n 3), at 4–9.

[11] See the following note for an objection to the claim that conviction is permissible when it yields the same expected value as acquittal.

[12] Someone may object that the permissibility of both acquittal and conviction when they yield equal expected value runs counter to the long-standing principle *in dubio pro reo*. According to this principle, in a situation of doubt between options, the adjudicator should choose the option that is less detrimental to the defendant. If the expected value of convicting is the same as that of acquitting, the principle *in dubio pro reo* would seem to demand that the apparent impasse be overcome by acquitting the defendant. A defiant reply to this objection is to say that, if someone endorses the principle of maximising expected value, it necessarily follows that they should be indifferent between options that maximise expected value, and that if this means departing from the principle *in dubio pro reo*, so be it.

the probability of guilt p is higher than the standard of proof, the expected value of convicting is greater than that of acquitting; hence, the adjudicator should convict. When p is lower than the standard of proof, the reverse is true; hence, the adjudicator should acquit.[13] To recapitulate, while conviction is warranted if, and only if, p is equal to, or higher than, the standard of proof, it is obligatory in the latter case. As shown in the Appendix, it is possible to derive from (1) above the formula expressing the standard of proof, or p^*:

$$p^* = \frac{1}{1+\dfrac{V_{cg}-V_{ag}}{V_{ai}-V_{ci}}} \tag{2}$$

This formula, which has enjoyed considerable support in the evidence law scholarship,[14] shows that the standard of proof is derived from the values of the four possible outcomes of the trial. More precisely, it shows that the key variables that determine the standard of proof are the difference between the values of the outcomes involving guilt and the difference between the values of the outcomes involving innocence. This is why, as mentioned in the previous chapter, it is important that these differences are accurately reflected in the value function.

In this chapter, and especially in the previous chapter, I have frequently said, or hinted at the idea, that the adjudicator is the decision-maker in the context of the choice whether to convict or acquit. Even though my defence of intermediate

There is, however, a more conciliatory reply, suggesting that the problem should not be overstated. It would be possible to complement the decision-theoretic standard of proof with a rule that implements the principle *in dubio pro reo* for cases of indifference between conviction and acquittal. While not an implication of decision theory, this rule would not be in conflict with it, since choosing acquittal in such cases would still maximise expected value. The additional rule could be seen as a tiebreaker of sorts, not inspired by the consideration of the expected values of acquitting and convicting, respectively, since these are, by hypothesis, equal, but possibly by considerations of mercy, and by the value of dealing consistently with cases of indifference across the system.

[13] In fact, the accuracy of these considerations depends on the ordering of the values of the outcomes. They are accurate under the two plausible orderings discussed later in this section. For a brief discussion of alternative, but implausible, orderings, see n 19 below.

[14] In a seminal article from 1968, John Kaplan presented a simplified version of the formula, including just the values of the false outcomes. See J. Kaplan, 'Decision Theory and the Factfinding Process' (1968) 20 Stanford Law Review 1065, at 1071–1077. Later works have convincingly criticised the omission of the values of the true outcomes from the formula. See M. L. Dekay, 'The Difference Between Blackstone-Like Error Ratios and Probabilistic Standards of Proof' (1996) 21 Law and Social Inquiry 95, at 115–117 and L. Laudan and H. D. Saunders, 'Rethinking the Criminal Standard of Proof: Seeking Consensus about the Utilities of Trial Outcomes' (2009) 7 International Commentary on Evidence 1, at 12–19. The complete version of the formula has been relied upon in a number of influential works on the standard of proof, including E. Lillquist, 'Recasting Reasonable Doubt: Decision Theory and the Virtues of Variability' (2002) 36 UC Davis Law Review 85, at 104–111; D. Hamer, 'Probabilistic Standards of Proof, their Complements and the Errors that are Expected to Flow from Them' (2004) 1 University of New England Law Journal 71, at 81–87; and D. A. Nance, *The Burdens of Proof: Discriminatory Power, Weight of Evidence, and Tenacity of Belief* (CUP 2016), at 21–42.

verdicts does not hinge on whether this characterisation of the adjudicator is accurate, I pause here to assess it briefly in the light of what we have just learnt about the decision-theoretic standard of proof. Indeed, in the next chapter I will rely on the few considerations that I am about to make. The choice between conviction and acquittal is a decision problem with a peculiar structure, in that it features a sort of split agency. I contend that it is for the legislator to attribute a value to each of the four outcomes of the trial and, therefore, to identify an appropriate standard of proof on the basis of such values, as directed by formula (2) above. Indeed, it is sensible to argue that such decisions should not be delegated to the adjudicator.[15] This is partly because the evaluation of the outcomes and the concomitant selection of the standard of proof are the sort of delicate decisions that we should want to result from an informed political and public debate (also remember that the construction of the value function depends on which theory of punishment is endorsed, a decision that should itself result from such a debate), and partly because translating these decisions into laws of general applicability is a necessary means to protect the equal treatment of defendants, a value that is essential for criminal justice, and which may easily be undermined if such decisions were instead in the province of each individual adjudicator.[16] However, it is the adjudicator who calculates the probability of guilt in the individual case, assesses whether the standard of proof has been satisfied, and, consequently, convicts or acquits the defendant. Given this division of labour, then, it is fair to say that the decision-maker is really the legislator. By constructing the value function and selecting the standard of proof, the legislator is vicariously deciding each individual case. The adjudicator's task is largely theoretical rather than practical:[17] they have to assess the probability of guilt. Their ensuing action does not presuppose a decision on their part, aside from the decision whether or not to follow the legislator's directives. In the light of these considerations, my references in the previous chapter to the theory of punishment endorsed by the adjudicator as being determinative of the applicable value function, hence of the result of adjudication, should be understood as references to the theory of punishment endorsed by the true decision-maker, ie the legislator.

[15] By saying this, I am not also claiming that the standard of proof should not vary depending on the relevant characteristics of the case. The legislator may justifiably choose different standards of proof for different types of case. I will return to this question in the next chapter.

[16] Kaplan's view, instead, was that the jury should be in charge of attributing values to the trial outcomes and, hence, of selecting the standard of proof: see Kaplan (n 14), at 1073–1077. Both Lillquist (n 14), at 147–176, and Nance (n 14), at 41–42, 252, argue that the jury should be able to make minor adjustments to the values previously expressed by the legislator. In fact, they both accept—indeed, welcome— the fact that the standard of proof may vary depending on the circumstances of the case, an issue that I will address in the next chapter. A similar view is expressed in R. D. Bartels, 'Punishment and the Burden of Proof in Criminal Cases: A Modest Proposal' (1981) 66 Iowa Law Review 899, at 905–910. A similar view to mine, instead, is defended by Mike Redmayne with respect to civil cases in M. Redmayne, 'Standards of Proof in Civil Litigation'(1999) 62 Modern Law Review 167, at 183–184.

[17] As explained in the previous chapter, in conceptualising the choice whether to acquit or to convict, I am not considering the legal-interpretive work involved in adjudicating.

Before moving to my defence of intermediate verdicts, it is worth clearing the path of a tempting objection to the decision-theoretic argument for selecting the standard of proof in a binary system. As I have shown, the argument identifies the standard starting from the values of the possible outcomes of the decision problem. Someone may object that the values of the possible outcomes of conviction depend on the probability of guilt. In particular, they may claim that the lower the probability on which the adjudicator bases their decision to convict, the worse the conviction is, whether true or false. This claim can be defended by considering that: (a) the lower the probability of guilt is, the greater is the risk of false conviction that the adjudicator is willing to impose on the defendant by convicting them; and (b) the greater is the risk of false conviction that the adjudicator is willing to impose, the lower is the degree of respect for the defendant's rights displayed in the decision; hence, the lower is the value of the conviction.[18] The decision-theoretic argument, however, treats the values of outcomes as fixed inputs that do not vary as a function of the probability of guilt. This, the objection contends, is a serious inaccuracy.

The objection begs the question of what degree of risk of false conviction it is acceptable to impose on the defendant by convicting them. Until we have answered this question, we are not in a position to tell whether the risk imposed does, indeed, make the outcomes of conviction worse: only the imposition of an unacceptable risk will make these outcomes worse than they would have been without considering the risk imposed. Setting the standard of proof, though, is precisely the way in which this question is addressed and answered. Indeed, by identifying the range of the probability of guilt that warrants conviction, the standard of proof identifies the degree of risk of false conviction that it is acceptable to impose on the defendant by convicting them. Convicting an individual when the probability of guilt does not meet the standard of proof imposes on them an unacceptable risk of error, which arguably reduces the value of their conviction, whether true or false. Until the standard is set, though, we are not in a position to tell whether the risk imposed by convicting is unacceptable and should, therefore, influence the evaluation of the outcome. This is why, during the process

[18] cf L. H. Tribe, 'Trial by Mathematics: Precision and Ritual in the Legal Process' (1971) 84 Harvard Law Review 1329, at 1381–1383. A similar, although less intuitive, argument can be made with respect to acquittals. Some may argue that the greater the probability of guilt on which the adjudicator bases their decision to acquit, the worse the acquittal is, whether true or false. This is because: (a) the greater the probability of guilt is, the greater the risk of victimisation by the defendant that the adjudicator is willing to impose on third parties by acquitting the defendant; and (b) the greater the risk of victimisation that the adjudicator is willing to impose on third parties is, the lesser the respect for the third parties' rights displayed in the decision, hence the lower the value of the acquittal is. Of course, this argument depends on the existence of a significant recidivism rate, and on the fact that punishment would have an incapacitating effect; hence, that it would actually prevent the victimisation that acquittal, instead, would allow.

of setting the standard of proof, the values of the possible outcomes of conviction are not affected by the probability of guilt.

4.3 The superiority condition

In order to identify the superiority condition, there is no need to flesh out the value function corresponding to the choice whether to convict or to acquit; that is, there is no need to arrange the values of the four standard outcomes in an interval scale. The superiority condition, though, is valid only for some orderings of the values of these outcomes. I explained in the previous chapter that the value functions corresponding to different theories of punishment may differ significantly: for instance, they may feature different intervals between the outcomes' values. However, each of these value functions is compatible with my defence of intermediate verdicts insofar as it reflects one of the orderings on which the superiority condition is premised.

It is unnecessary to discuss all the orderings for which the superiority condition is valid. It suffices to say that it is valid under the only two orderings that I consider plausible.[19] I briefly touched upon these orderings in the previous chapter, when discussing the possible value function of a theorist of punishment endorsing any of the deontological norms that I studied there. The first ordering is that according to which convicting the innocent is the worst outcome, convicting the guilty is the best, and acquitting the guilty is worse than acquitting the innocent. Thus, the ordering is $V_{cg} > V_{ai} > V_{ag} > V_{ci}$.[20] The second ordering is the permutation where, other things being equal, the value of acquitting the innocent is the highest in the value function, and the value of convicting the guilty is the second highest. Thus,

[19] After reading this section, and with the help of Fig. 4.1, one notices that the superiority condition is valid under all the orderings of the values of the standard outcomes which are such that there is an intersection between the line representing the expected value of convicting, and that representing the expected value of acquitting. Thus, the condition is valid with the orderings $V_{cg} > V_{ag} > V_{ai} > V_{ci}$, $V_{ag} > V_{cg} > V_{ci} > V_{ai}$, $V_{ai} > V_{ci} > V_{cg} > V_{ag}$, and $V_{ci} > V_{ai} > V_{ag} > V_{cg}$. Needless to say, all of these orderings are highly implausible, because they rank V_{ci} too high, or because they rank V_{ai} too low. The condition is also valid with the orderings $V_{cg} > V_{ai} > V_{ci} > V_{ag}$ and $V_{ai} > V_{cg} > V_{ci} > V_{ag}$—both implausible orderings, since they consider V_{ci} greater than V_{ag}—and with the orderings $V_{ag} > V_{ci} > V_{ai} > V_{cg}$, $V_{ag} > V_{ci} > V_{cg} > V_{ai}$, $V_{ci} > V_{ag} > V_{cg} > V_{ai}$, and $V_{ci} > V_{ag} > V_{ai} > V_{cg}$, all implausible orderings given the high ranking of V_{ci} and the low ranking of V_{cg}. Instead, the condition is not valid under the eight permutations, such as $V_{ci} > V_{cg} > V_{ag} > V_{ai}$, where the values of both possible outcomes of convicting, or of acquitting, are the two greatest or the two smallest, nor is it valid under the four permutations, such as $V_{cg} > V_{ag} > V_{ci} > V_{ai}$, where the two greatest or smallest values concern outcomes both involving guilt, or both involving innocence, and the values of outcomes involving conviction alternate in the ordering with those involving acquittal. In such cases, there would be no intersection between the lines representing the expected value of convicting and of acquitting, thus no standard of proof. The adjudicator should always convict or acquit, depending on which line is higher; in other words, the verdict system would not be binary, since it would countenance only one verdict. This is a highly implausible state of affairs.

[20] This ordering has been defended by Laudan and Saunders (n 14), at 24–29, and adopted as plausible by Tribe (n 18), at 1379.

the ordering is $V_{ai} > V_{cg} > V_{ag} > V_{ci}$.[21] The plausibility of these orderings resides in their reflecting the reasonable views that false outcomes are less valuable than true outcomes, and that, of the two false outcomes, convicting the innocent is worse than acquitting the guilty. In the previous chapter, I explained why I prefer the first ordering to the second, and I will not rehearse those arguments here. While the superiority condition is valid under both orderings, for the sake of simplicity I will work mainly with the ordering according to which the best outcome is the conviction of the guilty.

Figure 4.1 provides a visualisation of the decision-theoretic argument for the selection of the standard of proof in a binary system, which I presented in the previous section.[22]

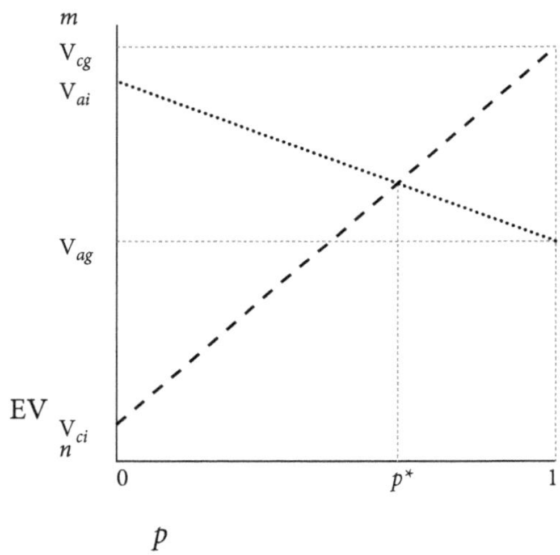

Figure 4.1 Visualisation of the decision-theoretic argument for the selection of the standard of proof in a binary verdict system

Expected value is measured on the vertical axis, whereas the probability of guilt is measured on the horizontal axis. The thick dashed line represents the expected value of convicting, while the dotted line represents the expected value of acquitting. Indeed, the expected value of each act is a linear function of the probability of guilt (consider that the expected value of convicting, for instance, can also be expressed as $f(p) = p(V_{cg} - V_{ci}) + V_{ci}$, a formula that fits the form of a linear function).

[21] This permutation is defended somewhat dogmatically by Patricia G. Milanich in her 'Decision Theory and Standards of Proof' (1981) 5 Law and Human Behavior 87, at 90–92.

[22] Similar graphs have been used previously in Dekay (n 14), at 113; Hamer, 'Probabilistic Standards of Proof' (n 14), at 84; and Laudan and Saunders (n 14), at 7, 31.

The intersection between the two lines, ie the point at which the expected value of convicting equals that of acquitting, occurs at the probability of guilt p^*, which represents the standard of proof. At probabilities of guilt greater than p^* the thick dashed line is higher than the dotted line: the principle of maximising expected value requires conviction. At probabilities of guilt smaller than p^* the reverse is true, thus the adjudicator should acquit. Finally, when the probability of guilt equals p^*, both acquittal and conviction maximise expected value; hence, they are both permissible.

While the lines represent expected value, their end points identify the values of the four outcomes. Indeed, when the probability of guilt is one, the expected value of convicting, and that of acquitting, equal the values of convicting the guilty, and of acquitting the guilty, respectively. When, instead, the probability of guilt is zero—hence, that of innocence is one—the expected value of convicting, and that of acquitting, equal the values of convicting the innocent, and of acquitting the innocent, respectively. The four values are reported on the vertical axis, so as to offer a visual representation of the value function on which the argument is premised. As can be seen, the ordering of the outcomes' values is one of the two plausible orderings identified earlier.

Visualising the decision-theoretic argument for the selection of the standard of proof in a binary system is instrumental to identifying the condition for the superiority of an intermediate verdict. In order to identify this condition, though, I must first clarify the notion of the *intermediacy* of a verdict. In referring to a verdict as 'intermediate' between acquittal and conviction, I mean a verdict such that: (a) the value of issuing it when the defendant is innocent—a value that I will express as V_{ii}—must fall between the value of acquitting the innocent and the value of convicting the innocent; and (b), the value of issuing it when the defendant is guilty—a value that I will express as V_{ig}—must fall between the value of acquitting the guilty and the value of convicting the guilty. I will add more flesh to this definition in section 4.4.1 below, but an intuitive way of capturing it for present purposes is to say that intermediacy requires that the verdict be less severe a measure than conviction, but more severe a measure than acquittal. As the reader will have noticed, this requirement restates one of the two 'dimensions' of intermediacy mentioned in the Introduction of the book. It will soon become clear that the intermediacy of a verdict, as just defined, makes it the case that if the verdict is superior to—and, therefore, should be issued instead of—acquittal and conviction at a particular range of the probability of guilt, this range must fall between the range of the probability of guilt at which acquittal is superior to the alternatives and the range of the probability of guilt at which conviction is superior to the alternatives. In other words, the evidential basis of a superior intermediate verdict is more robust than the evidential basis of 'not guilty', but less robust than the evidential basis of the 'guilty' verdict. As the reader will have noticed, this requirement restates the other 'dimension' of intermediacy mentioned in the Introduction of the book.

Matrix 2 illustrates the relationship between the acts, the states of the world, and the outcomes, in a verdict system including an intermediate verdict.

Act \ State	Innocence	Guilt
Conviction	*Convicting the innocent (ci)*	*Convicting the guilty (cg)*
Intermediate verdict	*Issuing the intermediate verdict against the innocent (ii)*	*Issuing the intermediate verdict against the guilty (ig)*
Acquittal	*Acquitting the innocent (ai)*	*Acquitting the guilty (ag)*

Matrix 2

As seen earlier, in a binary system the adjudicator should acquit the defendant when the probability of guilt is lower than the standard of proof, either convict or acquit when the probability of guilt equals the standard of proof,[23] and convict when the probability of guilt is higher than the standard of proof. In Figure 4.2

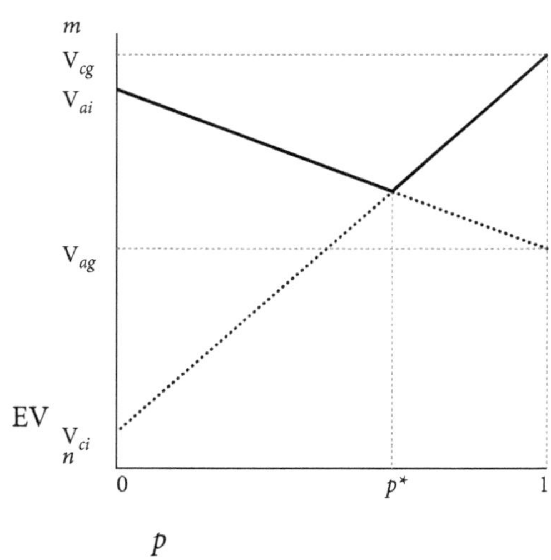

Figure 4.2 The ceiling of a binary verdict system

[23] See n 12 above.

below, the solid broken line represents the expected value of this strategy. I call this line the 'ceiling' of the verdict system, since it sets the limits of the system with respect to the maximisation of expected value. In other words, given the available verdicts, at any value of the probability of guilt the adjudicator cannot realise higher expected value than that represented by the ceiling of the system they are working with.

An intermediate verdict is superior to acquittal and conviction at any value of the probability of guilt if, and only if, the expected value of issuing the verdict is represented by a line that is higher than the ceiling of the relevant binary system at any such probability value. If the expected value of the verdict is so represented, then, issuing the verdict maximises expected value at some value of the probability of guilt. By looking at Figure 4.3 below, one appreciates that the line representing the expected value of issuing the intermediate verdict is higher than the ceiling of the binary system at any value of the probability of guilt if, and only if, such line is higher than this ceiling when the probability of guilt equals the standard of proof p^*. This is due to the intermediacy of the verdict. Consider that if V_{ii} were greater than V_{ai}, and V_{ig} were smaller than V_{ag}, or if V_{ii} were smaller than V_{ci}, and V_{ig} were greater than V_{cg}, the line corresponding to the additional, non-intermediate, verdict could be higher than the ceiling of the binary system at some value of the probability of guilt without being higher than this ceiling at p^*.[24] Given intermediacy, we can ignore this possibility.[25] Thus, we can conclude that an intermediate verdict is superior to acquittal, and to conviction, at any value of the probability of guilt if, and only if, *the expected value of issuing the verdict is represented by a line that is higher than the ceiling of the relevant binary system when the probability of guilt equals the standard of proof* p^*. This is a verbal formulation of the superiority condition. The condition can also be expressed with the following inequality:

$$p^* \cdot V_{ig} + (1 - p^*) \cdot V_{ii} > p^* \cdot V_{cg} + (1 - p^*) \cdot V_{ci} \quad (3)$$

The left-hand side of the inequality expresses the expected value of issuing the intermediate verdict when the probability of guilt equals p^*. The right-hand side of the inequality expresses the expected value of convicting when the probability of guilt equals p^*; but also, it expresses the expected value of acquitting with such probability of guilt, since, as seen earlier, the two values are equal. An intermediate

[24] Notice that if, for example, V_{ii} were greater than V_{ai}, and V_{ig} were equal to, or greater than, V_{ag}; or if V_{ig} were greater than V_{cg}, and V_{ii} were equal to, or greater than, V_{ci}, then the (non-intermediate) verdict would always satisfy the superiority condition, and would, effectively, supersede one, or both, of the standard verdicts.

[25] Notice that, if the verdict system were to incorporate a (superior) verdict such as the ones just hypothesised, the system would, effectively, be adding this verdict as a new extreme option in the choice set. Since my focus in this book is on intermediate options, I will not explore this possibility further.

verdict is superior to acquittal, and to conviction, if, and only if, inequality (3) above is verified: the expected value of issuing the intermediate verdict at p^* is greater than the expected value of convicting at p^*. Although I have been working with the ordering of the values of the standard outcomes according to which $V_{cg} > V_{ai} > V_{ag} > V_{ci}$, my argument works just as well with the plausible permutation whereby, other things being equal, V_{ai} is greater than V_{cg}. With the help of the figures, one easily notices that, given intermediacy, even under this permutation the line representing the expected value of issuing the intermediate verdict is higher than the ceiling of the relevant binary system at some value of the probability of guilt if, and only if, it is higher than this ceiling at p^*. Hence, the superiority condition is also valid with this alternative ordering.

Let us take stock. The starting point of my analysis is a binary system of verdicts characterised by a plausible ordering of the values of the standard trial outcomes; that is, either $V_{cg} > V_{ai} > V_{ag} > V_{ci}$ or $V_{ai} > V_{cg} > V_{ag} > V_{ci}$. The next step is to conceive of a verdict that is intermediate between acquittal and conviction, in the sense of 'intermediate' explained earlier. This intermediate verdict is superior to both acquittal and conviction within a certain range of the probability of guilt if, and only if, the expected value of issuing this verdict at p^* is greater than the expected value of acquitting (or of convicting) at p^*. Figure 4.3 visualises an intermediate verdict that satisfies the superiority condition, superimposed on a binary verdict system.

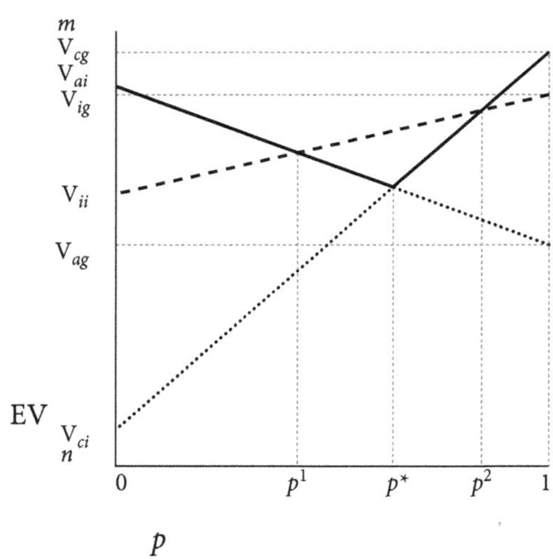

Figure 4.3 Visualisation of an intermediate verdict that satisfies the superiority condition, superimposed on a binary verdict system

The thick dashed line represents the expected value of issuing the intermediate verdict. The expected value of this act, too, is a linear function of the probability of guilt and the end points of the line identify, respectively, the value of issuing the intermediate verdict against the innocent, and the value of issuing the intermediate verdict against the guilty. The two intersections between the solid broken line and the thick dashed line identify p^1 and p^2, the two standards of proof that would be operative, instead of p^*, if the intermediate verdict were available. Given the additional option, the strategy for the adjudicator is as follows: they should acquit the defendant when the probability of guilt is lower than p^1, they should issue the intermediate verdict when the probability of guilt is between p^1 and p^2, and they should convict when the probability of guilt is higher than p^2. At a probability of guilt equal to p^1, both acquitting and issuing the intermediate verdict are permissible; at a probability of guilt equal to p^2, both issuing the intermediate verdict and convicting are permissible.[26]

Of course, one may countenance adding to the system a second intermediate verdict. In the Appendix, I identify and formalise the superiority condition for such an additional verdict. A similar assessment to that undertaken in the Appendix can be carried out for yet further intermediate verdicts to be added to the system. In this work, though, I limit my analysis to the adoption of a single intermediate verdict. This choice needs explaining. After all, one may ask, is the logical endpoint of my analysis not represented by a truly analogue system of verdicts where every increase in the probability of guilt is accompanied by a change in—in particular, by an increase in the severity of—the verdict that is issued against the defendant?[27] Is it not possible to replicate indefinitely—indeed, infinitely—the steps that I have followed to identify the superiority condition so as to identify superiority conditions for an ever-increasing number of intermediate verdicts?

My decision to stop at the addition of a single intermediate verdict is justified by two considerations. First, and most importantly, my main goal in this book is to challenge the dogma that criminal verdicts have to be binary; that *tertium non datur* when it comes to criminal adjudication. To this end, it is sufficient for me to defend the addition of one intermediate verdict to the system. I leave it to others to consider whether further verdicts should be added, and I hope that my work can serve as a basis for theirs. Second, if someone endorses my decision-theoretic argument, they will agree that justifying systems with more than one intermediate verdict

[26] On the possible role of the principle *in dubio pro reo* as a tiebreaker in these cases, see n12 above.

[27] In a recent article, Mark Spottswood has defended a similar system, with special focus on civil trials. See M. Spottswood, 'Continuous Burdens of Proof' (2021) 21 Nevada Law Journal 779. Spottswood's main arguments in favour of this system, when compared to the current US binary system, are that it increases deterrence, furthers equal treatment, spreads the risk of errors more fairly between the parties, and decreases the incentives to hide or destroy evidence. For earlier defences, see H. Lando, 'The Size of the Sanction should Depend on the Weight of the Evidence' (2005) 1 Review of Law and Economics 277; T. Fisher, 'Constitutionalism and the Criminal Law: Rethinking Criminal Trial Bifurcation' (2011) 61 University of Toronto Law Journal 811; T. Fisher, 'Conviction without Conviction' (2011) 96 Minnesota Law Review 833; and M. Wansley, 'Scaled Punishments' (2013) 16 New Criminal Law Review 309.

raises difficult ontological and epistemological problems. This fact can be appreciated by considering Figure 4.4 below, in conjunction with the Appendix. As I show in the latter, the condition for the superiority of a *genuine* second intermediate verdict over conviction, acquittal, and the first intermediate verdict, is more sophisticated than that for the superiority of the first intermediate verdict over conviction and acquittal: that is, it is more sophisticated than inequality (3) above. Indeed, for each genuinely additional intermediate verdict, the sophistication of the respective superiority condition is due to increase. The superiority of a genuinely additional intermediate verdict requires that the verdict be such that the expected value of issuing it is represented by a line that travels higher than *one corner only* of the ceiling of the system to which it is added. If, instead, the line travels higher than two or more corners, the new intermediate verdict simply supersedes one or more of the intermediate verdicts already included in such system. Thus, it is not a genuinely additional verdict. To see this, consider Figure 4.4. The solid broken line is the ceiling of a system including one intermediate verdict. The thick dotted line represents the expected value of issuing an intermediate verdict that is superior with respect to this ceiling, but not genuinely additional. This verdict supersedes the intermediate verdict already included in the system, such that the system resulting from the addition of the former still only features a single intermediate verdict. The thick dashed line, instead, represents the expected value of issuing an intermediate verdict that is superior and genuinely additional. This verdict does not supersede the intermediate verdict already included in the system, thus the system resulting from the addition of the former has two intermediate verdicts. The greater the number of intermediate verdicts in the system, then, the narrower is the scope for (a line representing the expected value of issuing) a genuinely additional superior intermediate verdict; in other words, the more sophisticated is the superiority condition for a genuinely additional intermediate verdict. Given this, one can appreciate that the greater the number of intermediate verdicts in the system, the less likely it is that an additional intermediate verdict satisfying the respective superiority condition actually exists (the ontological problem), and, if it does exist, that it can be successfully identified (the epistemological problem). I trust that the sceptical reader will find these considerations more persuasive after reading the upcoming sections, in which I tackle the issue of understanding the superiority condition for a single intermediate verdict, and the issue of identifying a concrete example of an intermediate verdict that meets the condition. They will see, for instance, that a truly analogue system providing for a term of imprisonment and/or a fine, increasing in proportion to the probability of guilt, while it may well be justified otherwise, cannot be the end point of my theory. This is for the simple reason that neither imprisonment nor a fine can plausibly meet the superiority condition in inequality (3) above; hence, they could not provide the content of the initial superior intermediate verdict from which the supposed analogue system would be developed.

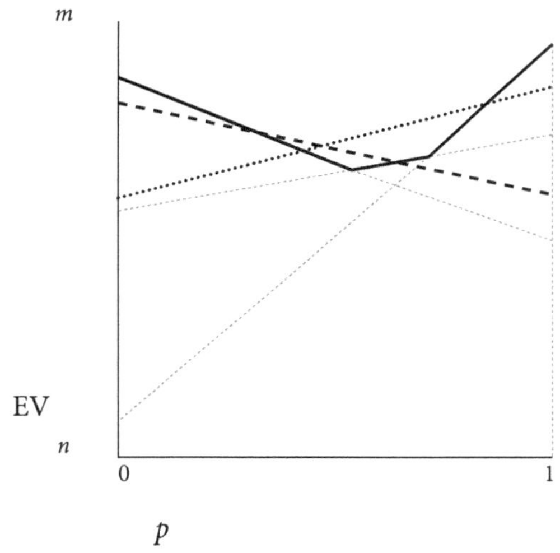

Figure 4.4 Genuinely additional and non-genuinely additional intermediate verdicts

4.4 Understanding the superiority condition

What should an intermediate verdict consist of in order to satisfy the superiority condition? In other words, what is the nature of a superior intermediate verdict? The reason for addressing these questions is that, ultimately, I want to be in a position to identify a concrete intermediate verdict that satisfies the superiority condition. In order to answer them, though, it is necessary to delve deeper into the meaning of the condition.

Inequality (3) gives us the formal expression of the superiority condition. An intermediate verdict is superior to conviction, and to acquittal, if, and only if, *the expected value of issuing the intermediate verdict at p^* is greater than the expected value of convicting at p^**. This alone does not seem very informative about the nature of a superior intermediate verdict. In order to identify a concrete instance of such a verdict, we need more than just some indication of the expected value that issuing the verdict would have at a given probability of guilt. It would be helpful to know something about the values that the intermediate outcomes should have for an intermediate verdict to be superior, so as to have an idea of what these outcomes—and, hence, the act that produces them—should consist of. More precisely, it would be helpful to know something about the respective positions that the values of the intermediate outcomes should have in the value function relative to the values of the outcomes produced by the verdicts with which we are already familiar; that is, the standard outcomes. This would allow us to identify a superior intermediate verdict through a comparison with acquittal and conviction. Fortunately, it is possible to tease out this information from inequality (3). This is done by deriving, from (3), other formulations of the superiority condition.

From (3), it is possible to derive the following inequality:

$$\frac{V_{ci} - V_{ii}}{V_{ig} - V_{cg}} > \frac{p^*}{1 - p^*} \tag{4}$$

If (3) is formulated referring to the expected value of acquitting, rather than that of convicting (remember that the two values are equal at p^*), we can derive from it another inequality:

$$\frac{V_{ai} - V_{ii}}{V_{ig} - V_{ag}} < \frac{p^*}{1 - p^*} \tag{5}$$

Finally, from (4) and (5) we can derive a third inequality:

$$\frac{V_{ii} - V_{ci}}{V_{ai} - V_{ii}} > \frac{V_{cg} - V_{ig}}{V_{ig} - V_{ag}} \tag{6}$$

The Appendix shows how (4) and (5) are derived from (3), and how (6) is derived from (4) and (5). Importantly, it also shows that (3), (4), (5), and (6) are equivalent. They are just different formulations of the superiority condition. This notwithstanding, for my purposes I consider (6) better than the alternatives. I have already pointed out the shortcomings of (3). Inequalities (4) and (5), instead, express the superiority condition in terms of the respective positions that the values of the intermediate outcomes—V_{ii} and V_{ig}—must have in the value function, given a particular standard of proof, or p^*. Take, for example, (4) and assume that $p^* = 0.9$. This is the probability that some scholars associate with the standard of proof beyond a reasonable doubt,[28] employed in a host of jurisdictions. Given such p^*, according to (4) an intermediate verdict is superior if, and only if, the interval between the value of convicting the innocent and that of issuing the intermediate

[28] See L. Laudan, 'The Rules of Trial, Political Morality, and the Costs of Error: Or, is Proof Beyond a Reasonable Doubt Doing More Harm than Good?' in L. Green and B. Leiter (eds), *Oxford Studies in Philosophy of Law* (OUP 2011), at 197; and Laudan and Saunders (n 14), at 21, 31. This probabilistic definition of the standard has been defended by adopting decision theory, and by relying on Blackstone's maxim as the source of the values of false conviction and false acquittal. This argument, though, has been convincingly confuted by Michael Dekay in Dekay (n 14). For a discussion on the quantification of the reasonable doubt standard in court, see P. Tillers and J. Gottfried, 'Case Comment—*United States v Copeland*, 369 F Supp 2d 275 (EDNY 2005): A Collateral Attack on the Legal Maxim that Proof Beyond a Reasonable Doubt Is Unquantifiable?' (2006) 5 Law, Probability and Risk 135.

verdict against the innocent is greater than nine times the size of the interval between the value of issuing the intermediate verdict against the guilty and the value of convicting the guilty.

For the purposes of identifying a concrete superior intermediate verdict, (4) and (5) are a step forward with respect to (3), insofar as they give some information about the structure of a value function incorporating the values of the outcomes of such a verdict. However, (6) is neater, simpler, and, thus, more intelligible than the alternatives. This is due to the fact that (6) defines the respective requisite positions in the value function of the values of the intermediate outcomes only by reference to the values of the four standard outcomes. It expresses the structure of the value function corresponding to a system including a superior intermediate verdict without resorting to any element external to the function itself, such as the standard of proof. According to (6), an intermediate verdict is superior if, and only if, the ratio of the interval between V_{ii} and V_{ci} to the interval between V_{ai} and V_{ii} is greater than the ratio of the interval between V_{cg} and V_{ig} to the interval between V_{ig} and V_{ag}. In order to appreciate the significance of this requirement, consider Figure 4.5 below, representing an intermediate verdict that satisfies the condition.

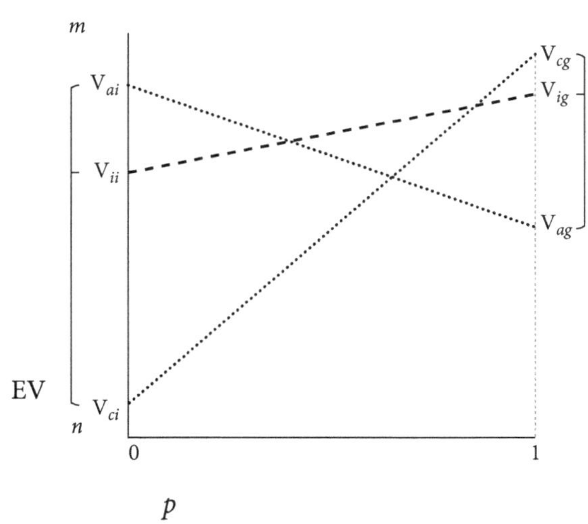

Figure 4.5 A visual aid to understand the superiority condition

In the figure, I have highlighted the interval between V_{ai} and V_{ci} and the interval between V_{ag} and V_{cg}. The interval between V_{ai} and V_{ci} expresses the difference in value between acquittal and conviction for the case in which the defendant is innocent; the interval between V_{ag} and V_{cg}, instead, expresses the difference in value between acquittal and conviction for the case in which the defendant is guilty. The requirement in inequality (6) concerns the position that the value of issuing the intermediate verdict against the innocent (V_{ii}) must have in the first interval, relative to the position that the value of issuing the intermediate verdict against the guilty (V_{ig}) has in the second, or vice versa. To be more precise, the requirement of an inequality between ratios of differences, stated in (6), can be expressed as the requirement that the value of issuing the intermediate verdict against the guilty be *disproportionately* close to the value of convicting the guilty, compared to how distant the value of issuing the intermediate verdict against the innocent is to the value of convicting the innocent. Or it can be expressed as the requirement that, when the defendant is guilty, the value of issuing the intermediate verdict must fall *disproportionately* close to the value of conviction (hence, *disproportionately* far from the value of acquittal), compared to where it falls when the defendant is innocent. The adverb 'disproportionately' is key here. The requirement is not that V_{ig} be closer to V_{cg} than V_{ii} is to V_{ci} in absolute terms (indeed, this is neither necessary nor sufficient for inequality (6) to be satisfied). Rather, it is that V_{ig} be 'closer' to V_{cg} than V_{ii} is to V_{ci} relative to the sizes of the intervals V_{ag} - V_{cg} and V_{ai} - V_{ci}, ie the intervals within which V_{ig} and V_{ii}, respectively, are expected to fall, given intermediacy. These two intervals, in fact, may not have the same size, as can be seen from Figure 4.5.

4.4.1 The nature of a superior intermediate verdict

In order to be in the position to identify a concrete superior intermediate verdict, it is necessary to give inequality (6) some more flesh, by reflecting on the evaluation of trial outcomes. The salient difference[29] between conviction and acquittal is the fact that the former typically involves punishment,[30] whereas the latter does not. Of course, this is not to deny that acquitted defendants experience hardship as a result of being tried, and possibly arrested and remanded in custody.[31] However, neither the stigma that may haunt the acquitted due to these detrimental experiences, nor the detrimental experiences themselves, can be viewed as defining features or consequences of acquittal,[32] not to mention as forms of punishment that

[29] Conviction and acquittal, understood as verdicts broadly construed, also differ because of the distinct speech acts that they involve. See the Introduction to the book on this point. This ulterior difference seems unimportant for the purposes of the current discussion, which focuses on the difference in value between acquitting and convicting, given innocence or guilt. I contend that such a difference in value is, by and large, determined by the hard treatment that each verdict may involve. However, as pointed out later in the paragraph, one can consider that the expressive dimension of the speech act of giving a 'guilty' verdict is itself a form of hard treatment and is, therefore, relevant to the evaluation of conviction.

[30] I say 'typically', rather than 'always', because the defendant may be given a pardon or, more likely, an absolute or conditional discharge.

[31] For a classic treatment of the idea that the process is itself a sanction, and can be perceived as such, see M. M. Feeley, *The Process is the Punishment: Handling Cases in a Lower Criminal Court* (Russell Sage Foundation 1979), in particular ch 7.

[32] On whether the stigma that may be associated with acquittal should be considered a product and, hence, a feature of this verdict, see Chapter 2, section 2.2.1.

are involved in such a verdict. Punishment is generally defined as the infliction of hard treatment; that is, treatment that is burdensome, harmful, or even painful.[33] This, at least, is the conduct element of punishment;[34] the element that has an impact on the defendant's life and, as a result, on the community. Someone may object that conviction involves more than just punishment, so understood. In particular, they may point out that the speech act of giving a 'guilty' verdict—which, as seen in the Introduction to the book, is a component of the verdict broadly construed—involves condemnation or censure.[35] Now, I treat this expressive feature of conviction as falling under the concept of hard treatment.[36] To clarify, my view is not merely that condemnation can be expressed through hard treatment.[37] Rather, I consider condemnation to be, in itself, a form of hard treatment. After all, condemnation is likely to harm someone's reputation, influencing the polity's behaviour towards, and perception of, the condemned in ways that are detrimental to them. Also—but this is a more tentative point—condemnation may foster a burdensome feeling of shame in the condemned, unsettling them by altering the perception that they have of themselves, and impelling them to engage in challenging, and potentially transformative, self-reflection. Condemnation being hard treatment, then, it is itself sufficient[38] to constitute punishment.

If the salient difference between acquittal and conviction is the fact that only the latter imposes hard treatment on the defendant, then the difference in value between the outcomes of the two verdicts given the defendant's guilt—that is, the interval V_{ag} - V_{cg}—and between the outcomes of the two verdicts given the defendant's innocence—that is, the interval V_{ai} - V_{ci}—must be determined by this fact. Of course, as seen in the previous chapter, how someone assesses this fact in their evaluation of the outcomes depends on their commitment to a certain theory of punishment. For instance, an expressivist may attribute a quantum of value to true conviction on the ground that condemning a guilty person sends them the appropriate disapproving message, hence fostering shame and self-reflection on their part; alternatively, they may subtract a quantum of value from false acquittal on the ground that it is a failure to send to the defendant the message that their behaviour warrants and, hence, a failure to foster their shame and self-reflection. A retributivist may

33 See H. L. A. Hart, *Punishment and Responsibility: Essays in the Philosophy of Law* (2nd edn, OUP 2008), at 4; R. A. Duff, *Punishment, Communication, and Community* (OUP 2001), at xiv; D. Boonin, *The Problem of Punishment* (CUP 2008), at 6–7; J. Feinberg, 'The Expressive Function of Punishment' in J. Feinberg, *Doing and Deserving: Essays in the Theory of Responsibility* (Princeton University Press 1970), at 98.

34 See the works in the previous note for other definitional elements.

35 See H. L. Ho, *A Philosophy of Evidence Law: Justice in the Search for Truth* (OUP 2008), at 28–31.

36 cf A. von Hirsch, *Censure and Sanctions* (Clarendon Press 1993); A. Ashworth and A. von Hirsch, *Proportionate Sentencing: Exploring the Principles* (OUP 2005), ch 2; Duff (n 33), ch 3. These works treat censure as separate from hard treatment.

37 See Feinberg (n 33), at 98–101.

38 Condemnation is often treated as a necessary condition for punishment. See, in particular, ibid, at 98 and Duff (n 33), at xv, 79–82.

attribute a quantum of value to true acquittal on the ground that it avoids the imposition of undeserved hard treatment; alternatively, they may subtract a quantum of value from false conviction on the ground that it imposes undeserved hard treatment, and so on. I use the adverb 'alternatively' to reiterate the point made in the previous chapter that the same reason should not be counted twice in determining the interval between the values of two outcomes, lest the interval scale is inaccurate.

In section 4.3, I defined a verdict as 'intermediate' if the value of issuing it against the innocent falls within the interval between the value of acquitting the innocent and that of convicting the innocent, and if the value of issuing it against the guilty falls within the interval between the value of convicting the guilty and that of acquitting the guilty. If the infliction of hard treatment on the defendant is the salient difference between conviction and acquittal, and is what determines the difference in the values of their respective outcomes given a relevant state of the world (that is, innocence or guilt), a verdict is intermediate if, and only if, it consists in a quantum of hard treatment that is less than the hard treatment involved in conviction,[39] but obviously more than the hard treatment involved in acquittal, which is nil.[40] To be more precise, intermediacy is satisfied if, and only if, issuing the intermediate verdict against the innocent consists in a quantum of hard treatment that is greater than that involved in acquitting the innocent, but smaller than that involved in convicting the innocent; and issuing the intermediate verdict against the guilty consists in a quantum of hard treatment that is greater than that involved in acquitting the guilty, but smaller than that involved in convicting the guilty.

As seen earlier, the superiority of an intermediate verdict requires that when the defendant is guilty, the value of the intermediate verdict be disproportionately close

[39] Notice that, for my purposes, it does not matter whether the hard treatment involved in the intermediate verdict can or cannot be characterised as punishment. Some may argue that punishment requires a categorical 'guilty' verdict. This view can be justified on the ground that punishment is for an offence, and that, therefore, for an authority to see itself as punishing, it must treat the offence as having, indeed, occurred. For elaboration on this point, see F. Picinali, 'Can the Reasonable Doubt Standard be Justified? A Reconstructed Dialogue' (2018) 31 Canadian Journal of Law and Jurisprudence 365, at 395–396; and Boonin (n 33), at 17–21. As pointed out in the Introduction to the book, it is difficult to see how an intermediate verdict could involve, or be perceived as involving, a categorical assertion of guilt. If so, and if this argument about punishment is correct, the hard treatment involved in the intermediate verdict is not punishment.

[40] In fact, this understanding of intermediacy, and that of superiority explained in the following paragraph, would not be undermined if acquittal were to involve a quantum of hard treatment: both understandings simply hinge on the fact that conviction involves greater hard treatment than acquittal does (whatever hard treatment that acquittal might involve), and that their respective values, given the relevant state of the world, are determined by this fact. See section 4.6 below for discussion of a significant detrimental feature of the verdict of acquittal in the English and Welsh system. cf. A. D. Leipold, 'The Problem of the Innocent, Acquitted Defendant' (2000) 94 Northwestern University Law Review 1297, at 1304–1313, pointing out that, in several US jurisdictions, the law authorises an acquitted person suffering some detrimental measures as a result of being arrested and/or tried; and J. Peay and E. Player, '"Not a Stain on Your Character?": The Finality of Acquittals and the Search for Just Outcomes' (2021) 11 Criminal Law Review 921, discussing harms to acquitted defendants in England and Wales which may not be intentionally inflicted by the State, but represent a 'form of collateral damage' (at 922) of the criminal process.

to the value of conviction (hence, disproportionately far from the value of acquittal), compared to when the defendant is innocent. In other words, the value of issuing the intermediate verdict against the guilty defendant must be disproportionately close to the value of true conviction, compared to how distant the value of issuing the intermediate verdict against the innocent defendant is to the value of false conviction. Now, the difference in value between the outcome of conviction and that of acquittal, given a relevant state of the world, hinges on the fact that only the former verdict involves hard treatment; indeed, a quantum of hard treatment that is greater than that involved in the intermediate verdict. Therefore, the value of the intermediate verdict will be disproportionately close to the value of conviction when the defendant is guilty, compared to when the defendant is innocent if, and only if, the verdict consists in a quantum of hard treatment that is greater when the verdict is imposed on the guilty than when it is imposed on the innocent.[41] In other words, superiority according to inequality (6) is satisfied if, and only if, *the intermediate verdict consists in harder treatment if the defendant receiving it is guilty than if they are innocent.*[42] As the reader may recall, in the Introduction to the book I mentioned that I would have reached the conclusion that issuing an intermediate verdict that satisfies the requirement stated in italics above is justified when the probability of guilt falls in the proximity of the standard of proof of a hypothetical binary system, such that the case is a close one, if tried within such a system. Indeed, as evident from our study of the superiority condition in the previous two sections, issuing an intermediate verdict that meets this condition should maximise expected value when the probability of guilt approximates such standard of proof. The question that needs answering now is whether a verdict that satisfies the requirement stated in italics above does exist. Before I address this question, though, there is an important caveat to make.

4.4.2 Heuristics for identifying a superior intermediate verdict

I have just presented necessary and sufficient conditions for intermediacy and superiority, respectively, in terms of the hard treatment imposed by a verdict.

[41] Consider that, if the quantum of hard treatment was constant across the scenarios of guilt and of innocence, one should expect proportionality. In other words, they should expect the two parts of inequality (6) to be, in fact, equal. See also the previous footnote.

[42] In this section, I have assumed that conviction imposes the same quantum of hard treatment on the innocent as it does on the guilty. Someone may object that conviction consists in harder treatment if the defendant is innocent, due to the sense of injustice that the innocent is, uniquely, likely to feel. Arguably, if this objection were sound, an intermediate verdict that consists in harder treatment if the defendant receiving it is guilty than if they are innocent would, a fortiori, satisfy inequality (6). The hypothetical fact that convicting the innocent consists in harder treatment than convicting the guilty would lower the value of convicting the innocent with respect to what this value would otherwise be. This would widen the interval $V_{ii} - V_{ci}$, thus increasing the ratio in the first part of the inequality. In any case, in the next section I will warn against relying on the possible emotional impact of a verdict for the purposes of constructing the value function.

However, I am not *claiming* that these are, in fact, necessary and sufficient conditions for a verdict to be, respectively, intermediate according to the definition given in section 4.3, and superior according to inequality (6). Let me clarify. Consider that intermediacy and the superiority condition concern the values of trial outcomes. Since the evaluation of trial outcomes—and, hence, of the imposition of hard treatment—depends on the particular theory of punishment that one endorses, whether the satisfaction of the conditions that I have identified in terms of hard treatment is, indeed, necessary and sufficient for intermediacy and superiority, respectively, depends on such a theory of punishment as well. For example, whether it is necessary and sufficient for intermediacy that a verdict involves a quantum of hard treatment that is greater than that involved in acquittal, but smaller than that involved in conviction, depends on how the relevant theory of punishment evaluates the imposition of such quantum of hard treatment on the guilty and the innocent, respectively. This theory may well consider that, keeping the kind of hard treatment constant across verdicts, imposing on the guilty a quantum of hard treatment that is smaller than that involved in conviction is less valuable than not imposing on them any hard treatment at all (that is, acquitting), since nothing short of the hard treatment involved in conviction can further the theory's goals. Or the theory may consider that imposing on the guilty a quantum of hard treatment that is greater than that involved in acquittal, but smaller than that involved in conviction, is less valuable than acquitting the guilty if, unlike the hard treatment involved in conviction, that involved in the hypothetical additional verdict is of a kind that does not further the theory's goals. In both cases, the condition for intermediacy that I have identified in terms of hard treatment would be satisfied, but intermediacy itself would not. The bottom line is that, in order to defend the claim that the conditions I have identified in terms of hard treatment are necessary and sufficient for intermediacy and superiority, respectively, one would have to show that they are, indeed, necessary and sufficient under all theories of punishment to which my decision-theoretic argument applies; that is, all theories that accept one of the plausible orderings of the values of the standard outcomes on which the argument is premised, such that inequality (6) is a valid superiority condition for them. I will not do so here, nor do I think that the claim would withstand this test.[43] Moreover, I am not defending any particular theory of punishment, thus I cannot even show that I have a preferred theory under which the claim of necessity and of sufficiency is true.

Instead, here I merely *treat* or *presumptively accept* the above conditions in terms of hard treatment as necessary and sufficient for intermediacy and superiority, respectively. And I do so on the basis of the arguments for these conditions presented in the previous section, which build on the correspondence between

[43] A notable complication is the fact that, in principle, there is no limit to the number of potential theories of punishment to which my argument would apply. Hence, the test could never be completed.

value and the imposition of hard treatment that characterises the four standard outcomes. Notice that this correspondence should hold for all theories of punishment to which my decision-theoretic argument applies. This is because it merely consists in there being, in the binary set-up, a relationship of dependence of value from the imposition of hard treatment, such that there is a difference in value between the outcome of conviction—which involves such imposition—and that of acquittal—which does not—given a relevant state of the world. My task in the next section is to identify a concrete verdict that has potential for being intermediate and superior under all theories of punishment to which my decision-theoretic argument applies. I conceive of the conditions in terms of hard treatment that I put forward in the previous section as *heuristics* for achieving this identification. If I were to work exclusively with intermediacy and superiority—which set requirements in terms of the values of trial outcomes—I would not be able to identify a concrete intermediate and superior verdict without relying on a fully fledged value function for the binary system, and on a corresponding theory of punishment that instructs on how value should be attributed to the intermediate outcomes. I do not have a value function and a theory of punishment to rely on, nor do I want to restrict my attention to one such theory only. Focusing on the imposition of hard treatment as a proxy for value allows me to make a prima facie case for the intermediacy and superiority of a particular verdict with respect to all theories of punishment—that is, theories that concern such imposition—to which my decision-theoretic argument applies, without relying on their value functions. Of course, this begs the question whether the verdict that I will identify is indeed intermediate and superior under any such theory of punishment. This depends on whether this verdict, while satisfying the heuristic requirements in terms of hard treatment, is intermediate and superior according to the original requirements, in terms of value. In the conclusion to this chapter, I will give a partial answer to this question. But I leave it to—in fact, I invite—the supporters of these theories of punishment to give the full answer, assuming that my prima facie case for this intermediate verdict will stimulate their interest. Importantly, even if the verdict that I will identify is not intermediate or superior under these theories, inequality (6) still represents, for them, the condition for the superiority of an intermediate verdict; hence, it gives guidance on how to identify such a verdict, relying on their respective value functions.

4.5 Conditional acquittal as a superior intermediate verdict

The search for a verdict that consists in harder treatment if the defendant receiving it is guilty than if they are innocent may strike some as being the quest for the philosophers' stone. After all, given our constant worry about the ineliminable risk of drawing the innocent into the machinery of criminal justice, and of burdening them with punishment, it would be somewhat relieving if we could rely on measures that are less harmful for the innocent than they are for the guilty. To be sure, I doubt that such measures are sufficiently available that they could supplant current forms of punishment. In any case, to call the binary system into question it is enough to identify a single verdict that satisfies the heuristic requirements that I have drawn from intermediacy and the superiority condition.

Take a defendant. You do not know whether they are guilty or innocent. What measure could consist in harder treatment for them if they are guilty than if they are innocent? Needless to say, typical forms of punishment such as a fine or imprisonment are hardly measures of this kind. The approach to this question that I consider most promising is to think of measures that impose a potential burden on the defendant, such that this burden is more likely to materialise if they are guilty than if they are innocent. To clarify, such a measure involves an expected cost as a form of hard treatment (whereas typical punishments involve an actual cost as a form of hard treatment). The expected cost consists in the cost of the potential burden for the defendant, discounted by the probability of it materialising. It follows that the evaluation of the possible outcomes of issuing an intermediate verdict consisting in this measure, ie issuing it against the innocent, and against the guilty, involves the evaluation of an expected cost imposed on the defendant. Insofar as the probability of the cost materialising is greater if the defendant is guilty than if they are innocent, the expected cost imposed in the former case is also greater. Therefore, the intermediate verdict consists in harder treatment if the defendant receiving it is guilty than if they are innocent.

For an example of a measure of this kind, consider a verdict imposing the enhancement of a possible future sentence. Let us assume that the verdict is intermediate: the imposition of the potential enhancement consists in harder treatment than acquittal but milder treatment than conviction. The enhancement is triggered if, after receiving the intermediate verdict, the defendant is convicted of a crime of the same type as that for which they received such a verdict. Let us assume that, at the time of the trial in which the defendant received the intermediate verdict, they had not already been convicted of a crime of the relevant type; indeed, they were not known to have committed any such crime.[44] Let us also make the important assumption that this type of crime is characterised by a recidivism rate that is significantly higher than their incidence in the general population, such that someone who has committed a crime of this type has a 'comparative propensity' to commit

[44] If the defendant had already committed a crime of the relevant type, whether they are guilty or innocent of the crime charged in the trial in which they received the intermediate verdict, they may well have the 'comparative propensity' (to commit crimes of this type) that I am about to mention in the text. This will depend, especially, on how 'fresh' the past criminal behaviour is (see the following note). If both the innocent and the guilty have such a propensity, the example I am giving does not work.

it again.[45] In these circumstances, if the defendant is guilty of the crime for which they received the intermediate verdict, they are more likely to commit a crime of the relevant type after the trial than if they are innocent.[46] Hence, they are more likely to trigger the sentence enhancement. The intermediate verdict, therefore, imposes on the defendant a greater expected cost if they are guilty than if they are innocent; it consists in harder treatment in the former case. The obvious problem with this intermediate verdict is that it fulfils (the heuristic requirement corresponding to) the superiority condition only in a relatively narrow set of cases: the cases that satisfy the specific assumptions on which the example is built. There is, however, an intermediate verdict that can have substantially wider application. I call it 'conditional acquittal'.

Conditional acquittal is loosely modelled on the suspension of res judicata—or *absolutio ab instantia*—a possible epilogue of the *ius commune* trial that I discussed in Chapter 1. In essence, this was an intermediate verdict allowing for the proceedings against the defendant to be reopened should new incriminating evidence become available. Conditional acquittal is, indeed, a verdict according to which the defendant can be tried again for the same crime if such evidence emerges. In fact, as I will discuss in the next section, the test for a new trial that I envisage is more sophisticated than this. We saw in Chapter 1 that the suspension of res judicata could also involve further restrictive conditions for the defendant. These are not part of conditional acquittal.

I call the intermediate verdict 'conditional acquittal' since it is, fundamentally, an acquittal with a condition attached to it: precisely, that the defendant can be retried if new incriminating evidence is discovered. By 'new' evidence I mean evidence that was not adduced in the trial resulting in the intermediate verdict because, at the time, it was not known *and* could not have been known, using reasonable diligence, by the investigating and prosecuting authorities.[47] This seems an obvious requirement. These authorities should not be allowed a 'second bite of the cherry' when their first attempt to obtain conviction has been marred by their failures—whether these failures consisted in negligent ignorance of evidence which is then discovered after the first trial, or in a poor tactical choice not to use known evidence, only to conclude after the first trial that such evidence could have secured conviction. If compared to the requirements that the evidence be merely

[45] In fact, this assumption is satisfied by a wide range of offences, according to fairly recent data about England and Wales. See M. Redmayne, *Character in the Criminal Trial* (OUP 2015), at 22–24, concluding that the available data 'suggest that a person with a recent previous conviction for a particular offence is considerably more likely than a person without a previous conviction to commit such an offence'. Consider, though, that the recidivism rate generally declines with the passing of time from the previous conviction (ibid, at 25–28).

[46] Given the assumption of significant recidivism, this may be true, even accounting for the possible deterrent effect of the enhancement.

[47] cf. ss 78(2) and 79(2)(c) of the English and Welsh Criminal Justice Act 2003, regulating retrials for serious offences. I will discuss aspects of this discipline later in the chapter.

unknown or unused, not only does the above requirement of 'new' evidence afford the defendant greater protection from an unreasonable use of State power, but it also gives the authorities a stronger incentive to prepare and present their initial case against the defendant as diligently as possible. Indeed, with the requirement of 'new' evidence in place, the authorities can hardly count on the possibility of a new trial as compensation for a sloppy investigation or trial tactic.[48] The question to address now is how such a verdict can satisfy the heuristic requirements concerning intermediacy and superiority.[49]

The verdict is intermediate between conviction and acquittal insofar as the punishment characterising conviction consists in harder treatment than imposing on the defendant the expected cost of a new trial, where the cost of such a trial should include, among other things, the expected cost of punishment in the event of conviction. Arguably, then, the verdict should be intermediate, at the very least, for crimes for which the minimum sentence[50] in the event of conviction is custodial—even if it may be suspended—or it is a sufficiently demanding community order. In fact, in Chapter 5 I will reconsider the intermediacy of conditional acquittal and advance a tentative argument to the effect that this verdict is intermediate in every case. Importantly, conditional acquittal meets the heuristic requirement concerning superiority insofar as the test for a new trial is more likely to be satisfied—hence, the new trial is more likely to materialise—when the defendant is guilty than when the defendant is innocent; given such a test, the expected cost—hence, the hard treatment—imposed on the defendant by the verdict is greater when they are guilty than when they are innocent. I argue that a test demanding *new*

[48] The stronger incentive to carry out a diligent investigation provided by the requirement that the evidence be 'new', in the sense clarified, shows that this requirement is not justified exclusively on grounds of fairness towards the defendant; it is also justified on epistemic grounds. The stronger incentive is, indeed, a device for the practical optimisation of Keynesian weight at the first trial. Keynesian weight is, roughly, the sum or amount of evidence taken into consideration in a fact-finding endeavour, and it is a distinct concept from the probability of the hypothesis to which this evidence pertains, eg guilt. A marginal increase in Keynesian weight may increase or decrease such probability, but it always 'reduces the *expected error*—or, alternatively, increases the *expected certainty*—associated with [the probability]' (D. A. Nance, 'Weight of Evidence' in C. Dahlman and others (eds), *Philosophical Foundations of Evidence Law* (OUP 2021), at 124 (italics in the original)). For the original problematisation of this concept, see J. M. Keynes, *A Treatise on Probability* (MacMillan 1921), at 71–78. For applications of this concept to the context of legal adjudication, see F. Picinali, 'Structuring Inferential Reasoning in Criminal Fact Finding: An Analogical Theory' (2012) 11 Law, Probability and Risk 197; D. Hamer, 'Probability, Anti-Resilience, and the Weight of Expectation' (2012) 11 Law, Probability and Risk 135; Nance, ibid; and Nance, *The Burdens of Proof* (n 14), chs 3, 4, and s 5.1.

[49] I will not discuss here which procedure might be followed for the retrial of the defendant to take place. A possibility would be a procedure along the lines of that provided by the English and Welsh Criminal Justice Act 2003 for retrials in cases of serious offences. In a nutshell, this involves an application to the Court of Appeal by the prosecutor (after obtaining the consent of the Director of Public Prosecutions) and a decision of the Court of Appeal on whether the test for the new trial is satisfied.

[50] By 'minimum sentence', I mean the minimum sentence imposed by statute, or the bottom end of the lowest category range prescribed by the sentencing guidelines for each offence. See <https://www.sentencingcouncil.org.uk/crown-court/> accessed 20 September 2021.

incriminating evidence with substantial probative value is a test that achieves the desired result.

4.5.1 The appropriate test for a new trial

In order to show that the test requiring new incriminating evidence with substantial probative value is more likely to be satisfied if the defendant is guilty than if they are innocent, it is important to review, briefly, the notions of relevant evidence, incriminating evidence, and probative value. An effective way of understanding these notions is to rely on the likelihood ratio $\frac{p(E/G)}{p(E/I)}$. '*E*' stands for the evidence, '*G*' stands for the hypothesis that the defendant is guilty, and '*I*' stands for the hypothesis that the defendant is innocent. Thus, the numerator expresses the probability that the evidence exists (more precisely, that it comes into existence) given that the defendant is guilty, and the denominator expresses the probability that the evidence exists (more precisely, that it comes into existence) given that the defendant is innocent. Evidence is relevant if the following inequality is verified: $\frac{p(E/G)}{p(E/I)} \neq 1$.[51] In other words, it is relevant when the probability of its existence if the defendant is guilty differs from the probability of its existence if the defendant is innocent. If the two probabilities were the same—and, therefore, their ratio was one—the evidence would be equally indicative of guilt and innocence: thus, it would not provide useful information to choose between the two hypotheses. Notice that saying that the evidence is relevant when the above inequality is verified is the same as saying that it is relevant when the probability of guilt, given the evidence, differs from the probability of guilt not conditioned on the evidence. Indeed, as shown in the Appendix, the above inequality is equivalent to this inequality: $p(G/E) \neq p(G)$, which reflects the standard definition of relevance to be found in *DPP v Kilbourne*.[52]

[51] The use of the Bayesian likelihood ratio to capture the notion of legal relevance dates back to the classic R. O. Lempert, 'Modeling Relevance' (1977) 75 Michigan Law Review 1021. See also Picinali, 'Structuring Inferential Reasoning in Criminal Fact Finding' (n 48). For a recent discussion of the potential and the limits of using the likelihood ratio in legal fact-finding, see N. Fenton and others, 'Bayes and the Law' (2016) 3 Annual Review of Statistics and its Application 51. Notice that the likelihood ratio—hence, the relevance—of the evidence depend on the other evidence that has already been taken into account. For instance, a match between the defendant's fingerprint and a fingerprint collected from the scene of the crime may well be irrelevant if clear and reliable CCTV footage already puts the defendant at the scene. Indeed, the probability of the match if the defendant is guilty *and is already put at the scene by the CCTV evidence* may well be the same as the probability of the match if the defendant is innocent *and is already put at the scene by the CCTV evidence*. See n 54 below and the works referenced there.

[52] [1973] AC 729 (HL), stating, at 756, that 'Evidence is relevant if it is logically probative or disprobative of some matter which requires proof... [R]elevant (i.e. logically probative or disprobative) evidence is evidence which makes the matter which requires proof more or less probable.'

Using the likelihood ratio, incriminating evidence can be defined as evidence for which the following inequality is verified: $\frac{p(E/G)}{p(E/I)} > 1$.[53] In other words, evidence is incriminating if it is more likely to exist if the defendant is guilty than if they are innocent, such that the evidence is more indicative of guilt than it is of innocence. This is the same as saying that evidence is incriminating if the probability of guilt, given the evidence, is greater than the probability of guilt not conditioned on the evidence. Indeed, as shown in the Appendix, $\frac{p(E/G)}{p(E/I)} > 1$ is equivalent to $p(G/E) > p(G)$, which reflects the commonsensical understanding of incriminating evidence.

The likelihood ratio is also useful to express the probative value of the evidence.[54] In the case of incriminating evidence, the numerator is greater than the denominator, so that their ratio is greater than one. As the value of the ratio increases above one, so does the probative value of the incriminating evidence. Evidence with a likelihood ratio of 100 is more probative of guilt than evidence with a likelihood ratio of 1.5. Indeed, assuming that the prior probability of guilt, ie the probability of guilt prior to considering the evidence, is the same, the former evidence increases the probability of guilt more than the latter one does.[55] A classic example of

[53] Conversely, exculpatory evidence can be defined as evidence for which the following inequality is verified: $\frac{p(E/G)}{p(E/I)} < 1$.

[54] See D. A. Nance, 'Naturalized Epistemology and the Critique of Evidence Theory' (2001) 87 Virginia Law Review 1551, at 1595–1599. Notice that the likelihood ratio—hence, the probative value—of the evidence depend on the other evidence that has already been taken into account. For example, the likelihood ratio of an eyewitness identification depends, arguably, on whether another eyewitness identification pertaining to the same time and venue has already been taken into account. This is because the probability of an identification if the defendant is guilty (or if they are innocent) may differ from the probability of an identification if the defendant is guilty (or if they are innocent) *and has already been identified as the perpetrator by another eyewitness*. For another example of this phenomenon, see ibid, at 1597. For similar remarks, see D. Hamer, 'The Significant Probative Value of Tendency Evidence' (2019) 42 Melbourne University Law Review 506, at 523–534. See also R. D. Friedman, 'A Close Look at Probative Value' (1986) 66 Boston University Law Review 733 and D. H. Kaye, 'Quantifying Probative Value' (1986) 66 Boston University Law Review 761, both discussing a measure of probative value 'in context' that expresses the extent to which the evidence alters the prior probability of guilt. This is distinct from the measure of the 'intrinsic' probative value of the evidence, conveyed by the likelihood ratio. While I do not deny that the former measure can be useful, my focus here is on the intrinsic probative value of the evidence. For criticisms of these approaches to the measurement of probative value, see M. S. Pardo and R. J. Allen, 'Generalizations and Reference Classes' in Dahlman and others (eds) (n 48).

[55] To see this, take the odds version of Bayes' theorem, according to which $\frac{p(G/E)}{p(I/E)} = \frac{p(G)}{p(I)} \cdot \frac{p(E/G)}{p(E/I)}$, that is, the odds of guilt after considering the new evidence (or posterior odds) equal the odds of guilt prior to considering the new evidence (or prior odds) multiplied by the likelihood ratio of the new evidence. Assume that the prior probability of guilt, *p(G)*, is 0.6, such that the prior probability of innocence, *p(I)*, is 0.4. With a likelihood ratio of 100, the posterior odds of guilt—that is, $\frac{p(G/E)}{p(I/E)}$ — are $\frac{0.6}{0.4} \cdot 100 = 150$. Converting these odds into a probability—which is done dividing the odds by one plus

incriminating evidence with substantial probative value is a DNA match resulting from lab testing. The probability of a match between a DNA sample collected at the scene of the crime and a DNA sample collected from the defendant is significantly greater if the defendant is the source of the sample found at the crime scene[56] than if they are not. With some simplification,[57] we can equate the probability of a match in the latter case with the so-called random match probability. This is the probability of finding an unknown person at random in a relevant population whose DNA corresponds to the sample found at the crime scene. While the numerator of the likelihood ratio for a DNA match is one,[58] the random match probability—that is, the denominator—is generally considered to be minuscule: as low as one in a billion. Hence, the likelihood ratio is very high. Another example of incriminating evidence with substantial probative value is the identification of the defendant as the perpetrator by a witness with no incentive to lie, who made the observation from a close distance, with good illumination, and with sufficient time to perceive the physiognomy of the defendant.[59] Arguably, the probability of such identification existing is substantially greater if the defendant is guilty than if they are innocent.

This brief digression into probabilistic definitions of core evidential concepts helps us to appreciate why a test authorising a new trial in the presence of incriminating evidence with substantial probative value would make the intermediate verdict of conditional acquittal compliant with the superiority condition; more precisely, with the corresponding heuristic requirement. Someone may hastily argue that if incriminating evidence is, indeed, evidence that is more likely to exist if the defendant is guilty than if they are innocent, a test for a new trial requiring new incriminating evidence, without making further demands about its probative value, would be more easily satisfied if the defendant is guilty of the crime for which they received the intermediate verdict than if they are innocent;

the odds—we obtain a (posterior) probability of guilt of 0.99. Other things being equal, with a likelihood ratio of 1.5, we obtain a (posterior) probability of guilt of 0.69. Notice that evidence with a lower likelihood ratio may well change the probability of guilt to a greater extent than evidence with a higher likelihood ratio does, if the prior probability differs in the two cases. This does not deny that the intrinsic probative value of the latter evidence is greater. For further discussion, see the previous note and the works cited therein.

[56] In fact, I am considering here the relevance of the match to the issue whether the DNA found at the crime scene is the defendant's, not to the ultimate issue of guilt. Consider that the defendant may well be the source of the sample found at the crime scene without being guilty of the crime. There may be a convincing innocent explanation for the presence of the defendant's DNA at the scene, and this explanation may well render the DNA evidence irrelevant to the ultimate issue of guilt.

[57] For detailed discussion of the nature and use of DNA evidence in court, with reference to the likelihood ratio as the means of expressing the probative value of this evidence, see R. Puch-Solis and others, *Practitioner Guide No. 2: Assessing the Probative Value of DNA Evidence, Guidance for Judges, Lawyers, Forensic Scientists and Expert Witnesses* (Royal Statistical Society 2012), in particular at 39–56.

[58] For an explanation of this fact, see ibid, at 45–46.

[59] For an overview of the empirical research on factors that may affect an eyewitness's perception, see D. Simon, *In Doubt: The Psychology of the Criminal Justice Process* (Harvard University Press 2012), ch 3.

hence, the expected cost imposed by the verdict would be greater in the former case. The problem with this argument is that the probability of the evidence existing is not the same as the probability of the evidence being found by the investigative authorities, and until the evidence is found, the test for a new trial cannot possibly be met. In other words, for us to be able to conclude that a given test for a new trial is more likely to be satisfied if the defendant is guilty than if they are innocent, it must be the case that the evidence that satisfies the test is more likely to be found by the authorities in the former case than in the latter. It is the probability of finding the evidence that ultimately matters.

While, undoubtedly, the probability of finding the evidence depends on the probability of its existence, it also depends on other factors, one of which is not constant across the scenarios of innocence and guilt. The resources, skills, motivation, and incentives of the investigative authorities, and the natural perishability of the evidence, are all factors that influence the probability of finding the evidence. But there is no reason to believe that they are more potent if the defendant is guilty than if they are innocent, or vice versa. The same holds for the fact that incriminating evidence has already been discovered and used in the first trial. True, the probability of finding new incriminating evidence after the trial decreases as a result of such prior discovery. But there is no reason to believe that such decrease would be different if the defendant is guilty than if they were innocent; and, in particular, that it would be more pronounced in the former case.[60] However, arguably, the guilty have an incentive to cover their tracks by suppressing—for example, hiding or destroying—incriminating evidence. Unless the innocent have reason to fear that they may be investigated for a crime they have not committed, they have no such incentive. In fact, the innocent may have no knowledge whatsoever that a crime has been committed—possibly because no crime has been committed—and, if they have such knowledge, they might trust that their innocence is not going to be questioned by the authorities, or they might not want to interfere with evidence that may be useful to identify the culprit. Accordingly, while, on the one hand, requiring incriminating evidence for a new trial should make it more likely that the requisite evidence will be found if the defendant is guilty than if they are innocent, on the other hand, the incentive that the guilty have to suppress incriminating evidence decreases the probability of this kind of evidence being found by the authorities, by decreasing the probability that incriminating evidence still exists at the relevant time. No similar decrease affects the probability of finding incriminating evidence if the defendant is innocent. Therefore, accounting for the incentive to

[60] Were the defendant guilty, one might expect that the case against them at the first trial would be built on more incriminating evidence than if they were innocent. That the case against the guilty would be so built, though, surely would not mean that, if the defendant were, instead, innocent, there would be more incriminating evidence to be found after the trial. It would simply be a result of the fact that incriminating evidence is more likely to exist if the defendant is guilty than if they are innocent.

suppress incriminating evidence reduces—but can it possibly eliminate?—the difference between the probability of finding incriminating evidence if the defendant is guilty and the probability of finding it if they are innocent.

I confess that I am not sure whether the incentive to suppress evidence has a significant differential impact on these two probabilities. There is reason to be cautious about the significance of such impact. At first glance, one may think that it does not matter when the guilty might experience the incentive to suppress the evidence and when they may act upon it: whether this is before, during, or after the first trial, it reduces the probability of finding incriminating evidence that may warrant a new trial following conditional acquittal. Consider, though, that evidence of the suppression of other evidence can itself be incriminating.[61] Now, if suppression occurs before or during the first trial, and the prosecution discovers this promptly, they will put forward evidence of suppression at the first trial. In such a case, the probability of finding new incriminating evidence when the first trial is over is effectively reduced by the act of suppression. Indeed, the evidence of this act is already known and spent by the prosecution, such that the existence of this evidence cannot compensate for said reduction. What about the case in which, irrespective of when suppression occurs, the evidence thereof, while obtainable, is not discovered before or during the first trial? Such evidence of suppression would be additional incriminating evidence out there; and it could offset the reduction in the probability of finding new incriminating evidence after the first trial, reduction that was initially produced by the act of suppression.

Be that as it may, in order to be reasonably confident that the test for a new trial is more likely to be satisfied if the defendant is guilty than if they are innocent, it is safer to formulate the test as requiring not just new incriminating evidence, but new incriminating evidence *with substantial probative value*; that is, evidence that is substantially more likely to exist if the defendant is guilty than if they are innocent.[62] The requirement of substantial probative value serves to compensate for the higher probability of suppression of the evidence if the defendant is guilty. Requiring substantial probative value means that, even if we account for the stronger incentive to suppress evidence experienced by the guilty, the probability of finding evidence of the kind that satisfies the test is still greater if the defendant is guilty than if they are innocent. To restate this point: since incriminating evidence with substantial probative value is substantially more likely to exist—and, hence, other things being equal, to be found—if the defendant is guilty than if they are innocent, even

[61] But see D. A. Nance, 'Adverse Inferences about Adverse Inferences: Restructuring Judicial Roles for Responding to Evidence Tampering by Parties to Litigation' (2010) 90 Boston University Law Review 1089, in particular at 1099–1103, pointing out that evidence of suppression is epistemically inferior to the evidence that has been suppressed.

[62] It is possible to make the attribute 'substantial' more precise, by quantifying the value that the likelihood ratio of the evidence should have for the test to be satisfied. I do not need to pursue this possibility here. While unquestionably vague, the attribute is sufficiently precise to support the arguments that I advance in this chapter.

if, due to factoring in the defendant's variable incentive to suppress incriminating evidence, the probability of finding incriminating evidence—including, of course, incriminating evidence with substantial probative value—decreases more in the scenario of guilt than in that of innocence, we are still more likely to find incriminating evidence with substantial probative value if the defendant is guilty than if they are innocent.[63] To exemplify, we are still more likely to come across the strong eyewitness identification evidence described earlier if the defendant is guilty than if they are innocent, even though the defendant is more likely to suborn an adverse witness in the former case than in the latter.

Let us take stock. The question that I have addressed is how to devise a test authorising a new trial such that the test is more likely to be met if the defendant receiving conditional acquittal is guilty than if they are innocent. The question is important because the superiority of conditional acquittal over acquittal and conviction depends on devising such a test. Insofar as the test is more likely to be met if the defendant is guilty than if they are innocent, the expected cost imposed on the defendant by the intermediate verdict is greater in the former case than in the latter; hence, the intermediate verdict consists in harder treatment if the defendant receiving it is guilty than if they are innocent. I have suggested that the relevant test can be identified by thinking about the type of evidence that is more likely to be found if the defendant is guilty than if they are innocent. The test can then be devised so as to require this type of evidence, such that the test is more likely to be satisfied in the former case than in the latter. Relying on the likelihood ratio, I have defined incriminating evidence as evidence that is more likely to exist if the defendant is guilty than if they are innocent. Arguably, if an item of evidence is more likely to exist if the defendant is guilty than if they are innocent, it is also more likely to be found by the authorities in the former case than in the latter. To see this, consider that variables such as the natural perishability of the evidence, the use of incriminating evidence in the first trial, and the investigators' skills, resources, motivation, and incentives to gather evidence—all factors that affect the probability of finding new incriminating evidence—are constant across the scenarios of guilt and innocence. If so, new incriminating evidence would seem to be evidence that is more likely to be found if the defendant is guilty than if they are innocent. And it would seem, therefore, that a test for a new trial requiring new incriminating evidence would be more likely to be satisfied in the former case than in the latter.

[63] Another role that the requirement of substantial probative value might perform is to disincentivise fraudulent behaviour on the part of the prosecution, consisting in holding back incriminating evidence at the first trial so as to reserve the possibility of a 'second bite at the apple' through a new trial, by making the evidence appear at a suitable time, while feigning ignorance of it. This behaviour would be fraudulent under a test for a retrial requiring 'new' evidence, according to the definition of this attribute given earlier. No reasonable prosecutor would hold back incriminating evidence with substantial probative value, since this evidence may play an important role in securing conviction. I am grateful to Dale Nance for inviting me to consider this point.

This argument, though, may be too fast. Incriminating evidence is subject to being suppressed by the defendant and, arguably, this behaviour is more likely to occur if the defendant is guilty than if they are innocent. This means that it may be unsafe to conclude, from the incriminating nature of the evidence alone, that evidence of this kind is more likely to be found if the defendant is guilty than if they are innocent. In order to compensate for the greater impact that the incentive to suppress incriminating evidence has on the probability of finding it if the defendant is guilty than if they are innocent, I have argued in favour of devising the test so as to require new incriminating evidence with substantial probative value; that is, evidence that is substantially more likely to exist if the defendant is guilty than if they are innocent. This is evidence like the DNA match or the eyewitness testimony described earlier. To support the reasonableness of these arguments, consider that, if we did not believe that incriminating evidence—and, especially, strongly incriminating evidence—against an individual is more likely to be found if they are guilty than if they are innocent, we should expect the innocent to have equal chances to, or greater chances than, the guilty of being suspected, arrested, remanded in custody, tried, and possibly even of being convicted. In other words, we should seriously doubt the possibility of doing criminal justice at all.

4.5.2 Other possible features of conditional acquittal

Conditional acquittal may produce a quantum of social stigma for those against whom it is issued, with the baggage of detrimental consequences that a blemished reputation may have on the defendant's personal and professional lives. This is ultimately because, as with any other intermediate verdict, the evidential basis of conditional acquittal sits between that of acquittal and that of conviction, a fact that inevitably expresses doubt about whether the defendant is guilty.[64] As mentioned in Chapter 2, though, whether an intermediate verdict does, indeed, produce stigma depends on whether there is any uptake of this doubt on the part of the polity, and this is a question that should be investigated empirically. Still, it is

[64] Here, I am relying on the considerations made in Chapter 2, section 2.2.1, according to which it is reasonable to expect that, if the intermediate verdict does produce social stigma, this is not due to how high the range of the probability of guilt corresponding to the verdict is. It is due, among other things, to the intermediate nature of the verdict. Notice that, if a significant extent of stigma indeed depended on where the standard of proof p^1 (authorising the intermediate verdict) is located, this extent should be factored into the evaluation of the intermediate outcomes. But if stigmatisation so depended upon the standard of proof, the values of intermediate outcomes could not be determined without knowing the standard first. Hence, the decision-theoretic model that I have relied upon would need tweaking. This is because, as shown in formula (2), this model treats the outcomes' values as inputs for the determination of the relevant standard of proof (whether this is p^1, p^*, or p^2) that do not depend on the standard itself. In the next chapter, I will consider, at greater length, a similar issue, with reference to the potential deterrent effect of an intermediate verdict.

plausible to assume that the comportment of interested parties towards, and their perception of, the defendant would be affected by the issuing of conditional acquittal. To be sure, one would expect this stigma to be less than that produced by conviction, since the defendant receiving conditional acquittal should be perceived as less likely to be guilty than if they had been convicted, and would not suffer the stigmatising hard treatment that may be involved in conviction.[65] Some role in triggering stigma might also be played by the name of the verdict itself. Consider that, unlike the names 'acquittal' and 'conviction'—and, especially, the categorical formulas uttered in the speech acts involved in these verdicts: 'not guilty' and 'guilty', respectively—the name 'conditional acquittal' expresses doubt about whether the defendant is guilty or innocent. It is part and parcel of this name to maintain and convey doubt, rather than trying to dispel it in one direction or the other. This lingering doubt is, indeed, the epistemic context within which a new trial may emerge as the opportunity to settle the question.

The stigma that the intermediate verdict may produce contributes to the hard treatment that the verdict involves, and should, therefore, be factored into the value function. In other words—to restate a point made in the Introduction to the book—if the legislator intends or expects the causing of social stigma, this should be treated as a component of the intermediate verdict broadly construed, and should, therefore, be factored into the legislator's assessment of the values of the intermediate outcomes. Since, as just seen, this stigma is probably less than that produced by conviction, and since causing stigma is a relatively mild form of hard treatment compared to other forms of hard treatment involved in conviction, the intermediate nature of the verdict should not be affected by its causing of social stigma. Also, there is no reason to believe that the stigma produced by an intermediate verdict would be greater (or smaller, for that

[65] Someone may contend that the values of the four standard outcomes are bound to change when the intermediate verdict is introduced. In particular, the value of acquitting the innocent increases, and that of acquitting the guilty decreases. As can be seen from Fig. 4.3, with the introduction of the intermediate verdict, acquittal corresponds to a range of the probability of guilt, the upper limit of which is lower than it is in the binary system. This is due to the fact that the intermediate verdict becomes available for cases falling in the higher section of the probability range corresponding to acquittal in the binary system. Therefore, acquittal acquires a greater exonerating effect: the acquitted is more likely to be perceived as innocent. This is beneficial if the acquitted is innocent, which explains why the value of acquitting the innocent would increase; and detrimental if the acquitted is guilty, which explains why the value of acquitting the guilty would decrease. In fact, someone may also argue that the increase in the standard of proof for conviction produced by the introduction of the intermediate verdict—a fact that is made evident in Fig. 4.3—has an impact on the value of convicting the innocent and on the value of convicting the guilty. The former may decrease, given that a conviction on firmer grounds may have a higher stigmatising effect. By the same token, the latter may increase. I do not dismiss completely the possibility that these effects may be produced by the introduction of the intermediate verdict. But I stress that whether the effects would exist, and what their sizes would be, are questions that need empirical investigation. Moreover, insofar as, with the introduction of the intermediate verdict, the line expressing the expected value of acquittal pivots clockwise, and the line expressing the expected value of conviction pivots anticlockwise—as the above argument suggests—the system resulting from the introduction of the intermediate verdict may well yield higher expected value if these effects are, indeed, present.

matter) when the defendant is guilty than when they are innocent. Therefore, this factor does not contribute to the satisfaction of the superiority condition: more precisely, of the corresponding heuristic requirement. Now, if retrials were a very rare occurrence in the criminal justice system, the expected cost of a new trial would be low, such that the hard treatment of conditional acquittal would consist mainly of the stigma it may produce. As pointed out earlier, though, the probability of finding the requisite evidence for a new trial also depends on the resources that the authorities invest in this task. Thus, if the intermediate verdict is taken seriously by the system, there is little risk that the probability of a retrial approximates zero, and that, therefore, the causing of stigma is pretty much all that there is in the hard treatment constituting the verdict. Admittedly, if this probability did approximate zero, the expected cost of a new trial would be so low that the difference between the impacts that the intermediate verdict would have, respectively, in the scenario of guilt, and in the scenario of innocence, would be very limited and, possibly, negligible. This would threaten the superiority of the verdict over acquittal and conviction. In theory, though, as long as the probability of a retrial is different from zero, and as long as a retrial is, indeed, more likely if the defendant is guilty, the expected cost and, hence, the hard treatment imposed by the intermediate verdict is greater when the defendant is guilty. Thus, the heuristic requirement concerning superiority is satisfied.[66] In the next chapter, I will reconsider the question of the probability of a new trial in light of the interest of the system in retrying a defendant when the crime is minor, and when the crime is serious.

Someone may object that, if we pay close attention to the emotional impact of conditional acquittal on the defendant, it is not at all clear that the verdict satisfies the heuristic requirement concerning superiority. Indeed, an innocent defendant may well feel a sense of injustice, or at least disappointment, at receiving the intermediate verdict rather than acquittal. Not only is the guilty defendant unlikely to experience such a negative feeling, but they might, instead, experience a feeling of relief, having avoided the tougher treatment of conviction. Insofar as this imbalance in the feelings experienced, respectively, by the innocent and by the guilty does indeed occur, it may offset the difference in the expected costs of a new trial that conditional acquittal imposes when the defendant is innocent and when they are guilty, respectively. As a result, the intermediate verdict may not consist in harder treatment when the defendant receiving it is guilty than when they are innocent. A possible reply to this objection is that the attention it pays to the emotional impact of the verdict is not sufficiently close after all. For example, innocent defendants, especially those with a strong case against them, may experience

[66] But see nn 92, 93, and 95 below, regarding other possible costs and benefits of the intermediate verdict that may affect its superiority.

relief at receiving the intermediate verdict rather than conviction, very much like the guilty may; and both in the short and in the long term, this feeling may well swamp any sense of injustice they might feel. Moreover, if the defendant knows that the test for a new trial is more easily met in the scenario of guilt, then the guilty defendant may well experience more anxiety about the possibility of a new trial than the innocent defendant. If either of these prognoses is correct, it is not at all clear that the differential impact of conditional acquittal studied in the previous section is offset as the objection suggests, not to mention the fact that this differential impact may be sufficiently robust to withstand any possible imbalance in feelings of the kind described by the objection. As seen in section 4.4.1, hard treatment is 'hard' because it is burdensome, harmful, or even painful; in other words, because of how it affects, and is perceived by, its recipient. I do not deny, then, that the emotional impact of a verdict contributes to the hard treatment that the verdict involves. However, unless we can count on reliable generalisations about how a verdict impacts on the emotions of its recipients, it is difficult to account for such an impact in assessing the values of the possible outcomes of the verdict. Without reliable generalisations, this assessment becomes an exercise in speculation; or it reflects the subjectivity of particular defendants only. The objection considered here, and my replies to it, are speculative insofar as they purport to apply to defendants in general. Insofar as they purport to capture the emotions of a group of defendants only, they have limited importance for the enterprise of producing a value function with general validity: discounting them may well reduce the accuracy of the value function in some cases, but this is an inevitable cost to pay for the sake of formulating a theory that aspires to generality. I have argued, earlier, that the prospect of a new trial, and of the punishment that may result from this trial, is an expected cost for the defendant. I do not think there is anything speculative in saying that this prospect is an expected cost for the generality of defendants, and that any given defendant—any given reasonable defendant, at least—would perceive it as such.

4.6 Acquittal, retrial, and double jeopardy

It is now time to address the elephant in the room. Sections 77 to 79 of the English and Welsh Criminal Justice Act 2003 already allow for an acquittal to be quashed and a retrial to be ordered when 'new and compelling' incriminating evidence emerges, and the new trial is in the interests of justice.[67] Notice that this test—at

[67] Consider that this measure is only available for a selected group of serious offences listed in pt 1 of sch 5 of the Act. For a concise critical discussion of these norms, see L. Campbell and others, *The Criminal Process* (5th edn, OUP 2019), at 419–424. A retrial after an acquittal is also authorised by ss 54–57 of the Criminal Procedure and Investigations Act 1996, in cases in which the acquittal was obtained by the defendant, or by someone acting on their behalf, through the interference with, or the

least, its evidential component—[68] is very similar to the one I defended earlier for conditional acquittal, given that 'compelling' evidence is defined by the statute as evidence that is 'reliable', 'substantial', and which 'appears highly probative' of guilt. This state of affairs gives rise to an objection to introducing conditional acquittal into a verdict system such as the current English and Welsh system.[69] Since, in such a system, retrials are already permissible in the event of acquittal, and since they are permissible under circumstances that are very similar to those reflected in the test involved in the intermediate verdict I defended, the evaluation of (the outcomes of) acquittal must already include the expected cost of a new trial that the intermediate verdict is meant to impose on the defendant. This means that the intermediate verdict, in fact, is hardly intermediate between acquittal and conviction, according to the meaning of intermediacy presented in section 4.3. Rather, it is substantially equivalent to acquittal. Because of this, the verdict cannot possibly satisfy the superiority condition: indeed, it appears to be nugatory.[70]

intimidation of, a witness or juror. cf the Double Jeopardy (Scotland) Act 2011, having particular regard to s 4, which authorises the retrial of the acquitted in the event of 'new evidence'.

[68] Consider that, unlike the test I defended earlier, the Act does not impose a requirement that the evidence was not known and could not have been known by the authorities, using reasonable diligence. New evidence is defined by s 78(2) simply as evidence that 'was not adduced in the proceedings in which the person was acquitted'. However, according to s 79(2)(c), one of the factors to be considered by the Court of Appeal when deciding whether ordering a retrial is in the interests of justice is 'whether it is likely that the new evidence would have been adduced in the earlier proceedings against the acquitted person but for a failure by an officer or by a prosecutor to act with due diligence or expedition'. See also *R v Dobson (Gary)* [2011] EWCA Crim 1255, para 10, stating that 'if the new evidence relied on by the prosecution would have been revealed for use at the first trial by a competent investigative and/or prosecutorial process, then the interests of justice may, on this ground alone, lead to the application being refused'. cf the Double Jeopardy (Scotland) Act 2011, s 4(7)(b), stating that an acquittal may be set aside only if 'the new evidence was not available, and could not with the exercise of reasonable diligence have been made available, at the trial in respect of the original offence'.

[69] Contrary to what was implied in the first few paragraphs of the Introduction to the book, then, the English and Welsh verdict system may not be considered a central case of a 'binary' verdict system, given the definition of binary verdict system offered there. See Introduction, in particular n 4. This is because—one may argue—in England and Wales acquittal is not 'plain vanilla': it involves the imposition of hard treatment in the form of the expected cost of a retrial, even if this would hardly be characterised as punishment by anyone. The crucial definitional features of the binary system, ie the presence of only two verdicts and, consequently, of only one standard of proof, are, however, satisfied. Against this characterisation of the English and Welsh acquittal, though, it may be argued that allowing for the retrial of the acquitted is, effectively, a reconfiguration of the status quo of innocence, in that it removes or circumscribes the right against retrying the acquitted, which was part of such status quo. Once the status quo is so reconfigured, however, acquittal cannot be considered as involving hard treatment, that is, as infringing upon such status quo. Under this alternative view, then, the English and Welsh acquittal would indeed be 'plain vanilla'.

[70] A related objection is that, if the English and Welsh status quo of innocence is already characterised by the absence, or the restriction, of the right against retrying the acquitted, the intermediate verdict of conditional acquittal does not, in fact, infringe upon this status quo, contrary to what I have suggested thus far. Notice that this objection fails if conditional acquittal produces stigma, thus being an infringing verdict for this reason alone (given that the English and Welsh status quo surely includes a right to reputation). If conditional acquittal produced stigma, though, the objection in the text may fail as well: the verdict would involve harder treatment than acquittal, and would, therefore, be intermediate according to the corresponding heuristic requirement (see n 40 above; see also Chapter 2, section 2.2.1

In short, my reply to this objection is that a system, such as the current English and Welsh system, which allows for the retrial of the acquitted on the basis of new incriminating evidence with substantial probative value, falls foul of the double jeopardy rule and is, therefore, unjustified. Instead, adopting conditional acquittal while prohibiting the retrial of the acquitted is not at odds with the rule. To justify this reply, though, I need to delve into the uneasy relationship between acquittal and retrial.

Traditionally, in England and Wales, jury acquittals were considered final, as were acquittals by the magistrates when the appeals process was over. Finality was justified on the basis of the double jeopardy rule, which in civil law jurisdictions is usually conveyed by the maxim *ne bis in idem*. The rule essentially states that someone should not be subjected to a new trial for an offence for which they have already been convicted or acquitted.[71] In particular, if acquitted of an offence, they should not, again, be put in jeopardy of being convicted for it through a new trial. The justification of this rule is not uncontroversial. Below, I briefly survey and assess the arguments that are usually advanced in support of the rule; in particular, of the part of the rule concerning the retrial of the acquitted.[72]

The first argument is that a retrial should not be allowed because it increases the risk of false conviction. This argument is weak. While allowing retrials does increase the risk of an innocent defendant being convicted—assuming that there are innocents in the pool of acquitted defendants, of course—this risk can be tamed by granting this opportunity only in the presence of new incriminating evidence with substantial probative value;[73] that is, as seen earlier, evidence that the authorities

for a defence of the claim that acquittal does not 'produce' stigma, and that, therefore, stigma cannot be considered a feature of this verdict). Having said this, conditional acquittal may still not satisfy the superiority condition in inequality (6). This depends, among other things, on how the expected cost of a new trial affects the values of the outcomes of acquittal. In any case, in this section I develop a stronger reply to both objections: the English and Welsh law on the retrial of the acquitted—and, hence, an aspect of the English and Welsh status quo of innocence—is unjustified. Once the right against retrying the acquitted is reinstated as part of such status quo, conditional acquittal does represent an infringement upon this right.

[71] A timely appeal of the verdict—if any appeal is, indeed, allowed by the law—is not a new trial for the purposes of the rule; hence, it is not in breach of it. For a concise account of the history of the rule, and a comparative overview of how the rule is enforced in common law and civil law jurisdictions, see C-F. Stuckenberg, 'Double Jeopardy and *Ne Bis in Idem* in Common Law and Civil Law Jurisdictions' in D. Brown and others (eds), *The Oxford Handbook of Criminal Process* (OUP 2019), at 457. This contribution includes an account of some complexities of the law of double jeopardy that are irrelevant for my purposes. Notably, the double jeopardy rule is contained in several supranational legal instruments, in particular in Art 14(7) of the International Covenant on Civil and Political Rights, and in Art 4 of the Additional Protocol no 7 of the European Convention on Human Rights. Notice that Art 4(2) of the Protocol allows for an exception to the rule in the event of 'evidence of new or newly discovered facts'.

[72] The arguments, with the exception of that from moral authority, restate arguments presented in Law Commission, *Double Jeopardy* (Law Com CP No 156, 1999), at 30–32.

[73] See Campbell and others (n 67), at 422; and I. Dennis, 'Rethinking Double Jeopardy: Justice and Finality in Criminal Process' (2000) Criminal Law Review 933, at 939.

are (significantly) more likely to find if the defendant is guilty than if they are innocent. One also has to remember that, as discussed previously in this chapter, trial rules already include a norm designed to keep the risk of false conviction within limits that are considered acceptable in light of the values of the possible outcomes of adjudication. This is the standard of proof.[74] This norm would, obviously, also be operative in the new trial.

A second argument against retrying acquitted defendants is that it is wrong to impose on them the distress and anxiety of a trial, after they have already been through that experience. This argument can be framed so as to also encompass the distress and anxiety that a new trial may cause to victims and witnesses. Now, while a second trial may surely cause distress to the defendant, the victims, and the witnesses, the same is true of the first trial. And yet, the distress caused to these individuals is not a sufficient reason not to try the defendant the first time. This is because considerations of distress are outweighed by the value of convicting the guilty, and by the evidence against the defendant, which persuades the prosecution of their guilt; in other words, they are outweighed by the expected value of true conviction. The same conclusion should apply with regard to a retrial. Even assuming that the distress caused by a retrial is greater for all involved than that caused by the first trial, distress is unlikely to be a decisive objection to trying a defendant again when, as a result of newly discovered evidence, the probability of their guilt is high.[75] To be more precise, there must be a probability threshold—plausibly a high one—such that if (and only if) the probability of guilt, conditioned also on the new incriminating evidence, surpasses such threshold, the argument from distress should not be an obstacle to a new trial.

A third argument against the retrial of acquitted defendants is that barring such retrial incentivises the authorities to investigate a case efficiently and exhaustively; if the authorities knew that they could count on a second trial, this incentive would be less strong. This argument, too, seems weak. Even with the possibility of a retrial, investigators and prosecutors can be subjected to pressures and checks that incentivise and impel them to perform their roles diligently.[76] More importantly, this argument does not apply with reference to a test for a new trial requiring evidence that, at the time of the first trial, was not known and could not have been known by the authorities, using reasonable diligence. Given the strictness of this test, the possibility of a retrial does not lower the incentive to investigate the case properly from the very start.[77] Indeed, if the authorities negligently overlook incriminating

[74] See Dennis (n 73), at 939. Of course, if someone could be retried arbitrarily, an indefinite number of times, the risk of false conviction may well become unacceptable notwithstanding the use of the decision-theoretic standard of proof in every trial. This, however, is far from the situation that is being considered here.

[75] See P. Roberts, 'Justice for All? Two Bad Arguments (And Several Good Suggestions) for Resisting Double Jeopardy Reform' (2002) 6 International Journal of Evidence and Proof 197, at 208–211.

[76] See ibid, at 212.

[77] See Dennis (n 73), at 941–942.

evidence before or during the first trial, they will not be able to rely on this evidence, should they later discover it, in order to obtain a second chance to try the defendant. As pointed out earlier in the chapter, with a test of this kind in place, the authorities can hardly count on the possibility of a new trial as compensation for a sloppy investigation.

According to a fourth argument against the retrial of the acquitted, for the State to have the authority to try the defendant, the State must trust—and be seen to trust—the reliability of its procedures. A State that demands to retry an acquitted defendant is, effectively, admitting that the acquittal is not reliable; hence, the State is undermining its own authority to bring the defendant to trial a second time.[78] In a similar vein, the double jeopardy rule has been characterised as part of a constitutional 'criminal justice deal' between the State and its citizens, departure from which would undermine the authority of the State and the relationship of trust between the State and its citizens.[79] If the State 'could accept or reject acquittal verdicts much as it suited [it], criminal proceedings would soon be exposed as a sham trial of guilt, and jury acquittal would lose its current practical and symbolic meaning. Public confidence in jury verdicts generally would be undermined, and government would have assumed an ominously authoritarian jurisdiction.'[80] Now, neither version of the argument centred on State authority undermines the possibility of justifying a retrial. Consider a test authorising a new trial only with the discovery of incriminating evidence which, at the time of the first trial, was not known and could not have been known by the authorities, using reasonable diligence. If such evidence emerges, a State that sets aside the acquittal may well be taken to admit that the verdict is unreliable. But this unreliability cannot be imputed to a failure in the agency of the State: the evidence that casts doubt on the reliability of the verdict is not evidence that, using reasonable diligence, the State could have discovered before this verdict was handed down. Hence, the authority of the State should not be undermined.[81] Moreover, if a retrial is authorised only in the presence of such evidence, unlike in the scenario envisaged in the quoted passage, the State is not left free to reject acquittals at its convenience. Consider, finally, the worry about undermining public confidence or public trust, raised in this passage. There must be a probability threshold, plausibly a high one, such that if (and only if) the probability of guilt—conditioned also on the new incriminating evidence—surpasses this threshold, the retrial is supported by convincing reasons. Therefore, a criminal justice system authorising a retrial under such epistemic circumstances would not—at least, should not—be perceived as operating arbitrarily

[78] See Campbell and others (n 67), at 423.

[79] See P. Roberts, 'Double Jeopardy Law Reform: A Criminal Justice Commentary' (2002) 65 Modern Law Review 393, at 410–412. See also Stuckenberg (n 71), at 460–461.

[80] Roberts, 'Double Jeopardy Law Reform' (n 79), at 411.

[81] cf Campbell and others (n 67), at 423.

or unreasonably. Absent such a perception, public confidence in the system would not be undermined. In fact, public confidence may well be increased to the extent that the public values securing the guilty to justice.

A fifth and final[82] argument against the retrial of the acquitted is the argument from finality. It draws on the consideration that it is valuable, both for the parties and for society as a whole, to treat a disputed issue as if it were resolved, or—to use the words of the Law Commission—that there is 'virtue in putting a line under emotive and contentious events, so that life can move on'.[83] Not only is it the case that the defendant has an interest in not being held back by doubts about their legal standing, but there is also an institutional interest in legal certainty; an interest in not leaving important legal relationships undefined.[84] As with the arguments from distress, and from public confidence, the argument from finality does not constitute a decisive objection against allowing the retrial of a defendant when, as a result of newly discovered evidence, the probability of their guilt surpasses a critical threshold. Legal certainty is, undoubtedly, important, but so is securing the guilty to justice. The argument from finality must, therefore, yield if (and only if) a retrial occurs when such critical probability threshold is surpassed.[85]

After this brief overview, one is left with the impression that the rule against double jeopardy is not absolute. In particular, there seems to be no conclusive argument against retrying an acquitted defendant as long as there is new incriminating evidence with substantial probative value, it being evidence that, at the time of the first trial, was not known and could not have been known by the authorities, using reasonable diligence. This is nothing but the test involved in the intermediate verdict that I have defended. And it is, by and large, the test provided by the Criminal Justice Act 2003.[86] This impression, however, is imprecise. True, insofar as it is supported by the above arguments, the double jeopardy rule admits of retrials.

[82] This is not meant to be an exhaustive list. In fact, see P. Westen and R. Drubel, 'Toward a General Theory of Double Jeopardy' (1978) The Supreme Court Review 81, at 129–132. Westen and Drubel argue that the rule against retrying those acquitted in jury trials is justified by the jury's legitimate authority to nullify the law by acquitting against the evidence. More specifically, their argument is that the jury has such an authority, but it is never possible to tell whether the jury exercised this authority in a particular case (hence, whether or not the acquittal is the result of a defect of reasoning, and whether or not it would also have been issued if the jury had considered incriminating evidence that emerged after the trial); and that, because of this impossibility, jury acquittals should be treated as final. Aside from the fact that it does not apply easily to acquittals from the bench (cf Westen and Drubel, ibid, at 134–135), the argument is unpersuasive. Even if nullification were a legitimate power, rather than just a power, of the jury, it is not clear why it would be a conclusive reason against retrial. Surely, while maintaining a general interest in the jury's exercise of an ultimate check on the use of State power, someone can argue that there are circumstances in which this interest is outweighed by opposing considerations. For instance, the presence of new evidence of guilt, and of an overall strong case against the defendant (possibly involving a serious crime causing social concern), may be circumstances of this kind.

[83] Law Commission (n 72), at 31.

[84] See Stuckenberg (n 71), at 460.

[85] See Campbell and others (n 67), at 422.

[86] But see n 68 above.

However, some of the surveyed arguments against retrying the acquitted have been found incapable of supporting an absolute prohibition against retrials, not because they yield when the above test for a retrial is implemented, but only because they yield when, as a result of newly discovered evidence, the probability of the defendant's guilt passes a critical threshold. This is the case for the arguments from distress, finality, and public confidence. I have argued that there must be a probability threshold such that if, and only if, the probability of guilt—conditioned also on the new incriminating evidence—surpasses such threshold, the case for a new trial outweighs considerations of distress and of finality, and it is sufficiently strong to secure public support, hence public confidence in the system that provides for this opportunity. Importantly, though, a test for a new trial requiring new incriminating evidence with substantial probative value does not guarantee that a retrial is authorised exclusively when the probability of guilt resulting from the consideration of the new incriminating evidence meets such a threshold. Therefore, it is possible that, if said test is chosen, there would be cases in which a retrial takes place when it really should not; that is, when the arguments from distress, finality, and public confidence are not overcome. Let me explain.

While the probability of guilt increases with the consideration of the new incriminating evidence, it also depends on the evidence already adduced against the defendant in the trial ending with their acquittal. More precisely, the posterior probability of guilt, ie the probability resulting from the consideration of the new evidence, depends on the prior probability of guilt, ie the probability resulting from the consideration of the evidence adduced in the first trial. Holding constant the probative value of the new evidence, the lower the prior probability of guilt, the lower the posterior probability of guilt;[87] hence, the more compelling the arguments from distress, finality, and public confidence against the retrial of the acquitted. There is a point where the evidence adduced in the first trial is so weak—thus, the prior probability of guilt is so low—that, even accounting for the substantial probative value of the new incriminating evidence, the posterior probability of guilt is insufficient to overcome these arguments.[88] Consider that the range of the probability of guilt corresponding to acquittal in a binary system goes from the standard

[87] One can appreciate this point by considering the odds version of Bayes' theorem, already employed in n 55 above. The odds of guilt given the new evidence can be expressed as $\frac{p(G/E)}{p(I/E)} = \frac{p(G)}{p(I)} \cdot \frac{p(E/G)}{p(E/I)}$, where $\frac{p(E/G)}{p(E/I)}$ is the likelihood ratio for the new evidence and $\frac{p(G)}{p(I)}$ are the prior odds of guilt. In this case, the prior odds of guilt are the odds of guilt given the evidence presented at the first trial. The lower the prior odds of guilt, the lower the odds of guilt given the new evidence and, hence, the lower the posterior probability of guilt.

[88] Consider this unheeded passage from the Law Commission's consultation paper leading to the 2003 reform: 'It would also be possible to require ... that the prosecution's case, as strengthened by the new evidence, should be of some minimum strength overall. If there were no such requirement, the exception [to the double jeopardy rule] might be invoked where the prosecution's case at the first trial was very weak

of proof for conviction all the way down to zero. This means that there may well be trials resulting in acquittal where the prior probability of guilt falls below the point just mentioned.[89] Hence, there is reason to expect that allowing the retrial of an acquitted person on the mere basis of new incriminating evidence with substantial probative value could, sometimes, be unjustified.[90] This is why a verdict system such as the current English and Welsh system is at odds with the double jeopardy rule: unjustified retrials are allowed under such a system, at least in principle.[91]

indeed, and the new evidence makes it much stronger, but still does not turn it into a very strong case overall. In our view, cases of this kind ought not to be included within the new exception. The law generally regards the existence of a prima facie case as sufficient justification to put a person on trial, in spite of the distress that will thus be caused; but in our view this cannot be so where the proposed defendant has already been once acquitted. We think there should be a requirement that the evidence available for the retrial, as a whole, must be of a certain minimum strength, over and above the ordinary requirement of a prima facie case.' (Law Commission (n 72), at 44). The Law Commission's point can be expressed using the odds version of Bayes' theorem (see n 55 above). Let us give a generous definition of 'substantial probative value' of the incriminating evidence in terms of a likelihood ratio of ten. In other words, this is evidence that is ten times more likely to exist if the defendant is guilty than if they are innocent. With a prior probability of guilt of 0.2, the posterior probability is 0.7, a probability that, arguably, is too low to justify a retrial in the face of considerations of finality, distress, and public confidence. The Law Commission ultimately recommended that 'the new evidence should be regarded as compelling if, in the opinion of the court, it makes it *highly probable that the defendant is guilty*' (see Law Commission, *Double Jeopardy and Prosecution Appeals* (Law Com No 267, 2001), at 52 (italics added)). This is not the definition of 'compelling' adopted by s 78 of the 2003 Act, which does not refer to the posterior probability of guilt, but only to the probative nature of the evidence. See n 91 below. Here I will not engage in a comparison between the non-binary system that I have envisaged and a binary system that were to implement the Law Commission's proposal, but I admit that it would be an interesting comparison to make.

89 As I will soon recognise, public confidence in the system is unlikely to be undermined by how a single case is dealt with. The point made here, though, is that it may be undermined by the fact that the system allows for cases in which the defendant is retried notwithstanding a low posterior probability of guilt.

90 I want to stress the word 'sometimes'. Of course, if the new evidence is a DNA match going to the issue of the identity of the perpetrator (and assuming that this is the only or main contested issue in the case), it is to be expected that, notwithstanding that the prior probability of guilt is low, the posterior probability of guilt is sufficiently high to overcome the arguments from distress, finality, and public confidence. But this may not be the case with other items of evidence that may well have substantial probative value, albeit less than the DNA match. Think of the testimony of an eyewitness, of an alleged confession to a private individual, of evidence of motive, or of other forms of expert evidence going to the issue of identity. The system is unjustified because it leaves open the possibility of a retrial in cases in which it should not be possible.

91 I should point out that in both *R v Andrews* [2008] EWCA Crim 2908 and *R v Celaire* [2009] EWCA Crim 633, the Court of Appeal appears to treat a high probability of conviction in the new trial as a reason to allow the new trial in the particular cases it decides. However, the court's terse prose surely falls short of interpreting the test in the Criminal Justice Act 2003 as imposing such a requirement. This is no surprise, since the words of the statute do not lend themselves to this interpretation, and there is a long line of cases arguing that the relevant statutory provisions 'require no real gloss', and that the test must be understood 'in the sense explained in the statute itself' (see, among others, *R v Reilly* [2017] EWCA Crim 1333 , para. 29). Moreover, in *Andrews* and *Celaire*, the court offers no articulation of the 'high probability of conviction' ground for retrial in light of considerations of finality, distress, and public confidence. Finally, while the probability of conviction depends on the probability of guilt, the two are not the same, and it is a high probability of guilt that is needed to overcome such considerations. The fact that someone against whom there is not a strong case is very likely to be convicted—say, due to pervasive bias, or to the sensational nature of the new evidence—cannot be sufficient. Consider also the Crown Prosecution Service, *Retrial of Serious Offences: Legal Guidance*, available at <https://www.cps.gov.uk/legal-guidance/retrial-serious-offences> accessed 17 June 2021, stating that '[t]he DPP has agreed that he would only want to proceed in cases in which, as a result of the new evidence a conviction

4.6.1 Conditional acquittal as a response to the challenge of double jeopardy

Incorporating in the verdict system the intermediate verdict of conditional acquittal, while at the same time prohibiting the retrial of the acquitted, avoids the problem raised at the end of the previous section. One may ask how conditional acquittal can overcome the arguments from finality, distress, and public confidence, given that it authorises a retrial in the presence of new incriminating evidence with substantial probative value. Is a system adopting conditional acquittal not undermined by the same reasons that undermine a binary verdict system such as the English and Welsh system, which permits the retrial of the acquitted on the basis of a similar test? The short answer to these questions is that conditional acquittal would only be issued in cases in which the probability of guilt is sufficiently high that, with the discovery of incriminating evidence with substantial probative value, the posterior probability of guilt would be such as to outweigh arguments from distress, finality, and public confidence. The longer answer starts by looking at the roles that the arguments from distress, and from finality, play in the assessment of whether conditional acquittal is justified under the decision-theoretic model and, if it is justified, in the identification of the range of the probability of guilt at which the verdict should be issued.

Notice that the considerations pertaining to finality and distress mentioned in the preceding discussion on double jeopardy can be factored into the evaluation of the outcomes of conditional acquittal. In fact, insofar as issuing conditional acquittal—that is, imposing the possibility of a new trial—denies finality, with the impact that this has on the defendant, and possibly also on others, and insofar as the potential new trial allowed by this verdict causes distress to the defendant, to victims, and to witnesses, these facts can be treated as features of the intermediate

is highly probable, either by a plea of guilty or by the verdict of the jury and any acquittal by a jury would appear to be perverse'. The Court of Appeal has described this guidance as 'entirely appropriate, and consistent with the relevant legislative framework' (*R v Andrews*, ibid, para 28). The passage in the CPS guidance, though, is about the policy of the DPP, not the meaning of the statutory test. And the guidance makes no attempt to articulate the 'high probability of conviction' ground in light of considerations of finality, distress, and public confidence. Someone may argue that these considerations are incorporated into the 'interests of justice' test set by s 79 of the Criminal Justice Act 2003. This interpretation, though, is not without problems. First, notice that the salient factors of the 'interests of justice' test, stated in s 79(2), do not include considerations of finality, distress, or public confidence. There is a reference to trial fairness, which clearly cannot capture the breadth of such considerations. Otherwise, the salient factors pertain to the staleness of the offence allegedly committed, and to the diligence of the police, and of the prosecution. Second, we have seen earlier that whether arguments from finality, distress, and public confidence are overcome depends on the probability of guilt at the time of the new trial. If the English and Welsh test had a requirement concerning such probability, one would expect to find it in the evidential prong of the test, not in the 'interests of justice' one. Finally, the case law offers indications that conflict with the argument at issue. See, in particular, *R v Andrews* (ibid), stating, at paras 40–41, that considerations advanced against the 2003 reform, such as those concerning finality, should not generally be part of the 'interests of justice' test because—allegedly—they have already been overcome with the passing of the Act.

outcomes that affect their respective values.[92] If they are so treated, considerations of distress, and of finality, are relevant to finding out whether conditional acquittal meets the superiority condition: as we know, the satisfaction of this condition depends on the values of the intermediate outcomes. In fact, not only are such considerations relevant to this task, they are also instrumental to identifying the range of the probability of guilt at which issuing conditional acquittal maximises expected value, and is, therefore, warranted, if such a range does exist. Consider Figure 4.3 above. The probability range in question is that between the standards of proof p^1 and p^2. As can be seen from the figure, where these standards lie depends on the values of the possible outcomes of the trial. More precisely, in order to identify each of these standards, we need to use a formula similar to formula (2), where the values taken into account are those of the possible outcomes of the two verdicts between which the standard sits, ie acquittal and the intermediate verdict for p^1, and

[92] Here is a tentative account of these features, with the caveat that whether they are considered relevant, and how they are evaluated, ultimately depends on the theory of punishment that one endorses. On this point, see the previous chapter and the remainder of this section. Let us start with finality. Denying finality essentially means leaving the defendant's legal status undefined and uncertain. The denial of finality is a feature of both intermediate outcomes, since conditional acquittal allows for the retrial of the defendant. The defendant's status of 'conditionally acquitted' is, indeed, inherently changeable, due to the possibility of a new trial taking place. As far as the defendant is concerned, the uncertainty produced by conditional acquittal involves an expected cost, precisely the expected cost of a new trial (and, possibly, a quantum of anxiety due to such expectation). This expected cost is the key component of the hard treatment involved in conditional acquittal, and is already factored into the decision-theoretic argument for this verdict advanced earlier. I am not at all persuaded that the uncertainty concerning the legal status of the defendant produces a cost for the victim. One may argue that it does, since it prevents closure. But it is not at all clear that a 'plain vanilla' acquittal, which does not involve such uncertainty, would not prevent closure as well. The alleged link between uncertainty and lack of closure is, therefore, debatable. Conditional acquittal may, instead, be beneficial to the victim, as I point out below. Arguably, though, the uncertainty concerning the legal status of the defendant may have detrimental consequences for other individuals. Whether for moral or prudential reasons, some people may decide not to engage with the defendant personally or professionally, due to the Damoclean sword of a new trial hanging over the defendant's head, and the related worry that the new trial may disrupt the potential relationships in question. This can be considered a cost for these individuals. And I surmise that it is a cost both when the defendant is innocent and when they are guilty: after all, it can surely be valuable for people to engage personally and professionally with the guilty. On a closer look, the supposed loss in engagement with the defendant is a cost for the defendant as well. And, indeed, the defendant themselves may decide not to enter certain relationships due to the worry of a new trial, with the detrimental consequences that this choice may have for them. This cost for the defendant may be treated as part of the hard treatment imposed by conditional acquittal. Consider, now, distress. It is reasonable to expect that a new trial will cause distress to the defendant. Such distress can easily be factored into the expected cost of a new trial that conditional acquittal imposes on the defendant as a form of hard treatment. What about victims and witnesses? Again, it is reasonable to expect that a new trial will cause distress to them. This, too, is an expected cost of conditional acquittal, this time imposed on individuals other than the defendant. Consider, though, that, between witnesses and victims, the latter are the most likely to experience distress due to a new trial; or, at least, their distress is likely to be greater insofar as the new trial prompts them to relive their experiences of victimisation. And yet, victims may well feel that such distress is dwarfed by the value of a new opportunity to secure the defendant to justice. Some prosecution witnesses may feel the same. From the psychological perspective of these individuals, then, a retrial may be a good thing overall, such that the net effect is actually an expected benefit. The upshot of this tentative analysis is that the most significant features amongst those of the intermediate outcomes pertaining to the denial of finality, and the causing of distress, are already accounted for in the decision-theoretic argument for conditional acquittal, being part of the expected cost that this verdict imposes on the defendant.

the intermediate verdict and conviction for p^2. If considerations of distress, and of finality, affect the values of the intermediate outcomes, they also affect p^1 and p^2.

The crucial point is that, once these considerations have been accounted for in the evaluation of the intermediate outcomes, *if* the decision-theoretic model shows that there is indeed a probability range such that, when the probability of guilt falls within this range, issuing conditional acquittal maximises expected value, the denial of finality and the distress that are involved in this verdict, and in the trial that may result from it, are perforce justified. In particular, this probability range—that is, the range of the prior probability of guilt corresponding to conditional acquittal—will perforce be such that, when new incriminating evidence with substantial probative value is discovered—that is, when the evidential test defining the intermediate verdict is satisfied—the posterior probability of guilt is sufficient to overcome the arguments against retrials based on distress and finality. Why so? Notice that these arguments have been built into the decision-theoretic model: more specifically, into the value function with which the model operates. Therefore, they have been relied upon to assess superiority, and to identify p^1 and p^2. If the model shows that, when the probability of guilt falls within these standards, the adjudicator is justified in issuing conditional acquittal—that is, in imposing the possibility of a retrial if evidence of the requisite kind is found—the arguments from finality and distress do not have any residual role to play that may threaten the justification of the intermediate verdict, and of the retrial that may follow.[93] Notice that, in the case of a binary system of verdicts allowing for the retrial of the acquitted on the basis of new incriminating evidence with substantial probative value, considerations of distress and finality can, surely, be incorporated into the values of the possible outcomes of acquittal. However, since the system has only two possible verdicts, these considerations are only instrumental to identifying the standard of proof for conviction on the basis of formula (2), and not also to identifying a minimum probability threshold such that, when the prior probability of guilt falls below this threshold, a retrial cannot be authorised. A retrial could, potentially, be authorised in any case of acquittal, thus raising the issue discussed in the previous section.

[93] One may worry that factoring considerations of finality and distress into the evaluation of intermediate outcomes may compromise the satisfaction of intermediacy and/or of the superiority condition by conditional acquittal. If this were so, these considerations would undermine the justification of the intermediate verdict from within the decision-theoretic model; but see the previous footnote, showing that, by and large, these considerations are already factored into the decision-theoretic argument for conditional acquittal presented thus far. As seen in the previous chapter, and as I will point out again shortly, the evaluation of trial outcomes ultimately depends on one's theory of punishment (here, I am committing to none in particular). Therefore, whether the satisfaction of the superiority condition is undermined by considerations of finality or distress is also dependent on the chosen theory. The main point advanced here, though, is that, insofar as considerations of distress and finality do not undermine intermediacy and superiority, the decision-theoretic model provides an answer to the challenge of double jeopardy: it gives us a rational way of identifying the posterior probability of guilt at which a retrial is warranted. No such answer is provided by the current English and Welsh regime.

The foregoing discussion highlights an important—perhaps obvious—point. We have seen earlier that, holding constant the innocence or the guilt of the defendant, the difference in the values of trial outcomes is determined by whether these outcomes involve the imposition of hard treatment. However, as already evidenced by the discussion in the previous chapter about the construction of a value function, the evaluation of such imposition (or of the lack thereof) need not consist exclusively in the assessment of the costs and benefits that the imposition has for the defendant. It can, and often will, also include the assessment of the costs and benefits that the imposition of hard treatment on the defendant (or the lack thereof) may have for other individuals, or for society as a whole. An obvious example of this phenomenon is valuing the conviction of the guilty on the ground that it prevents crime, and is, therefore, beneficial to society.[94] Arguments from finality, and from distress, offer other examples, drawing attention to the impact that conditional acquittal may have beyond the defendant.[95] Needless to say, all of these costs and benefits, whether affecting the defendant or others, have to be identified and evaluated in light of the theory of punishment that one endorses. As argued in the previous chapter, it is this theory that determines which values to assign to which outcome, and for what reason.

So far, I have addressed the arguments against retrials based on finality and distress. What about the argument that public confidence in the system is undermined if the system allows for retrials in the absence of convincing reasons for retrying the defendant; that is, when the probability of their guilt is not sufficiently high? The denial of finality and the potential distress caused by a possible new trial

[94] Unlike a pure deterrence theory of punishment, rehabilitative or communicative theories may value the imposition of hard treatment especially in virtue of the benefits that, according to such theories, this imposition has for the defendant. In this sense, they can be said not to use the defendant merely as a means to a further goal. For an attempt to elaborate a deterrence theory of punishment that is compatible with the 'means principle', see V. Tadros, *The Ends of Harm: The Moral Foundations of Criminal Law* (OUP 2011).

[95] Indeed, decision theory sets no limit as to which costs and benefits (whether for the defendant, or for others) can be considered in the assessment of trial outcomes. For example, the assessment of the imposition of conditional acquittal on the innocent may include the expected social costs and benefits of the trial procedure itself (eg the expected monetary cost of a new trial for the State, and the expected gain in remuneration and experience by the personnel involved), the expected cost of false conviction in the new trial, and the expected benefit of true acquittal in the new trial. The assessment of the imposition of conditional acquittal on the guilty, on the other hand, may include the expected social costs and benefits of the trial procedure itself, the expected cost of false acquittal in the new trial, and the expected benefit of true conviction in the new trial. Of course, in calculating the magnitude of these expected costs and benefits, one needs to remember that a new trial is more likely to occur if the defendant is guilty. To be sure, the assessment of the outcomes of conditional acquittal can be more comprehensive than this: indeed, infinitely comprehensive. This is, in fact, true for any trial outcome. As pointed out in the text, which costs and benefits are taken into account, and how they are evaluated, depends on one's theory of punishment: here, I am committing to none in particular. A theory of punishment may well include a practical criterion of saliency, according to which costs and benefits that the theory recognises, but which are too little or too remote, are not taken into account. Indeed, a criterion of this kind is necessary for the workability not just of the decision-theoretic model, but of any argument that claims to identify the standard of proof or the preferable verdict system on the basis of the evaluation of trial outcomes.

are aspects of any token conditional acquittal. They can, therefore, be treated as features of the intermediate outcomes, and accounted for in the outcomes' values. The possible drop in public confidence, instead, is not so much an aspect, or a consequence, of any token case in which conditional acquittal is issued. Rather, it may be the consequence of the very fact that the criminal justice system countenances retrials; that is, of the legislator's decision to reform the verdict system by adopting conditional acquittal, hence permitting retrials.[96] Considerations of public confidence, therefore, cannot easily be incorporated into the decision-theoretic model: this model offers a representation of decision-making in the token criminal case, not of system-level reform decisions, this being a point that I will reconsider in the next chapter. And yet, the model allows us to identify the conditions under which permitting retrials by adding conditional acquittal to the verdict system would not—or, at least, should not—undermine public confidence. Relying on the model, the legislator can find out whether there is a probability range such that, when the probability of guilt falls within that range, conditional acquittal yields higher expected value than 'plain vanilla' acquittal and conviction. Importantly, the decision-theoretic model prompts the legislator to address this question, and to identify the relevant probability range, on the basis of a value function that incorporates all the stakes considered relevant in a token case, including, as seen earlier, considerations of finality, and of distress. If the result of this analysis is that such a probability range does exist, the adjudicator is justified, when the probability of guilt falls within this range, in issuing conditional acquittal; that is, in imposing the possibility of a retrial if evidence of the requisite kind is found. It follows that, if conditional acquittal is issued justifiably, and if the requisite evidence is found, the retrial is justified as well. More precisely, the range of the probability of guilt at which issuing conditional acquittal is warranted will be such that the posterior probability of guilt resulting from the discovery of the requisite evidence is sufficiently high to warrant a retrial. A legal reform allowing for retrials when these epistemic circumstances are present should, therefore, command public confidence. After all, the confidence that reasonable people are expected to have in a reform depends on the reasons in support of such a reform. If the reform is justified on the basis of the rational and comprehensive decision-theoretic analysis just envisaged, public confidence should follow. In the next chapter, I will have more to say in defence of the claim that a decision-theoretic justification of an intermediate verdict should be expected to foster—or, at least, not undermine—the public confidence in a system that adopts such a verdict.

The upshot of this discussion is that the decision-theoretic argument for conditional acquittal offers a rational way of identifying the critical probability threshold such that, when the probability of guilt meets this threshold, arguments from

[96] One may argue that the frequency of the use of this intermediate verdict by the courts may also have a bearing on public confidence.

finality, distress, and public confidence are overcome, and allowing for a retrial is not at odds with the double jeopardy rule. This threshold is met by any posterior probability of guilt resulting from updating a prior probability falling within the range that warrants conditional acquittal, in light of new incriminating evidence with substantial probative value.[97] If conditional acquittal is justified on decision-theoretic grounds, then, it is also a justified exception to the double jeopardy rule.

4.7 Concluding remarks

In this chapter, I have shown that if a binary system of verdicts is premised on a value function that reflects a plausible ordering of the values of the four possible outcomes of the trial, ie $V_{cg} > V_{ai} > V_{ag} > V_{ci}$ or $V_{ai} > V_{cg} > V_{ag} > V_{ci}$, then there is a probability range such that, when the probability of guilt falls within that range, expected value is maximised by issuing a verdict that is intermediate between acquittal and conviction, and satisfies what I have called the 'superiority condition'. My next step was to draw from the superiority condition—which is a simple mathematical formula—a heuristic for the identification of a concrete intermediate verdict that has the potential for being superior under any theory of punishment to which my decision-theoretic argument applies, ie any theory that endorses one of the above orderings, such that the superiority condition is valid for this theory. According to the heuristic, the superiority condition is satisfied if, and only if, the intermediate verdict consists in harder treatment if the defendant receiving it is guilty than if they are innocent.[98] This heuristic requirement is derived from the superiority condition by reasoning about the correspondence between value and hard treatment, which characterises the four standard outcomes.

Looking back at the extant and historical intermediate verdicts studied in Chapter 1, one appreciates that, while these verdicts may, indeed, be intermediate within their respective systems, they may not meet the heuristic requirement concerning superiority. I doubt that the *ius commune poena extraordinaria*, and the Italian acquittal '*per insufficienza di prove*', issued at the end of the trial phase, can

[97] We can identify this threshold with the posterior probability of guilt resulting from updating a prior probability, corresponding to the lower end of the range that warrants conditional acquittal (ie p^1), in light of new incriminating evidence with substantial probative value. Of course, to identify this threshold with precision, we would need a definition of 'substantial probative value' in terms of a corresponding minimum likelihood ratio. I am not pursuing this definition here.

[98] Notice that, if the satisfaction of the heuristic requirement is, indeed, a necessary condition for superiority, a non-infringing intermediate verdict could not be justified on the basis of the decision-theoretic argument that I have offered. This is because a non-infringing intermediate verdict, if there is any such thing, cannot involve hard treatment. See n 6 above, and accompanying text. On a closer look, one sees that a non-infringing verdict could not be an intermediate verdict either, according to the definition of intermediacy given in section 4.3. Insofar as the satisfaction of the heuristic concerning intermediacy identified in section 4.4.1 is, indeed, a necessary condition for intermediacy, for a verdict to be intermediate it must involve hard treatment. cf Chapter 2, n 82.

be characterised as consisting in harder treatment if the defendant receiving them is guilty than if they are innocent. If I am right in this regard, I have not advanced the case for these intermediate verdicts with this chapter. The *ius commune* suspension of res judicata may be a case apart, though. Indeed, my defence of conditional acquittal—which, in essence, is the authorisation of a retrial when new incriminating evidence is found—can be seen as an attempt to reinterpret and justify aspects of this ancient and now-defunct legal device. What about the Scottish 'not proven' verdict? As pointed out in Chapter 1, since the Double Jeopardy (Scotland) Act 2011, this intermediate verdict allows for a retrial in the presence of new incriminating evidence. 'Not proven' may, therefore, meet the heuristic requirement insofar as the applicable test for a new trial is akin to that characterising conditional acquittal. While I cannot engage in a careful comparison between these two tests here, it is arguable that the they are, by and large, equivalent.[99] Importantly, though, even if 'not proven' did indeed meet the heuristic requirement concerning superiority, this would not necessarily mean that the current Scottish verdict system would be justified on decision-theoretic grounds.[100]

Conditional acquittal authorises a retrial in the presence of new incriminating evidence with substantial probative value, this being evidence that, at the time of the first trial, was not known by the authorities, and could not have been known by them, using reasonable diligence. My defence of this verdict offered an opportunity to address the conflictual relationship between acquittal and retrial that characterises the law on double jeopardy. While defending the retrial of those conditionally acquitted, I argued against the retrial of the acquitted, as provided by the Criminal

[99] See, especially, s 4(3)(a) of the Act, mentioning, as a condition for the retrial, that 'there is new evidence that the person committed the original offence . . .', and s 4(7), stating that 'The court may set aside the acquittal only if satisfied that – (a) the case against the person is strengthened substantially by the new evidence, (b) the new evidence was not available, and could not with the exercise of reasonable diligence have been made available, at the trial in respect of the original offence . . . '. To see how the test is interpreted and applied by the courts, consider the leading decision *HM Advocate v Sinclair* [2014] HCJAC 131, in particular paras 97–104. This test focuses on the overall strength of the case, rather than the probative value of the new evidence. In this respect, it seems to differ from the test characterising conditional acquittal. However, the case cannot be 'strengthened substantially' unless the new evidence has substantial probative value. On this rather obvious point, see, in particular, para 100 of the decision.

[100] To begin with, consider that, under the Double Jeopardy (Scotland) Act 2011, a new trial is also allowed in the event of full acquittal, and the test for a new trial is the same for all cases of acquittal. This gives rise to the objection with which I started section 4.6 of this chapter: the substantial equivalence between full acquittal and 'not proven' means that the latter may not be intermediate, not to mention superior, according to the definitions of intermediacy and of superiority given in this chapter. But see n 70 above. Also, the standard of proof for conviction in the Scottish system is the reasonable doubt standard, whereas the system does not include any specific standard regulating the choice between acquittal and 'not proven'. For the system to be justified on decision-theoretic grounds, it would have to feature two standards of proof, ie p^1 and p^2, each derived by adopting a formula similar to formula (2), where the values taken into consideration are those of the possible outcomes of the two verdicts between which each standard sits; that is, full acquittal and 'not proven' for p^1; 'not proven' and conviction for p^2. Each standard should be specified, and there is no guarantee that p^2 would correspond to the reasonable doubt standard. Finally, the retrial of the fully acquitted in the Scottish system may be unjustified for the same reasons that undermine the justification of the retrial of the acquitted in the English and Welsh system. See section 4.6 above. Consider that s 4(7)(c) of the Double Jeopardy (Scotland) Act

Justice Act 2003. On reflection, my proposal to introduce an intermediate verdict is more modest than the reader might at first have feared: as far as the English and Welsh system is concerned, the verdict I defend simply reallocates to a different range of the probability of guilt a form of hard treatment that the law already provides.[101]

Within the evidence law literature discussing the decision-theoretic argument for the selection of the standard of proof in a binary system, it was pointed out that it is difficult to justify, on decision-theoretic grounds, a standard of proof as high as proof beyond a reasonable doubt,[102] which is associated, by some, with a probability of 0.9.[103] The claim is that any reasonable assignment of value to the four standard outcomes of the trial produces a standard of proof that is lower than 0.9. Be that as it may, in this chapter I have shown that, whatever the standard of proof of the relevant binary system, if a superior intermediate verdict is adopted, the standard of proof for conviction increases. Indeed, as can be seen from Figure 4.3 above, p^2 is always higher than p^*, given superiority. True, the intermediate verdict imposes a quantum of hard treatment when the probability of guilt satisfies a standard of proof lower than p^*. But the most severe measures that the criminal justice system employs would be justified only when guilt is proven to a higher standard than that of the binary system. This indicates that the introduction of an intermediate verdict, and especially of a verdict such as conditional acquittal, may well be a shift towards less, rather than more, punitiveness.

In the previous chapter, I showed that, in the context of the adjudicator's problem whether to convict or acquit, both consequentialists and deontologists about punishment can follow the principle of maximising expected value without thereby relinquishing any tenets of their respective theories. Building on this, the present chapter has shown that, if a theory of punishment endorses one of two plausible orderings of the values of the standard outcomes of the trial—not a demanding requirement—this theory must accept that an intermediate verdict that satisfies the superiority condition maximises expected value, if issued when the probability of guilt falls within a certain range. This is an interesting result in itself, which opens the door to the possibility of justifying concrete forms of intermediate

2011 conditions the new trial on the satisfaction of the requirement that 'on the new evidence and the evidence which was led at [the original] trial, it is highly likely that a reasonable jury . . . would have convicted' the defendant. This requirement, though, is not equivalent to that of a sufficiently high posterior probability of guilt, and it is such probability that is needed to overcome considerations of distress, finality, and public confidence, against retrying the acquitted. On this point see n 91 above.

101 But see n 70 above, for a possible difference between the hard treatment involved in conditional acquittal and that involved in the acquittal that currently features in the English and Welsh system. See also n 69 above.

102 See T. Connolly, 'Decision Theory, Reasonable Doubt, and the Utility of Erroneous Acquittals' (1987) 11 Law and Human Behaviour 101, at 107–111.

103 See n 28 above.

verdicts from the perspective of both consequentialist and deontological theories of punishment.[104] Having drawn from inequality (6) the heuristic requirement that the intermediate verdict should consist in harder treatment if the defendant receiving it is guilty than if they are innocent, I then identified conditional acquittal as a verdict that meets this requirement, and has, therefore, potential for being intermediate and superior under any of the theories of punishment for which inequality (6) is valid. As explained in section 4.4.2, in fact, satisfying the heuristic requirement is no guarantee of actual superiority. My case for conditional acquittal, then, is a prima facie case only. A fully fledged value function is needed to assess whether it is, indeed, a superior intermediate verdict. In other words, its superiority depends on the theory of punishment endorsed.

I have not shown that conditional acquittal does indeed meet the superiority condition under any of the theories of punishment to which my argument applies. I leave it to the supporters of these theories to address this question. However, I want to briefly defend the claim that conditional acquittal is a valuable form of hard treatment under any plausible theory of punishment; in other words, that the imposition of conditional acquittal *on the guilty* furthers the goals of any such theory, whether these are retribution, deterrence, Duff's three Rs, and/or something else. Now, unlike the hard treatment that, according to any given theory of punishment, should be involved in conviction, the hard treatment involved

[104] Notice that the argument presented in Chapter 3, according to which a deontologist can follow the principle of maximising expected value without fearing a departure from the deontological norms studied there, still holds once an intermediate verdict is introduced into the verdict system. Consider that, given intermediacy, $V_{cg} > V_{ig} > V_{ag}$. If so, for any of the interpretations of 'categorical belief' (hence, of knowledge) surveyed in the previous chapter, when the restriction requiring conviction or the permission allowing conviction apply (ie when the adjudicator knows that the defendant is guilty), the principle of maximising expected value requires conviction as well, rather than the intermediate verdict, or acquittal. Remember that, according to the third interpretation of 'categorical belief', a categorical belief in guilt is the degree of belief in guilt that justifies acting as the adjudicator would act if they were certain that the defendant is guilty (that is, in light of the above ordering of values, it justifies convicting), given the values of the possible outcomes of the decision problem. With the addition of an intermediate verdict, this degree of belief is represented by a probability of guilt that is equal to, or greater than, p^2. With such a probability of guilt, expected value is, indeed, maximised by convicting. Also consider that, given intermediacy, $V_{ai} > V_{ii} > V_{ci}$. If so, for any of the interpretations of 'categorical belief' (hence, of knowledge) surveyed in the previous chapter, when the restriction requiring acquittal applies (ie when the adjudicator knows that the defendant is innocent), the principle of maximising expected value requires acquittal as well, rather than the intermediate verdict, or conviction. Remember that, according to the third interpretation of 'categorical belief', a categorical belief in innocence is the degree of belief in innocence that justifies acting as the adjudicator would act if they were certain that the defendant is innocent (that is, in light of the above ordering of values, it justifies acquitting), given the values of the possible outcomes of the decision problem. With the addition of an intermediate verdict, this degree of belief is represented by a probability of guilt that is equal to, or lower than, p^1. With such a probability of guilt, expected value is, indeed, maximised by acquitting. In any case, were the three deontological norms in conflict with the principle of maximising expected value, then, as argued in Chapter 3, a deontologist adjudicator would have to follow the principle when these norms do not apply, ie when the adjudicator does not have the requisite knowledge. This would leave scope for the deontologist adjudicator to issue an intermediate verdict, according to the argument that I have defended in this chapter.

in conditional acquittal may not be seen as furthering the theory's goals. If this were so, the theory would view conditional acquittal as imposing on defendants a fruitless cost, irrespective of whether they were innocent or guilty. Notice that, if a theory of punishment viewed conditional acquittal in these terms, the verdict could not possibly be intermediate, according to the definition given in section 4.3; hence, it could not be the sort of verdict that I am trying to justify. Indeed, intermediacy requires that the verdict be considered valuable when imposed on the guilty, and that it be considered detrimental when imposed on the innocent. If the verdict were not so considered, the value of imposing it on the guilty could hardly be greater than that of not imposing any hard treatment on them—that is, of acquitting them—and the value of imposing it on the innocent could hardly be smaller than that of acquitting the innocent. Arguably, any plausible theory of punishment would consider the imposition of conditional acquittal on the innocent as detrimental. I contend that any plausible theory would also consider the imposition of this verdict on the guilty as valuable.

Conditional acquittal is the imposition of an expectation. What is expected is something that any plausible theory of punishment already countenances and justifies: a trial and, in the event of conviction, the hard treatment of choice, ie the kind of hard treatment that furthers the theory's goals. What conditional acquittal does, then, is to impose on the defendant the possibility of procedures and treatments that a theory already considers valuable. I fail to see how, if these procedures and treatments can further the theory's goals when imposed on the guilty, imposing on the guilty the possibility of them occurring could not. Indeed, a theory of punishment that cannot justify imposing on the guilty (in fact, on any individual) the possibility of these measures can hardly justify setting up a criminal justice system: a choice which involves precisely this imposition. When assessing the value of issuing conditional acquittal against the guilty, one should also consider that, as seen earlier, arguments against a retrial based on finality and distress yield when the probability of guilt is sufficiently high. If so, they surely yield when the defendant is *ex hypothesi* guilty. This means that the denial of finality, and the causing of distress, involved in the intermediate outcomes should not undermine the beneficial nature of issuing conditional acquittal against the guilty.[105] Now, if

[105] As for the stigma that may be produced by conditional acquittal, consider that stigma—whether intended by the legislator or not—is an (inevitable?) epiphenomenon of conviction. Moreover, an epiphenomenon that is increasing considerably during the age of Internet (see S. E. Lageson and S. Maruna, 'Digital Degradation: Stigma Management in the Internet Age' (2018) 20 Punishment and Society 113; and A. Corda and S. E. Lageson, 'Disordered Punishment: Workaround Technologies of Criminal Records Disclosure and the Rise of a New Penal Entrepreneurialism' (2019) 60 British Journal of Criminology 245). Hence, stigma is an element of hard treatment that any realistic theory of punishment must justify (thus considering the imposition of stigma on the guilty valuable) or, at least, come to terms with (thus considering the imposition of stigma on the guilty not valuable, but a factor that is outweighed by the value of imposing other components of hard treatment).

conditional acquittal is, indeed, intermediate under any plausible theory of punishment, the fact that this verdict consists in harder treatment when the defendant receiving it is guilty than when they are innocent is a strong indication that it satisfies the superiority condition in inequality (6) under any such theory. But, again, I leave it to others to address this question properly.

I concluded the last chapter by offering a restatement of a hypothetical from Frank Jackson, in which the physician, Jill, is facing a decision about which treatment to give to her patient, John. In my view, the restatement triggers the intuition that there is a probability range such that if the probability that John has the relevant condition is within this range, expected value is maximised by choosing the option that is intermediate between giving a whole pill of the relevant medicine and not giving any treatment. The hypothetical incorporates a feature that, arguably, plays an important role in triggering the intuition; a feature shared with the three hypotheticals presented in the Introduction to the book. This is the fact that the intermediate option is more beneficial if the fact at issue is true than it is detrimental if such fact is false.[106] To be more precise, this option has a greater impact in terms of relieving the condition if John is, indeed, affected by the condition than it does in terms of causing discomfort if John does not have the condition. This feature renders, or contributes to rendering,[107] the intermediate option intuitively appealing from the perspective of Jill, when she experiences significant doubt about whether John has the condition. Indeed, if he does have the condition, the intermediate option will produce notable benefit by performing, albeit to a limited extent, the healing function of giving the full pill; if he does not have it, instead, this option will worsen the state of affairs only marginally. The differential impact of the intermediate option in Jill's case strikes me as comparable to the differential in hard treatment required by the heuristic concerning the superiority of an intermediate verdict. Even if someone considers this heuristic requirement in isolation—that is, independently of the decision-theoretic argument that I relied upon to derive it—an intermediate verdict that satisfies the requirement still seems an intuitively appealing option

[106] The benefits and harms of Jill's intermediate option are calculated by comparison with the state of affairs at the time of the decision.

[107] As in the examples offered in the Introduction to the book, in Jill's case, too, the intermediate option presents smaller error costs than the extreme options. This, too, seems a relevant consideration in favour of choosing the intermediate option, in the event of doubt. But see Introduction, n 10, on this point. A decision-theoretic analysis of Jill's case would be necessary to assess whether the differential impact characterising the intermediate option makes it the case that there is a probability range such that, when the probability that John has the condition falls within that range, the intermediate option maximises expected value. I cannot undertake such an analysis here.

when the probability of guilt is somewhere in the proximity of the standard of proof of a binary system, such that the adjudicator experiences significant doubt about whether to convict or acquit. This intuitive appeal flows from the fact that, if issued, the verdict is more similar to conviction if the defendant receiving it is guilty than if they are innocent.[108]

[108] But see the Conclusion to this book, on this point. Notice that I have been careful not to say that an intermediate verdict satisfying the heuristic requirement concerning superiority is more beneficial if imposed on the guilty than it is detrimental if imposed on the innocent. In fact, someone may contend that the benefit of imposing a quantum of hard treatment on the guilty is outweighed by the cost of imposing the same, or even a smaller, quantum of hard treatment on the innocent. Hence, a verdict that satisfies the heuristic requirement may well be more detrimental if imposed on the innocent than it is beneficial if imposed on the guilty. This is a notable difference between this intermediate option and that in Jill's case, or in each of the three examples given in the introduction. This is why I have referred to the differential impact in hard treatment demanded by the heuristic requirement as 'comparable', rather than 'equivalent', to the differential impact of the intermediate option in Jill's case.

5
A Battery of Objections

5.1 Introduction

In this final chapter, I address a series of objections. Some of these objections are specifically targeted at the decision-theoretic justification of intermediate criminal verdicts offered in the previous chapter. They criticise aspects of this justification, rather than the adoption of an intermediate verdict per se. Other objections, instead, attack precisely the addition of an intermediate verdict to the verdict system. Here is what is on the menu. In section 5.2, I consider an objection to the effect that the decision-theoretic model that I rely upon gives a representation of criminal adjudication that is simplistic. In section 5.3, I consider a further three objections, each claiming that the model cannot register a particular important effect that the adoption of an intermediate verdict is likely to produce in the criminal justice system. In section 5.4, I address worries concerning the implementation of the decision-theoretic model. In section 5.5, I address two objections according to which the legal system already features devices that are equivalent to an intermediate verdict. These objections suggest that, if the system should be amended at all, it would be preferable to enhance these devices rather than adopting an intermediate verdict. To conclude, in section 5.6 I address the objection that an intermediate verdict offers the adjudicator the opportunity to dodge their decision-making responsibilities; in other words, that the verdict may be used as a 'cop-out'.

None of these objections is framed as an objection to the specific intermediate verdict that I defended in the previous chapter; that is, conditional acquittal. In fact, I will argue, with reference to some of these objections, that they become considerably weaker if framed in these terms. I advance no claim that the set of objections addressed in this chapter is exhaustive. Indeed, I address other objections to intermediate verdicts throughout the book, especially in my reconstruction of the debates relating to the *ius commune*, the Italian, and the Scottish intermediate verdicts. And, no doubt, there will be more criticisms—possibly fatal ones—that I have not considered. What I present in this chapter, together with the argument from the presumption of innocence addressed in Chapter 2, are the main objections that were raised during exchanges with colleagues, or that emerged as a result of thinking hard about the issue of intermediate verdicts.

Justice In-Between, Federico Picinali, Oxford University Press. © Federico Picinali 2022.
DOI: 10.1093/oso/9780198864592.003.0006

5.2 Not all cases are alike

The decision-theoretic model on which I have based my defence of conditional acquittal concerns adjudication in a token criminal case, and identifies the condition under which an intermediate verdict is superior to both acquittal and conviction in such a case. It may be objected, though, that criminal cases can vary dramatically, such that it is unreasonable to represent the phenomenon of criminal adjudication through a token case, and to draw from the analysis of such a case conclusions concerning adjudication as a whole. In particular, by so representing this phenomenon, the decision-theoretic model seems to posit that the values of the four standard outcomes are constant across all criminal cases. This, however, is very unlikely.

There are several factors, likely to contribute to the values of the standard outcomes under many theories of punishment, that may vary from one case to another. Consider, among others, the seriousness of the crime charged; the presence and number of victims; the type and extent of the applicable punishment; the dangerousness of the defendant, as indicated by their criminal history; and whether the defendant has dependants. The variation of each of these factors may affect the values of at least some of the outcomes. For instance, other things being equal, falsely convicting a defendant is, arguably, worse the greater the applicable punishment is, and it is, arguably, worse if the defendant has dependants who would be affected by the conviction. Similarly, other things being equal, falsely acquitting a defendant is, arguably, worse the more serious the crime charged is, and it is, arguably, worse the greater the risk is that they will recidivate, if not punished.

If the values of the four standard outcomes vary depending on these and other factors, though, the standard of proof of the binary system is bound to vary as well, such that, under the decision-theoretic model, there could not be a unique standard of proof applying in all criminal trials. Indeed, the standard of proof is determined by formula (2), set out in the previous chapter, which features as inputs the values of the four standard outcomes.[1] Also, the variation of the values of these

[1] This problem is discussed in F. Picinali, 'Two Meanings of "Reasonableness": Dispelling the "Floating" Reasonable Doubt' (2013) 76 Modern Law Review 845, at 847–850; E. Lillquist, 'Recasting Reasonable Doubt: Decision Theory and the Virtues of Variability' (2002) 36 UC Davis Law Review 85, at 147–162; and R. D. Bartels, 'Punishment and The Burden of Proof in Criminal Cases: A Modest Proposal' (1981) 66 Iowa Law Review 899, at 907–908. It seems unreasonable to expect that the variation of the values of the four standard outcomes would be such that the value of the ratio $\frac{V_{cg} - V_{ag}}{V_{ai} - V_{ci}}$ (which features in formula (2)) would remain constant, and that, therefore, the standard of proof would be the same across the system. On this point, see Lillquist, ibid, at 150–151. cf A. Walen, 'Proof Beyond a Reasonable Doubt: A Balanced Retributive Account' (2015) 76 Louisiana Law Review 355, at 436–437, giving a decision-theoretic retributive justification of the reasonable doubt standard, and arguing that, in the generality of cases, the standard of proof would be the same. For non-decision-theoretic defences of a variable standard of proof, see H. L. Ho, *A Philosophy of Evidence Law: Justice in the Search for Truth* (OUP 2008), ch 4, and G. Ribeiro, 'The Case for Varying Standards of Proof' (2019) 56 San Diego Law Review 161. See also S. Moss, 'Pragmatic Encroachment and Legal Proof' (2021) 31 Philosophical

outcomes might have repercussions for the justification of an intermediate verdict. Since the superiority of the verdict with respect to acquittal, and to conviction, depends on the position that the values of the intermediate outcomes have in the value function relative to the values of the standard outcomes—as indicated by inequality (6)—if the latter values vary across the system, an intermediate verdict that is superior in one case might not be superior in another. What is more, the values of intermediate outcomes themselves may vary across the system. This seems to be the case for conditional acquittal, at least. Indeed, the stigma that the verdict may produce might vary depending on the seriousness of the crime charged. Also—and I will look at this point in more detail later—the expected cost of a new trial arguably depends on the seriousness of the crime, and on the related factor of the severity of the punishment warranted by this crime. Both stigma and the expected cost of a new trial affect the values of the intermediate outcomes; or, they should be expected to affect such values under any plausible theory of punishment.

The objection, then, boils down to pointing out that the decision-theoretic model gives the false impression of a homogeneous system, in which the values of the outcomes are fixed once and for all. In fact, the reality is much more complicated than this. The variables that the model takes as unchanging do, indeed, acquire different values. This has ramifications for the setting of the standard of proof in the binary system, and for the justification of intermediate verdicts: ramifications that the decision-theoretic model seems to gloss over. Notice that the objection may well hold for any theory of punishment. Insofar as a theory acknowledges that varying factors, such as those mentioned above, play a role in the evaluation of trial outcomes, it is highly implausible that, under such a theory, the values of these outcomes could remain constant across all cases.

In replying to this objection, I consider, first, the implications that it has for the selection of the standard of proof in the binary system. Building on this discussion, I will later consider the objection's implications for the justification of intermediate verdicts, and of conditional acquittal in particular. Let me start by saying that I agree that, if one relies on decision theory, they should accept that the standard of proof of a binary system may vary from one case to another as a function of factors such as those highlighted by the objection, which inform the values of the standard outcomes. Indeed, I expect that the standard of proof will vary across the range of criminal cases. While the model that I have relied upon in Chapter 4 is, undoubtedly, too simple to account for the complexity of the phenomenon of criminal adjudication, I will show that, with some adjustments, the accuracy of the model can be improved dramatically. Consider, also, that the variability of the standard of proof is not a problem exclusive to the decision-theoretic justification

Issues 258, arguing that conviction requires knowledge of guilt, and that whether the fact-finder knows that the defendant is guilty depends on what is at stake in adjudication, which includes the variable consequences that the defendant may face if convicted.

of the standard. Any theory that aims at justifying the standard of proof on the basis of the values of trial outcomes has to confront the issue that the standard may vary as a function of the variability of these values. As I have argued in Chapter 3, justifying the standard of proof without regard for the values of trial outcomes is not at all a sensible strategy. The problem discussed here, then, affects any reasonable theory of the standard.

In Chapter 4, I defended the view that it is for the legislator to assess the values of trial outcomes and, on this basis, select the standard of proof. I appealed, there, to the delicacy of these operations, and to the importance that like cases be treated equally. Having now unveiled the problem of the variability of the outcomes' values and, consequently, of the standard of proof, some may argue that the adjudicator is better positioned to undertake these tasks. Unlike the legislator, the adjudicator has access to the relevant factors that pertain to the particular case, and can, therefore, tailor the standard of proof to the case, in the light of the impact that these factors have on the outcomes' values.[2] This is all very well, but if sentencing guidelines can indeed cater for the relevant specifics of future cases in which they will be applied, so can the legislator identify, in the abstract, factors that are relevant to the evaluation of trial outcomes, and evaluate such outcomes accordingly. I do not see anything distinctively problematic about the latter task. Of course, the resulting assessment may not be as fine-grained as it would be if it had been made by a reliable and sensible adjudicator, tuned into the theory of punishment that reflects the values of their community. But it is hardly uncommon for legal rules to be rough around the edges. And, more importantly, the arguments from delicacy and equal treatment indicate that a quantum of imprecision can be tolerated for the sake of more important values that risk being undermined if the task of selecting the standard is assigned to adjudicators. Still, the question remains as to how the legislator should handle the problem of the variability of the standard of proof in the binary system.

I present here what I consider to be the two main strategies that the legislator could follow. Both require that the legislator classifies by type of case the array of cases that could, potentially, be tried in the criminal justice system. To clarify, these strategies require that the legislator identifies mutually exclusive types of potential cases, based on the factors that are responsible for the variation of the outcomes' values,[3] such that each type will present a distinctive set of values of the four

[2] See Lillquist (n 1), at 147–176, and D. A. Nance, *The Burdens of Proof: Discriminatory Power, Weight of Evidence, and Tenacity of Belief* (CUP 2016), at 41–42, 252. Both Lillquist and Nance accept—indeed, welcome—the fact that the standard of proof may vary depending on the circumstances of the case. They argue that this variability should be realised by letting the jury make minor adjustments to the values previously expressed by the legislator. A similar view is found in Bartels (n 1), at 905–910.

[3] Precisely because the assessment is made by the legislator with regard to potential cases, the factor consisting in the severity of punishment cannot possibly represent the punishment actually meted out in an individual case. Indeed, this would be true even if the assessment were made by the adjudicator, since sentencing takes place after the standard of proof has been identified and employed. This factor,

standard outcomes. The types identified by the legislator should cover the whole array of potential cases. Of course, which factors are taken into account for the purposes of the classification will depend on the theory of punishment endorsed. For example, as seen in Chapter 3, if someone endorses a theory according to which instrumental reasons for punishing should not be factored into the evaluation of trial outcomes, they will not consider the dangerousness of the defendant—and, hence, the benefit of incapacitating the defendant—as factors that increase the values of both true and false conviction or, alternatively, decrease the values of both false and true acquittal. Therefore, these factors will not be relevant to their classification. In reality, the class of cases represented by each type identified by the legislator may turn out not to be internally homogenous: despite formally falling under the same type, actual cases may present relevant characteristics that were not accounted for in the classification and, hence, they may present different sets of values of the four outcomes. This inaccuracy can be minimised by adopting a sufficiently fine-grained classification. But, again, inaccuracy is part and parcel of rulemaking.

Given this classification of the array of potential cases, the first strategy to handle the problem of the variability of the standard requires calculating, for each of the four standard outcomes, the average of the values that it acquires in the different types of cases that determine the classification. These four average values should then be plugged into formula (2), so that a single standard of proof is chosen for the whole system. However, it does not take much thinking to see that this solution is unsatisfactory. Consider that the number of potential cases of each type may not be constant across all types. If there is such variation, it would be fairer if the value of each standard outcome to be plugged into (2) were a *weighted* average of the values that the outcome acquires in the different types of cases featured in the system. To clarify, in calculating the average, the value that an outcome acquires in a given type of cases should be weighted by the number, or the rate, of cases of that type that the system is likely to process in the period in which the standard of proof will be operative. This number, or rate, could be inferred from statistics about the array of actual cases dealt with by the system during a representative period of time, and should be checked periodically against new statistics. This guarantees that, in the determination of the standard of proof, for each standard outcome the values that characterise a higher number of potential cases carry more weight than the values that characterise a lower number. Still, there would be a single standard of proof for the whole system.

While having a single standard of proof is optimal from the perspective of implementation, it is suboptimal from the perspective of accuracy. The worry is that many cases would be decided on a standard of proof that does not accurately reflect the actual stakes. The second strategy to handle the problem of the variability of

instead, can be conceived of as referring to the range of punishment that is available for a particular crime or, possibly, to the minimum or maximum of this range, or to an average of the two.

the standard of proof sacrifices optimality from the perspective of implementation, in order to gain more accuracy. The strategy is straightforward: there should be as many standards of proof as there are types that make up the array of cases that are potentially tried in the system. This strategy leaves plenty of scope for trading off accuracy with ease of implementation. The more coarse-grained the classification, the fewer the standards of proof; hence, the easier the implementation. For example, in order to reduce complexity, the legislator may decide to ignore personal factors such as the criminal history of the defendant, or their family situation, focusing instead on the nature of the crime. Also, if two or more types of case present standards of proof that are very close to one another, the legislator may decide to merge these different types and apply, for the resulting type, a standard of proof that is the weighted average of the standards of proof of the original types. Of course, all of these simplifying decisions will need justifying in light of the balance between ease of implementation and accuracy.

Let us now consider how the system would be altered with the addition of an intermediate verdict such as conditional acquittal. As pointed out earlier, the values of each outcome of conditional acquittal are likely to vary across the system. This is because the hard treatment involved in the verdict depends on the seriousness of the crime charged, and on the related factor of the severity of the punishment that is warranted by that crime. Let me explain. Consider, first, that if the verdict produces stigma, this may well vary with the seriousness of the crime charged.[4] Second, the expected cost that a new trial has for the defendant will vary on the basis of the seriousness of the crime, and the related factor of the severity of punishment. Indeed, not only is the cost of a new trial for the defendant greater when the punishment that they can receive if convicted in such trial is greater, but also, the probability of a new trial arguably depends on the seriousness of the crime. When the crime at issue is serious, the system has interests in retrying the defendant if the evidential circumstances allow for this; hence, the investigating authorities will make significant efforts to identify the new evidence that will warrant a retrial. When the crime is minor, instead, the system may not care about having another go at the defendant, and these authorities will put little to no effort into identifying the new evidence. This means that, *ceteris paribus*, the probability of a retrial will be higher in a case involving a serious crime than in a case involving a minor one. Now, if indeed the cost of a retrial increases with the severity of the possible punishment, and the probability of a retrial increases with the seriousness of the crime, one can conclude that the expected cost of a retrial will be greater in a case involving a serious crime than in a case involving a minor one.

[4] cf S. Ispa-Landa and C. E. Loeffler, 'Indefinite Punishment and the Criminal Record: Stigma Reports Among Expungement-Seekers in Illinois' (2006) 54 Criminology 387. This US study indicates that individuals with a criminal history experience ongoing stigma (causing loss of employment, housing, and educational opportunities), whether their criminal history is extensive and serious or, instead, limited and minor.

Notwithstanding that the values of the intermediate outcomes may vary across the system, the intermediacy of conditional acquittal may well be preserved in every case. Indeed, it is plausible to argue that, whether the defendant is innocent or guilty, the stigma and the expected cost involved in conditional acquittal are always harder treatment than acquittal and milder treatment than conviction. Insofar as this is sufficient for intermediacy,[5] the value of the intermediate outcome involving innocence should sit between the values of convicting the innocent and of acquitting the innocent, whereas the value of the intermediate outcome involving guilt should sit between the values of convicting the guilty and of acquitting the guilty. One might worry that, in the case of minor crimes, a new trial is harder treatment than the punishment involved in conviction, and that issuing conditional acquittal would, therefore, consist in harder treatment than convicting. However, besides the fact that the stigma that conditional acquittal may produce would likely be lower than that produced by conviction, one has to consider that the new trial is just a possibility, not a necessity, and that, for minor crimes, the expected cost of the new trial is indeed very low, for the reasons mentioned earlier. If necessary, though, in order to guarantee intermediacy, one could take the option of reducing the severity of the punishment that would be available in the second trial, as compared to that available in the first, to the extent that is needed to render the expected cost imposed by conditional acquittal a milder treatment than conviction.

However, there is reason to believe that conditional acquittal would not be superior to acquittal, and to conviction, in all cases. There may be a threshold of seriousness of a crime, below which the system is just not interested in retrying those who have not been convicted. To be sure, whether such a threshold exists and, if so, where it sits, are matters for the legislator to decide.[6] But if it does exist, then the probability of a new trial for crimes below the threshold would be nil. If so, the expected cost of a new trial that conditional acquittal would impose on the defendant, if implemented, would also be nil: the hard treatment involved in the intermediate verdict would consist exclusively of the stigma that the verdict may produce.[7] Since the differential impact of the verdict on the innocent and the guilty, respectively, depends on the expected cost of a retrial, if this expected cost were nil, the differential impact would disappear. As argued in the previous chapter, superiority

[5] As pointed out in the previous chapter (see section 4.4.2), the satisfaction of the heuristic requirement concerning intermediacy is no guarantee of actual intermediacy.

[6] In this regard, it is significant to note that a post-acquittal retrial under the English and Welsh Criminal Justice Act 2003 is available only for a selected group of serious offences listed in pt 1 of sch 5 of the Act. In the autumn of 2021, I submitted two freedom of information requests to the Ministry of Justice, inquiring about the number of acquittals for the relevant offences, the number of applications for a retrial, and the number of Court of Appeal retrial orders. In the period between 2016 and 2020, the number of all acquittals for offences in sch. 5 ranged between 2300 per year and 605 per year (these figures do not include cases in which someone was acquitted of one offence but convicted of another). In the period between 2006 and 2020, the applications for a retrial have been, at most, four per year, and the Court of Appeal orders have been, at most, two per year. Taken together, these data indicate that the probability of being retried, if acquitted of any of the relevant offences, is quite low.

[7] This hard treatment should be sufficient for intermediacy, but consider what follows.

may well depend on this differential impact. If this is correct, conditional acquittal could not be superior to acquittal and conviction. This means that, for crimes falling below the relevant threshold of seriousness, the verdict system would have to be binary. Should the legislator consider that there is a relevant classification of this set of insufficiently serious crimes, in light of internal variations of the values of the four standard outcomes, they could identify the applicable standard(s) of proof by following either the weighted average strategy, or the 'as many standards as there are types' strategy. If there is no relevant classification, of course, a single standard of proof applies to the whole set.

What about crimes above the threshold of seriousness? In such cases, the system is interested in retrying those who have not been convicted, if the evidential circumstances allow for this. Hence, the probability of a new trial is not nil, and the differential impact discussed in the previous chapter is operative. There should, therefore, be a probability range such that conditional acquittal is superior to acquittal and conviction, if issued when the probability of guilt falls within that range.[8] This range is identified by the standards of proof p^1 and p^2, which control the adjudicator's decision when the intermediate verdict is added to the verdict system. In order to identify the probability thresholds corresponding to these standards, we need to use a formula similar to formula (2) from the previous chapter, where the values taken into consideration are those of the possible outcomes of the two verdicts between which the standard sits; that is, acquittal and conditional acquittal for p^1, and conditional acquittal and conviction for p^2. For reasons explained earlier, though, the values of the intermediate outcomes, and of the standard outcomes, may vary across the set of crimes falling above the threshold of seriousness. If so, p^1 and p^2 are likely to vary as well, across such a set. Here, the legislator faces a now-familiar choice. The starting point is to classify by type of cases the set of cases falling above the threshold of seriousness, based on the relevant factors that vary across the set, such that each type of cases has a distinctive series of values of the six possible outcomes. Given this classification, ease of implementation is maximised by adopting the weighted average strategy for both standards of proof, so that there would be only one p^1 and one p^2 for the whole set.[9] Alternatively, the legislator may trade a decrease in ease of implementation for an increase in accuracy, and enforce a distinctive pair of standards for each type of cases in this set.

[8] Of course, this depends on whether the satisfaction of the heuristic requirement concerning superiority is, indeed, sufficient for superiority. As pointed out in the previous chapter (see section 4.4.2), this may not be the case. Also consider that, as suggested earlier, superiority might be affected by a possible variation of the values of the standard outcomes in cases falling above the threshold of seriousness. If there were a type of cases, above this threshold, for which the intermediate verdict is not superior, these cases should be tried with a binary set-up. See also n 6 above, keeping in mind that the probability of being retried, if acquitted, under the English and Welsh Criminal Justice Act 2003 need not be the same as that of being retried, when receiving an intermediate verdict, under a hypothetical system including conditional acquittal. The latter probability need not be so low that the differential impact of conditional acquittal is negligible.

[9] I do not see how adopting the weighted average strategy could possibly lead to values that compromise the intermediacy of the verdict, or make it the case that inequality (6) is not satisfied, considering that, *ex hypothesi*, the conditions of intermediacy and inequality (6) are satisfied for each type of cases falling above the threshold of seriousness. If I were wrong about this, though, the legislator would

The bottom line is that, notwithstanding that the values of outcomes vary across the array of criminal cases, the resulting verdict system need not be complex at all. Using the weighted average strategy, the legislator could identify a single standard of proof for the binary set-up that applies to minor crimes, and a single pair of p^1 and p^2 for the non-binary set-up that applies to more serious crimes. If this is seen as too inaccurate a reflection of the values at stake, for either set of crimes the legislator can implement the 'as many standards as there are types' strategy, choosing the classification that best balances the conflicting goals of accuracy and ease of implementation.

5.3 Effects not registered in the decision-theoretic justification

Reforming the verdict system with the adoption of an intermediate verdict may produce a series of important effects on the system as a whole. It may be argued that the decision-theoretic model is incapable of registering these effects. This is because the model focuses on decision-making in a token case, whereas these effects are not the result of the decision in any token case: therefore, they cannot be meaningfully accounted for in the description and evaluation of the possible trial outcomes, and of the intermediate outcomes in particular. Indeed, the effects in question are the result of the availability itself of an intermediate verdict; that is, of the legislator's choice to reform the verdict system by adopting such a verdict. No representation of such a system-level reform decision (in particular, of the outcomes it may produce) is found in the decision-theoretic model. Now, if these effects are plausible and significant, and if, indeed, they cannot be registered in the decision-theoretic model, the justification of intermediate verdicts offered in the previous chapter appears incomplete. Here, I consider two possible systemic effects of the introduction of an intermediate verdict that present this problem: the effect on the behaviour of prosecutors, and the effect on the legitimacy of the criminal justice system. However, I will start my analysis by considering a distinct effect: the deterrent effect related to the probability of hard treatment. As with the other effects just mentioned, with regard to this effect, too, it is possible to argue that it cannot be registered in the decision-theoretic model. However, in this case, the alleged impossibility is due to a more technical reason, pertaining to the particular way in which the model derives the standard of proof.

5.3.1 Deterrence and the stringency of the standard of proof

It is arguable that the stringency of the standard of proof influences the behaviour of individuals. In particular, other things being equal, the lower the standard of proof,

have to adopt the 'as many standards as there are types' strategy, choosing the appropriate level of precision of the classification by balancing accuracy and ease of implementation.

the greater the incentive not to commit crime should be. This is because the agent is likely to perceive that, if they act criminally, the probability of being subjected to hard treatment is greater when a lower standard is in place.[10] If this view is correct, it follows that the introduction of an intermediate verdict that involves hard treatment should influence the rate of criminality: in particular, it should decrease it. Indeed, the intermediate verdict makes hard treatment available at probabilities of guilt that are lower than the probability at which hard treatment is available under the binary system. It should not come as a surprise, then, that an argument from deterrence has been employed to defend a non-binary system of verdicts where hard treatment increases gradually with the probability of guilt, and attaches to probabilities that are below the current standard of proof.[11] Indeed, as seen in Chapter 1, in the 19th century an argument from deterrence was advanced in support of the *poena extraordinaria*. The question is whether the decision-theoretic model can reflect the comparative assessment of the deterrent effects produced, respectively, by the binary system, and by a verdict system comprising an intermediate option. All those who value deterrence would consider this assessment relevant to the choice whether to reform the binary system. In their eyes, the decision-theoretic justification would be inadequate if it could not reflect this assessment.

But why should the model be unable to reflect it? After all, in Chapter 3 we saw that the possible deterrent effect of conviction can be accounted for in the evaluation of the possible outcomes of convicting, for the purposes of constructing the relevant value function. Insofar as a token conviction contributes to this effect, this

[10] This insight is at the heart of Louis Kaplow's theory of standards of proof, defended in his 'Burden of Proof' (2011) 121 Yale Law Journal 738, in particular at 752–772. In fact, Kaplow highlights both the deterrent effect on criminal activity and the chilling effect on lawful activity that may be produced by lowering the standard of proof, the former being a benefit of the change, and the latter being a cost. Kaplow discusses how the two quantities can be calculated, by unpacking their distinct components (at 764 ff). He concludes that the optimal standard of proof 'will have the feature that the deterrence benefit just equals the chilling cost' (at 769).

[11] See T. Fisher, 'Constitutionalism and the Criminal Law: Rethinking Criminal Trial Bifurcation' (2011) 61 University of Toronto Law Journal 811; T. Fisher, 'Conviction without Conviction' (2011) 96 Minnesota Law Review 833; and M. Spottswood, 'Continuous Burdens of Proof' (2021) 21 Nevada Law Journal 779. cf H. Lando, 'The Size of the Sanction should Depend on the Weight of the Evidence' (2005) 1 Review of Law and Economics 277. Lando's argument is premised on the claim that hard treatment has no deterrent effect, and is, therefore, 'wasted', if it is inflicted on the innocent. I do not see how this claim can be true without making the debatable assumption that potential criminals know whether a defendant is innocent or guilty. If the claim is true, though, according to Lando it follows that, as the probability of guilt increases, so should the severity of hard treatment. This is because, as the probability of guilt increases, and thus that of innocence decreases, the risk that the hard treatment would be wasted on an innocent person decreases as well; therefore, the additional cost involved in inflicting an increasingly harder treatment is outweighed by the gradual increase in expected deterrence, and related benefits, that such a sanctioning regime would produce. Fisher points out that, because of its stress on the risk of wasting punishment on the innocent, Lando's argument seems to advocate for the imposition and the gradation of hard treatment only with very high probabilities of guilt. Indeed, it would seem that only at very high probabilities of guilt can such risk be contained within reasonable levels. To defend the imposition and the gradation of hard treatment at lower probabilities, too, Fisher complements Lando's argument with the consideration that allowing for hard treatment in the event of relatively low probabilities of guilt increases deterrence, since potential criminals are deterred more by the 'certainty' of hard treatment than by its severity (Spottswood employs this argument as well, see ibid, at 788–792), and since doing so decreases the rate of false acquittal, an outcome that undermines deterrence. As the following will show, I am quite sceptical of these arguments.

strategy for factoring the effect into the decision-theoretic model is sensible. The same strategy should be followed for the evaluation of the intermediate outcomes. Insofar as a token intermediate outcome contributes to deterrence, this should be factored into the value of such outcome. By doing so, the deterrent potential of the intermediate verdict could be reflected in the model, and would contribute to the expected value of choosing this option. Therefore, deterrence would be accounted for in the crucial comparison between this expected value and that of the options available in the binary system: acquitting and convicting.

Consider, though, that the objection alerts us to a complicating factor. Its basic claim is that the probability of hard treatment is relevant to its deterrent effect. Now, the probability that the hard treatment involved in a particular verdict will materialise depends on the stringency of the applicable standard of proof, since the verdict can be issued only when the applicable standard is satisfied. According to the objection, then, the deterrent effect of that verdict also depends on the stringency of the standard of proof. Importantly, the deterrent effect of the verdict contributes to the values of the verdict's possible outcomes; that is, it contributes to such values insofar as the decision-maker believes, and values the fact, that the effect is triggered by the very act of issuing the verdict, rather than just by the abstract availability of the verdict as an option in adjudication. And the decision-maker may so believe on the ground that this act is the event that makes salient for potential criminals both considerations about the severity of the verdict and, crucially, considerations about the probability of receiving the verdict, given the stringency of the applicable standard of proof, should they decide to break the law. Being triggered by the act of issuing the verdict, then, the deterrent effect of the verdict—including, crucially, the effect dependent on the stringency of the standard of proof—contributes to the values of the verdict's outcomes. Therefore, these values, too, depend on the stringency of the standard: the lower is the standard, the stronger are the considerations against committing crime made salient by issuing the verdict and, hence, the higher are the values of the verdict's outcomes. As seen in Chapter 4, though, this dependence is not reflected in the decision-theoretic model, which treats the outcomes' values as variables that are determined independently of the relevant standard of proof, and serve, in fact, as the premises for the identification of such standard. Notice, then, that the problem raised by the objection affects the decision-theoretic justification of intermediate verdicts because it affects, *in primis*, the decision-theoretic argument for setting the standard of proof in a binary system, on which such justification is grounded. This argument and, hence, the superiority condition, are premised on the possibility of constructing a value function for the decision problem of adjudication, prior to knowing where the relevant standard(s) of proof lie on the probability spectrum.[12] If the objection

[12] As far as the superiority condition is concerned, it is the value function that tells us where the intersections are between the line representing the expected value of the intermediate verdict and the lines representing the expected values of acquitting and convicting, and hence whether the expected value of issuing the intermediate verdict is higher than that of the other options when the probability of guilt equals p^*. The intersections identify the standards of proof p^1 and p^2.

is right, though, the values of the possible outcomes of conviction[13] cannot fully be determined without knowing, first, the standard of proof. Until the standard is known, these values can reflect the deterrent effect due to the severity of the hard treatment involved in conviction, but not also the effect due to the stringency of the standard.. But, according to the decision-theoretic model, the standard cannot be identified without knowing the values of the trial outcomes. This, apparently, produces a chicken-and-egg problem that casts doubt on the accuracy of the formulas employed in the previous chapter, and which, seemingly, could be solved only by failing to register, in the model, the deterrent effect due to the stringency of the standard of proof. A deterrence theorist may not accept this solution.

Does this objection point to a flaw in the decision-theoretic model, such that the model should be jettisoned, or at least amended?[14] I do not think so. In line with the standard law and economics approach, the objection assumes that individuals deliberate rationally about whether to commit a crime, and are motivated exclusively, or mainly, by the expected material costs and benefits that their potential behaviour would have for them. These would include, in particular, the expected costs of the prospective application of the law to such behaviour. Therefore, the stringency of the standard[15] of proof, which affects the probability of hard treatment, is considered by the objection to be amongst the relevant motivational factors.[16]

[13] The same considerations apply to the relationship between the values of the intermediate outcomes and p^1: until this standard is set, these values can only reflect the deterrent effect due to the severity of the hard treatment involved in the intermediate verdict, and not also the alleged effect due to the stringency of the standard. According to the decision-theoretic model, though, this standard cannot be identified without knowing the values of the intermediate outcomes.

[14] Even if the objection were right about the relationship of interdependence between the values of the possible outcomes of conviction and the standard of proof, it would not follow from this that we would be stuck with a chicken-and-egg problem that renders the decision-theoretic argument for the standard of proof unworkable. It would be possible to account for the interdependence by revising formula (2) as follows:

$$p^* = \frac{1}{1+\dfrac{V_{cg}(p^*)-V_{ag}}{V_{ai}-V_{ci}(p^*)}} \qquad (2.1)$$

V_{cg} (p^*) and V_{ci} (p^*) stand to indicate that the value of each outcome of conviction depends on the standard of proof. In order to solve (2.1), though, we need to know how these values depend on the standard of proof, and we need to know this with a level of precision that is far greater than the rough correlations suggested by the objection.

[15] Or 'standards', in case of a non-binary system.

[16] Some may contend that deterrence does not require that agents engage in a conscious cost–benefit analysis. Rather, it may result from an implicit influence that information about the severity and the probability of punishment exerts on the agent's decision-making. To clarify, the hypothesis is that—especially in the age of social media—agents encode this information through being exposed to accounts by their peers, or by media outlets, and that this produces an emotional response—say, a certain degree of fear of punishment—which ultimately influences their decision-making about whether to act criminally. While this hypothesis is plausible, and has some empirical backing (see J. T. Pickett and others, 'Toward a Bifurcated Theory of Emotional Deterrence' (2018) 56 Criminology 27), the empirical study of the causes of fear (of apprehension, or of punishment) and, especially, of its role in criminal decision-making is still underdeveloped (ibid, at 29, 44–47), such that caution is needed in this area. More importantly, I expect that the more implicit and affective the dynamics of deterrence are, the less

However, only a part of society—arguably, a small one—is likely to deliberate in this manner concerning criminal agency, and to do so in a way that is sensitive to the actual regulations.[17] In everyday life, individuals often do not make rational choices at all, ie they do not act as indicated by the balance of the reasons that they recognise, and often they do not even deliberate on whether, or how, to act before acting. It suffices to read a handful of criminal law cases to infer, reasonably, that this is true also for many criminal actions.[18] Moreover, for many people who deliberate, the decision whether or not to commit a crime is unlikely to be made exclusively, or mainly, on the basis of the expected material benefits and costs that acting criminally has for them: in particular, it is unlikely to be made on the basis of the expected costs of the prospective application of the law to their potential criminal behaviour. Rather, for many people, this decision is determined by their commitment to respecting the law, by their fear of the social censure that may result from being seen to break the law (irrespective of whether they are also convicted for such a breach), and by their belief about the moral rightness or wrongness of the conduct at issue: moral attributes that are not, themselves, determined, or fully determined, by the aforementioned cost–benefit assessment.[19] Finally, those who do deliberate about acting criminally, and are motivated exclusively, or mainly, by the expected material costs and benefits that so acting has for them may fall prey to cognitive biases that produce a departure from rational decision-making,[20] such that their decisions may not adequately be responsive to the relevant reasons, including the standard of proof and the related probability of hard treatment.

If I am right, then, the group of individuals that can be deterred by altering the expected costs of the prospective application of the law to their potential behaviour is relatively small. Still, one may contend that it is sufficiently large to be significant in the evaluation of trial outcomes: if a verdict, be it conviction or an intermediate verdict, can deter such individuals, this effect should be accounted for in the assessment of the verdict's possible outcomes. A survey of the literature on deterrence, though, casts doubt on the objection, even when circumscribed to this deterrable group. It is, indeed, doubtful that the behaviour of deterrable

fine-tuned is the responsiveness of one's decisions to the relevant reasons, such that significant changes in the severity or probability of punishment, and especially changes in the stringency of the standard of proof, may not lead to any significant change in behaviour. On this point, see ibid, at 45, claiming that policies that raise the risk of sanction, or the risk of apprehension, may not generate the respective fears, and may not, therefore, produce deterrence.

[17] For similar arguments see Nance (n 2), at 65–69.

[18] See T. R. Tyler, 'Procedural Justice, Legitimacy, and the Effective Rule of Law' (2003) 30 Crime and Justice 283, at 305, making the reasonable argument that deterrence strategies are ineffective in cases of crimes committed on the 'spur of the moment', or in the 'heat of passion'.

[19] See D. S. Nagin, 'Deterrence in the Twenty-First Century' (2013) 42 Crime and Justice 199, at 204. cf the distinct types of law-abiding citizens highlighted in H. L. A. Hart, *The Concept of Law* (OUP 1961), at 88–91; F. Schauer, *The Force of Law* (Harvard University Press 2015).

[20] See, among others, A. Tversky and D. Kahneman, 'Judgment under Uncertainty: Heuristics and Biases' (1974) 185 Science 1124 and D. Kahneman and A. Tversky, 'On the Reality of Cognitive Illusions' (1996) 103 Psychological Review 582.

individuals is influenced by the stringency of the standard of proof the satisfaction of which warrants the imposition of hard treatment. The literature provides some evidence that 'swift-and-certain' sanctioning regimes have a deterrent effect.[21] The evidence comes from a couple of studies in which, as the name of the regime suggests, sanctions were immediate and followed the illegal behaviour without fail. It is, therefore, unsafe to extrapolate from these studies alone the broad claim that the deterrent effect of hard treatment is directly proportional to the probability of it being inflicted; or, for that matter, the claim that the effect is inversely proportional to the stringency of the standard of proof. In general, the literature provides more robust evidence of a deterrent effect being produced by the 'certainty' of hard treatment than of a deterrent effect being produced by its severity.[22] This seems to give some support to the objection. However, the evidence concerning the deterrent effect of certainty is provided almost exclusively by studies that focus on the probability of apprehension by the police, rather than the probability of being prosecuted if detected, tried if prosecuted, and—what matters most for our purposes—sanctioned if tried.[23] What is more, the literature leaves considerable doubt about the accuracy of individual perceptions of the types of hard treatment provided by the legal system, and of how, and when, they are administered; importantly, it leaves considerable doubt about the responsiveness of these perceptions to changes in the sanctioning regime, which may include, for instance, the lowering of the standard of proof for conviction, or the introduction of an intermediate verdict. In fact, as yet, little is known on these matters.[24] Conversely, there is evidence showing that individuals have reasonably accurate perceptions of salient changes in policing strategies, and that these changes can, indeed, produce a deterrent effect. This has led researchers to argue that an effective deterrence strategy should concentrate on policing, rather than the design of the sanctioning regime.[25]

After considering the literature, one is left with the impression that, even if there were a significantly large group of individuals who were susceptible to being deterred, the claim that the stringency of the standard of proof authorising hard treatment influences their behaviour is just a theoretical possibility, without sufficient empirical backing, for the time being. As far as we know, deterrable individuals are tuned into the probability of detection, but may have little knowledge

[21] See A. Chalfin and J. McCrary, 'Criminal Deterrence: A Review of the Literature' (2017) 55 Journal of Economic Literature 5, at 27–28. See also A. Raskolnikov, 'Criminal Deterrence: A Review of the Missing Literature' (2020) 28 Supreme Court Economic Review 1, at 39–41, pointing out that attempts to replicate the findings of the studies at issue have largely failed.

[22] See Nagin (n 19), at 201–202, 243–244. See also Chalfin and McCrary (n 21), at 38; and Raskolnikov (n 21), at 32–35.

[23] See Nagin (n 19), at 201–202.

[24] See ibid, at 204–205, 251; and Chalfin and McCrary (n 21), at 12.

[25] See Chalfin and McCrary (n 21), at 22–23, 38–40; and Nagin (n 19), at 201–202.

about the probability of being sanctioned if detected. In particular, they may have little knowledge about the stringency of the standard of proof, and about how such stringency interacts with other variables—such as the probabilities of detection and of prosecution, and the strength of the available incriminating evidence—for the purposes of estimating the probability of being sanctioned.[26] Moreover, even if they had knowledge of these matters, the decision-making of these individuals may well be indifferent to them, being largely focused on the more salient and imminent worry of detection. Notice, instead, that it is more plausible to expect the deterrable individual to have some rough knowledge of the severity, rather than the probability, of the applicable hard treatment. Insofar as this knowledge produces a deterrent effect, this can be factored into the assessment of trial outcomes without incurring the objection.

If and when a significant deterrent effect due to the stringency of the standard of proof is detected, the decision-theoretic model will need to be amended or complemented so that the effect is taken into account. This is the case only if the decision-maker values deterrence, of course. To those who have faith that this effect exists, and insist on the inadequacy of the model without waiting for the evidence, I will just say that, if they turn out to be right, the effect does support the introduction of an intermediate verdict,[27] and of conditional acquittal in particular. In other words, following a different avenue from mine, they may reach roughly the same conclusion that I have reached. It is true that conditional acquittal is not a particularly severe verdict. The available evidence, however, shows that social stigma does have a deterrent effect for some people.[28] And the causing of social stigma is likely to be a component of the hard treatment involved in conditional acquittal.[29] Accordingly, it is not far-fetched to argue that the supposed inverse proportionality between deterrence and the stringency of the standard of proof warranting hard treatment would also feature in the case of this intermediate verdict, such that incorporating this verdict into the choice set increases deterrence.[30]

[26] See Nance (n 2), at 68–69.
[27] See the works cited in n 11 above.
[28] See Nagin (n 19), at 244–245.
[29] I doubt that the expected cost of a retrial could have a significant deterrent effect, considering that many salient events have to occur before the retrial materialises, in particular apprehension, charge, trial, intermediate verdict, and discovery of the requisite evidence. Still, a potential criminal may worry about being 'stuck in the system' for a long time (whether because of conviction, or because of the intermediate verdict).
[30] In Chapter 4, we saw that, with the introduction of a superior intermediate verdict, the standard of proof for conviction becomes higher. Assuming that the stringency of this standard of proof is inversely proportional to deterrence, this fact should decrease the deterrent effect produced by conviction; that is, by the most severe form of hard treatment that the system provides. This would counter the increase in deterrence produced by the availability of hard treatment at lower probabilities of guilt, thanks to the introduction of the intermediate verdict. However, while the shift of the standard of proof for conviction is a feature of the decision-theoretic model, it need not be a feature of a different case for intermediate verdicts, such as that which the faithful deterrent theorist may put forward. See n 11 above.

5.3.2 The behaviour of prosecutors

Arguably, the stringency of the standard of proof in a binary system influences the behaviour of the enforcement authorities[31] and, especially, the decisions of prosecutors whether to charge defendants. Other things being equal, the lower the standard of proof, the greater the prosecutor's incentive to charge the defendant is. This is because the lower the standard, the more probable it is that the prosecution will obtain a conviction if they opt for charging, and a conviction is, of course, generally seen by prosecutors as a desirable outcome. If this view is correct, someone may argue that the introduction of an intermediate verdict that involves hard treatment should be expected to influence the rate of prosecutions. Indeed, with such an intermediate verdict in place, the prosecution can obtain a desirable result—precisely, hard treatment, even if this is less severe than with conviction—more easily than under the binary system. We should, therefore, expect that, with the addition of an intermediate verdict, some cases will be prosecuted that would not be prosecuted in the binary system, because they would be considered too weak to meet the standard of proof for conviction.[32] Someone may also argue that the addition of an intermediate verdict reduces the prosecution's incentive to strike a plea deal with the defendant. If the intermediate verdict is more desirable to the prosecution than a plea deal, the fact that this verdict is easier to obtain than conviction should reduce the appeal that a deal has for the prosecution, hence reducing the rate of deals actually struck. The combined effect of the alleged increase in the number of prosecutions, and of the alleged decrease in the rate of plea deals, would be an increase in the number of cases going to trial. A system with an intermediate verdict may, therefore, produce more trial outcomes—including a number of intermediate outcomes—than the binary system.

Now, the increase in cases going to trial is surely relevant to the choice whether to adopt an intermediate verdict. And yet there does not seem to be any meaningful way of reflecting such increase in the decision-theoretic model. Notice that the evaluation of a trial outcome can account for the effect that an outcome of that kind has on the system. For example, insofar as conviction contributes to preventing crime through incapacitation and, possibly, through deterrence, this systemic effect can be accounted for in the evaluation of its outcomes. It seems, however, that the alleged increase in the number of cases going to trial cannot be registered

[31] On this point, see D. Epps, 'The Consequences of Error in Criminal Justice' (2015) 128 Harvard Law Review 1065, at 1106–1108, focusing especially on the likely effects that the 'Blackstone principle' has on the behaviour of enforcement authorities; and Kaplow (n 10), at 815–819, analysing the synergy between the standard of proof and the level of enforcement effort in the production of the optimal balance between deterrence benefit and chilling cost; and, at 849–851, discussing the relationship between the standard of proof and the scope for the enforcement authorities to abuse their power.

[32] In fact, the rate of cases being prosecuted may also be influenced by possible changes in the rate of criminality due to the introduction, and the issuing, of the intermediate verdict, a phenomenon discussed critically in the previous section.

in this way. After all, this is not the effect of any token intermediate outcome (or combination of such outcomes); rather, it results from the very availability of the intermediate verdict as an option for the adjudicator. The decision-theoretic justification of intermediate verdicts being unable to register this effect, it appears incomplete and, therefore, inadequate. This is the objection considered here.

In replying to the objection, let me start by saying that I agree that if there were an increase in cases going to trial, produced by the introduction of an intermediate verdict—or, indeed, if there were any significant change in the rates of such cases, and of plea deals—this would be a relevant consideration in the choice whether to adopt this verdict, and that I cannot think of a sensible way of incorporating this information in the decision-theoretic model.[33] If this increase were real, then, the decision-theoretic justification would not give us a complete account of the reasons in favour of, and against, adopting the intermediate verdict. This does not mean, though, that such justification should be ditched. Rather, the increase in cases going to trial should be treated as an additional, separate consideration, to be taken into account alongside the decision-theoretic justification, when making the choice whether to adopt an intermediate verdict. I do not see anything problematic with this dual decision-making approach. Indeed, for the set of cases that would be tried under both the binary system and the system with an intermediate verdict, the decision-theoretic model is sufficient to justify the issuing of this verdict, if it meets the superiority condition, and if the probability of guilt falls within the relevant range; the additional cases that would go to trial only as a result of switching from the former to the latter system would need independent consideration.

The real challenge, in fact, lies precisely in assessing the alleged increase in cases going to trial. Is it a good or a bad thing?[34] This depends on the distribution of the outcomes of the additional set of cases. To clarify, it depends on the rates of false conviction, true conviction, false acquittal, true acquittal, and intermediate outcomes characterising this additional set. And it depends on the value of this distribution, by which I mean the aggregate value of all the outcomes of these cases, given their distribution. The distribution's value would tell us whether the additional set is a reason in favour of, or against, introducing an intermediate verdict.

It is worth opening a parenthesis here. Once someone realises that the significance that the increase in cases has for the choice whether to introduce an intermediate verdict or not depends on the value of their distribution, they might wonder why one should stop at the assessment of these cases only. The whole question of the

[33] One may argue that each instance of the intermediate verdict being issued contributes to persuading prosecutors to try weaker cases (since it shows them that adjudicators are willing to resort to the intermediate option), and that, if so, the effect described by the objection may be fully accounted for in the evaluation of intermediate outcomes. I am not convinced by this argument (also because, as I will explain shortly, the effect itself is difficult to evaluate). If it were correct, though, it would undermine the objection.

[34] I leave aside the consideration of the monetary cost of trying more cases. While a relevant consideration, it is of secondary importance here.

justification of adopting an intermediate verdict could be reframed in terms of a comparison between the distribution of outcomes of a binary system and the (expected) distribution of outcomes of a hypothetical system adopting such a verdict. If the latter is more valuable, in the sense just explained, the adoption of the intermediate verdict is justified.[35] It goes without saying that, irrespective of whether the alleged increase in cases going to trial occurs, the two distributions are bound to differ. One would reasonably expect that, in the presence of an intermediate verdict, both the rate of acquittal (whether true or false) and that of conviction (whether true of false) would be lower than they would be absent such option. This is because, as we have seen in Chapter 4, the probability range corresponding to the intermediate verdict encroaches on the probability ranges that, in a binary system, correspond, respectively, to acquittal and conviction. The divergence between the two distributions also depends on the obvious fact that no intermediate outcome would feature in the binary system.

The problem with this justificatory strategy, though, is that it requires reliance on data that are difficult to gather, or simply not available. As a result, the comparison between the two verdict systems via this strategy is bound to be highly speculative. The main difficulty lies with calculating the distribution of outcomes that a system produces, or is expected to produce. Consider actual binary systems: attempts have been made to calculate the rates of certain outcomes,[36] with recent studies signalling improvements in the quality of the data produced.[37]

[35] A similar approach is advocated for by some scholars working on the choice of the criminal standard of proof in a binary system. In essence, these scholars aim to compare the performance of the current standard with that of alternative standards by comparing the distribution of outcomes that each produces, or is expected to produce. See L. Laudan, *Truth, Error and Criminal Law: An Essay in Legal Epistemology* (CUP 2006), at 74–76; L. Laudan, *The Law's Flaws: Rethinking Trial and Errors* (College Publications 2016), chs 3, 4, and 5; W. Cullerne-Browne, 'The Criminal Justice System as a Problem in Binary Classification' (2018) 22 International Journal of Evidence and Proof 363; and W. Cullerne-Browne, 'Measuring Justice' (2019) 23 International Journal of Evidence and Proof 399. Laudan's and Cullerne-Browne's approaches are significantly different, but they both require a measurement of the (expected) distribution of (at least some) outcomes. In both approaches, the evaluation of the appropriateness of the current standard of proof, and of other standards that were to be implemented in its stead, depends on such a measurement.

[36] See, eg Laudan, *The Law's Flaws* (n 35), ch 3, estimating the rate of false positives and false negatives for all violent offences. Laudan's focus is on the current criminal justice system of the United States, which is why his reliance on some old empirical studies, as well as on sources that concern other jurisdictions, is perplexing. A more modest and precise task is undertaken by M. D. Risinger, 'Innocents Convicted: An Empirically Justified Factual Wrongful Conviction Rate' (2007) 97 Journal of Criminal Law & Criminology 761, which estimates the wrongful conviction rate for capital rape-murders in the 1980s in the US, relying on data concerning DNA exonerations.

[37] See S. R. Gross and others, 'Rate of False Conviction of Criminal Defendants who are Sentenced to Death' (2014) 111 Proceedings of the National Academy of Sciences of the United States of America 7230, calculating the rate of false conviction amongst death sentences in the US; K. Walsh and others, 'Estimating the Prevalence of Wrongful Convictions' (2017), available at https://www.ncjrs.gov/pdffiles1/nij/grants/251115.pdf accessed 4 February 2022, calculating the rate of false conviction in murder and sexual assault cases in Virginia; C. E. Loeffler and others, 'Measuring Self-Reported Wrongful Convictions Among Prisoners' (2019) 35 Journal of Quantitative Criminology 259. Besides providing an estimate of the rate of false conviction in the United States by relying on self-reporting by a sample of prisoners, the authors of this study show that the rate is likely to vary significantly depending on the

Nonetheless, the data that we have fall far short of providing a sufficiently complete[38] and reliable picture of the distribution of outcomes that these systems churn out. And there is doubt as to whether such a picture could ever be provided. This is largely because we often lack a reliable way of telling whether the defendant is guilty or innocent—and hence, whether an outcome is true or false—other than trial fact-finding itself.[39] What is more, when it comes to comparing the binary system with a hypothetical system including an intermediate verdict, this justificatory strategy requires that we calculate the expected distribution of outcomes that would be produced by the latter term of the comparison: this is the principal obstacle to using the strategy. To appreciate the extent of the problem, consider the difficulty of calculating the expected rate of cases in which an innocent defendant would receive an intermediate verdict. A possible avenue would be to assess the evidence available in each case decided by the current binary system in a given period, and whether such evidence, while not sufficient for conviction in the alternative system, would be sufficient to satisfy the lower standard of proof warranting the intermediate verdict. Even if carried out with a representative sample of cases, these operations would be very complicated indeed, and their outcome would be of dubious reliability. Moreover, they would only give us the rate of intermediate verdicts, not the rate of *innocent defendants* receiving such verdicts.[40]

Tracing our steps backwards, we can see that the failure of the justificatory strategy based on a comparison between the values of outcomes' distributions points to the difficulty of making any use of the objection's claim that the adoption of an intermediate verdict would increase the number of cases going to trial. Whether or not this increase would, indeed, occur, its significance for the choice whether to adopt an intermediate verdict depends on calculating the value of the hypothetical distribution of outcomes for the set of additional cases. In other words, it depends on data that are hardly accessible to us; hence, it can only be the subject of speculation. Of

crimes for which the participants have been convicted. They also provide an estimate of implausible or false claims of innocence; and M. Zalman and R. J. Norris, 'Measuring Innocence: How to Think about the Rate of Wrongful Convictions' (2021) 24 New Criminal Law Review 601, offering a critical survey of the research to date on the rate of false conviction in the United States, and stating (at 652) that 'precisely calculating such a rate is impossible'.

38 The studies that I am aware of are concerned mostly with the rate of false conviction. See the previous notes.

39 I must add the caveat that in a binary system with a high standard of proof, not even fact-finding, through the verdict of acquittal, provides a reliable indication of innocence.

40 For further examples of this justificatory strategy, which inevitably fall short of comparing fully fledged and reliable distributions of outcomes, see H. Phalen, 'Overcoming the Opposition to a Third Verdict: A Call for Future Research on Alternative Acquittals' (2018) 50 Arizona State Law Journal 401, at 411–414; F. Picinali, 'Do Theories of Punishment Necessarily Deliver a Binary System of Verdicts? An Exploratory Essay' (2018) 12 Criminal Law and Philosophy 555, in particular at 561–562; Fisher, 'Conviction without Conviction' (n 11), at 859–862; Fisher, 'Constitutionalism and the Criminal Law: Rethinking Criminal Trial Bifurcation' (n 11), at 830–833; and M. Wansley, 'Scaled Punishments' (2013) 16 New Criminal Law Review 309, at 346–362.

course, it is possible that, if the additional cases were, on average, weaker than the cases currently brought to trial in the binary system—which is plausible, according to the objection—many of them would end up in intermediate outcomes or acquittals. But without knowing whether the defendants receiving the intermediate verdict or the 'not guilty' verdict are innocent or guilty, the significance of the fact that many cases would end up as hypothesised is shrouded. In fact, besides the problem of calculating the distribution of outcomes of the additional set of cases, there is the preliminary issue of identifying this potential set. A possible, but crude, way of doing this would be to ask prosecutors whether, had an intermediate verdict been available, they would have brought charges in cases that they decided not to prosecute under the binary system. Identifying cases that can be regarded as additional may be seen as an easier problem than calculating the expected distribution of their outcomes, but it certainly adds to the difficulty of evaluating the alleged increase in the number of cases going to trial. The bottom line is that this increase may well occur, but it is difficult to make anything of it, other than worrying about the extra budget needed to process the additional set of cases.[41]

To conclude on this objection, I want to challenge the view that the alleged increase in cases going to trial is a necessary epiphenomenon of the introduction of an intermediate verdict. I do not think this is true, especially not in the case of a verdict such as conditional acquittal. Assuming that it is considered desirable to do so, it seems possible to introduce an intermediate verdict, while preventing, or rendering insignificant, the increase at issue. This can be done through regulation and prosecutorial culture. First, it is important to adopt a test for the decision to prosecute that discourages prosecutions aimed at obtaining the intermediate verdict. For instance, in England and Wales the 2018 Code for Crown Prosecutors prescribes a test whose evidential limb requires 'sufficient evidence to provide a realistic prospect of conviction'.[42] This evidential requirement would be fit for the purpose described above. Notice that what would be required is a realistic prospect of *conviction*, not of an intermediate verdict. If so, the availability of a verdict that is warranted with weaker evidence than that needed for conviction should not make it easier to satisfy the test. With a test of this kind in place, it is arguable that the addition of an intermediate verdict should not increase the number of cases

[41] *Mutatis mutandis* the problems discussed here also affect the evaluation of a possible change in the number of plea deals that may be produced by the introduction of the intermediate verdict: which plea deals would or would not occur in the event of such introduction? What distribution of outcomes would these plea deals produce (ie are the defendants involved innocent or guilty)? Moreover, these problems affect the evaluation of a possible, but counter-intuitive, decrease in cases going to trial, due to the introduction of the intermediate verdict: what cases would not be brought to trial when the intermediate verdict is introduced? What is the value of the distribution of the outcomes of these cases in the binary system?

[42] See ss 4.6–4.8 of the Code, available at <https://www.cps.gov.uk/publication/code-crown-prosecutors> accessed 24 September 2021. For a discussion of different interpretations of the evidential limb, see L. Campbell and others, *The Criminal Process* (OUP 2019), at 200–202. The Code also provides for a less stringent test (the 'threshold test') to be applied in special cases: see ss 5.1–5.10.

brought to trial: at least, it should not increase such number if the test is applied conscientiously.[43] Second, and precisely because the test may not be so applied, there should be an active scrutiny of prosecutorial decisions. The relevant prosecution agency—such as the English and Welsh Crown Prosecution Service—or possibly the courts, through judicial review,[44] should exercise checks on charging decisions. Third, and most importantly, a prosecutorial culture should be fostered according to which intermediate verdicts are not a target, but are, at most, a 'silver lining'. This would not be difficult in the case of conditional acquittal. After all, while conditional acquittal must be valuable for the system if it is to be justified, it nevertheless represents a failed prosecution. Aside from the stigma it may produce, this verdict offers to the prosecution the opportunity to have another 'go' at the defendant, if the evidential circumstances allow for it. That the first go was not a success is a necessary premise of the verdict.

These final considerations are also relevant to the claim that prosecutors may be less interested in plea deals if an intermediate verdict is introduced: this is unlikely to be the case for an intermediate verdict such as conditional acquittal. Even with respect to more severe intermediate verdicts, though, one should consider that a plea deal secures conviction, whereas the intermediate verdict is ... well, intermediate, and it is just a possibility, even if probable. Moreover, the plea deal involves the admission of responsibility on the part of the defendant. I suspect that this would be a more desirable evidential vindication for a prosecutor than the satisfaction of the standard of proof for the intermediate verdict. Finally, the claim that the availability of an intermediate verdict would reduce the prosecution's incentive to strike a deal and, hence, the rate of plea deals, does not consider that the incentive that a party has to strike a deal is not insulated from the behaviour of the other party. To clarify, while the availability of an intermediate verdict may well reduce the initial incentive of the prosecutor to strike a deal, it may also increase the incentive of the defendant to do so, precisely because the likelihood of a trial outcome that is detrimental to the defendant has increased. Hence, the defendant may be willing to accept a worse deal than they would have accepted absent the intermediate verdict. Under these conditions, the prosecutor may well prefer a deal to the possibility of an intermediate verdict. Given the plausibility of these bargaining dynamics, the availability of the verdict need not necessarily reduce the rate of plea deals.[45] Be that as it may, conditional acquittal involves a quantum of hard

[43] I concede, though, that the number might decrease marginally given that—as seen in Chapter 4—the standard of proof for conviction increases with the introduction of a superior intermediate verdict and, therefore, the cases satisfying the test may be fewer. For reasons discussed earlier, it is difficult to assess the value of this possible decrease.

[44] For an overview of the current role of courts as reviewers of charging decisions in England and Wales, see Campbell and others (n 42), at 228–230.

[45] cf M. Spottswood, 'Proof Discontinuities and Civil Settlements' (2021) 22 Theoretical Inquiries in Law 201. Using a data simulation approach that reflects the realities of American civil litigation, Spottswood shows that providing for intermediate options is likely to increase the rate of settlements.

treatment that is unlikely to appeal to prosecutors more than the hard treatment and evidential vindication they would manage to secure with a plea deal in serious cases,[46] these being the cases in which, as seen in section 5.2, the intermediate verdict would be available.[47]

If I am right that the number of cases brought to trial need not necessarily change due to the introduction of an intermediate verdict, then it is unnecessary to worry about this issue in the justification of such a verdict. The number of cases brought to trial is a fact that we can safely account for with a *ceteris paribus* clause.

5.3.3 Legitimacy

Another objection to the decision-theoretic justification of intermediate verdicts contends that it cannot capture the effect that the adoption of an intermediate verdict involving hard treatment is likely to have on the legitimacy of the criminal justice system. Given intermediacy, the standard of proof the satisfaction of which authorises issuing the verdict is lower than the standard of proof for conviction in the binary system. This, the objection argues, is problematic. By adopting the intermediate verdict as a possible option for the adjudicator, the legislator accepts a risk of imposing hard treatment on the innocent that is greater than that accepted in the binary system. This raises the worry that the public will perceive the legislator as allowing risky gambles—importantly, riskier than the ones allowed in a binary setting—with the lives of the law-abiding citizen.[48] Insofar as this perception is real

[46] cf Phalen (n 40), at 415, arguing that, in the presence of a 'not proven' verdict, US prosecutors would push more strongly for a plea deal, since this intermediate verdict may not be perceived by them as desirable.

[47] Consider that, while charge and fact bargaining exist in England and Wales, a true form of sentence bargaining does not. The bargain on the sentence 'is with the law' (Campbell and others (n 42), at 326), not with the prosecution. It is the law that entitles the defendant to a sentence discount if they plead guilty, and that sets the limits of this discount. In cases in which the prosecution cannot exercise any leverage by bargaining on the charges, or on the facts stated in the indictment, the relevant question is whether the number of defendants 'bargaining with the law' by pleading guilty varies with the introduction of an intermediate verdict. I can only speculate here, considering also that the choice to plead guilty is influenced by factors other than the likely outcome of the trial (eg attitude to risk, legal advice). My suggestion is that this number need not change significantly. If, on the one hand, going to trial may seem more appealing given that—as seen in Chapter 4—with the introduction of an intermediate verdict the standard of proof for conviction increases, the availability of such a verdict, on the other hand, would likely counterbalance this increase in the trial's appeal: in fact, it may outweigh it, if the verdict is sufficiently severe. These opposite vectors should also inform the initial attitude of the defendant in cases in which the prosecution is an actual party to the bargaining. A comparison between the rates of guilty pleas in Scotland, and in England and Wales, could provide interesting information concerning the impact that an intermediate verdict, in particular a relatively benign one such as 'not proven', may have on such rate. However, it has emerged, thanks to a recent freedom of information request by James Chalmers, that the Scottish Government does not hold information on the rate of guilty pleas. See <https://www.gov.scot/publications/foi-202100199803/> accessed 4 August 2021.

[48] cf L. H. Tribe, 'Trial by Mathematics: Precision and Ritual in the Legal Process' (1971) 84 Harvard Law Review 1329, at 1372–1375, cautioning against making explicit the risk of false conviction that the system is willing to accept.

and widespread—the objection continues—some people may lose confidence in the criminal justice system and become less disposed to accept and interiorise the system's decisions. If so, the legitimacy of the system in the eyes of the public may well be diminished; this being a claim that we have already encountered in the context of the 19th century debate on the *ius commune* intermediate verdicts.

The objection I have in mind recognises that the effect that the adoption of the intermediate verdict may have on the legitimacy of the system may not be sufficiently strong to countervail the reasons in favour of adopting such a verdict. But it insists that this effect is an important consideration in assessing the justification for this reform. The problem—the objection contends—is that the decision-theoretic model does not seem capable of registering this consideration. This is because the alleged effect is produced by the legislator's choice to adopt an intermediate verdict, and possibly by the frequency with which such verdicts are issued by the courts. It is not the result of any token intermediate verdict, hence it cannot be accounted for in the evaluation of the intermediate outcomes.[49]

My reply to the objection starts from questioning this last claim, ie the claim that the alleged drop in public confidence and legitimacy cannot be registered in the value function. True, in Chapter 4 I made a similar claim when discussing the relationship between conditional acquittal and the double jeopardy rule. However, it is

[49] Drawing on Charles Nesson's seminal article 'The Evidence or the Event? On Judicial Proof and the Acceptability of Verdicts' (1985) 98 Harvard Law Review 1357, someone might put forward a distinct objection based on a concern for legitimacy. The gist of this objection is that an intermediate verdict sends the wrong message to the public. Being intermediate between two categorical verdicts, this verdict is inherently 'probabilistic'. If so—and unlike the factual 'guilty' verdict—the intermediate verdict might project a decision rule, rather than the conduct rule that the defendant has allegedly violated (on the distinction between decision and conduct rules, see the classic M. Dan-Cohen, 'Decision Rules and Conduct Rules: On Acoustic Separation in Criminal Law' (1984) 97 Harvard Law Review 625). To clarify, the intermediate verdict can be seen as telling the public what consequence will befall them if the evidence against them satisfies a particular probability threshold. This message conceals, and detracts from, the more important substantive message that conduct of a particular kind is prohibited, and will be met with consequences. The former message invites the public to behave opportunistically, violating the substantive norm if they believe that the decision rule will not be satisfied. In other words, 'it invites people to act not according to what they know is lawful, but according to what they think can be proved against them' (Nesson, ibid, at 1357). Instead, the latter message—which, allegedly, is sent by the categorical 'guilty' verdict—invites people to conform with the substantive law, and encourages them to interiorise this law as a crucial source of guidance in their decision-making. The objection contends that a system with verdicts that routinely project the decision rule, rather than the conduct rule, is bound to lose legitimacy in the long run. This is because the system will be perceived by the public as doing two contradictory things: on the one hand, it states conduct rules, and, on the other, it gives information to the public on how to get away with their violations of such rules. Now, I find this objection highly speculative in what it claims about how people are likely to perceive verdicts, and intermediate verdicts in particular. Consider also that the adoption of an intermediate verdict does not displace categorical 'guilty' verdicts. Assuming that the objection is correct about the fact that categorical 'guilty' verdicts send to the public the desired message about the conduct rule, these verdicts will continue to send such a message, even when the intermediate verdict is added to the verdict system. In fact, notwithstanding their formulation, 'guilty' verdicts, too, are inherently probabilistic. And laypeople are likely to be familiar with this fact: any reasonable person knows that—notwithstanding the facade of the categorical assertion of guilt—the risk of false conviction is inevitable; in other words, that the standard of proof for conviction cannot be absolute certainty. If an intermediate verdict is sending the wrong message because of its probabilistic nature, so is the guilty verdict.

plausible to argue otherwise. In particular, someone could argue that it is the very act of the adjudicator consisting in issuing the intermediate verdict that may foster the public perception that the system is unreasonably gambling with the lives of innocent people. If this view is correct, whoever worries about a possible loss in legitimacy can factor this into the evaluation of the intermediate outcomes, as a cost.[50] It is not possible to say, in the abstract, whether accounting for this cost as just described may compromise the intermediacy and/or the superiority of a verdict that is otherwise intermediate and superior. Of course, this will ultimately depend on the extent of the phenomenon of loss of legitimacy, and on the legislator's evaluation of it.[51]

Be that as it may, the crux of my reply to the objection is a different one, and it chimes with considerations made in Chapter 4 concerning the ability of a decision-theoretic justification of an intermediate verdict to foster—or, at least, not to undermine—public confidence. The objection plausibly holds that the public worries about the risk of imposing hard treatment on the innocent. But is it not equally plausible to hold that the public also worries about the risk of not imposing hard treatment on the guilty? After all, even accepting that the former outcome is worse than the latter, would a reasonable person not worry about both risks? If the public does worry about both, though, their confidence in the criminal justice system will depend on their perception of how the system handles both risks, rather than just the risk of imposing hard treatment on the innocent. In other words, the legitimacy of the system, in the eyes of the public, will ultimately depend on the reasonableness of the method that the system relies upon in order to decide what the acceptable risks of imposing hard treatment on the innocent, and of not imposing it on the guilty, are. Notice that the decision-theoretic model provides a method that is eminently suited for this task. According to the model, issuing a verdict is justified if, and only if, doing so maximises expected value. Whether a verdict maximises expected value depends on a comparison with the expected value yielded by the other available options. Therefore, issuing a verdict that involves hard treatment can only be justified if it yields higher expected value than acquitting. This means that the justification for issuing such a verdict requires taking into account both the risk that the hard treatment involved in the verdict is imposed on the innocent, and the risk that no hard treatment is imposed on the guilty. The former risk is conveyed through the expected value of issuing the verdict against the innocent,

[50] Indeed, the cost would be present whether the defendant is innocent or guilty, since the adjudicator takes the 'unreasonable' risk of imposing hard treatment on the innocent in both cases.

[51] Notice that, according to the objection, the loss of legitimacy depends on the stringency of the standard of proof warranting the intermediate verdict—hence, the hard treatment involved in the verdict—since the degree of risk of imposing such hard treatment on the innocent depends on where this standard lies. If this is correct, the strategy of accounting for such loss in the values of the intermediate outcomes may lead to a chicken-and-egg problem similar to that discussed earlier with reference to deterrence. I will not discuss this problem here, since my main reply to the objection does not rely on adopting this strategy.

which contributes to the overall expected value of issuing the verdict; the latter risk is conveyed through the expected value of acquitting the guilty, which contributes to the overall expected value of acquitting. Now, insofar as the legislator relies on this method for designing decision-making options, and for setting the epistemic conditions under which they are justified, and insofar as the legislator does so sensibly, I do not see why they should be accused of taking unreasonable risks. If the risks they take are reasonable, I do not see why such risk-taking should undermine public confidence and legitimacy.

To conclude on this objection, let me point out that research on procedural justice shows that people's willingness to accept, comply with, and interiorise the constraints of the law depends to a considerable extent on their evaluation of the fairness of the procedures followed by law enforcement authorities, including the courts.[52] Indeed, assessments of procedural fairness are more important in shaping acceptance and interiorisation than assessments of the fairness of the outcome.[53] The key factors that people take into account in their evaluation of procedural fairness are the neutrality of the authorities, their lack of bias, their reliance on objective indicators rather than personal views, and whether the authorities treat those involved with dignity and respect, acknowledging their claims and concerns.[54] Whether these factors are operative in decision-making does not depend on whether decision-making is binary. Insofar as these findings are accurate, then, there is no reason to expect that a system adopting an intermediate verdict would necessarily fare worse than a binary system in fostering public acceptance and interiorisation of the law's message.

5.4 Can the decision-theoretic model be implemented?

The decision-theoretic model that I have employed is premised on a particular division of labour between legislator and adjudicator. The legislator is in charge of producing a value function and, consequently, of selecting the standard(s) of proof for adjudication in the individual case. The adjudicator, instead, is in charge of assessing the evidence available in the individual case, and of determining whether this evidence meets the standard(s) of proof chosen by the legislator. The model is, therefore, built on some assumptions. In particular, as far as

[52] See Tyler, 'Procedural Justice, Legitimacy, and the Effective Rule of Law' (n 18), and T. R. Tyler, 'Psychological Perspectives on Legitimacy and Legitimation' (2006) 57 Annual Review of Psychology 375, at 379–384. For Tyler's earlier classic study on legitimacy, procedural justice, and compliance see T. R. Tyler, *Why People Obey the Law* (Princeton University Press 2006). For a study confirming the validity of Tyler's procedural justice model of compliance with respect to policing in England and Wales, see J. Jackson and others, 'Why Do People Comply with the Law? Legitimacy and the Influence of Legal Institutions' (2012) 52 British Journal of Criminology 1051.

[53] See Tyler, 'Procedural Justice, Legitimacy, and the Effective Rule of Law' (n 18), at 284, 292–297, 300, 311–312.

[54] ibid, at 298, 250.

the legislator is concerned, the model assumes that, having assessed the outcomes' values in light of the theory of punishment that they endorse, the legislator is capable of conveying these values through a numerical value function, taking the form of an interval scale. As far as the adjudicator is concerned, instead, the model assumes that, having assessed the evidence, the adjudicator is capable of determining whether it satisfies the probability threshold(s) represented by the standard(s) of proof. No doubt, some may worry that these assumptions are unwarranted, and that this undermines the possibility of implementing the model. In this section, I try to assuage this worry.

Let us start with the assumption concerning the legislator. The value of an outcome depends on facts that define the outcome. These facts are, therefore, reasons to value the outcome in a particular way. When we compare or add reasons—both essential operations of reasoning—we engage in measurement. This measurement, though, is usually vague and nuanced, often abridged. This raises doubt about the possibility of conveying the measurement of an outcome's value through numbers, as the decision-theoretic model requires. And yet, we are used to expressing numerically the value of objects, services, or, more generally, states of affairs. Here, I am not thinking exclusively of the monetary price that we attribute to countless things we value. Among the many other examples, consider the numerical feedback that we often give about what we purchase online, and about our experiences with a service; the numerical evaluation of our research output in exercises such as the UK Research Excellence Framework; or the numerical feedback that students routinely give about our teaching, our course materials, services provided by the university, etc. These instances of numerical evaluation are not trivial: the viability of a business, our academic careers, and the standing and funding of a university may depend on them.

For another telling academic example, think of our evaluation of student essays.[55] There are some numerical properties in an essay, for instance the number of words, the number of readings underpinning it, and the number of hours spent thinking about, or writing it. But surely the essay's evaluation depends on properties of it that are not intrinsically numerical: thoughtfulness, coherence, clarity of exposition, originality, comprehensiveness, just to mention a few. And yet, we do express the essay's quality with a number; moreover, a number on an interval scale ranging from zero to 100.[56] This is the same kind of scale required by the decision-theoretic model. Not only do we do this, but we also perform calculations

[55] This example is inspired by P. Weirich, *Realistic Decision Theory: Rules for Nonideal Agents in Nonideal Circumstances* (OUP 2004), at 61.

[56] While the characterisation of the grading scale as an interval scale is accurate in theory, it may not be accurate in practice, insofar as some markers tend to consider certain intervals to be wider than other numerically equivalent intervals, because the former determine a change in classification. For example, they may consider that the interval between 69 and 70 is wider than the interval between 67 and 68, since grades in the range 60 to 69 are upper second-class grades, whereas grades of 70 or higher are first-class grades. In an interval scale, the width of an interval is determined by the numerical value alone.

with that number. If the essay counts for only a certain percentage of the course grade, we discount the number by that percentage and sum the discounted numbers corresponding to the distinct assessments in the course, in order to obtain the final grade. The final grades are then used in yet other mathematical operations, in order to determine the classification of the degree, which is itself a number. The academic experience of a student, their professional career, and the credibility of the awarding institution, ultimately depend on the soundness of our numerical grading and calculations.

Another familiar example of quantification of value is provided by criminal sentencing. In sentencing, the adjudicator calculates a comprehensive measure of how much punishment a crime is worth by taking into account a variety of reasons, such as the culpability of the defendant, the harm caused, mitigating and aggravating factors, and the purpose(s) that the sentence should serve.[57] Having done this, the adjudicator translates this measure of 'punishment worthiness' into a quantity of time that the defendant should spend in prison or doing community service, and/or into a quantity of money that the defendant should pay to the State. Needless to say, these operations are of the utmost importance. The welfare of the defendant and their loved ones, as well as the legitimacy of the criminal justice system, depend on them being carried out appropriately.

I do not want to give the impression of downplaying the difficulty of an operation such as conveying the value of trial outcomes numerically. This is, indeed, a difficult task.[58] My point here is that, if we were not capable of accomplishing this task, even with unavoidable imprecision, we would also be incapable of accomplishing many similar tasks that we routinely accomplish in our lives, and in our practice of the law; moreover, tasks that are of crucial importance for our economy, our students, our academic institutions, our criminal justice system, and many other aspects of living in a community. I doubt that, with respect to these tasks, we have just deluded ourselves into thinking that we are competent quantifiers of value.

Let us now consider the assumption that the adjudicator is capable of determining whether the available evidence satisfies the probability threshold(s) represented by the standard(s) of proof. Notice that the decision-theoretic model does not require that the adjudicator relies on devices such as the likelihood ratio or Bayes' theorem, respectively, for expressing the probative value of individual items of evidence, and for updating the probability of guilt as new items of evidence are taken into consideration.[59] The model does not give any prescription about the

[57] Here, I am relying on Sentencing Council, *General Guideline: Overarching Principles* (2019), available at <https://www.sentencingcouncil.org.uk/overarching-guides/magistrates-court/item/general-guideline-overarching-principles/> accessed 24 September 2021.

[58] For a tentative discussion of how to accomplish the task, see L. Laudan and H. D. Saunders, 'Re-Thinking the Criminal Standard of Proof: Seeking Consensus about the Utilities of Trial Outcomes' (2009) 7 International Commentary on Evidence 1, at 19–29.

[59] Both devices have been met with a considerable degree of scepticism by English and Welsh courts. See, in particular, *R v Adams* [1996] 2 Cr App R 467, *R v Adams (No 2)* [1998] 1 Cr App R 377, and *R v T*

mechanisms that the adjudicator should rely upon to assess the available body of evidence. All that it asks is that, once the evidence has been assessed, the adjudicator be generally[60] capable of telling whether the evidence satisfies particular probability thresholds. Now, we routinely express our degree of belief in facts using the language of probabilities, without relying on any mathematical calculations in the reasoning process that starts with assessing the available evidence and ends with asserting a probability.[61] We may do so, for instance, when answering a friend's question about the chances that we will attend an event, when conveying our views about the winning chances of an individual or team in a sporting contest, when answering the many market surveys that we are inundated with in our daily lives, or when participating in academic empirical research. There is nothing arcane or incoherent in the expectation that the adjudicator be capable of assessing the evidence of guilt against a probability threshold, even if they have not undertaken any mathematical analysis of the evidence.[62] What is more, the decision-theoretic model does not demand that the probability threshold(s) representing the standard(s) of proof be expressed numerically. The legislator may choose to translate the standard(s) of proof into a corresponding verbal formula. While this may not be easy, it is not an unprecedented task.[63] After all, for those who believe

[2011] 1 Cr App R 9. Notice that, in Chapter 4, I relied on the likelihood ratio to devise a test for a new trial that is more likely to be satisfied when the defendant receiving conditional acquittal is guilty than when they are innocent; but nothing in what I said commits me to the view that the adjudicator should use the likelihood ratio in fact-finding. At most, I am committed to the view that the likelihood ratio has to be used by whatever authority is in charge of assessing whether the test for a new trial has been satisfied. For these purposes, though, the ratio need not be expressed in numbers. Words can be used to convey the probabilities at the numerator and at the denominator.

[60] It is to be expected that there would be cases in which the adjudicator is in doubt as to whether the relevant threshold has been met.

[61] Of course, our probabilistic judgements are not free from error. For a general discussion of cognitive limitations that can affect probabilistic judgements, and a review of the psychological literature, see K. M. Clermont, *Standards of Decision in Law: Psychological and Logical Bases for the Standard of Proof, Here and Abroad* (Carolina Academic Press 2013), at 61–82. See also the works cited in n 20 above.

[62] See P. Tillers and J. Gottfried, 'Case Comment—*United States v Copeland*, 369 F Supp 2d 275 (EDNY 2005): A Collateral Attack on the Legal Maxim that Proof Beyond a Reasonable Doubt Is Unquantifiable?' (2006) 5 Law, Probability and Risk 135, at 142, 147; D. H. Kaye, 'Do We Need a Calculus of Weight to Understand Proof Beyond a Reasonable Doubt?' in P. Tillers and E. Green (eds), *Probability and Inference in the Law of Evidence: The Uses and Limits of Bayesianism* (Kluwer 1988), at 135–136; and Nance (n 2), at 84–95. On the limits and advantages of quantifying standards of proof, see also M. Spottswood, 'Burdens of Proof' in C. Dahlman and others (eds), *Philosophical Foundations of Evidence Law* (OUP 2021), s 2.4.

[63] See D. A. Schum, *The Evidential Foundations of Probabilistic Reasoning* (Northwestern University Press 1994), at 264–265, mentioning studies that have tried to match fuzzy attributes such as very improbable, improbable, probable, and very probable with numerical probability intervals. See, in particular, Sherman Kent's chart in his 'Words of Estimative Probability' (1964) General CIA Records, Document no CIA-RDP93T01132R000100020036-3, at 55. A version of the article is available here: <https://www.cia.gov/static/0aae8f84700a256abf63f7aad73b0a7d/Words-of-Estimative-Probability.pdf> accessed 28 June 2021. For a study on the interpersonal comparison of verbal probability statements, see M. K. Dhami and T. S. Wallsten, 'Interpersonal Comparison of Subjective Probabilities: Toward Translating Linguistic Probabilities' (2005) 33 Memory and Cognition 1057.

that standards of proof *are* probabilities, the use of words to convey numerical probabilities is already a reality in the legal system.[64]

To conclude on the question of implementation, I want to remind the reader of two things. First, as pointed out at the start of this chapter, my theory does not entail a complex system of verdicts. I have argued that crimes falling below a certain threshold of seriousness could be tried with a binary system, applying the same standard of proof across the board. Crimes that sit above that threshold could, instead, be tried with a system that includes conditional acquittal, where the standards of proof regulating the choices between acquittal and the intermediate verdict, and between the intermediate verdict and conviction, need not change across this set of crimes. Second, in Chapter 1, I reported some reassuring data about mock jurors' experiences with the Scottish 'not proven' verdict.[65] In particular, the data show that the availability of 'not proven'[66] is associated with a slightly lower level of dissatisfaction with the experience of serving on a jury; that its availability does not affect the length of deliberation, the extent of juror participation, the number of evidential issues discussed, or the extent and accuracy of the discussion of legal issues; and that mock jurors that are given the option of 'not proven' express greater confidence in their decision, irrespective of the verdict chosen. Of course, there are differences between the Scottish verdict system and the system I have envisaged. In particular, the standard of proof warranting conditional acquittal is meant to be specified, whereas that warranting 'not proven' is not specified. However, the two systems are sufficiently similar that the findings on 'not proven' make one hopeful that lay fact-finders would have a similar—one may even say 'a similarly positive'—experience with conditional acquittal. If anything, the fact that the standard of proof warranting conditional acquittal is specified should make the tasks of both lay and professional fact-finders more intelligible to them, and to the public.

[64] See, among others, Nance (n 2), at 42, according to whom the preponderance of the evidence standard and the reasonable doubt standard can be understood as expressing probability ranges; and T. Anderson and others, *Analysis of Evidence* (2nd edn, CUP 2005), at 246, describing the reasonable doubt standard, the clear and convincing evidence standard, and the probable cause standard as 'verbal probabilistic edges'. Empirical studies conducted on the reasonable doubt standard (for a useful summary see Lillquist (n 1), at 111–117), and on the being sure of guilt standard (see M. Zander, 'The Criminal Standard of Proof: How Sure is Sure?' (2000) 150 New Law Journal 1517), indicate that there is variation in the numerical probability of guilt that both laypeople and legal professionals assign to each standard. This is an issue to bear in mind if the standards of proof of the envisaged system are to be expressed verbally. To be sure, a quantum of variation in the understanding of a standard is inevitable, and expressing the standard with a numerical probability would surely not eliminate the possibility of divergences in the application of the standard to the same body of evidence by different people.

[65] See Chapter 1, section 1.4.1 and footnotes therein.

[66] The term of comparison is, of course, a binary system.

5.5 Existing equivalent devices

I now consider two objections claiming that the English and Welsh criminal justice system, and legal system more generally, already feature devices that are equivalent to an intermediate verdict. These objections also claim that, because of the existence of such equivalent devices, the intermediate verdict is not necessary: if there is any need to provide a middle ground between conviction and acquittal, the system should rely on such devices. After all—the objections conclude—since these devices are already part of the system, employing them would be a less radical, safer, and more coherent avenue to follow. My goal here is, especially, to challenge the claims of equivalence.

5.5.1 Lesser included and preparatory offences

English and Welsh criminal law features the phenomenon of lesser included offences. These are offences that comprise only some of the elements of another offence, and which, for this reason, are punished less severely than the richer offence. A classic example is given by theft and robbery. Section 1(1) of the Theft Act 1968 states that '[a] person is guilty of theft if he dishonestly appropriates property belonging to another with the intention of permanently depriving the other of it; and "thief" and "steal" shall be construed accordingly'. Section 8(1) of the Act states that '[a] person is guilty of robbery if he steals, and immediately before or at the time of doing so, and in order to do so, he uses force on any person or puts or seeks to put any person in fear of being then and there subjected to force'. Given these definitions, theft is a lesser included offence with respect to robbery: the latter cannot be committed without the former being committed, and requires elements not required by the former.

Prosecutors may charge a defendant with both the richer offence and the lesser included offence, and adjudicators may return a 'guilty' verdict for the lesser included offence if all its constituent elements are proven to the standard of proof for conviction, while the additional elements defining the richer offence are not proven. Some may argue that this decision-making mechanism is equivalent to a verdict system that features an option between acquittal and conviction; more precisely, that norms criminalising lesser included offences are devices equivalent to an intermediate verdict. This argument rests on the contention that conviction for the lesser included offence effectively consists in imposing milder hard treatment than that involved in conviction for the richer crime, when the evidence of guilt for the richer crime is weaker than is required to convict the defendant of this crime. If the claim of equivalence were accurate, it would mean that something akin to an intermediate verdict is already operative in the English and Welsh criminal justice system. This may raise doubts about the opportunity of amending the verdict system. If the substantive criminal law has already been experimented with in order to provide a middle ground between acquittal and conviction, it may be safer and more coherent to rely on this instrument—that is, to enact more norms that criminalise lesser included offences—in order to seek the maximisation of expected value that has driven my justification of intermediate verdicts,[67] or whatever other goal one aims to achieve with the adoption of such a verdict.[68]

The claim of equivalence between an intermediate verdict and norms criminalising lesser included offences is, however, false. When an intermediate verdict is issued against the defendant, the justification for so doing depends on there being evidence that shows, to the satisfaction of a standard of proof lower than that for conviction, that the defendant may have committed the offence charged; the justification for issuing an intermediate verdict does not depend on whether or not behaviour worthy of punishment has already been proven to the standard of proof for conviction. Instead, when a defendant is proven to have committed a lesser included offence, and is convicted for it, the general view is that punishment is justified by the consideration that the lesser included offence is, per se, worthy of punishment; not by the consideration that the lesser included offence is evidence of some other behaviour that is the actual target of the criminal law. Take the case of theft. Whoever is proven to have stolen is punished for theft because theft itself is deemed worthy of punishment, not because theft is considered to be evidence of robbery. The consideration that there is evidence, short of proof, of a target offence—which plays a crucial role in the justification for issuing an intermediate verdict—is not a prominent component, or even just a component, of the justifications for punishing theft that one would expect the lawmaker, a legal practitioner, or a legal scholar to offer. In sum, the claim of equivalence between an intermediate verdict and norms criminalising lesser included offences is undermined by the discrepancy between the reasons that justify issuing the former, and the reasons that are generally taken to justify punishment for breaching the latter. This discrepancy shows that norms criminalising lesser included offences are not understood, or employed, as devices equivalent to an intermediate verdict. Therefore, it is unreasonable to argue that, by criminalising such offences, the criminal justice system has already incorporated, and made available, devices akin to such a verdict.[69]

[67] On the view that lesser included offences can be understood as instruments for decision-theoretic compromise between acquittal and conviction, see J. Kaplan, 'Decision Theory and the Factfinding Process' (1968) 20 Stanford Law Review 1065, at 1078–1082.

[68] cf D. Teichman, 'Convicting with Reasonable Doubt: An Evidentiary Theory of Criminal Law' (2018) 93 Notre Dame Law Review 757, elaborating a descriptive and normative theory of substantive criminal law, according to which lesser included offences are, and should be, used in order to graduate the sanction as a function of the evidence of the more serious crimes that include them.

[69] For other offences to test this reply to the objection, see assault and battery, both lesser included offences with respect to the offence proscribed by s 47 of the English and Welsh Offences Against the Person Act 1861.

This reply may not satisfy everyone. Some may shift the focus from lesser included offences to preparatory offences, which may or may not be 'lesser included' with respect to the offence that is being prepared. They may argue that at least some preparatory offences are 'evidentiary' in nature; in other words, they are punished exclusively because they are considered to be evidence of another offence, which is the real target of the criminal law, and may often be too difficult to prove. When a defendant is proven to have committed a preparatory offence of this kind, and is punished accordingly—the rejoinder continues—this is not done because the behaviour that was proven is deemed worthy of punishment in itself. Rather, it is done only because, even if there is not sufficient evidence to convict the defendant for the 'complete' offence, the behaviour that was proven is taken to be evidence that they may have committed such offence. Some possession offences may be thought to provide examples of evidentiary offences. For instance, one may argue that drug possession,[70] or the possession of articles that can be used to steal or burgle,[71] are punished not because they are deemed worthy of punishment in themselves, but exclusively because they are considered to be evidence of other offences: respectively, drug possession with intent to supply, or the actual supply of drugs, and theft or burglary.

My first response to this rejoinder is to question whether preparatory offences, or even just some of them, are, indeed, evidentiary offences. Arguably, these behaviours are punished also, if not principally, because, as preparatory acts for the complete offence, they are believed to increase the risk of this offence being committed. To clarify, while the complete offence is punished because it is believed to harm values that the system is intended to protect, the preparatory offence is punished because it is deemed to put at risk these very values by making completion more likely, and because it is deemed to foster public insecurity as a result of the risk it creates.[72] If, however, this 'putting at risk', and the consequent public insecurity, are the considerations that drive the decision to punish the preparatory offence, the offence is punished because it is deemed worthy of punishment in itself, irrespective of its supposed evidential role. This fact alone undermines the claim of equivalence between the norms criminalising preparatory offences and an intermediate verdict.

There is also a clear instrumental reason that, arguably, plays a role in the decision to proscribe these offences:[73] doing so allows law enforcement to intervene before the protected values are actually harmed through the complete offence.

[70] See s 5(2) of the English and Welsh Misuse of Drugs Act 1971.

[71] See the offence of 'going equipped for stealing', under s 25 of the English and Welsh Theft Act 1968.

[72] For critical discussion, see P. Ramsay, 'Preparation Offences, Security Interests, Political Freedom' in R. A. Duff and others (eds), *The Structures of the Criminal Law* (OUP 2011).

[73] Notice that I am not committing to any view as to whether preparatory offences should, indeed, be criminalised. Here I am merely discussing the possible reasons why they are criminalised, in order to counter the claim that they are evidentiary offences.

Notice that this instrumental reason presupposes an expectation on the part of the system that is in tension with the claim that preparatory offences are criminalised because they are considered to be evidence of completion. This is the expectation that, while preparatory acts have been taken, the complete offence has not indeed occurred, and that it will not occur if law enforcement is allowed to step in timeously. After all, the logic of the preventive use of criminal law involves, precisely, bringing forward the limit between permissible and impermissible action so that the harm to protected values is merely risked, but does not materialise. The limit, instead, is not brought forward on the basis of the inference that this harm has, indeed, materialised if preparations for it have been made.[74]

Still, even if the objection were correct about the fact that the law currently criminalises evidentiary offences—or if such offences were, in any case, criminalised—an intermediate verdict would not be equivalent to the substantive law mechanism that the criminalisation of these offences would represent. Indeed, under this mechanism, each element of the evidentiary offence would need to be proven to the standard of proof for conviction, while an intermediate verdict may be available even if no element of the offence is proved to such a standard. Therefore, it is not the case that a hypothetical evidentiary offence could be considered proven in every instance in which a hypothetical intermediate verdict would be warranted. More importantly, even assuming equivalence, there would be reasons to prefer the adoption of an intermediate verdict to a widespread criminalisation of evidentiary offences. In fact, it is doubtful whether criminalising evidentiary offences could ever be justified. For one thing, criminalising conduct just because it is evidence of other behaviour may blur the message that the criminal law sends to the polity, creating confusion as to which values it promotes. Assuming that the criminal law is designed to protect and promote certain values, the law will hardly get these values across to the public through prohibiting conduct that, while being evidence of behaviour that undermines a protected value, does not itself harm or put at risk any such value. The worry is that the evidentiary conduct may be perceived by the public as harming or threatening values that are dear to the system, when this is not, in fact, the case. In the long run, this perception may produce the unwanted effect of mobilising the community behind values that differ from those that the system was intended to guard and promote. A related problem is that, adopting the substantive law mechanism, cases would occur where, while it emerges that the complete offence has not taken place, the evidentiary offence is established. In these cases, the criminal law would send a contradictory message to prosecutors, adjudicators, and the criminals themselves, by signalling that, on the one hand, conduct significant enough to amount to a crime has been committed,

[74] For in-depth treatment of the complex phenomenon of preventive criminal law, see A. Ashworth and others (eds), *Prevention and the Limits of the Criminal Law* (OUP 2013); and A. Ashworth and L. Zedner, *Preventive Justice* (OUP 2014).

but that, on the other hand, it is not conduct worth caring about after all, since its evidentiary role is undermined.

To conclude, I am not convinced that the law currently criminalises evidentiary offences; that, if it does, or if such offences were criminalised, the relevant substantive norms are, or would be, equivalent to an intermediate verdict; and that, if these norms are, or were, equivalent to an intermediate verdict, they represent, or would represent, a better option than such a verdict. Moreover, the objection considered here is even weaker if framed in terms of an equivalence between existing norms proscribing lesser included/preparatory offences and the particular intermediate verdict that I defend: conditional acquittal. This is because no existing criminal law norm carries with it punishment that is comparable to the hard treatment involved in this verdict.

5.5.2 The interaction between civil and criminal justice

The standard of proof applicable in civil trials in England and Wales is proof on the balance of probabilities, which is significantly lower than the reasonable doubt—or being sure of guilt—[75] standard applicable in criminal trials. It is, therefore, possible for a defendant who has been acquitted of a crime to be held liable for a corresponding tort in a civil court.[76] While being from overseas, the notorious case of OJ Simpson offers a ready illustration of such interaction between civil and criminal justice (I must add the caveat that jury nullification may have affected Simpson's criminal case). In 1995 Simpson was acquitted of the murders of Ron Goldman and Nicole Brown Simpson after a highly mediatic trial that came to be regarded as 'the trial of the 20th century'. One year later, Simpson was held liable for the wrongful death of Ron Goldman as a result of a civil suit brought by the Goldman family. In cases of this kind, the interaction between civil and criminal justice seems to produce a decision-making mechanism that is equivalent to an intermediate verdict: in the presence of evidence of guilt that is not sufficient to justify criminal conviction, hard treatment short of that warranted by conviction is, nonetheless, imposed on

[75] According to s 5(3) of the *Crown Court Compendium, Part I: Jury and Trial Management and Summing Up* (August 2021), the being sure of guilt standard is equivalent to the reasonable doubt standard. See <https://www.judiciary.uk/publications/crown-court-compendium-published/> accessed 24 September 2021.

[76] Consider that courts in England and Wales have, occasionally, held that, when a plaintiff alleges criminal conduct in a civil case, the criminal standard of proof should apply. This, however, is by no means a uniform view in the case law. See M. Redmayne, 'Standards of Proof in Civil Litigation' (1999) 62 Modern Law Review 167, at 192–194, criticising this approach; and I. Dennis, *The Law of Evidence* (7th edn, Sweet & Maxwell 2020), at 484–486. Notably, in a recent decision, the Court of Appeal has denied the existence of 'a principle that where the court is faced with applications ... in which the basis of the application relates to criminal or quasi criminal behaviour, the criminal standard is necessitated by a proper appreciation of the requirements of fairness under article 6.1' of the European Convention on Human Rights. See *Birmingham City Council v Jones* [2018] 3 WLR 1695, at 1712. See also paras 58–59, at 1713–1714.

the defendant.[77] Would the enhancement of this interaction not be preferable to the adoption of an intermediate verdict? After all, the interaction between civil and criminal justice is already a well-established feature of our legal system. A possible way of enhancing this feature, with an eye to replicating an intermediate verdict, would be to allow whoever has a claim for damages against the defendant to bring this claim into the criminal trial—as happens in Italy, for instance—[78] but still to adjudicate the civil action using the balance of probabilities standard, and the criminal action using the reasonable doubt—or being sure of guilt—standard.[79]

As interesting as this proposal seems, the claim of equivalence between the civil/criminal interaction and intermediate verdicts is false. I will limit myself to a few considerations. First, the overlap between the civil and the criminal normative systems is not complete. In other words, not every crime is also a tort. Consider crimes that do not produce an identifiable loss for anyone, such that no one would be entitled to bring a tort suit against the defendant. While there may not be many such crimes, some do exist. To give a few examples, consider drug-related offences, such as the import or export of a controlled substance, its possession, or its production; the possession of articles that can be used to steal or burgle, already mentioned earlier; and any attempted crime that does not cause damage or harm. In these cases, absent an intermediate verdict, there would be no middle ground available between acquittal and conviction. None could be provided by the civil/criminal interaction. Second, even when there is an overlap between the two normative systems, this may not be realised in practice. The defendant may be sued, but not charged, because the behaviour they are accused of is not considered sufficiently serious to make the criminal prosecution in the public interest, or because there is not sufficient incriminating evidence to pass the evidential test for bringing charges. More importantly, for our purposes, the defendant may be charged, but not sued, for instance because the victim does not have the resources to sue. The possibility of this mismatch in practice also results from the fact that decisions as

[77] See Fisher, 'Conviction without Conviction' (n 11), at 848–849. The parallel between an intermediate verdict and the interaction between civil and criminal justice is also drawn in B. S. Jackson, 'Truth or Proof? The Criminal Verdict' (1998) 11 International Journal for the Semiotics of Law 227, at 234. While I focus, here, on this interaction, another interaction that may be seen as equivalent to an intermediate verdict is that between disciplinary and criminal proceedings. The member of a professional body (most notably, a teacher, a police officer, a doctor, or a lawyer) who is acquitted by a criminal court may be subjected to disciplinary proceedings in order to establish professional misconduct. A lower standard of proof than the criminal standard would apply in such proceedings. While potentially severe, the consequences of a positive finding may not be as serious as criminal conviction. By and large, the considerations that I make in this section also apply to a possible claim of equivalence between an intermediate verdict and the interaction between disciplinary and criminal proceedings.

[78] See arts 74 and 75 of the 1988 Code of Criminal Procedure.

[79] In Italy, instead, once the civil claim is brought into the criminal trial, both actions are decided on the reasonable doubt standard. However, if, pursuant to art 622 of the Code of Criminal Procedure, the Supreme Court (ie, Corte di Cassazione) annuls only the part of a criminal judgment that pertains to the civil claim, and instructs a lower court to reconsider this claim, the criminal and the civil actions are effectively severed, such that the lower court will apply the civil standard of proof. See Corte di Cassazione Civile no 22520/2019.

to whether to start the different types of proceedings are the prerogatives of different agents. In particular, while in England and Wales a private individual or association may bring a prosecution, within certain limits,[80] the public prosecutor cannot bring a civil suit against the defendant. If the criminal action is brought, the absence of an overlap in practice means that, again, no middle ground is available between acquittal and conviction, if no intermediate verdict is in place. Third, even if the overlap is realised in practice, one has to remember that decision-making in the civil case is governed by the balance of probabilities standard. This may not be the standard of proof that warrants an intermediate verdict in the criminal trial. As discussed previously, where the latter standard sits should depend on applying a formula similar to formula (2) from the previous chapter, but involving the values of the outcomes of acquittal, and of the intermediate verdict. This means that, even if being held civilly liable could be understood as a middle ground between acquittal and conviction that delivers criminal justice, it would be a middle ground that may not be justified by the decision-theoretic model that I have relied upon. Fourth, and most importantly, the functions of criminal law and of tort law are markedly different, such that being held civilly liable cannot be seen as a device for delivering criminal justice. An appropriate discussion of this point would take us far beyond the scope of this book. It suffices to say that crimes, and the way in which they are processed and responded to, involve an element of public concern, and of public engagement,[81] that is generally absent from the private disputes regulated by the law of torts. It is, therefore, reasonable to argue that a finding against the defendant in a civil action could hardly perform the role of an intermediate criminal verdict. For instance, it could hardly be seen as a societal response, or foster the social stigma that may constitute an intentional component of the hard treatment involved in this verdict. This seems true even if—as per the proposal mentioned earlier—the civil and criminal actions were dealt with in the same proceedings: if the defendant is only held civilly liable, after all, the evident message sent by the proceedings is that the criminal justice system has no business with them. Also consider that, as shown in Chapters 3 and 4, the justification for issuing an intermediate verdict ultimately depends on the value function of the theory of punishment that one endorses. In fact, no criminal verdict could be justified if it did not foster the values of the relevant theory of punishment. Civil judgments are not tested for, nor justified on the basis of, their ability to foster the values of a

[80] See s 6(1) of the Prosecution of Offences Act 1985, and the Crown Prosecution Service, *Private Prosecutions: Legal Guidance*, available at <https://www.cps.gov.uk/legal-guidance/private-prosecutions> accessed 28 June 2021.

[81] This element, for instance, is central to Antony Duff's theory of the criminal law. See A. Duff, *The Realm of Criminal Law* (OUP 2018), chs 4 and 5.

particular theory of punishment. This is for the simple reason that civil remedies are not normally considered an instance of punishment.[82] Fifth, and finally, the alleged equivalence cannot reasonably be claimed with respect to the particular intermediate verdict that I defend; that is, conditional acquittal. Being held liable in a civil court does not warrant a new criminal trial. If, after acquittal, new incriminating evidence surfaces in a subsequent tort case, it is this evidence, rather than the outcome of the civil case, that may warrant a retrial.[83]

[82] The obvious exception to this statement is that of punitive damages. See, in particular, V. Wilcox, 'Punitive Damages in England' in H. Koziol and V. Wilcox (eds), *Punitive Damages: Common Law and Civil Law Perspectives* (Springer 2009).

[83] A plea deal may be considered another device that is equivalent to an intermediate verdict. In fact, it has been argued that plea deals are an expression of the logic 'weaker evidence (than that required for conviction at trial), milder hard treatment (than that involved in conviction at trial)'. See Fisher, 'Conviction without Conviction' (n 11), at 849–851; S. Bray, 'Not Proven: Introducing a Third Verdict' (2005) 72 University of Chicago Law Review 1299, at 1308; and Wansley (n 40), at 312–314. A notable difference between a plea deal and an intermediate verdict is that the former involves conviction. With a deal, the defendant is guilty in the eyes of the system, and plausibly also in those of the community. This alone undermines the claim of equivalence. I am also sceptical about the idea that a plea deal is an expression of the logic just mentioned. In particular, I am not convinced by the claim that a plea deal is generally indicative of weaker evidence of guilt than that required for conviction at trial. After all, to the extent that such deals are made 'in the shadow of trial' (for critical discussion of this theory, see S. Bibas, 'Plea Bargaining Outside the Shadow of Trial' (2004) 117 Harvard Law Review 2464), one would expect that, in a considerable number of cases, the defendant would not plead guilty unless there was incriminating evidence that could meet the standard of proof for conviction at trial. Moreover, even accepting that some guilty pleas are false and/or that they are made not in consideration of the strength of the evidence, but because of irresistible incentives, bad representation, or ignorance of the consequences, one would hope that the system is not so rotten that a guilty plea per se cannot be considered significant incriminating evidence. Also consider that, while charge and fact bargaining both exist in England and Wales, a true form of sentence bargaining does not. The bargain on the sentence 'is with the law' (Campbell and others (n 42), at 326), not with the prosecution. It is the law that entitles the defendant to a sentence discount if they plead guilty, and that sets the limits of this discount (it cannot exceed one-third of the sentence). While the prosecution can indirectly bargain on the sentence by dropping a charge, or by restating the facts in the indictment, it cannot do so directly, other than by bringing the law to the attention of the defendant. For instance, in a weak case, it is not for the prosecution to offer the defendant a sufficient sentence reduction that would make the prospect of a plea deal more appealing than going to trial. It is the law that makes the offer; the maximum reduction is fixed, and the actual reduction is just a function of how early the plea is made, not of the strength of the evidence of guilt. See Sentencing Council, *Reduction of Sentence for a Guilty Plea: Definitive Guideline* (2017), available at <https://www.sentencingcouncil.org.uk/publications/item/reduction-in-sentence-for-a-guilty-plea-definitive-guideline-2/> accessed 28 June 2021. The fact that the prosecution is, effectively, bypassed in sentence bargaining, the fact that the reduction cannot be greater than a third of the sentence, and the fact that the extent of the reduction does not depend on the strength of the incriminating evidence (in particular, the reduction is not inversely proportional to the strength of the evidence), all reinforce the expectation that most defendants would not plead guilty absent a strong case against them. On top of these considerations, I restate the point already made with reference to the other devices studied in this, and in the previous, section: the claim of equivalence considered here loses all its credibility if made with reference to conditional acquittal. To conclude, may diversion mechanisms such as simple cautions or conditional cautions (see Campbell and others (n 42), at 164-171) be considered equivalent to an intermediate verdict? Notice that these frequently used mechanisms require the admission of guilt on the part of the suspect. For this reason alone, a possible claim of equivalence would be unconvincing.

5.6 Are intermediate verdicts a 'cop-out'?

There are a host of studies in consumer psychology evidencing the phenomenon of 'extremeness aversion', also referred to as 'compromise behaviour'.[84] This is the fact that 'the attractiveness of an option is enhanced if it is an intermediate option in the choice set and is diminished if it is an extreme option'.[85] To illustrate, take three options: *A*, a low-range and low-priced camera; *B*, a mid-range and mid-priced camera; and *C*, a high-range and high-priced camera. Due to extremeness aversion, the rate of choosing *B*, relative to the rate of choosing *A*, is lower when *A* and *B* are the only options than when *C* is added to the choice set, such that *B* becomes the intermediate option.[86] Notice that the greater attractiveness of an option when it becomes intermediate in the choice set can be seen as a departure from rational choice, insofar as the extreme option that is added to the set does not provide any new information about the already existing options.[87] In other words, why should *B*'s popularity relative to *A*'s increase once *C* is added to the choice set, if this addition does not provide the decision-maker with any new information as to the value of *A* or *B*? Or if someone chooses *A* over *B* in a binary choice set, why should they switch to *B* once such an uninformative addition has been made to the set?[88] Be that as it may, studies on extremeness aversion, by and large, provide evidence that consumers—indeed, decision-makers more generally—[89] have a tendency towards compromise. Is this a reason to worry about the adoption of an intermediate criminal verdict?

[84] For a recent meta-analysis of the vast literature on the topic, see N. Neumann and others, 'A Meta-Analysis of Extremeness Aversion' (2016) 26 Journal of Consumer Psychology 193. The authors state, at 194, that 'despite finding substantial variation in effect magnitudes due to method choices, our analysis of 142 experimental cases provides empirical evidence that compromise behavior is manifest in consumer choice and appears to be a robust behavioral phenomenon'.

[85] See I. Simonson and A. Tversky, 'Choice in Context: Tradeoff Contrast and Extremeness Aversion' (1992) 29 Journal of Marketing Research 281, at 281.

[86] See ibid, at 290.

[87] See Neumann and others (n 84), at 195; A. Chernev, 'Extremeness Aversion and Attribute-Balance Effects in Choice' (2004) 31 Journal of Consumer Research 249, at 249; and P. K. Padamwar and others, 'Range Effect on Extremeness Aversion' (2018) 45 Decision 345, at 346–347.

[88] In fact, insofar as extremeness aversion is measured in terms of 'relative-share changes', it may be detected even if no one who chooses *A* with the binary choice set switches to *B* when *C* is added to the set. Detection would merely require the increase in the rate of choosing *B*, relative to that of choosing *A*, when *C* is added to the set. For example, if the choosing rates of *A* and of *B* were, respectively, 40% and 60% in the binary choice set, extremeness aversion would be detected if, with the addition of *C*, the choosing rate of *A* became 5% and that of *B* became 45% (with *C* attracting the remaining 50% of participants). This may happen irrespective of whether there is any switch between choosing *A* and choosing *B*. But see Neumann and others (n 84), at 195–196, for alternative measures of the phenomenon.

[89] Extremeness aversion has also been detected in studies concerning legal adjudication, where the options offered to the participants consisted in conviction for crimes of varying seriousness. See M. Kelman and others, 'Context-Dependence in Legal Decision Making' (1996) 25 Journal of Legal Studies 287, in particular at 290–295. For a discussion of the implications of these findings for legal decision-making, see ibid, at 300–309. See also C. R. Sunstein, 'Behavioral Analysis of Law' (1997) 64 University of Chicago Law Review 1175, at 1181–1182.

To begin with, some may worry that adopting an intermediate verdict could foster irrational decision-making of a similar kind to that just described. In Chapter 1, we saw that empirical evidence on the Scottish 'not proven' verdict confirms that the availability of this intermediate option lures mock jurors away from both the 'not guilty' and 'guilty' verdicts.[90] There, I pointed out that the lower rate of conviction amongst mock jurors who were given the option of 'not proven' may signal decision-making inconsistency. In particular, if neither the incriminating evidence nor the standard of proof for conviction change when the intermediate option is added, one would expect that a rational decision-maker who would convict with the binary choice set would also convict with the richer set. Indeed, the detected behaviour of mock jurors seems to share a problematic aspect of the irrational behaviour described in the previous paragraph. The new choice added to the set does not provide new information about the conditions under which conviction is warranted,[91] and yet, the addition decreases the rate of conviction. Notice, though, that this critical assessment is not valid any more if one adopts the decision-theoretic model presented in the previous chapter. Under this model, the addition of a superior intermediate verdict changes the conditions under which both acquittal and conviction are warranted. This is because the probability range corresponding to the intermediate verdict encroaches on the probability ranges that correspond to acquittal and conviction in the binary verdict system. Indeed, $p^1 < p^* < p^2$. In other words, the standard of proof below which acquittal is required is lower when the intermediate verdict is added to the choice set, and, crucially, the standard of proof for conviction is higher after the addition. This means that adding the intermediate option to the choice set changes the significance of the extreme options. Under these conditions, and holding constant the incriminating evidence, it can be perfectly rational for a decision-maker who would have convicted, or acquitted, with a binary choice set to issue the intermediate verdict when this option becomes available.[92]

Still, some may worry that the adoption of an intermediate verdict may foster compromises which, if not irrational, are at least non-virtuous. The worry is that, in cases characterised by decisional difficulty or closeness, the intermediate option may tempt, and prompt, the adjudicator to dodge their decision-making responsibilities. To clarify, if, at the time of deliberation, the adjudicator is left with the impression that the case is not a clear acquittal or a clear conviction, they may seize the intermediate verdict as an opportunity to avoid fuller deliberation. Rather

[90] See Chapter 1, section 1.4.1, and corresponding footnotes.

[91] Notice that, in the case of the Scottish verdict system, this is not true for the 'not guilty' verdict. Arguably, the addition of 'not proven' changes the conditions under which 'not guilty' is warranted; in particular, it reduces the probability range corresponding to 'not guilty'. This is why no decision-making inconsistency is evidenced by the detected reduction in the rate of 'not guilty' verdicts when 'not proven' is added to the set.

[92] cf Fisher, 'Constitutionalism and the Criminal Law' (n 11), at 837–838.

than assessing the evidence carefully and being open to the possibility that this evidence, once so assessed, may warrant any of the available options, the adjudicator may lazily cut the deliberation short and choose the option that presents the smallest error cost.[93] This is the option sitting in-between acquittal and conviction.[94] I have already considered this objection in Chapter 1, when studying the debate on the Scottish 'not proven' verdict. There, I pointed out that there is some empirical evidence that mock jurors understand 'not proven' as making possible such a non-virtuous compromise.[95] However, I also pointed out that, while the decisional difficulty of a case increases the propensity of mock jurors to choose 'not proven', this may actually be due to the fact that they see this verdict as the option that best fits the evidence. More precisely, they may choose 'not proven' when, after careful consideration of the evidence, they are in doubt about whether the standard for conviction is met, but clearly recognise the existence of significant incriminating evidence. Notice that, in this case, the compromise is a virtuous one. The intermediate verdict is not chosen in spite of the evidence, or regardless of the evidence. It is chosen *because* of the evidence.

Having said this, I certainly do not dismiss the possibility that adopting an intermediate verdict might encourage non-virtuous behaviour on the part of the adjudicator, be this a panel or an individual. After all, if an adjudicator has a disposition, or any reason, to do their job hastily, having an option that avoids the risk of false acquittal and, especially, the risk of false conviction may well encourage them to give in to this disposition, or this reason, by choosing this option without further deliberation. To be sure, this is an issue that requires more empirical investigation, tailored to the specific intermediate verdict that one envisages. The important point here, though, is that the ultimate driver of virtuous adjudication is the virtuousness of the adjudicator, not the verdict system. Indeed—as we are reminded by the behaviour of juror seven in Sidney Lumet's celebrated *12 Angry Men*—a non-virtuous adjudicator may well render adjudication non-virtuous, even when the choice set is binary.[96] Conversely, a virtuous adjudicator would behave virtuously, even if given

[93] Among the epistemic virtues that are not displayed in this behaviour, and which, arguably, an adjudicator should put in practice are thoroughness, caution, patience, and judiciousness. For discussion, see N. Cooper, 'The Intellectual Virtues' (1994) 69 Philosophy 459, at 461–463.

[94] Strictly speaking, an intermediate outcome is always an error, given that the defendant is either innocent (hence, they should be acquitted) or guilty (hence, they should be convicted). But the error represented by any intermediate outcome is less costly than the possible error of conviction (false conviction), and, depending on the severity of the intermediate verdict, it is also less costly than the possible error of acquittal (false acquittal). Arguably, in the cases of both 'not proven' and conditional acquittal, both intermediate outcomes are preferable to false acquittal.

[95] See R. Ormston and others, *Scottish Jury Research: Findings from a Large-Scale Mock Jury Study* (Scottish Government, Social Research Series 2019), at 40, 48 and J. Chalmers and others, 'Beyond Doubt: The Case Against "Not Proven"' (2021) Modern Law Review, DOI: 10.1111/1468-2230.12707, at 27-28.

[96] Interpreted by Jack Warden, juror seven is largely indifferent to the case, and is anxious to attend a baseball match. He changes his vote to 'not guilty' when he sees that the tide is moving in the direction of acquittal. He apparently does so because he wants the deliberation to end as quickly as possible. The jury's overall deliberation is hailed by many as an example of virtuous decision-making. But this is in

an intermediate option. Now, if what we want is virtuous decision-making in criminal adjudication, we are not going to achieve this desideratum simply by avoiding an option that might encourage the non-virtuous to behave non-virtuously. We can only achieve it by educating adjudicators to virtuous decision-making.[97] Once we have nurtured this culture, though, the possible worry that the intermediate option might encourage non-virtuous behaviour should not detract from the reasons that we have for making this option available.

5.7 Concluding remarks

In this chapter, I have attempted to fend off a series of challenging objections to the decision-theoretic justification offered in the previous chapter, and, more generally, to the adoption of an intermediate verdict. I may not have convinced everyone that all of these objections are superable. This discussion may have actually pointed some in the direction of further, stronger, objections. If so, these will be part of the conversation on the merits of adopting an intermediate verdict, which the book aims to revive. Notwithstanding that this conversation started several hundred years ago, I doubt that we have run out of new and interesting things to say on the matter.

spite of juror seven's behaviour. The point I am making here is that, had the jury been composed exclusively of individuals with the same disposition as juror seven, the deliberation would have been far from virtuous, notwithstanding the binary choice set.

[97] For a defence of this project, and of the claim that the study of virtue epistemology should have a prominent role in the field of evidence law theory, see A. Amaya, 'Virtues in Evidential Reasoning in Law' (unpublished manuscript on file with the author). For an application of virtue epistemology to criminal fact-finding, see F. Picinali, 'The Threshold Lies in the Method: Instructing Jurors About *Reasoning* Beyond Reasonable Doubt' (2015) 19 International Journal of Evidence and Proof 139.

Conclusion

This study started with an account of the intermediate verdicts that developed in the Late Middle Ages, and led to the defence of a hypothetical intermediate verdict that is reminiscent of one of its medieval predecessors. The verdict that I have defended is called conditional acquittal, and consists in imposing on the defendant the possibility of being retried if new incriminating evidence with substantial probative value is found. Conditional acquittal shares the essential traits of an intermediate option that featured in the *ius commune* criminal trial of continental Europe, and which was employed in some European jurisdictions well into the 19th century: the suspension of res judicata, or *absolutio ab instantia*.

Having cleared the path from the argument that the presumption of innocence is incompatible with intermediate criminal verdicts (see Chapter 2), I attempted to justify conditional acquittal on decision-theoretic grounds (see Chapter 4). I showed that conditional acquittal satisfies the requirement of a particular differential impact between the case in which the defendant receiving the verdict is guilty and the case in which the defendant is innocent. Indeed, conditional acquittal consists in harder treatment in the former case than in the latter, as the requirement demands. I have drawn this requirement from the 'superiority condition', a simple mathematical formula. This is the condition that an intermediate verdict must satisfy in order to maximise expected value within a certain range of the probability of guilt and, hence, in order to be justified on decision-theoretic grounds.[1] I have pointed out that the requirement of a differential impact represents a heuristic for the identification of a concrete superior intermediate verdict; that is, a concrete intermediate verdict that satisfies the superiority condition. The relationship between the heuristic requirement and the superiority condition is such that a verdict that satisfies the former has potential for satisfying the latter under any theory of punishment to which my decision-theoretic argument applies; but it will not necessarily do so. This means that showing that an intermediate verdict satisfies the superiority condition is providing a justification for this verdict; showing that it satisfies the heuristic requirement is providing only a prima facie justification. My

[1] To clarify, if the verdict maximises expected value within a certain range of the probability of guilt, then issuing the verdict when the probability of guilt falls within that range is justified on decision-theoretic grounds, hence incorporating the verdict into the verdict system so that it would be issued under such circumstances is also justified on decision-theoretic grounds.

Justice In-Between, Federico Picinali, Oxford University Press. © Federico Picinali 2022.
DOI: 10.1093/oso/9780198864592.003.0007

case for conditional acquittal, then, is a prima facie justification (see Chapter 4, section 4.4.2). Whether it is, indeed, a superior intermediate verdict is a hypothesis that must be tested by constructing a fully fledged value function reflecting the theory of punishment that one endorses.

I argued that, in the decision problem of adjudication, both consequentialists and deontologists about punishment can follow the principle of maximising expected value without relinquishing any tenets of their respective theories of punishment (see Chapter 3). In fact, I argued that a deontologist must follow this principle when adjudicating under conditions of lack of knowledge about the responsibility of the defendant. If, indeed, consequentialists and deontologists about punishment follow the principle of maximising expected value in the decision problem of adjudication, they will consider that there is a justification for issuing an intermediate verdict when doing so maximises expected value. As I just pointed out, the case I have made for the superiority of conditional acquittal is a prima facie case only: I have not shown that this intermediate verdict is justified on decision-theoretic grounds under any theory of punishment. I hope, though, that my defence of conditional acquittal will encourage both consequentialists and deontologists about punishment to study whether such a verdict is justified under their respective theories. In any case, the discovery of the superiority condition is, in itself, a valuable outcome, since it paves the way for justifying an intermediate verdict—be it conditional acquittal or not—on decision-theoretic grounds.

I have remarked on the fact that, even when considered in isolation—that is, independently of the decision-theoretic argument that I relied upon to derive it—the heuristic requirement has intuitive appeal (see Chapter 4, section 4.7). More precisely, an intermediate verdict that consists in harder treatment if the defendant receiving it is guilty than if they are innocent seems an intuitively appealing option when the probability of guilt is somewhere in the proximity of the standard of proof of a binary system, such that the adjudicator experiences significant doubt about whether to convict or acquit. This intuitive appeal flows from the fact that, if issued, the verdict is more similar to conviction if the defendant receiving it is guilty, than if they are innocent. Or, the verdict is more incisive in performing the function of conviction, if the defendant is guilty, than it is in imposing the wrongful burden of conviction, if the defendant is innocent. This intuitive appeal notwithstanding, whether there is, indeed, a probability range such that the adjudicator is justified in issuing the intermediate verdict when the probability of guilt falls within that range, depends on whether doing so maximises expected value. In other words, a justification for issuing the intermediate verdict cannot be provided by the intuitive appeal. The intuition may give the hint that issuing the intermediate verdict is warranted, under some epistemic conditions. If it is indeed warranted, though, this is not due to the intuition, but to what is being intuited: that, under such epistemic conditions, the verdict is the superior option from a decision-theoretic perspective.[2]

There are a series of questions pertaining to conditional acquittal that I have not addressed in the book. What procedure should be followed for the authorisation of the new trial that the intermediate verdict makes possible? Should this resemble the current procedure for authorising the retrial of the acquitted under the English and Welsh Criminal Justice Act 2003, which, in a nutshell, involves the prosecution's application to the Court of Appeal, and the court's decision as to whether the test for a new trial is met? Should the prosecution and/or the defence be allowed to appeal against conditional acquittal and, if so, on what grounds? Should there be a time limit after which the conditionally acquitted defendant cannot be retried?[3] Should conditional acquittal be available as an option at the retrial?[4] Should conditional acquittal be admissible as character evidence in a trial for a different offence allegedly committed by the defendant? Should conditional acquittal produce a criminal record, such that it may be disclosed when the conditionally acquitted person applies for employment, when they apply for particular licences, when they seek admission to certain professions, etc? These questions are important and some of them, at least, raise difficult issues. However, they concern the implementation of conditional acquittal, or peripheral aspects of the verdict's nature. Addressing them goes beyond my attempt to justify this intermediate verdict.[5]

I argued that the current English and Welsh law on the retrial of the acquitted is unjustified since it cannot overcome some arguments in support of the double jeopardy rule (see Chapter 4, section 4.6). More specifically, this law also allows for a retrial in cases in which the probability of guilt is not sufficiently high to overcome arguments from finality, distress, and public confidence. I also argued that the

[2] While, in the book, I have not provided a decision-theoretic analysis of the three everyday life decision problems mentioned in the Introduction, or of Jill's reworked case, discussed in Chapter 3, the intuitions triggered by these scenarios should, indeed, be tested with such an analysis, in order to find out whether the respective non-binary choice sets are justified.

[3] On the issue of time limits, albeit with reference to the retrial of the acquitted, see Law Commission, *Double Jeopardy* (Law Com CP No 156, 1999), at 48–49, and Law Commission, *Double Jeopardy and Prosecution Appeals* (Law Com No 267, 2001), at 56–57. Under the Criminal Justice Act 2003, there is no time limit for retrying the acquitted. However, according to s 79 of the Act, the lapse of time from when the offence was allegedly committed is relevant to the assessment of whether a retrial is in the interests of justice.

[4] On the issue of whether it should be possible to retry the acquitted more than once for the same offence, see Law Commission, *Double Jeopardy* (n 3), at 50, and Law Commission, *Double Jeopardy and Prosecution Appeals* (n 3), at 59–60.

[5] Notice that it may be possible to deal with some of these questions from within the decision-theoretic justification of conditional acquittal. For instance, one may consider that whether or not there is a time limit for the retrial affects the values of the intermediate outcomes. If it were the case that the absence of a time limit compromises the superiority of conditional acquittal, then this intermediate verdict would be justified only if an appropriate time limit for the retrial is in place.

decision-theoretic model that I have employed offers a way of accounting for (or addressing) these arguments, such that if the issuing of conditional acquittal in a particular case is justified according to the model, these arguments are conclusively overcome, and the possibility—or the actuality—of a new trial cannot be objected to on double jeopardy grounds. Notice that, even if someone rejected the decision-theoretic argument for conditional acquittal, the double jeopardy discourse would still provide reasons to prefer adopting such an intermediate verdict to the current English and Welsh law on retrials. If a retrial is allowed only when the original trial ended with the intermediate verdict, once new incriminating evidence with substantial probative value is discovered, the case against the defendant should always be sufficiently robust to warrant trying them again in the face of considerations of finality, distress, and public confidence.[6] This is not true when the retrial is allowed in the event of acquittal, as happens under the current law: the probability of guilt resulting from the first trial may be so low that, even with the discovery of new incriminating evidence with substantial probative value, the case against the defendant would not be sufficiently strong to warrant a retrial. Paradoxically, those who support the current law, and are unimpressed by these arguments, will find in my defence of conditional acquittal an additional reason to prefer such law to a binary system with 'plain vanilla' acquittal; that is, acquittal that does not admit of a retrial. I argued that a test for a new trial requiring new incriminating evidence with substantial probative value—that is, a test that is essentially equivalent to the evidential limb of the test provided by the Criminal Justice Act 2003—is more likely to be satisfied if the defendant is guilty than if they are innocent (see Chapter 4, section 4.5.1). Hence, a retrial is more likely to materialise if the acquitted defendant is, in fact, guilty. This fact may contribute to countering a possible criticism of the current law to the effect that it increases the risk of false conviction to an unreasonable extent.[7]

The availability of an intermediate verdict should be expected to reduce the rate of conviction. This is because, according to the decision-theoretic argument for intermediate verdicts, with the adoption of an intermediate verdict the standard of proof for conviction increases (see Chapter 4, section 4.3). An intermediate verdict may impose a quantum of hard treatment when the probability of guilt satisfies a standard of proof lower than the standard of the binary system. For instance, conditional acquittal does so by imposing the possibility of a new trial. However, the most severe measures that the criminal justice system employs, ie those involved in conviction, would be justified only when guilt is proven to a higher standard than that of the binary system. This shows that the introduction of an intermediate verdict may well be a shift towards less, rather than more, punitiveness. While some

[6] In fact, this depends on the stringency of the standard of proof warranting the intermediate verdict. The lower the standard chosen, the lower the probability of guilt of a defendant receiving conditional acquittal may be and, hence, the weaker the case against such a defendant at the time of retrial may be.

[7] To be sure, this criticism would be weak, especially in light of the data on post-acquittal retrials presented in Chapter 5, n 6.

may welcome this fact, others may be concerned that adopting an intermediate verdict—especially a relatively benign one such as conditional acquittal—may be problematic in relation to crimes that are already characterised by a worryingly low rate of conviction. Rape is the paradigmatic case.[8] The tempting response to this concern would be not to adopt an intermediate verdict in trials for rape; after all, it is surely possible to implement the intermediate verdict for certain types of crimes, but not for others (see Chapter 5, section 5.2). However, this concern may be dealt with from within the decision-theoretic argument for the intermediate verdict. Arguably, the low rate of conviction in rape trials makes conviction for this crime, whether true or false, more valuable than it would otherwise be, since conviction contributes to countering the disheartening and disempowering message that the low rate itself sends to victims. Any instance of conviction, then, invites victims to come forward without fear of being disbelieved, or of going through the ordeal of an investigation, and of a trial, for no expected gain. Having adjusted the values of the possible outcomes of conviction as suggested,[9] if the superiority of the intermediate verdict is not compromised, adoption of the verdict is justified even in trials for rape. To be sure, these are tentative considerations.[10] But they do show that there is potential in the decision-theoretic model for accommodating concerns of the kind discussed here.

Intermediate criminal verdicts have been around for centuries. And yet, the echo of the lively debates that have accompanied them can barely be felt in contemporary jurisdictions that adopt a binary verdict system. My primary goal in this book was to raise a question and bring it to the attention of those working in such jurisdictions who may never have considered it: can intermediate criminal verdicts be justified? Once the question is raised, it is natural to want to attempt an answer. My answer may have convinced some, but not others. I hope, though, that the book has succeeded in showing that there is something valuable to be gained from addressing the question.

[8] See A. Topping and C. Barr, 'Rape Convictions Fall to Record Low in England and Wales' *The Guardian* (London, 30 July 2020), available at <https://www.theguardian.com/society/2020/jul/30/convictions-fall-record-low-england-wales-prosecutions> accessed 3 August 2021; and J. Knight QC, 'Why do so Few Rapes Result in a Conviction?' *Al Jazeera* (7 May 2020), available at <https://www.aljazeera.com/opinions/2020/5/7/why-do-so-few-rapes-result-in-a-conviction> accessed 3 August 2021. See also Ministry of Justice and Home Office, *Review into the Criminal Justice System Response to Adult Rape and Serious Sexual Offences Across England and Wales – Research Report* (June 2021), in particular at 13, stating that '[v]olumes of prosecutions for adult rape have fallen by 59 per cent and convictions by 47 per cent between 2015–16 and 2019–20 … This has coincided with an increase of 79 per cent in police recorded adult rape offences over the same period.'

[9] With the use of the graphs and formulas in Chapter 4, one can see that the suggested increase in such values produces the lowering of the standard of proof for conviction, both in the binary system and in the system including the intermediate verdict.

[10] Eg, someone may argue that the low rate of conviction also affects the values of the possible outcomes of acquittal, in particular that it lowers them, insofar as these outcomes strengthen the negative message that the low rate itself sends to victims.

Appendix

(a) How to derive (2) from (1)

$$p \cdot V_{cg} + (1-p) \cdot V_{ci} \geq p \cdot V_{ag} + (1-p) \cdot V_{ai}$$

The standard of proof is the probability of guilt at which the expected value of convicting is equal to the expected value of acquitting. Therefore, in order to find this probability, we transform the inequality into an equality.

$$p \cdot V_{cg} + (1-p) \cdot V_{ci} = p \cdot V_{ag} + (1-p) \cdot V_{ai}$$

$$p \cdot V_{cg} + V_{ci} - p \cdot V_{ci} = p \cdot V_{ag} + V_{ai} - p \cdot V_{ai}$$

$$p \cdot V_{cg} - p \cdot V_{ag} - p \cdot V_{ci} + p \cdot V_{ai} = V_{ai} - V_{ci}$$

$$p \cdot (V_{cg} - V_{ag} - V_{ci} + V_{ai}) = V_{ai} - V_{ci}$$

$$p = \frac{V_{ai} - V_{ci}}{V_{cg} - V_{ag} + V_{ai} - V_{ci}}$$

$$p = \frac{1}{\frac{V_{cg} - V_{ag} + V_{ai} - V_{ci}}{V_{ai} - V_{ci}}}$$

$$p = \frac{1}{1 + \frac{V_{cg} - V_{ag}}{V_{ai} - V_{ci}}}$$

$$p^{*} = \frac{1}{1 + \frac{V_{cg} - V_{ag}}{V_{ai} - V_{ci}}}$$

(b) How to derive (4) from (3)

$$p^* \cdot V_{ig} + (1-p^*) \cdot V_{ii} > p^* \cdot V_{cg} + (1-p^*) \cdot V_{ci}$$

$$p^* \cdot V_{ig} - p^* \cdot V_{cg} > (1-p^*) \cdot V_{ci} - (1-p^*) \cdot V_{ii}$$

$$p^* \cdot (V_{ig} - V_{cg}) > (1-p^*) \cdot (V_{ci} - V_{ii})$$

$$\frac{p^*}{1-p^*} \cdot (V_{ig} - V_{cg}) > (V_{ci} - V_{ii})$$

$$\frac{p^*}{1-p^*} < \frac{V_{ci} - V_{ii}}{V_{ig} - V_{cg}}$$

The direction of the inequality changes when we divide both parts by $(V_{ig} - V_{cg})$. In fact, this difference has negative value, given the intermediacy of the additional verdict.

(c) How to derive (5) from (3)

NB, here (3) is formulated referring to the expected value of acquitting, which at p^* equals the expected value of convicting.

$$p^* \cdot V_{ig} + (1-p^*) \cdot V_{ii} > p^* \cdot V_{ag} + (1-p^*) \cdot V_{ai}$$

$$p^* \cdot V_{ig} - p^* \cdot V_{ag} > (1-p^*) \cdot V_{ai} - (1-p^*) \cdot V_{ii}$$

$$p^* \cdot (V_{ig} - V_{ag}) > (1-p^*) \cdot (V_{ai} - V_{ii})$$

$$\frac{p^*}{1-p^*} \cdot (V_{ig} - V_{ag}) > (V_{ai} - V_{ii})$$

$$\frac{p^*}{1-p^*} > \frac{V_{ai} - V_{ii}}{V_{ig} - V_{ag}}$$

(d) How to derive (6) from (4) and (5)

Given that $\frac{V_{ci} - V_{ii}}{V_{ig} - V_{cg}} > \frac{p^*}{1-p^*}$ and that $\frac{V_{ai} - V_{ii}}{V_{ig} - V_{ag}} < \frac{p^*}{1-p^*}$ then

$$\frac{V_{ci}-V_{ii}}{V_{ig}-V_{cg}} > \frac{p^*}{1-p^*} > \frac{V_{ai}-V_{ii}}{V_{ig}-V_{ag}}$$

$$\frac{V_{ci}-V_{ii}}{V_{ig}-V_{cg}} > \frac{V_{ai}-V_{ii}}{V_{ig}-V_{ag}}$$

$$\frac{V_{ci}-V_{ii}}{(V_{ai}-V_{ii})\cdot(V_{ig}-V_{cg})} > \frac{1}{V_{ig}-V_{ag}}$$

$$\frac{V_{ci}-V_{ii}}{V_{ai}-V_{ii}} < \frac{V_{ig}-V_{cg}}{V_{ig}-V_{ag}}$$

The direction of the inequality changes when we multiply both parts by $(V_{ig}-V_{cg})$. In fact, this difference has negative value, given the intermediacy of the additional verdict. Given intermediacy, $(V_{ci}-V_{ii})$ is negative as well. Thus, the numerator of each part of the inequality has negative value.

We can, however, render both numerators positive by inverting the order of the terms of the difference that each represents. Doing so changes the direction of the inequality.

$$\frac{V_{ii}-V_{ci}}{V_{ai}-V_{ii}} > \frac{V_{cg}-V_{ig}}{V_{ig}-V_{ag}}$$

(e) The equivalence between (4) and (5)

The equivalence between (4) and (5) should be intuited from considering that the former is derived from (3), formulated referring to the expected value of convicting, that the latter is derived from (3), formulated referring to the expected value of acquitting, and that at p^* these two values are the same, such that the two versions of (3) are equivalent. However, it is worth giving a full demonstration of the equivalence.

Given that $p^* = \dfrac{1}{1+\dfrac{V_{cg}-V_{ag}}{V_{ai}-V_{ci}}}$ then

$p^*\cdot V_{cg}+(1-p^*)\cdot V_{ci} = p^*\cdot V_{ag}+(1-p^*)\cdot V_{ai}$ (for this step see the intermediate workings in point (a) above)

$$p^*\cdot(V_{cg}-V_{ag}) = (1-p^*)\cdot(V_{ai}-V_{ci})$$

$$\frac{p^*}{1-p^*} = \frac{V_{ai}-V_{ci}}{V_{cg}-V_{ag}}$$

Given that $\dfrac{V_{ci}-V_{ii}}{V_{ig}-V_{cg}} > \dfrac{p^*}{1-p^*}$ [ie (4)], then

$$\frac{V_{ci}-V_{ii}}{V_{ig}-V_{cg}} > \frac{V_{ai}-V_{ci}}{V_{cg}-V_{ag}}$$

$$(V_{ci}-V_{ii})\cdot(V_{cg}-V_{ag}) < (V_{ai}-V_{ci})\cdot(V_{ig}-V_{cg})$$

The direction of the inequality changes when we multiply both parts by $(V_{ig}-V_{cg})$. In fact, this difference has negative value, given the intermediacy of the additional verdict.

$$V_{ci}\cdot V_{cg}-V_{ci}\cdot V_{ag}-V_{ii}\cdot V_{cg}+V_{ii}\cdot V_{ag} < V_{ai}\cdot V_{ig}-V_{ai}\cdot V_{cg}-V_{ci}\cdot V_{ig}+V_{ci}\cdot V_{cg}$$

$$-V_{ci}\cdot V_{ag}-V_{ii}\cdot V_{cg}+V_{ii}\cdot V_{ag} < V_{ai}\cdot V_{ig}-V_{ai}\cdot V_{cg}-V_{ci}\cdot V_{ig}$$

$$V_{ii}\cdot V_{ag}+V_{ai}\cdot V_{cg}+V_{ci}\cdot V_{ig} < V_{ai}\cdot V_{ig}+V_{ii}\cdot V_{cg}+V_{ci}\cdot V_{ag}$$

For convenience, let us call this inequality the Final Inequality.

Now, given that $\frac{p^*}{1-p^*}=\frac{V_{ai}-V_{ci}}{V_{cg}-V_{ag}}$ and that $\frac{V_{ai}-V_{ii}}{V_{ig}-V_{ag}}<\frac{p^*}{1-p^*}$ [ie (5)], then

$$\frac{V_{ai}-V_{ii}}{V_{ig}-V_{ag}} < \frac{V_{ai}-V_{ci}}{V_{cg}-V_{ag}}$$

$$(V_{ai}-V_{ii})\cdot(V_{cg}-V_{ag}) < (V_{ai}-V_{ci})\cdot(V_{ig}-V_{ag})$$

$$V_{ai}\cdot V_{cg}-V_{ai}\cdot V_{ag}-V_{ii}\cdot V_{cg}+V_{ii}\cdot V_{ag} < V_{ai}\cdot V_{ig}-V_{ai}\cdot V_{ag}-V_{ci}\cdot V_{ig}+V_{ci}\cdot V_{ag}$$

$$V_{ai}\cdot V_{cg}-V_{ii}\cdot V_{cg}+V_{ii}\cdot V_{ag} < V_{ai}\cdot V_{ig}-V_{ci}\cdot V_{ig}+V_{ci}\cdot V_{ag}$$

$$V_{ii}\cdot V_{ag}+V_{ai}\cdot V_{cg}+V_{ci}\cdot V_{ig} < V_{ai}\cdot V_{ig}+V_{ii}\cdot V_{cg}+V_{ci}\cdot V_{ag}$$

This is the Final Inequality. Hence, both (4) and (5) are equal to the Final Inequality.

(f) The equivalence between (6), (3), (4), and (5)

$$\frac{V_{ii}-V_{ci}}{V_{ai}-V_{ii}} > \frac{V_{cg}-V_{ig}}{V_{ig}-V_{ag}}$$

$$(V_{ig}-V_{ag})\cdot(V_{ii}-V_{ci}) > (V_{cg}-V_{ig})\cdot(V_{ai}-V_{ii})$$

$$V_{ig}\cdot V_{ii}-V_{ig}\cdot V_{ci}-V_{ag}\cdot V_{ii}+V_{ag}\cdot V_{ci} > V_{cg}\cdot V_{ai}-V_{cg}\cdot V_{ii}-V_{ig}\cdot V_{ai}+V_{ig}\cdot V_{ii}$$

$$-V_{ig} \cdot V_{ci} - V_{ag} \cdot V_{ii} + V_{ag} \cdot V_{ci} > V_{cg} \cdot V_{ai} - V_{cg} \cdot V_{ii} - V_{ig} \cdot V_{ai}$$

$$V_{cg} \cdot V_{ii} + V_{ig} \cdot V_{ai} + V_{ag} \cdot V_{ci} > V_{cg} \cdot V_{ai} + V_{ig} \cdot V_{ci} + V_{ag} \cdot V_{ii}$$

$$V_{cg} \cdot V_{ai} + V_{ig} \cdot V_{ci} + V_{ag} \cdot V_{ii} < V_{cg} \cdot V_{ii} + V_{ig} \cdot V_{ai} + V_{ag} \cdot V_{ci}$$

This is the Final Inequality (see point (e) above). (6), too, is equal to the Final Inequality. Hence, it is equivalent to (4) and to (5), and, of course, to (3), the inequality that (4) and (5) are derived from.

(g) The superiority condition for a genuinely additional second intermediate verdict

Take as a starting point a system with a single intermediate verdict, such as that illustrated in Figure 4.3.

The condition under which a second intermediate verdict is superior to acquittal, conviction, and the first intermediate verdict, *and is genuinely additional*, is that the line representing the expected value of the second intermediate verdict be higher than the ceiling of the system either at the probability of guilt represented by p^1, or at the probability of guilt represented by p^2. Notably, if this line were higher than the ceiling at both of these values of the probability of guilt, the second intermediate verdict would supersede the first, such that the former would not be genuinely additional.

Therefore, the superiority condition can be expressed with the following disjunctive:

Either

$$p^1 \cdot V_{i2g} + (1 - p^1) \cdot V_{i2i} > p^1 \cdot V_{ig} + (1 - p^1) \cdot V_{ii}$$

Or

$$p^2 \cdot V_{i2g} + (1 - p^2) \cdot V_{i2i} > p^2 \cdot V_{ig} + (1 - p^2) \cdot V_{ii}$$

Where V_{i2g} stands for the value of issuing the second intermediate verdict when the defendant is guilty, and V_{i2i} stands for the value of issuing the second intermediate verdict when the defendant is innocent.

(h) The equivalence between $\frac{p(E/G)}{p(E/I)} \neq 1$ and $p(G/E) \neq p(G)$

Consider that $I = \bar{G}$. Now, $\frac{p(E/G)}{p(E/\bar{G})} \neq 1$ means that E and G are probabilistically dependent. If they were independent, then $\frac{p(E/G)}{p(E/\bar{G})} = 1$. If, however, E and G are probabilistically dependent, then $p(G/E) = p(G) \cdot \frac{p(E/G)}{p(E)} \neq p(G)$.

The equivalence can also be proved as follows. Applying Bayes' theorem $p(G/E)=p(G)\cdot\frac{p(E/G)}{p(E)}$. Considering that $p(I)=p(\bar{G})$, using the law of total probability the equation can also be written as $p(G/E)=p(G)\cdot\frac{p(E/G)}{p(G)\cdot p(E/G)+p(I)\cdot p(E/I)}$. If $p(E/G)$ is equal to $p(E/I)$ (such that $\frac{p(E/G)}{p(E/I)}=1$) then $p(G/E)=p(G)\cdot\frac{p(E/G)}{p(E/G)\cdot(p(G)+p(I))}$. But since $p(G)+p(I)=1$, then $p(G/E)=p(G)\cdot\frac{p(E/G)}{p(E/G)}=p(G)$. In short, if $\frac{p(E/G)}{p(E/I)}=1$, then $p(G/E)=p(G)$; if $\frac{p(E/G)}{p(E/I)}\neq 1$, then $p(G/E)=p(G)\cdot\frac{p(E/G)}{p(E)}\neq p(G)$. For the inequality $p(G/E)\neq p(G)$ to be verified it has to be the case that $\frac{p(E/G)}{p(E/I)}\neq 1$. Hence, if $p(G/E)\neq p(G)$ then $\frac{p(E/G)}{p(E/I)}\neq 1$.

(i) The equivalence between $\frac{p(E/G)}{p(E/I)}>1$ and $p(G/E)>p(G)$

Consider that $I=\bar{G}$. Now, $\frac{p(E/G)}{p(E/\bar{G})}>1$ means that the two events E and G are probabilistically dependent and positively correlated: the occurrence of E raises the probability of G occurring, that is $p(G/E)>p(G)$.

The equivalence can also be proved as follows. Consider that

$$\frac{p(G/E)}{p(I/E)}=\frac{p(G)\cdot\frac{p(E/G)}{p(E)}}{p(I)\cdot\frac{p(E/I)}{p(E)}}=\frac{p(G)}{p(I)}\cdot\frac{p(E/G)}{p(E/I)}.$$

If $\frac{p(E/G)}{p(E/I)}>1$, then $\frac{p(G/E)}{p(I/E)}>\frac{p(G)}{p(I)}$.

Since $p(I)=p(\bar{G})$, then $p(G)+p(I)=1$ and $p(G/E)+p(I/E)=1$. If so, it must be the case that if $\frac{p(G/E)}{p(I/E)}>\frac{p(G)}{p(I)}$, then $p(G/E)>p(G)$. In short, if $\frac{p(E/G)}{p(E/I)}>1$, then $p(G/E)>p(G)$. To see this, consider that the inequality $\frac{p(G/E)}{p(I/E)}>\frac{p(G)}{p(I)}$ is equivalent to the inequality $\frac{1-p(I/E)}{p(I/E)}>\frac{1-p(I)}{p(I)}$, and, for the latter inequality to be verified, $p(I/E)$ must be lower than $p(I)$, which is to say that $1-p(I/E)$ must be greater than $1-p(I)$, that is, the inequality $p(G/E)>p(G)$ must be verified. Following the same steps, one sees that if $\frac{p(E/G)}{p(E/I)}\leq 1$ then $p(G/E)\leq p(G)$. Hence, for the inequality $p(G/E)>p(G)$ to be verified, it has to be the case that $\frac{p(E/G)}{p(E/I)}>1$. That is, if $p(G/E)>p(G)$ then $\frac{p(E/G)}{p(E/I)}>1$.

Bibliography

Aarnio, A, *The Rational as Reasonable: A Treatise on Legal Justification* (Dordrecht: D Reidel Publishing Company 1987)

Aboodi, R and others, 'Deontology, Individualism, and Uncertainty: A Reply to Jackson and Smith' (2008) 105 The Journal of Philosophy 259

Ademollo, A, *Giudizio Criminale in Toscana Secondo la Riforma Leopoldina dell'Anno 1838. Cenni Teorici Pratici* (Florence: Tipografia di Sansone Coen 1840)

Alessi Palazzolo, G, *Prova Legale e Pena: La Crisi del Sistema Tra Evo Medio e Moderno* (Naples: Jovene Editore 1979)

Alexander, L, 'Deontology at the Threshold' (2000) 37 San Diego Law Review 893

Alexander, L and Moore, M S, 'Deontological Ethics' in E N Zalta (ed), *Stanford Encyclopedia of Philosophy* (2016)

Alexander, L and Ferzan, K, *Crime and Culpability: A Theory of Criminal Law* (Cambridge: CUP 2009)

Alexy, R, *A Theory of Legal Argumentation: The Theory of Rational Discourse as Theory of Legal Justification* (R Adler and N MacCormick trs, Oxford: OUP 1989)

Alexy, R, 'The Reasonableness of the Law' in G Bongiovanni and others (eds), *Reasonableness and Law* (Dordrecht: Springer 2009) 3–15

Allen, R J, 'The Nature of Juridical Proof' (1991) 13 Cardozo Law Review 373

Allen, R J and Pardo, M S, 'Relative Plausibility and Its Critics' (2019) 23 International Journal of Evidence and Proof 5

Allen, R J and Pardo, M S, 'Inference to the Best Explanation, Relative Plausibility, and Probability' in C Dahlman and others (eds), *Philosophical Foundations of Evidence Law* (Oxford: OUP 2021) 201–214

Amaya, A, 'Epistemic Ambivalence in Law' (2021) 31 Philosophical Issues 7

Amaya, A, 'Virtues in Evidential Reasoning in Law' (unpublished manuscript on file with the author)

Ambrosoli, F, 'Delle Sentenze Dubitative nei Processi Criminali' (1852) *Giornale per le Scienze Politico-Legali*, Tomo III, Fascicolo 4

Anca, G A, 'Insufficienza di Prove' (1993) 7 Digesto delle Discipline Penalistiche 147

Anderson, T and others, *Analysis of Evidence* (2nd edn, Cambridge: CUP 2005)

Anscombe, G E M, *Intention* (2nd edn, Cambridge, Mass: Harvard University Press 2000)

Anscombe, G E M, 'Practical Inference' in M Geach and L Gormally (eds), *Human Life, Action and Ethics: Essays by G. E. M. Anscombe* (Exeter: Imprint Academic 2005) 109–147.

Ashworth, A, 'Four Threats to the Presumption of Innocence' (2006) 10 International Journal of Evidence and Proof 241

Ashworth, A and von Hirsch, A, *Proportionate Sentencing: Exploring the Principles* (Oxford: OUP 2005)

Ashworth, A and Zedner, L, *Preventive Justice* (Oxford: OUP 2014)

Ashworth, A and others (eds), *Prevention and the Limits of the Criminal Law* (Oxford: OUP 2013)

Atiq, E H, 'What Unconditional Credence in Individual Desert Claims does Retributivism Require?' (2018) University of Illinois Law Review Online 138

Audi, R, *Practical Reasoning* (London: Routledge 1989)

Barbato, J M, 'Scotland's Bastard Verdict: Intermediacy and the Unique Three-Verdict System' (2005) 15 Indiana International and Comparative Law Review 543

Bartels, R D, 'Punishment and The Burden of Proof in Criminal Cases: A Modest Proposal' (1981) 66 Iowa Law Review 899

Beccaria, C, *Dei Delitti e Delle Pene* (Turin: Einaudi 1965)

Bennett, A, 'Not Proven: The Verdict' (2002) 12 Scots Law Times 97

Berman, N M, 'Punishment and Justification' (2008) 118 Ethics 258

Berman, N M, 'Two Kinds of Retributivism' in R A Duff and S Green (eds), *Philosophical Foundations of Criminal Law* (Oxford: OUP 2011) 433–457

Bettiol, G, *Istituzioni di Diritto e Procedura Penale* (Padua: CEDAM 1966)

Bibas, S, 'Plea Bargaining Outside the Shadow of Trial' (2004) 117 Harvard Law Review 2464

Boonin, D, *The Problem of Punishment* (Cambridge: CUP 2008)

Bradley, R, *Decision Theory with a Human Face* (Cambridge: CUP 2017)

Bratman, M E, *Intention, Plans, and Practical Reason* (Cambridge, Mass: Harvard University Press 1987)

Bray, S, 'Not Proven: Introducing a Third Verdict' (2005) 72 University of Chicago Law Review 1299

Briggs, R, 'Normative Theories of Rational Choice: Expected Utility' in E N Zalta (ed), *Stanford Encyclopedia of Philosophy* (2017)

Brink, D O, 'Some Forms and Limits of Consequentialism' in D Copp (ed), *The Oxford Handbook of Ethical Theory* (Oxford: OUP, 2007) 380–417

Broome, J, 'The Structure of Good: Decision Theory and Ethics' in M Bacharach and S Hurley (eds), *Foundations of Decision Theory* (Oxford: Basil Blackwell 1991) 123–146

Brudner, A, *Punishment and Freedom: A Liberal Theory of Penal Justice* (Oxford: OUP 2009)

Brugnoli, G, *Della Certezza e Prova Criminale: Col Confronto di Varie Legislazioni d'Europa ed in Specie d'Italia* (Modena: Tipografia di Carlo Vincenzi 1846)

Byrd, B S, 'Kant's Theory of Punishment: Deterrence in its Threat, Retribution in its Execution' (1989) 8 Law and Philosophy 151

Campbell, L, 'Criminal Labels, the European Convention on Human Rights and the Presumption of Innocence' (2013) 76 Modern Law Review 681

Campbell, L and others, *The Criminal Process* (Oxford: OUP 2019)

Carmignani, G, *Teoria delle Leggi della Sicurezza Sociale* (Pisa: Fratelli Nistri e co 1832)

Carrell, S and Brooks, L, 'Call for Abolition of Not Proven Verdict in Scottish Law', *The Guardian* (London, 13 November 2018), available at <https://www.theguardian.com/law/2018/nov/13/call-for-abolition-of-not-proven-verdict-in-scottish-law> (accessed 12 May 2021)

Chalfin, A and McCrary, J, 'Criminal Deterrence: A Review of the Literature' (2017) 55 Journal of Economic Literature 5

Chalmers, J and Leverick, F, '"Substantial and Radical Change": A New Dawn for Scottish Criminal Procedure?' (2012) 75 Modern Law Review 837

Chalmers, J and others, 'Three Distinctive Features, but what is the Difference? Key Findings from the Scottish Jury Project' (2020) 11 Criminal Law Review 1012

Chalmers, J and others, 'A Modern History of the Not Proven Verdict' (2021) 25 Edinburgh Law Review 151

Chalmers, J and others, 'Beyond Doubt: The Case Against "Not Proven"' (2021) Modern Law Review , DOI: 10.1111/1468-2230.12707

Chang, R, 'Introduction' in R Chang (ed), *Incommensurability, Incomparability, and Practical Reason* (Cambridge, Mass: Harvard University Press 1997) 1–34

Chernev, A, 'Extremeness Aversion and Attribute-Balance Effects in Choice' (2004) 31 Journal of Consumer Research 249

Chiavario, M, 'Case note: *Corte Costituzionale* n 124/1972' (1972) 3 Giurisprudenza Costituzionale 1325

Clermont, K M, *Standards of Decision in Law: Psychological and Logical Bases for the Standard of Proof, Here and Abroad* (Durham, NC: Carolina Academic Press 2013)

Cohen, J L, *The Probable and the Provable* (Oxford: OUP 1977)

Cohen, J L, 'The Role of Evidential Weight in Criminal Proof' in P Tillers and E D Green (eds), *Probability and Inference in the Law of Evidence: The Uses and Limits of Bayesianism* (Dordrecht: Kluwer Academic Publishers 1988) 113–128

Colyvan, M and others, 'Modelling the Moral Dimension of Decisions' (2010) 44 Nous 503

Connolly, T, 'Decision Theory, Reasonable Doubt, and the Utility of Erroneous Acquittals' (1987) 11 Law and Human Behaviour 101

Conso, G, 'È da Rivedere, non da Eliminare l'Assoluzione per Insufficienza di Prove' (1967) 4 Giurisprudenza Italiana 101

Conso, G, 'L'Assoluzione per Insufficienza di Prove: Prospettive "De Iure Condendo"' in *La Frode in Assicurazione. L'Assoluzione per Insufficienza di Prove. Atti del Convegno di Studi Giuridici a Cura della Camera Penale di Trieste, 22–25 Aprile 1967* (Padua: CEDAM 1968) 259–280

Conso, G and others, *Il Nuovo Codice di Procedura Penale. Dalle Leggi Delega ai Decreti Delegati. Vol IV. Il Progetto Preliminare del 1988* (Padua: CEDAM 1990)

Conso, G and others, *Il Nuovo Codice di Procedura Penale. Dalle Leggi Delega ai Decreti Delegati. Vol V. Il Progetto Definitivo e il Testo Definitivo del Codice* (Padua: CEDAM 1990)

Cooper, N, 'The Intellectual Virtues' (1994) 69 Philosophy 459

Corda, A and Lageson, S E, 'Disordered Punishment: Workaround Technologies of Criminal Records Disclosure and the Rise of a New Penal Entrepreneurialism' (2019) 60 British Journal of Criminology 245

Cordero, F, *Procedura Penale* (2nd edn, Milan: Giuffrè Editore 1971)

Crown Prosecution Service, *Private Prosecutions: Legal Guidance*, available at <https://www.cps.gov.uk/legal-guidance/private-prosecutions> (2019) (accessed 28 June 2021)

Crown Prosecution Service, *Retrial of Serious Offences: Legal Guidance*, available at <https://www.cps.gov.uk/legal-guidance/retrial-serious-offences> (accessed 28 June 2021)

Cullerne-Browne, W, 'The Criminal Justice System as a Problem in Binary Classification' (2018) 22 International Journal of Evidence and Proof 363

Cullerne-Browne, W, 'Measuring Justice' (2019) 23 International Journal of Evidence and Proof 399

Curley, L J and others, 'The Bastard Verdict and Its Influence on Jurors' (2019) 59 Medicine, Science and the Law 26

Damaška, M R, *Evidence Law Adrift* (New Haven: Yale University Press 1997)

Damaška M R, *Evaluation of Evidence: Pre-Modern and Modern Approaches* (Cambridge: CUP 2019)

Dan-Cohen, M, 'Decision Rules and Conduct Rules: On Acoustic Separation in Criminal Law' (1984) 97 Harvard Law Review 625

Dekay, M L, 'The Difference Between Blackstone-Like Error Ratios and Probabilistic Standards of Proof' (1996) 21 Law and Social Inquiry 95

Dennis, I, 'Rethinking Double Jeopardy: Justice and Finality in Criminal Process' (2000) 12 Criminal Law Review 933

Dennis, I, *The Law of Evidence* (7th edn, London: Sweet & Maxwell 2020)

Dhami, M K and Wallsten, T S, 'Interpersonal Comparison of Subjective Probabilities: Toward Translating Linguistic Probabilities' (2005) 33 Memory and Cognition 1057
Dolinko, D, 'Retributivism, Consequentialism, and the Intrinsic Goodness of Punishment' (1997) 16 Law and Philosophy 507
Drizin, S and Leo, R, 'The Problem of False Confessions in the Post-DNA World' (2004) 82 North Carolina Law Review 891
Duff, A, *Punishment, Communication, and Community* (Oxford: OUP 2001)
Duff, A, 'Presuming Innocence' in L Zedner and J V Roberts (eds), *Principles and Values in Criminal Law and Criminal Justice* (Oxford: OUP 2012) 51–66
Duff, A, 'Who Must Presume Whom to be Innocent of What' (2013) 42 Netherlands Journal of Legal Philosophy 170
Duff, A, *The Realm of Criminal Law* (Oxford: OUP 2018)
Duff, A and others, *The Trial on Trial: Vol I: Truth and Due Process* (Oxford and Portland, Oregon: Hart 2004)
Duff, A and others, *The Trial on Trial: Vol III: Towards a Normative Theory of the Criminal Trial* (Oxford and Portland, Oregon: Hart 2007)
Duff, P, 'The Not Proven Verdict: Jury Mythology and "Moral Panics"' (1996) 41 Juridical Review 1
Dworkin, R, *A Matter of Principle* (Oxford: Clarendon Press 1985)
Eggleston, R, *Evidence, Proof and Probability* (2nd edn, London: Butterworths 1983)
Epps, D, 'The Consequences of Error in Criminal Justice' (2015) 128 Harvard Law Review 1065
Fantl, J and McGrath, M, 'Evidence, Pragmatics, and Justification' (2002) 111 Philosophical Review 67
Fantl, J and McGrath, M, 'On Pragmatic Encroachment in Epistemology' (2007) 75 Philosophy and Phenomenological Research 558
Fantl, J and McGrath, M, 'Pragmatic Encroachment: It's Not Just About Knowledge' (2012) 9 Episteme 27
Farmer, L, 'Innocence, the Burden of Proof and Fairness in the Criminal Trial: Revisiting *Woolmington v DPP* (1935)' in J D Jackson and S J Summers (eds), *Obstacles to Fairness in Criminal Proceedings: Individual Rights and Institutional Reforms* (Oxford: Hart 2018) 57–73
Feinberg, J, 'The Expressive Function of Punishment' in J Feinberg, *Doing and Deserving: Essays in the Theory of Responsibility* (Princeton: Princeton University Press 1970)
Feeley, M, *The Process is the Punishment: Handling Cases in a Lower Criminal Court* (New York: Russell Sage Foundation 1979)
Feldman, F, 'Actual Utility, the Objection from Impracticality, and the Move to Expected Utility' (2006) 129 Philosophical Studies 49
Fenton, N and others, 'Bayes and the Law' (2016) 3 Annual Review of Statistics and its Application 51
Ferguson, P R, 'The Presumption of Innocence and Its Role in the Criminal Process' (2016) 27 Criminal Law Forum 131
Ferrajoli, L, *Diritto e Ragione. Teoria del Garantismo Penale* (9th edn, Rome: Editori Laterza 2008)
Ferrer Beltrán, J, 'Legal Proof and Fact Finders' Beliefs' (2006) 12 Legal Theory 293
Filangieri, G, *La Scienza della Legislazione. Edizione Integrale* (Naples: Grimaldi & C Editori 2003)
Finnis, J, *Natural Law and Natural Rights* (Oxford: Clarendon Press 1980)

Fisher, T, 'Constitutionalism and the Criminal Law: Rethinking Criminal Trial Bifurcation' (2011) 61 University of Toronto Law Journal 811
Fisher, T, 'Conviction without Conviction' (2011) 96 Minnesota Law Review 833
Foucault, M, *Discipline and Punish: The Birth of the Prison* (London: Penguin Books 1991)
Fraher, R M, 'Conviction According to Conscience: The Medieval Jurists' Debate Concerning Judicial Discretion and the Law of Proof' (1989) 7 Law and History Review 23
Franklin, J, *The Science of Conjecture: Evidence and Probability Before Pascal* (Baltimore, Maryland: John Hopkins University Press 2001)
Friedman, R D, 'A Close Look at Probative Value' (1986) 66 Boston University Law Review 733
Friedman, R D, 'Answering the Bayesioskeptical Challenge' (1997) 1 International Journal of Evidence and Proof 276
Galoob, S R, 'Retributivism and Criminal Procedure' (2017) 20 New Criminal Law Review 465
Gardner, J, 'Introduction' in H L A Hart, *Punishment and Responsibility: Essays in the Philosophy of Law* (2nd edn, Oxford: OUP 2008) xiii–liii
Gebbie, G C and others, '"Not Proven" as a Juridical Fact in Scotland, Norway and Italy' (1999) 7 European Journal of Crime, Criminal Law, and Criminal Justice 262
Ghiara, A, 'Presunzione di Innocenza, Presunzione di "Non Colpevolezza" e Formula Dubitativa, anche alla Luce degli Interventi della Corte Costituzionale' (1974) 17 Rivista Italiana di Diritto e Procedura Penale 72
Giannoulopoulos, D, *Improperly Obtained Evidence in Anglo-American and Continental Law* (Oxford and Portland, Oregon: Hart 2019)
Glover, R, *Murphy on Evidence* (14th edn, Oxford: OUP 2015)
Gow, N, 'The Case for Not Proven' (1993) 143 New Law Journal 753
Graham, P A, 'In Defense of Objectivism about Moral Obligation' (2010) 121 Ethics 88
Green, M, 'Speech Acts' in E N Zalta (ed), *Stanford Encyclopedia of Philosophy* (2020)
Griffin, J, 'Incommensurability: What's the Problem?' in R Chang (ed), *Incommensurability, Incomparability, and Practical Reason* (Cambridge, Mass: Harvard University Press 1997) 35–51
Gross, S R and others, 'Rate of False Conviction of Criminal Defendants who are Sentenced to Death' (2014) 111 Proceedings of the National Academy of Sciences of the United States of America 7230
Hamer, D, 'Probabilistic Standards of Proof, Their Complements and the Errors that are Expected to Flow from Them' (2004) 1 University of New England Law Journal 71
Hamer, D, 'Probability, Anti-Resilience, and the Weight of Expectation' (2012) 11 Law, Probability and Risk 135
Hamer, D, 'The Significant Probative Value of Tendency Evidence' (2019) 42 Melbourne University Law Review 506
Hart, H L A, *The Concept of Law* (Oxford: OUP 1961)
Hart, H L A, *Punishment and Responsibility: Essays in the Philosophy of Law* (2nd edn, Oxford: OUP 2008)
Ho, H L, *A Philosophy of Evidence Law: Justice in the Search for Truth* (Oxford: OUP 2008)
Hope, L and others, 'A Third Verdict Option: Exploring the Impact of Not Proven on Mock Juror Decision Making' (2008) 32 Law and Human Behavior 241
Hume, D, *Commentaries on the Law of Scotland, Respecting Crimes, vol II* (4th edn, Edinburgh: Bell 1844)
Husak, D, 'Why Punish the Deserving?' in D Husak, *The Philosophy of Criminal Law: Selected Essays* (Oxford: OUP 2010)

Husak, D, 'Retributivism *in Extremis*' (2013) 32 Law and Philosophy 3
Hsien, N, 'Is Incomparability a Problem for Anyone?' (2007) 23 Economics and Philosophy 65
Ichikawa, J J and Steup, M, 'The Analysis of Knowledge' in E N Zalta (ed), *Stanford Encyclopedia of Philosophy* (2018)
Illuminati, G, *La Presunzione d'Innocenza dell'Imputato* (Bologna: Zanichelli 1979)
Illuminati, G, 'Presunzione di Non Colpevolezza' in *Enciclopedia Giuridica, vol XXVII* (Rome: Treccani 1991) 1–10
Ispa-Landa, S and Loeffler, C E, 'Indefinite Punishment and the Criminal Record: Stigma Reports Among Expungement-Seekers in Illinois' (2006) 54 Criminology 387
Jackson, B S, 'Truth or Proof? The Criminal Verdict' (1998) 11 The International Journal of the Semiotics of Law 227
Jackson, F, 'Decision-Theoretic Consequentialism and the Nearest and Dearest Objection' (1991) 101 Ethics 461
Jackson, F and Smith, M, 'Absolutist Moral Theories and Uncertainty' (2006) 103 The Journal of Philosophy 267
Jackson, J D and Summers, S J, *The Internationalisation of Criminal Evidence: Beyond the Common Law and Civil Law Traditions* (Cambridge: CUP 2012)
Jackson, J and others, 'Why Do People Comply with the Law? Legitimacy and the Influence of Legal Institutions' (2012) 52 British Journal of Criminology 1051
Judicial College, *Crown Court Compendium, Part I: Jury and Trial Management and Summing Up* (August 2021)
Judicial Institute for Scotland, *Jury Manual* (April 2021)
Kahneman, D and Tversky, A, 'On the Reality of Cognitive Illusions' (1996) 103 Psychological Review 582
Kamm, F M, 'Aggregation and Two Moral Methods' (2005) 17 Utilitas 1
Kant, I, *The Metaphysics of Morals* (Mary Gregor ed, Cambridge: CUP 1996)
Kaplan, J, 'Decision Theory and the Factfinding Process' (1968) 20 Stanford Law Review 1065
Kaplan, M, *Decision Theory as Philosophy* (Cambridge: CUP 1996)
Kaplow, L, 'Burden of Proof' (2011) 121 Yale Law Journal 738
Kassin, S M and others, 'Police-Induced Confessions: Risk Factors and Recommendations' (2010) 34 Law and Human Behavior 3
Kaye, D H, 'The Laws of Probability and the Laws of the Land' (1979) 47 University of Chicago Law Review 34
Kaye, D H, 'Quantifying Probative Value' (1986) 66 Boston University Law Review 761
Kaye, D H, 'Do we Need a Calculus of Weight to Understand Proof Beyond a Reasonable Doubt?' in P Tillers and E Green (eds), *Probability and Inference in the Law of Evidence: The Uses and Limits of Bayesianism* (Dordrecht: Kluwer 1988) 129–145
Kelman, M and others, 'Context-Dependence in Legal Decision Making' (1996) 25 Journal of Legal Studies 287
Kent, S, 'Words of Estimative Probability' (1964) General CIA Records, Document Number CIA-RDP93T01132R000100020036-3, available at <https://www.cia.gov/static/0aae8f84700a256abf63f7aad73b0a7d/Words-of-Estimative-Probability.pdf> (accessed 11 November 2021)
Keynes, J M, *A Treatise on Probability* (London: MacMillan 1921)
Kitai, R, 'Protecting the Guilty' (2003) 6 Buffalo Criminal Law Review 1163
Knight, J, 'Why do so Few Rapes Result in a Conviction?', *Al Jazeera* (7 May 2020), available at <https://www.aljazeera.com/opinions/2020/5/7/why-do-so-few-rapes-result-in-a-conviction> (accessed 3 August 2021)

Kolber, A J, 'Punishment and Moral Risk' (2018) 2018 University of Illinois Law Review 487
Lageson, S E and Maruna, S, 'Digital Degradation: Stigma Management in the Internet Age' (2018) 20 Punishment and Society 113
Langbein, J H, *Torture and the Law of Proof: Europe and England in the Ancien Régime* (Chicago: The University of Chicago Press 1977)
Langbein, J H, *The Origins of Adversary Criminal Trial* (Oxford: OUP 2003)
Lando, H, 'The Size of the Sanction Should Depend on the Weight of the Evidence' (2005) 1 Review of Law and Economics 277
Laudan, L, *Truth, Error and Criminal Law: An Essay in Legal Epistemology* (Cambridge: CUP 2006)
Laudan, L, 'Need Verdicts Come in Pairs?' (2010) 14 International Journal of Evidence and Proof 1
Laudan, L, 'The Rules of Trial, Political Morality, and the Costs of Error: Or, Is Proof Beyond a Reasonable Doubt Doing More Harm than Good?' in L Green and B Leiter (eds), *Oxford Studies in Philosophy of Law* (Oxford: OUP 2011) 195–223
Laudan, L , *The Law's Flaws: Rethinking Trial and Errors* (London: College Publications, 2016)
Laudan, L and Saunders, H D, 'Rethinking the Criminal Standard of Proof: Seeking Consensus about the Utilities of Trial Outcomes' (2009) 7 International Commentary on Evidence 1
Law Commission, *Double Jeopardy* (Law Com CP No 156, 1999)
Law Commission, *Double Jeopardy and Prosecution Appeals* (Law Com No 267, 2001)
Lazar, S, 'Anton's Game: Deontological Decision Theory for an Iterated Decision Problem' (2016) 29 Utilitas 88
Lazar, S, 'Deontological Decision Theory and Agent-Centered Options' (2017) 127 Ethics 579
Lazar, S, 'In Dubious Battle: Uncertainty and the Ethics of Killing' (2018) 175 Philosophical Studies 859
Lazar, S, 'Limited Aggregation and Risk' (2018) 46 Philosophy and Public Affairs 117
Lazar, S, 'Deontological Decision Theory and the Grounds of Subjective Permissibility' in M Timmons (ed), *Oxford Studies in Normative Ethics, vol 9* (Oxford: OUP 2019) 204–222
Lazar, S, 'Duty and Doubt' (2020) 8 Journal of Practical Ethics 28
Lazar, S and Graham, P A, 'Deontological Decision Theory and Lesser-Evil Options' (2019) 198 Synthese 6889
Lee, Y, 'Deontology, Political Morality, and the State' (2011) 8 Ohio State Journal of Criminal Law 385
Leipold, A D, 'The Problem of the Innocent, Acquitted Defendant' (2000) 94 Northwestern University Law Review 1297
Lempert, R O, 'Modeling Relevance' (1977) 75 Michigan Law Review 1021
Lempert, R O, 'The New Evidence Scholarship: Analyzing the Process of Proof' in P Tillers and E D Green (eds), *Probability and Inference in the Law of Evidence: The Uses and Limits of Bayesianism* (Dordrecht: Kluwer 1988) 61–102
Leone, G, *Lineamenti di Diritto Processuale Penale* (4th edn, Naples: Jovene 1956)
Lillquist, E, 'Recasting Reasonable Doubt: Decision Theory and the Virtues of Variability' (2002) 36 UC Davis Law Review 85
Lindley, D V, 'Subjective Probability, Decision Analysis and their Legal Consequences' (1991) 154 Journal of the Royal Statistical Society, Series A (Statistics in Society) 83
Lippke, R L, *Taming the Presumption of Innocence* (Oxford: OUP 2016)
Lippke, R L, 'Fundamental Values of Criminal Procedure' in D K Brown and others (eds), *The Oxford Handbook of Criminal Process* (Oxford: OUP 2019) 25–42

Litt, N W D, 'Curiosities of Criminal Justice' (1975) 48 Police Journal 5
Loeffler, C E and others, 'Measuring Self-Reported Wrongful Convictions Among Prisoners' (2019) 35 Journal of Quantitative Criminology 259
Logan, W, 'Informal Collateral Consequences' (2013) 88 Washington Law Review 1103
Lord Kilbrandon, *Other People's Law. The Hamlyn Lectures; 18th Series* (London: Stevens & Sons 1966)
Lord McCluskey, 'Not Proven: A Reply' (2002) 17 Scots Law Times 148
McCauley, F, 'Canon Law and the End of the Ordeal' (2006) 26 Oxford Journal of Legal Studies 473
MacCormick, N, *Practical Reason in Law and Morality* (Oxford: OUP 2008)
McMahon, M, *Public Consultation on a Proposal for a Bill to Replace the Current System of Three Verdicts in Criminal Trials with Two, and to Increase the Majority Required for Conviction*, 28 June 2012
McMahon, M, *Summary of Consultation Responses*, 29 October 2013
McNaughton, D and Rawling, P, 'Deontology' in D Copp (ed), *The Oxford Handbook of Ethical Theory* (Oxford: OUP 2007) 424–454
Mangini, R and others (eds), *Codice di Procedura Penale. Illustrato con i Lavori Preparatori* (Rome: Tipografia della Camera dei Deputati 1930)
Manzini, V, *Trattato di Diritto Processuale Penale Italiano, vol IV* (5th edn, Turin: UTET 1956)
Manzini, V, *Trattato di Diritto Processuale Penale Italiano, vol I* (6th edn, Turin: UTET 1967, with updates by G Conso and G D Pisapia)
Marzaduri, E, 'Commento all'Art. 530—Sentenza di Assoluzione' in M Chiavario (ed), *Commento al Nuovo Codice di Procedura Penale, vol 5* (Turin: UTET 1989) 509–530
Meccarelli, M, *Arbitrium: Un Aspetto Sistematico degli Ordinamenti Giuridici in Età di Diritto Comune* (Milan: Giuffrè Editore 1998)
Meccarelli, M, 'Tortura e Processo nei Sistemi Giuridici dei Territori della Chiesa: Il punto di Vista Dottrinale (Secolo XVI)' in B Durand (ed), *La Torture Judiciaire: Approches Historiques et Juridiques, vol II* (Lille: Centre d'Historie Judiciaire 2002) 677–707
Meccarelli, M, 'Le Categorie Dottrinali della Procedura e l'Effettività della Giustizia Penale nel Tardo Medioevo' in J Chiffoleau and others (eds), *Pratiques Sociales et Politiques Judiciaires dans les Villes de l'Occident à la Fin du Moyen Âge* (Rome: Ècole Française de Rome 2007) 573–594
Meccarelli, M, 'Criminal Law: Before a State Monopoly' in H Pihlajamäki and others (eds), *The Oxford Handbook of European Legal History* (Oxford: OUP 2018) 632–654
Milanich, P G, 'Decision Theory and Standards of Proof' (1981) 5 Law and Human Behavior 87
Miletti, M N, 'Ombre Sull'Innocenza. La Formula Dubitativa nel Processo Penale dell'Italia Liberale' (2020) 2 Quaderno di Storia del Penale e della Giustizia 177
Ministero della Giustizia e Degli Affari di Culto, *Lavori Preparatori del Codice Penale e del Codice di Procedura Penale. Volume IX, Osservazioni e Proposte sul Progetto Preliminare di un Nuovo Codice di Procedura Penale, Parte III* (Rome: Tipografia delle Mantellate 1930)
Ministero della Giustizia e Degli Affari di Culto, *Lavori Preparatori del Codice Penale e del Codice di Procedura Penale. Volume IX, Osservazioni e Proposte sul Progetto Preliminare di un Nuovo Codice di Procedura Penale, Parte IV* (Rome: Tipografia delle Mantellate 1930)
Ministry of Justice, *Criminal Court Statistics Quarterly, England and Wales, July to September 2020*, 17 December 2020
Ministry of Justice and Home Office, *Review into the Criminal Justice System Response to Adult Rape and Serious Sexual Offences Across England and Wales—Research Report*, June 2021

Mittermaier, C G A, *Teoria della Prova nel Processo Penale* (F Ambrosoli tr, Milan: Libreria di Francesco Sanvito 1858)
Moore, M, 'On Reasonableness' (1996) 13 Journal of Applied Philosophy 167
Moore, M S, 'Patrolling the Border of Consequentialist Justifications: The Scope of Agent-Relative Restrictions' (2008) 27 Law and Philosophy 35
Moore, M S, *Placing Blame: A Theory of the Criminal Law* (Oxford: OUP 2010)
Moran, M, *Rethinking the Reasonable Person: An Egalitarian Reconstruction of the Objective Standard* (Oxford: OUP 2003)
Morelli, F, *Le Formule di Proscioglimento: Radici Storiche e Funzioni Attuali* (Turin: Giappichelli 2014)
Moss, S, *Probabilistic Knowledge* (Oxford: OUP 2018)
Moss, S, 'Knowledge and Legal Proof' in T S Gendler and others (eds), *Oxford Studies in Epistemology, vol VII* (Oxford: OUP, forthcoming 2022)
Moss, S, 'Pragmatic Encroachment and Legal Proof' (2021) 31 Philosophical Issues 258
Munday, R, *Cross and Tapper on Evidence* (13th edn, Oxford: OUP 2018)
Munro, V, *Piecing Together Puzzles: Complainers' Experiences of the Not Proven Verdict* (Coventry: University of Warwick 2020), available at <http://wrap.warwick.ac.uk/137857/> (accessed 7 April 2021)
Nagin, D S, 'Deterrence in the Twenty-First Century' (2013) 42 Crime and Justice 199
Nance, D A, 'Civility and the Burden of Proof' (1994) 17 Harvard Journal of Law and Public Policy 647
Nance, D A, 'Naturalized Epistemology and the Critique of Evidence Theory' (2001) 87 Virginia Law Review 1551
Nance, D A, 'Adverse Inferences about Adverse Inferences: Restructuring Judicial Roles for Responding to Evidence Tampering by Parties to Litigation' (2010) 90 Boston University Law Review 1089
Nance, D A, *The Burdens of Proof: Discriminatory Power, Weight of Evidence, and Tenacity of Belief* (Cambridge: CUP 2016)
Nance, D A, 'Truth, Justification, and Knowledge in the Epistemology of Adjudication' in B Zhang and S Tong (eds), *Proceedings of the International Conference on Facts and Evidence* (Beijing: China University of Political Science and Law Press 2018) 101–135
Nance, D A, 'Weight of Evidence' in C Dahlman and others, *Philosophical Foundations of Evidence Law* (Oxford: OUP 2021) 123–136
Nesson, C, 'The Evidence or the Event? On Judicial Proof and the Acceptability of Verdicts' (1985) 98 Harvard Law Review 1357
Neumann, N and others, 'A Meta-Analysis of Extremeness Aversion' (2016) 26 Journal of Consumer Psychology 193
Nobili, M, *Il Principio del Libero Convincimento del Giudice* (Milan: Giuffrè Editore 1974)
Nozick, R, *Anarchy, State and Utopia* (New York: Basic Books 1974)
Nozick, R, *The Nature of Rationality* (Princeton: Princeton University Press 1993)
Oddie, G and Milne, P, 'Act and Value: Expectation and the Representability of Moral Theories' (1991) 57 Theoria 42
Ormston, R and others, *Scottish Jury Research: Findings from a Large-Scale Mock Jury Study* (Scottish Government, Social Research Series 2019)
Otsuka, M, 'Saving Lives, Moral Theory, and the Claims of Individuals' (2006) 34 Philosophy and Public Affairs 109
Packer, H L, *The Limits of the Criminal Sanction* (Stanford: Stanford University Press 1968)
Padamwar, P K and others, 'Range Effect on Extremeness Aversion' (2018) 45 Decision 345

Pagano, F M, *Principj del Codice Penale e Logica de' Probabili per Servire di Teoria alle Pruove nei Giudizj Criminali. Opera Postuma con Alcune Note* (Naples: Da' Torchi di Raffaello di Napoli 1828)

Pardo, M S, 'The Gettier Problem and Legal Proof' (2010) 16 Legal Theory 37

Pardo, M S and Allen, R J, 'Generalizations and Reference Classes' in C Dahlman and others, *Philosophical Foundations of Evidence Law* (Oxford: OUP 2021) 301–313

Passarella, C, 'From Scotland to Italy and Back: Enrico Ferri, the Verdict of Not Proven and its Consequences on the Accused' (2020) Forum Historiae Iuris, available at <https://forhistiur.net/2020-11-passarella/> (accessed 5 May 2021)

Peay, J and Player, E, '"Not a Stain on Your Character?": The Finality of Acquittals and the Search for Just Outcomes' (2021) 11 Criminal Law Review 921

Perelman, C, *Justice* (New York: Random House, 1967)

Perelman, C, *The New Rhetoric and the Humanities: Essays on Rhetoric and its Applications* (W Kluback tr, Dordrecht: D Reidel Publishing Company 1979)

Perelman, C and Olbrechts-Tyteca, L, *Traité de l'Argumentation: La Nouvelle Rhétorique* (2nd edn, Brussels: Editions de l'Institut de Sociologie de l'Université Libre de Bruxelles 1970)

Peterson, M, *An Introduction to Decision Theory* (2nd edn, Cambridge: CUP 2017)

Phalen, H, 'Overcoming the Opposition to a Third Verdict: A Call for Future Research on Alternative Acquittals' (2018) 50 Arizona State Law Journal 401

Picinali, F, 'Structuring Inferential Reasoning in Criminal Fact Finding: An Analogical Theory' (2012) 11 Law, Probability and Risk 197

Picinali, F, 'Two Meanings of "Reasonableness": Dispelling the "Floating" Reasonable Doubt' (2013) 76 Modern Law Review 845

Picinali, F, 'Innocence and Burdens of Proof in English Criminal Law' (2014) 13 Law, Probability and Risk 243

Picinali, F, 'The Threshold Lies in the Method: Instructing Jurors About *Reasoning* Beyond Reasonable Doubt' (2015) 19 International Journal of Evidence and Proof 139

Picinali, F, 'Do Theories of Punishment Necessarily Deliver a Binary System of Verdicts? An Exploratory Essay' (2018) 12 Criminal Law and Philosophy 555

Picinali, F, 'Can the Reasonable Doubt Standard be Justified? A Reconstructed Dialogue' (2018) 31 Canadian Journal of Law and Jurisprudence 365

Picinali, F, 'The Presumption of Innocence: A Deflationary Account' (2021) 84 Modern Law Review 708

Pickett, J T and others, 'Toward a Bifurcated Theory of Emotional Deterrence' (2018) 56 Criminology 27

Pisani, M, *Introduzione al Processo Penale* (Milan: Giuffrè Editore 1988)

Pisapia, G D, 'Relazione di Sintesi al Convegno' in *La Frode in Assicurazione. L'Assoluzione per Insufficienza di Prove. Atti del Convegno di Studi Giuridici a Cura della Camera Penale di Trieste, 22–25 Aprile 1967* (Padua: CEDAM 1968) 427–439

Pisapia, G D, *Compendio di Procedura Penale* (Padua: CEDAM 1975)

Pisapia, G D, *Compendio di Procedura Penale* (4th edn, Padua: CEDAM 1985)

Puch-Solis, R and others, *Practitioner Guide No 2: Assessing the Probative Value of DNA Evidence: Guidance for Judges, Lawyers, Forensic Scientists and Expert Witnesses* (Royal Statistical Society 2012)

Ramsay, P, 'Preparation Offences, Security Interests, Political Freedom' in R A Duff and others (eds), *The Structures of the Criminal Law* (Oxford: OUP 2011) 203–228

Rape Crisis Scotland, 'End Not Proven', available at <https://www.rapecrisisscotland.org.uk/campaigns-end-not-proven/> (accessed 12 May 2021)

Raskolnikov, A, 'Criminal Deterrence: A Review of the Missing Literature' (2020) 28 Supreme Court Economic Review 1
Rawls, J, *Political Liberalism* (New York: Columbia University Press 1993)
Rawls, J, *Justice as Fairness: A Restatement* (Erin Kelly ed, Cambridge, Mass: Belknap Press 2001)
Redmayne, M, 'Standards of Proof in Civil Litigation' (1999) 62 Modern Law Review 167
Redmayne, M, *Character in the Criminal Trial* (Oxford: OUP 2015)
Reiman, J and van den Haag, E, 'On the Common Saying that it is Better that Ten Guilty Persons Escape than that One Innocent Suffer: *Pro* and *Con*' (1990) 7 Social Philosophy and Policy 226
Ribeiro, G, 'The Case for Varying Standards of Proof' (2019) 56 San Diego Law Review 161
Risinger, M D, 'Innocents Convicted: An Empirically Justified Factual Wrongful Conviction Rate' (2007) 97 Journal of Criminal Law and Criminology 761
Roberts, P, 'Taking the Burden of Proof Seriously' (1995) 10 Criminal Law Review 783
Roberts, P, 'Double Jeopardy Law Reform: A Criminal Justice Commentary' (2002) 65 Modern Law Review 393
Roberts, P, 'Justice for All? Two Bad Arguments (And Several Good Suggestions) for Resisting Double Jeopardy Reform' (2002) 6 International Journal of Evidence and Proof 197
Roberts, P, 'Presumptuous or Pluralistic Presumptions of Innocence? Methodological Diagnosis towards Conceptual Reinvigoration' (2021) 198 Synthese 8901
Roberts, P and Hunter, J (eds), *Criminal Evidence and Human Rights: Reimagining Common Law Procedural Traditions* (Oxford: Hart 2012)
Roberts, P and Zuckerman, A, *Criminal Evidence* (Oxford: OUP 2010)
Rovelli, C, *Helgoland* (Milan: Adelphi 2020)
Sartor, G, 'A Sufficientist Approach to Reasonableness in Legal Decision-Making and Judicial Review' in G Bongiovanni and others (eds), *Reasonableness and Law* (Dordrecht: Springer 2009) 17–68
Scanlon, T M, *What We Owe to Each Other* (Cambridge, Mass: Harvard University Press 1998)
Schauer, F, *The Force of Law* (Cambridge, Mass: Harvard University Press 2015).
Scheffler, S, *The Rejection of Consequentialism: A Philosophical Investigation of the Considerations Underlying Rival Moral Conceptions* (Oxford: OUP 1982)
Schum, D A, *The Evidential Foundations of Probabilistic Reasoning* (Evanston, IL: Northwestern University Press 1994)
Schwartz, R D and Skolnick, J H, 'Two Studies on Legal Stigma' (1962) 10 Social Problems 133
Schwikkard, P J, *Presumption of Innocence* (Kenwyn: Juta 1999)
Scottish Government, *Criminal Proceedings in Scotland, 2016–2017* (2018)
Scottish Government, *Criminal Proceedings in Scotland, 2017–2018* (2019)
Scottish Government, *Criminal Proceedings in Scotland, 2018–2019* (2020)
Scottish Government, *Criminal Proceedings in Scotland, 2019–2020* (2021)
Scottish Government, *Data Relating to Not Proven Verdicts and Guilty Pleas: FOI Release (10 June 2021)*. Available at <https://www.gov.scot/publications/foi-202100199803/> (accessed 4 August 2021)
Scottish Office, *Juries and Verdicts: Improving the Delivery of Justice in Scotland* (1994)
Scottish Office, *Firm and Fair. Improving the Delivery of Justice in Scotland* (1994)
Sentencing Council, *Reduction of Sentence for a Guilty Plea: Definitive Guideline* (2017), available at <https://www.sentencingcouncil.org.uk/publications/item/reduction-in-sentence-for-a-guilty-plea-definitive-guideline-2/> (accessed 28 June 2021)

Sentencing Council, *General Guideline: Overarching Principles* (2019), available at <https://www.sentencingcouncil.org.uk/overarching-guides/magistrates-court/item/general-guideline-overarching-principles/> (accessed 11 November 2021)

Sentencing Council, *Sentencing Guidelines for use in Crown Court*, available at <https://www.sentencingcouncil.org.uk/crown-court/> (accessed 11 November 2021)

Setiya, K, 'Intention' in E N Zalta (ed), *Stanford Encyclopedia of Philosophy* (2018)

Shapiro, S J, *Legality* (Cambridge, Mass: Harvard University Press 2011)

Sibley, M, 'The Rational Versus the Reasonable' (1953) 62 The Philosophical Review 554

Simon, D, *In Doubt: The Psychology of the Criminal Justice Process* (Cambridge, Mass: Harvard University Press 2012)

Simonson, I and Tversky, A, 'Choice in Context: Tradeoff Contrast and Extremeness Aversion' (1992) 29 Journal of Marketing Research 281

Smithson, M and others, 'Guilty, Not Guilty, or...? Multiple Options in Jury Verdict Choices' (2007) 20 Journal of Behavioral Decision Making 481

Spector, H, 'Decisional Nonconsequentialism and the Risk Sensitivity of Obligation' (2016) 32 Social Philosophy and Policy 91

Spottswood, M, 'Burdens of Proof' in C Dahlman and others (eds), *Philosophical Foundations of Evidence Law* (Oxford: OUP 2021) 108–122

Spottswood, M, 'Continuous Burdens of Proof' (2021) 21 Nevada Law Journal 779

Spottswood, M, 'Proof Discontinuities and Civil Settlements' (2021) 22 Theoretical Inquiries in Law 201

Spragens, T A, 'Democratic Reasonableness' in S P Young (ed), *Reasonableness in Liberal Political Philosophy* (London: Routledge 2009) 85–106

Stalnaker, R C, *Inquiry* (Cambridge, Mass: MIT Press 1984)

Stanley, J, *Knowledge and Practical Interests* (Oxford: Clarendon Press 2005)

Steele, K and Stefánsson, H O, 'Decision Theory' in E N Zalta (ed), *Stanford Encyclopedia of Philosophy* (2016)

Stein, A, *Foundations of Evidence Law* (Oxford: OUP 2005)

Stewart, H, 'The Right to be Presumed Innocent' (2014) 8 Criminal Law and Philosophy 407

Stuckenberg, C F, 'Double Jeopardy and *Ne Bis in Idem* in Common Law and Civil Law Jurisdictions' in D Brown and others (eds), *The Oxford Handbook of Criminal Process* (Oxford: OUP 2019) 457–475

Sunstein, C R, 'Behavioral Analysis of Law' (1997) 64 University of Chicago Law Review 1175

Tadros, V, *The Ends of Harm: The Moral Foundations of Criminal Law* (Oxford: OUP 2011)

Teichman, D, 'Convicting With Reasonable Doubt: An Evidentiary Theory of Criminal Law' (2018) 93 Notre Dame Law Review 757

Tenenbaum, S, 'Action, Deontology, and Risk: Against the Multiplicative Model' (2017) 127 Ethics 674

Thayer, J B, 'Presumption of Innocence in Criminal Cases' (1897) 6 Yale Law Journal 185

Tillers, P and Gottfried, J, 'Case Comment—*United States v Copeland*, 369 F Supp 2d 275 (EDNY 2005): A Collateral Attack on the Legal Maxim that Proof Beyond a Reasonable Doubt is Unquantifiable?' (2006) 5 Law, Probability and Risk 135

Topping, A and Barr, C, 'Rape Convictions Fall to Record Low in England and Wales' *The Guardian* (London, 30 July 2020), available at <https://www.theguardian.com/society/2020/jul/30/convictions-fall-record-low-england-wales-prosecutions> (accessed 3 August 2021)

Trechsel, S, *Human Rights in Criminal Proceedings* (Oxford: OUP 2005)

Tribe, L H, 'Trial by Mathematics: Precision and Ritual in the Legal Process' (1971) 84 Harvard Law Review 1329

Tversky, A and Kahneman, D, 'Judgment Under Uncertainty: Heuristics and Biases' (1974) 185 Science 1124

Tyler, T R, 'Procedural Justice, Legitimacy, and the Effective Rule of Law' (2003) 30 Crime and Justice 283

Tyler, T R, *Why People Obey the Law* (Princeton: Princeton University Press 2006)

Tyler, T R, 'Psychological Perspectives on Legitimacy and Legitimation' (2006) 57 Annual Review of Psychology 375

Vaki, Y and Rabin, Y, 'Two Kinds of Acquittals—Different Kinds of Doubts' (2021) 32 Criminal Law Forum 97

Voltaire, *Commentaire sur le Livre 'Des Délits et Des Peines'* (1767), available at <https://gallica.bnf.fr/ark:/12148/bpt6k65400223.texteImage> (accessed 11 May 2021)

von Hirsch, A, *Censure and Sanctions* (Oxford: Clarendon Press 1993)

von Newman, J and Morgenstern, O, *Theory of Games and Economic Behavior* (2nd edn, Princeton: Princeton University Press 1947)

von Wright, G H, 'Images of Science and Forms of Rationality' in G H von Wright, *The Tree of Knowledge and Other Essays* (Leiden: Brill 1993) 172–192

Voorhooeve, A, 'How Should we Aggregate Competing Claims?' (2014) 125 Ethics 64

Walen, A, 'Proof Beyond a Reasonable Doubt: A Balanced Restributive Account' (2015) 76 Louisiana Law Review 355

Walen, A, 'Retributive Justice' in E N Zalta (ed), *Stanford Encyclopedia of Philosophy* (2020)

Walsh K and others, 'Estimating the Prevalence of Wrongful Convictions' (2017), available at <https://www.ncjrs.gov/pdffiles1/nij/grants/251115.pdf> (accessed 11 November 2021)

Wansley, M, 'Scaled Punishments' (2013) 16 New Criminal Law Review 309

Weatherson, B, 'Can we do without Pragmatic Encroachment?' (2005) 19 Philosophical Perspectives 417

Weatherson, B, 'Knowledge, Bets, and Interests' in J Brown and M Gerken (eds), *Knowledge Ascriptions* (Oxford: OUP 2012) 75–103

Weigend, T, 'Assuming that the Defendant is Not Guilty: The Presumption of Innocence in the German System of Criminal Justice' (2014) 8 Criminal Law and Philosophy 285

Weirich, P, *Realistic Decision Theory: Rules for Nonideal Agents in Nonideal Circumstances* (Oxford: OUP 2004)

Westen, P and Drubel, R, 'Toward a General Theory of Double Jeopardy' (1978) The Supreme Court Review 81

Whitman, J Q, *The Origins of Reasonable Doubt: Theological Roots of the Criminal Trial* (New Haven: Yale University Press 2008)

Wierzbicka, A, *English: Meaning and Culture* (Oxford: OUP 2006)

Wigmore, J H, *A Treatise on the Anglo-American System of Evidence in Trials at Common Law, vol 9* (3rd edn, Boston: Little Brown 1940)

Wilcox, V, 'Punitive Damages in England' in H Koziol and V Wilcox (eds), *Punitive Damages: Common Law and Civil Law Perspectives* (New York: Springer 2009) 7–53

Williams, B, 'A Critique of Utilitarianism' in J J C Smart and B Williams, *Utilitarianism: For and Against* (Cambridge: CUP 1973) 77–150

Willock, I D, *The Origins and Development of the Jury in Scotland* (Edinburgh: The Stair Society 1966)

Zalman, M and Norris, J M, 'Measuring Innocence: How to Think about the Rate of Wrongful Convictions' (2021) 24 New Criminal Law Review 601

Zander, M, 'The Criminal Standard of Proof: How Sure is Sure?' (2000) 150 New Law Journal 1517

Zimmerman, M J, *Living with Uncertainty: The Moral Significance of Ignorance* (Cambridge: CUP 2008)

Index

For the benefit of digital users, indexed terms that span two pages (e.g., 52–53) may, on occasion, appear on only one of those pages.

Figures are indicated by *f* following the page number